PATHWAYS

Pathways
APPROACHES TO THE STUDY OF
SOCIETY IN INDIA

T. N. MADAN

DELHI
OXFORD UNIVERSITY PRESS
BOMBAY CALCUTTA MADRAS
1995

Oxford University Press, Walton Street, Oxford OX2 6DP

Oxford New York
Athens Auckland Bangkok Bombay
Calcutta Cape Town Dar es Salaam Delhi
Florence Hong Kong Istanbul Karachi
Kuala Lumpur Madras Madrid Melbourne
Mexico City Nairobi Paris Singapore
Taipei Tokyo Toronto
and associates in
Berlin Ibadan

ISBN 0 19 563650 3

Phototypeset by Imprinter, 89, New Rajdhani Enclave, Delhi 110092
Printed by Rajkamal Electric Press, Delhi 110033
and published by Neil O'Brien, Oxford University Press
YMCA Library Building, Jai Singh Road, New Delhi 110001

To
UMA MADAN *née* CHATURVEDI

किं स्विद् वक्ष्यामि किम् उ नू मनिष्ये

CONTENTS

PREFACE   ix
ACKNOWLEDGEMENTS   xiii
NOTE ON EPIGRAPHS   xv

PART ONE: PATHFINDERS   1

1. TRADITION AND MODERNITY IN THE SOCIOLOGY
   OF D.P. MUKERJI   3
2. D.N. MAJUMDAR ON THE DEVELOPMENT OF CULTURES   24
3. AN INTRODUCTION TO M.N. SRINIVAS'S ŒUVRE   37
4. LOUIS DUMONT AND THE STUDY OF SOCIETY IN INDIA   52
5. IMAGES OF INDIA IN AMERICAN ANTHROPOLOGY   85

PART TWO: IN SEARCH OF A PATH: A PERSONAL ACCOUNT   109

6. ON LIVING INTIMATELY WITH STRANGERS   111
7. ON THE MUTUAL INTERPRETATION OF CULTURES   131
8. ON CRITICAL SELF-AWARENESS   147
9. THE SOCIAL CONSTRUCTION OF CULTURAL IDENTITIES
   IN RURAL KASHMIR   167
10. TWO FACES OF BENGALI ETHNICITY: BENGALI
    MUSLIM OR MUSLIM BENGALI   202
11. ASIA AND THE MODERN WEST: INDIAN AND JAPANESE
    RESPONSES TO WESTERNIZATION   226

REFERENCES   247
INDEX   277

PREFACE

This is a book about sociological and social anthropological approaches to the study of society in India. It is offered to those readers who sympathize with the view that no author is an island complete unto himself, that every scholar has predecessors, consociates, and succesors.

The essays collected here were written between 1971 and 1991, and are grouped into two parts. Part I—'Pathfinders'—contains five chapters dealing with selected aspects of the work of D. P. Mukerji, D. N. Majumdar, M. N. Srinivas, Louis Dumont, and some American anthropologists. Between themselves these scholars represent a wide range of methods and perspectives including neo-evolutionism, functionalism, structuralism, Marxism, and ethnosociology. While D. P. Mukerji and D. N. Majumdar were my teachers at the University of Lucknow in the early 1950s, I have learnt much from the other scholars too by studying their works and through personal contact with most of them. They are all 'pathfinders' in their distinctive ways and have been widely influential. This, of course, does not mean that I myself have always followed in their footsteps.

Part II of the book—'In Search of a Path: A Personal Account'—consists of two sets of three chapters each. The first three essays (nos. 6, 7, 8) describe the scope of social anthropological studies as I have understood and articulated it from time to time. The movement is from a somewhat muted unease about the exclusivism of the idea of anthropology as the study of 'other cultures' towards a more pointed and, I hope, convincing plea for anthropology as the mutual interpretation of cultures and, ultimately, as critical self-awareness. Anthropology as knowledge about how other people live their lives does not mean much, it seems to me, unless it helps us to live our own lives better.

The following three chapters (nos. 9, 10, 11) illustrate the method of understanding through the comparison or mutual interpretation of cultures. The first of these essays is based on my own fieldwork in the Kashmir Valley. It reflects a well-established empirical approach in anthropological research which seeks to portray social situations and even whole societies through intensive observation of day-to-day activities *in situ*. Whatever written materials (e.g. unpublished village records and published books) are drawn upon for information, are treated as a secondary source or supplementary texts. What is presented to the reader is not the minute details of everyday life, but an over-all pattern, a picture, constructed from stable interpersonal relations and social encounters. Society itself is conceived as socially constructed in this perspective, not through a deliberate fabricative endeavour, but mostly spontaneously. It is not suggested that the actors whose actions constitute society are unthinkig pawns at the mercy of 'social forces'. They have shared understandings about their society, the so-called first-order interpretations, which are also regarded as data by the anthropologist. Thus, Chapter 9 presents the differing perceptions of Kashmiri rural society among Hindus and Muslims, and shows how these support a larger social framework, a single society that stood in place for centuries until quite recently.

Chapter 10, like the preceding one, is concerned with the phenomenon of cultural pluralism, but within Muslim society itself, and with the Hindu-Muslim interface at the macro-level. There are many historical, cultural and social structural resemblances between the Kashmir Valley and Bangladesh. Notably, the majority population in both areas (about 95 per cent in Kashmir and 85 per cent in Bangladesh) consists of Muslims, most of whom are descended from converts to Islam. The cultural life of these Muslim peoples bears the imprint of their Hindu past. This fact makes for considerable co-operation between them and the Hindus at the local level, but conflict at the macro-level also is present. The factor that is most significant at the latter level is 'power' expressed in political and economic terms. To understand such a complex web of relations, one has to adopt the historical perspective. I am not, however, a historian and have not made any attempt to look into the original sources, but depended wholly on published accounts. Both these chapters (9 and 10) attempt to show that cultural identity is constructed from the dialectic of 'self-ascription' and 'other-ascription', and that it has more to do with 'process' than with 'substance'.

The last chapter broadens the scope of inter-cultural comparison further: it is concerned with Japanese and Indian reactions to the impact of the West in the nineteenth century. Once again the data are drawn from published sources. Given the vast scope of the inquiry, the discussion within the format of an essay is inevitably couched in very general terms, and the portrayal is by broad brush strokes, as it were. The purpose is more to highlight contrasting cultural perspectives of national elites rather than to provide historical details.

Although the writing of the articles was spread over twenty years, and was concerned with authors having divergent theoretical positions, or with varied themes, I would like to claim a certain unity for the book. It arises from, first, the fact that the general perspectives and substantive analyses of the various scholars that I have discussed in Part I do not appear here in sealed capsules, as it were, but are examined in their mutual relatedness. Secondly, my own views and ethnographical or historical discussions in Part II will be seen to have been influenced by the 'pathfinders' (as I call them), although my intellectual indebtedness is greater to some than to the others.

Notwithstanding the complementarity of the essays constituting the two parts of the book, the fact that the writing has been spread over time is not inconsequential. The date of composition and of publication of each essay is, therefore, given in an initial footnote to each chapter. I have refrained from any major revisions, additions or deletions (except in the third section of Chaptr 4) and confined the changes to occasional rewording in the interests of clarity. Prefatory remarks at the beginning of Chapter 4, postscripts at the end of Chapters 3, 4, 5, 9, and 10 have, however, been newly written. A few additional references to later, relevant publications have also been introduced in the original texts. Chapter 8 repeats a few points of information or interpretation from two earlier chapters; I have allowed these to remain for they are woven into the text.

The debts incurred in the writing of these essays have been many. At the beginning of each chapter, I have acknowledged my gratitude to the generous friends and colleagues who read drafts, gave advice, or helped in other ways. All that remains for me to do here is to thank Aradhya Bhardwaj, for compiling the bibliography and the index, and Connie Costigan, for her painting which appears on the jacket of this book. I also wish to express my gratitude to the authorities and faculty of the Institute of Economic Growth for their indulgence, to the Oxford University Press for their support, and to my wife, Uma, for being what she is. The felicity of my Lucknow University days derives in very large measure from my association with her there. She has stood by my side ever since. The book is dedicated to her.

Delhi   T. N. Madan
1 July 1992

ACKNOWLEDGEMENTS

I thank the following copyright holders for their permission to reproduce materials, with or without changes, published by them earlier. Full bibliographical details are given in the acknowledgements note of each chapter.

The D. P. Mukerji Memorial Lecture Endowment Committee (Lucknow University) for the essay that appears as Chapter 1 of this book;

Ethnographic and Folk-Culture Society, Lucknow, for Chapter 2;

Institute of Economic Growth, Delhi, for Chapters 3, 4, 6, 9 and 10;

The Riverdale Company, Glenn Dale, Maryland (USA) for Chapter 5;

The Wenner-Gren Foundation for Anthropological Research, Inc., New York (USA), for Chapter 7;

Oxford University Press, Delhi for Chapter 8;

Sage Publications India Private Ltd., for Chapter 11.

Note on the Epigraphs

The sources of the epigraphs used at the beginning of each part of the book and of each chapter are given below. Full bibliographical details are given in the list of references.

Part I	: Confucius 1989
Chapter 1	: Mukerji 1952: 13; Popper 1963: 122
Chapter 2	: Majumdar 1956–7: 131
Chapter 3	: Srinivas 1966: 157–8
Chapter 4	: Dumont 1966a: 30, 1957a: 7
Chapter 5	: Whitman 1980; Ramanujan 1986
Part II	: Eliot 1971a
Chapter 6	: Gibran 1962
Chapter 7	: Coomaraswamy 1948: 21; Lévi- Strauss 1966a: 127
Chapter 8	: Goethe 1959
Chapter 9	: Merleau-Ponty 1964: 159; Stanner 1957
Chapter 10	: Eliot 1971b
Chapter 11	: Stryk and Ikemoto 1981

The Sanskrit quotation forming part of the dedication is from the Rig Veda VI.9.6

PART ONE

PATHFINDERS

D. P. MUKERJI
D. N. MAJUMDAR
M. N. SRINIVAS
LOUIS DUMONT
DAVID MANDELBAUM *ET AL.*

The Master said, To learn and at due times to repeat what one has learnt, is that not after all a pleasure?

THE ANALECTS OF CONFUCIUS

Tradition and Modernity
in the Sociology of D. P. Mukerji

1

> For the important and immediate task of reconstructing Indian
> culture through intelligent adaptation to and assimilation of the
> new forces in the light of a reinterpreted past, Sociology is the
> most useful study.

D. P. MUKERJI

> I do not think that we could ever free ourselves entirely from the
> bonds of tradition. The so-called freeing is really only a change
> from one tradition to another. But we can free ourselves from the
> taboos of a tradition; and we can do that not only by rejecting it,
> but also by critically accepting it. We free ourselves from the
> taboo if we think about it, and if we ask ourselves whether we
> should accept it or reject it.

KARL POPPER

In this essay I make an attempt to examine briefly some central ideas in
the work of Dhurjati Prasad Mukerji (1894–1961).[1] He was one of the
founding fathers of sociology in India and taught during the second
quarter of the century at Lucknow University, where it was my privilege
to have been his student, in the early 1950s, during his last years there.

This chapter is a revised version of the first D. P. Mukerji Memorial Lecture delivered
under the auspices of the D. P. Mukerji Memorial Lecture Endowment Committee at
the University of Lucknow on February 25, 1977. I am grateful to the Committee—
particularly to its first Secretary, the late Professor V. B. Singh—for the honour of asking
me to give the Lecture. I would like to warmly thank Dr K. P. Gupta and Professors
Ramkrishna Mukherjee, A. K. Saran and K. J. Shah for their helpful criticisms of an
earlier draft of the essay. I am also beholden to Professors Clemens Heller and Yogendra
Singh for earlier publication of the text during their editorship of *Social Science Information*
(17,6,1978: 777–800) and *Sociological Bulletin* (26,2,1977: 155–76) respectively.

[1] As is well known, D. P. Mukerji wrote in both Bengali and English, but I have
read only his English works. In this essay I have drawn mainly on four of his five
monographs and three of his four collections of essays. The excluded books are *Problems of Indian Youth* (1946), a collection of essays and addresses, and *Introduction to
Indian Music* (1945). References to his works are by date alone; references to other sources
are by author's name and date.

After taking degrees in history and economics at Calcutta University, and opting for a career in teaching, Mukerji went to Lucknow in 1924 in response to the invitation of Radhakamal Mukerjee, who had been appointed Professor and Head of the Department of Economics at the newly established university there. Although there were significant differences of intellectual concerns and approach between them, they were in agreement about the importance of the comparative or sociological perspective in the teaching of economics. While Bombay University had established a sociology department around the same time (in 1919), and Calcutta University had introduced the teaching of anthropology (in 1920), Lucknow University opted for an interdisciplinary department. Courses in cultural anthropology were added in 1928 when D. N. Majumdar was brought over to Lucknow from Calcutta by Radhakamal Mukerjee (see Chapter 2). In the years to come DP (as Professor Mukerji was known among friends, colleagues, and students alike) was to establish a great reputation as a scholar of wide ranging interests, which included literature and music, and a highly influential teacher.

I would like to mention here that, apart from its inherent interest, I have another reason for wanting to turn to DP's own work. It so happens that considerable misrepresentation of his work has occurred in recent years. One might ignore what is said informally, but some grievous distortions have appeared in print.[2] In fact, two tendencies are noticeable. The more general of these has been to simply ignore DP's work. His books are out of print and not readily available in libraries, but where they are to be found they are not read. They rarely find a place in courses of studies. A reason for this may well be the contemporary concern with immediate goals and with a narrow empiricism. Besides, one would have to admit that not all of what DP published was of lasting value. Nevertheless, the neglect is quite unjust, and not only to him but, in fact more so, to ourselves, precisely because he was an uncompromising critic of narrow dogmatisms. Moreover, how can we hope to build sound scholarly traditions in India if we do

---

[2] See, for example, Srinivas and Panini 1973. This fairly long essay contains only two paragraphs about D. P. Mukerji (pp. 189–90), and nearly every statement in them is either factually incorrect or otherwise misleading. It is indeed surprising that the authors should suggest that DP 'viewed the processes of change under British rule as similar to changes under earlier alien rulers', or that they should think that he changed his views about 'synthesis' in his later writings. His concern for the cultural 'specificity' of India is misrepresented as an emphasis on 'uniqueness', and this after they have themselves drawn attention to the influence of Marxism on DP.

not take the work of our predecessors seriously? Surely, their experience should be as relevant to our tasks today, if not more so, as the concerns of intellectuals in other parts of the world.

Then there is the misrepresentation I mentioned, arising out of a casual acquaintance with DP's work. It would seem that not only his critics but also some of his admirers have arrived at evaluations of his work without studying it closely. This is harder to explain and, needless to stress, the more dangerous tendency.

DP's work demands to be seriously examined as was done, for instance, in his lifetime by one of the very ablest of his students and colleagues, Professor A. K. Saran (see Saran 1959 and 1965). I undertake here to make a small contribution to this important task in the hope more of perhaps persuading others to do the same, and do it better than I am able to do here.

Tradition and Modernity

The theme I have chosen for discussion is the relationship of tradition and modernity in DP's thought. It is true that this bipolarity is now becoming quite outmoded. Yet, I think, there would be a consensus among intellectuals and policy-makers in defining our national endeavours today as the quest for modernization: or, as DP would have put it, the effort to give a push to history towards the next higher stage. We may have become weary of the concept of modernization, but the important question is, have we carefully formulated the reasons for this weariness? And did we earlier develop adequately the argument for modernization and examine its nature and scope?

I am not sure we have done these things; and it is my belief that DP is an excellent guide to not only the clarification of the concept of modernity, but also to this self-questioning. He drew attention to some of the hazards that attend the task; and his own work illustrates others. Thus, he would have argued that our modernity is spurious, a sham, and indeed a major obstacle in the path of genuine modernization. But his criticism ultimately fails to point to a satisfactory solution. I should like to construct this argument in some detail.

Let me begin with DP's early work to examine the seeds of his ideas regarding tradition and modernity that came to flower later on. It is interesting to note here that he considered his first two books, *Personality and the Social Sciences* (1924) and *Basic Concepts of Sociology* (1932), 'personal documents'—products of his endeavour to formulate an adequate concept of social science. From the very beginning he organized his ideas around the notion of Personality. He took up the position that the abstract individual should not be the focus of social science theories, and pleaded for a 'holistic', psycho-sociological approach. It was this 'synthesis of the double process of individuality and the socialization of the uniqueness of individual life, this perfect unity' that he called Personality (1924: ii).

Looking back at his work of a lifetime, he said in his presidential address to the first Sociological Conference in 1955 that he had come to sociology from economics and history because he was interested in developing his personality through knowledge (1958: 228). The office of a comprehensive social science, transcending the prevailing compartmentalization of social sciences, was conceived by him to be the development of an integrated though many faceted personality. This is an idea which, as A. K. Saran (1962a: 167) has pointed out, is 'in some ways parallel to the ideal suggested by Moore in his *Principia Ethica*'.

Thus, at the very beginning of his intellectual career DP committed himself to a view of knowledge and of the knower. Knowledge was not, as he put it, mere 'matter-of-factness', but ultimately, after taking the empirical datum and the scientific method for its study into account, philosophic (1932: iv–v). Economics had to be rooted in concrete social reality, that is it had to be sociological; sociology had to take full cognizance of cultural specificity, that is it had to be historical; history had to rise above a narrow concern with the triviality of by-gone events through the incorporation in it of a vision of the future, that is it had to be philosophical. Given such an enterprise, it is obvious that the knower had to be a daring adventurer with a large vision rather than a timid seeker of the safety of specialization. He pointedly asked in the mid-forties (1946: 11):

> We talk of India's vivisection, but what about the vivisection of knowledge which has been going on all these years in the name of learning, scholarship and specialization? A 'subject' has been cut off from knowledge, knowledge has been excised from life, and life has been amputated from living social conditions. It is really high time for Sociology to come to its own. It may not offer *the* Truth. Truth is the concern of mystics and philosophers. Meanwhile, we may as well be occupied with the discipline which is most truthful to the wholeness and the dynamics of

the objective human reality.[3]

The philosophical approach which DP wished to see cultivated was that of rationalism, of 'Practical and Speculative Reason'. Reason was to be understood as a tool, 'not of understanding merely, but of the development of Personality' (1932: x). It seems a reasonable conjecture, though one could hardly assert it, that at this time he may have been under the influence of the teachings of Hegel. In fact, such an influence seems to have persisted till the very end, prominently in his concern with reason and human dignity, his attitude towards the past, wanting to preserve whatever was judged as valuable in it, and his fascination for dialectics. But, then, these values could also have been imbibed from the Hindu Upanishadic tradition.

DP's concern in the 1920s and 30s was with the mental make-up of modern Indian intellectuals and their world-view, which he rightly judged to be a borrowing of the Western liberal outlook with its various preoccupations, most notably the notions of 'progress' and 'equality'. These and the related concepts of 'social forces' and 'social control' were subjected to critical analysis in *Basic Concepts of Sociology*. It is in his discussion of the relation of 'progress' to 'personality' that, it seems to me, we come across early intimations of his later views on the nature of modernization.

Rejecting the evolutionist notion of 'progress' as a natural phenomenon, DP stressed the element of 'purpose' in the life of human beings. Development is not growth, he admonished us, but the broader process of the unfolding of potentialities (in this he followed Hegel and Marx though he did not say so explicitly), and added that the 'emergence of values and their dynamic character' must receive adequate consideration (1932: 9). He further wrote (ibid.: 15):

Progress can best be understood as a problem covering the whole field of '

[3] Cp. Eliot 1940, *Two Choruses from the 'Rock'*: 'Where is the Life we have lost in living?/Where is the wisdom we have lost in knowledge?/Where is the knowledge we have lost in information?'

I would like to record here that the most lasting impression that DP made on me, as indeed on many other students, was of his luminous conviction that genuine scholarship was socially useful no less than personally satisfying, that the life of ideas was not for the contented and the lazy but only for the sceptical and the restless, and that the life of an intellectual was an honourable life and intellectuals were the very salt of the earth. Given the contemporary cynicism about and among intellectuals, DP's faith needs reassertion. The rewards he sought were large, and so were the risks. I have often wondered how deeply his brief stint with the 1937 Congress government in UP hurt him.

human endeavour. It has a direction in time. It has various means and tactics of development. Fundamentally, it is a problem of balancing of values.

The scope of the problem is as wide as human society, and as deep as human personality. In so far as human values arise only in contact with human consciousness at its different levels, the problem of progress has unique reference to the changing individual living in a particular region at a particular time in association with other individuals who share with him certain common customs, beliefs, traditions, and possibly a common temperament.

It seems to me permissible to derive from the foregoing statement the conclusion that 'modernization' is the special form which 'progress' takes for people in the Third World countries today. If this is granted,[4] then the following words need to be pondered (1932: 29–30):

Progress ... is ... a movement of freedom .... What is of vital significance is that our time-adjustments should be made in such a way that we should be free from the necessity of remaining in social contact for every moment of our life. This is an important condition of progress. In leisure alone can man conquer the tyranny of time, by investing it with a meaning, a direction, a memory and a purpose. Obstacles to leisure, including the demands of a hectic social life, often mistaken for progress, must be removed in order that the inner personality of man may get the opportunity for development. This is why the Hindu philosopher wisely insists on the daily hour of contemplation, and after a certain age, a well-marked period of retirement from the turmoil of life. The bustle of modern civilization is growing apace and the need for retirement is becoming greater.

The above passage has a contemporary ring; and it is very relevant. If we paraphrase it, using words and phrases that are more familiar today, we get a succinct reference to the unthinking craving for and the human costs of modernization, including alienation, to the values of individual freedom and human dignity, and to social commitment. For DP progress was, as I have already quoted him saying, a problem of balancing of values; and so is modernization. When we introduce values into our discourse, and the rationalist perspective that he recommended will have it in no other way, we are faced with the problem of the hierarchy of values, that is with the quest for ultimate

[4] K. P. Gupta (1977) objects to such a formulation: 'I think it is undesirable to link the concepts of "social progress" and modernization ... because it [the linkage] provides a convenient bridge to legitimize the shift from the universal concern with progress in all societies to the narrower and prejudicial concern solely with the Third World development.'

or fundamental values. For these DP turned to the Upanishads, to *shantam, shivam, advaitam*, that is harmony, welfare, unity.

> The first is the principle of harmony which sustains the universe amidst all its incessant changes, movements and conflicts. The second is the principle of co-ordination in the social environment. The third gives expression to the unity which transcends all the diverse forms of states, behaviours and conflicts, and permeates thought and action with ineffable joy.... On this view, progress ultimately depends on the development of personality by a conscious realization of the principles of Harmony, Welfare and Unity (1932: 35).

This appeal to Vedanta, while discussing the Western notion of progress, is a disconcerting characteristic of DP's thought throughout. He sought to legitimize it by calling it 'synthesis', which itself he described as a characteristic of the historical process, the third stage of the dialectical triad. He thus evaded, it would seem, a closer examination of the nature and validity of synthesis. Its existence was assumed and self-validating. One's disappointment and criticism of DP's position is not on the ground of the source of this trinity of values—I am reminded of the research student at an Indian university who told me of her deep disappointment that DP was at heart a Hindu—but on the ground that Harmony, Welfare and Unity are too vague and esoteric, as they make their elusive appearance in DP's discourse; and he does not show how they may be integrated with such values of the West as are embodied in its industrial civilization. On the positive side, however, it must be addded that his preoccupation with ultimate values should be assessed in the light of his deep distrust of the installation of Science as the redeemer of mankind and of Scientific Method (based on a narrow empiricism and exclusive reliance on inductive inference) as the redeemer of the social sciences.

I have heard it said that DP's intellectual life reveals a striking lack of continuity between his early work, when he was interested almost exclusively in broad conceptual issues rather than in understanding the nature and problems of Indian society, and his later work, when he became increasingly immersed in India. Also, it is asserted that, this transition in his ideas was marked by a growing salience of a Marxist, or pseudo-Marxist (depending upon the critic's own ideological position), orientation in his work. That the emphases in his work changed with the passage of time may not be denied—and what is wrong with that? —but to maintain that there is a sharp break in the two phases of his work would seem to be unwarranted.

DP, it would seem, was always deeply sensitive to the social environment around him. To the extent that the society in which he lived
the life of a scholar was undergoing change, there was a discernible
shift in his intellectual concerns also, and he was conscious of this.
He even wrote about it: 'In my view, the thing changing is more real
and objective than change per se' (1958: 241). He was a very sensitive
person, and many of those who knew him intimately will recall how
a turn in events—whether of the university, the city, the country or
the world—would cast a gloom on him or bring him genuine joy.
He had an incredible capacity for intense subjective experience: it
perhaps killed him in the end. (One of his favourite books was Goethe's
Werther.) In all his writings he addressed himself to his contemporaries:
he had an unstated contempt for those who write for posterity with
an eye on personal fame and some kind of immortality, and I think
he was right in this attitude.[5]

It would seem that what DP was most conscious of in his earlier
writings was the need to establish links between the traditional culture
of which he was a proud though critical inheritor and the modern
liberal education of which he was a critical though admiring product.
The two—Indian culture and modern education—could not stay apart
without each becoming impoverished—as indeed had been happening
—and therefore had to be synthesized in the life of the people in general
and of the middle classes and intellectuals in particular. In this respect,
DP was a characteristic product of his times. He was attracted by the
image of the future which the West held out to traditional societies
and, at the same time, he was attached to his own tradition, the core
of which was the Hindu tradition. The need to defend what he regarded
as the essential values of this tradition thus became a compelling
concern, particularly in his later writings.

Dualities never ceased to bother DP, and he always sought to
resolve the conflict implicit in persistent dualism through transcendence. This transcendence was to him what history was all about—
or ought to be. But history was not for him a tablet already inscribed,
once for all, and for each and every people. Hence his early criticism
that, in the hands of Trotsky, Lenin and Bukharin, history had degenerated into 'pure dialectic' (1932: 184). This criticism was repeated by
him again and again. In 1945, he complained that the Marxists had made
the 'laws of dialectics' behave like the 'laws of *Karma*'—'predetermining

---

[5] I am reminded of R. G. Collingwood who wrote in his famous autobiography
that good writers always write for their contemporaries (Collingwood 1970: 39).

every fact, event and human behaviour in its course; or else, they are held forth as a moral justification for what is commonly described as opportunism' (1945: 18).

For DP historiography was meaningless unless it was recognized that the decision to 'write history' entailed the decision to 'act history' (1945: 46). And history was being enacted in India in the 1930s, if it ever was during DP's lifetime, by the middle classes and, under their leadership, by the masses. What they were doing increasingly bothered him, for history had not only to be enacted but to be enacted right. The question of values could not be evaded. The middle classes whose intellectual life was his concern in his earlier work were also his concern in his later work, but now it was their politics that absorbed him. In this respect his concern avowedly with himself was in fact sociological, for he believed that no man is an island unto himself, but embedded not merely in his class but also in his total socio–cultural environment. The focus was on modern Indian culture and the canvas naturally was the whole of India.

Modern Indian Culture

The year 1942 saw the publication of *Modern Indian Culture: A Socio-logical Study* and a second revised edition was completed in 1947, the year of independence, but also of partition. It was written under the impending shadow of the vivisection of India; anguish and sorrow are the mood of the book. The problem, as he saw it, was first to explain why the calamity of communal division had befallen India, and then to use this knowledge to shape a better future. Sociology had to be the handmaiden of history and it was no mean role; indeed it was a privilege. His analysis led him to the conclusion that a distortion had entered into the long-established course of Indian history and crippled it. The happening responsible for this was British rule. But let me first quote DP's succinct statement of the character of modern Indian culture (1948: 1):

> . . . As a social and historical process . . . Indian culture represents certain common traditions that have given rise to a number of general attitudes. The major influences in their shaping have been Buddhism, Islam, and Western commerce and culture. It was through the assimilation and conflict of such varying forces that Indian culture became what it is today, neither Hindu nor Islamic, neither a replica of the Western modes of living and thought nor a purely Asiatic product.

In this historical process, synthesis had been the dominant organizing principle and the Hindu, the Buddhist and the Muslim had together shaped a world-view in which, according to DP, 'the fact of Being was of lasting significance'. His favourite quotation from the Upanishads was *charaiveti*, keep moving forward. This meant that there had developed an indifference to 'the transient and the sensate' and a preoccupation with the subordination of 'the little self' to and ultimately its dissolution in 'the Supreme Reality' (1948: 2). This world-view DP called 'the mystical outlook'. He maintained that Islam could have on its arrival in India shaken Hindu society in its very roots, but Buddhism served as a cushion. Buddhism itself had failed to tear Hindu society asunder and had succeeded only in rendering it more elastic. Muslim rule was an economically progressive force but, on the whole, it brought about only a variation in the already existent socio-economic structure (ibid.: 65–7) and provided no real alternatives to native economic and political systems. 'The Muslims just reigned, but seldom ruled' (ibid.: 24).

British rule, however, did prove to be a real turning point in as much as it succeeded in changing the relations of production, or to use DP's own words, 'the very basis of the Indian social economy' (1948: 24). New interests in land and commerce were generated; a new pattern of education was introduced; physical and occupational mobility received a strong impetus. Overshadowing all these developments, however, was the liquidation of an established middle class, and 'the emergence of a spurious middle class',

> who do not play any truly historical part in the socio-economic evolution of the country, remain distant from the rest of the people in professional isolation or as rent receivers, and are divorced from the realities of social and economic life.... Their ignorance of the background of Indian culture is profound.... Their pride in culture is in inverse proportion to its lack of social content (ibid.: 25).

It was this middle class which helped in the consolidation of British rule in India but later challenged it successfully; it was also this same middle class which brought about the partition of the country. Its rootlessness made it a 'counterfeit class' and therefore its handiwork (whether in the domain of education and culture, in the political arena, or in the field of economic enterprise) had inevitably something of the same spurious quality. 'The politics and the culture of a subject country', DP wrote, 'cannot be separated from each other' (1948: 207). To expect such an 'elite' to lead an independent India along the path of genuine modernization, DP asserted with remarkable prescience, would be unrealistic. He warned that before they could be expected to remake India, modernize it, the elite themselves must be remade. And he wrote a forthright, if not easy, prescription for them: 'conscious adjustment to Indian traditions and symbols' (1948: 215), for 'culture cannot be "made" from scratch' (ibid.: 214).

It is important to understand why he made this particular recommendation, why he wanted the withdrawal of foreign rule to be accompanied by a withdrawal into the self which, let me hasten to add, was quite different from a withdrawal into the past or inaction. DP was not only *not* a revivalist, he was keenly aware of the imminent possibility of revivalism and its fatal consequences. He noted that it would be the form that political hatred disguised as civil hatred would take after independence. But he was not hopeless, for he fondly believed that revivalism could be combated by giving salience to economic interests through a 'material programme' that would cut across communal exclusiveness. He envisaged India's emancipation from the negative violence of the constrictive primordial loyalties of religion and caste through the emergence of class consciousness (1948: 216). He was silent on class conflict, however, and his critics may justifiably accuse him of not seeing his analysis through to its logical conclusion. His optimism was the sanguine hope of an Indian liberal intellectual rather than the fiery conviction of a Marxist revolutionary.

In any case, we know today, three decades after DP's expression of faith on this score, that class does not displace caste in India. Nor do they coexist in compartments: they combine but they do not fuse. DP's vision of a peaceful, progressive India born out of the 'union' of diverse elements, of distinctive regional cultures, rather than out of the type of 'unity' that the British imposed from above, however, remains eminently valid even today. The *accommodation* of various kinds of conflicting loyalties within a national framework, rather than national *integration*, is the strategy which new African and Asian states faced with cultural pluralism are finding to be both feasible and advantageous. We all know how Pakistan broke up in 1971 (see Chapter 10).

DP's plea for a reorientation to tradition was, then, of a positive nature—an essential condition for moving forward, for restoring historical dynamism, for reforging the broken chain of the sociocultural process of synthesis. Employing Franklin Giddings's classification of traditions into primary, secondary and tertiary, he suggested

that by the time of the British arrival, Hindus and Muslims had yet
not achieved a full synthesis of traditions at all levels of social existence. There was a greater measure of agreement between them
regarding the utilization and appropriation of natural resources and
to a lesser extent in respect of aesthetic and religious traditions. In the
tertiary traditions of conceptual thought, however, differences survived prominently.

It was into this situation that the British moved in, blundering their
way into India, and gave Indian history a severe jolt. As already stated,
they destroyed indigenous merchant capital and the rural economy,
pushed through a land settlement based on alien concepts of profit
and property, and established a socially useless educational system.
Such opportunities as they did create could not be fully utilized, DP
said, for they cut across India's traditions, and 'because the methods of
their imposition spoilt the substance of her need for new life' (1948: 206).

The Making of Indian History

At this point it seems pertinent just to point out that, while DP
followed Marx closely in his conception of history and in his characterization of British rule as uprooting, he differed significantly not
only with Marx's assessment of the positive consequences of this rule,
but also with his negative assessment of the pre-British traditions. It is
important to note this because some Marxists have claimed DP on
their side, despite his repeated denials that he was a Marxist; he jestingly
claimed to be only a 'Marxologist' (Singh 1973: 216). Some non-
Marxists also have, it may be added, described him as a Marxist.

It will be recalled that Marx had in his articles on British rule in
India asserted that India had a long past but 'no history at all, at least
no known history';[6] that its social condition had 'remained unaltered
since its remotest antiquity'; that it was 'the British intruder who
broke up the Indian handloom and destroyed the spinning-wheel';
that it was 'British steam and science' which 'uprooted, over the whole
surface of Hindustan, the union between agriculture and manufacturing
industry'. Marx had listed England's 'crimes' in India and proceeded
to point out that she had become 'the unconscious tool of history'
whose actions would ultimately result in a 'fundamental revolution'
(see Marx 1853a, 1853b). He had said: 'England had to fulfil a double
mission in India: one destructive and the other regenerating—the
annihilation of old Asiatic society, and the laying of the material
foundations of Western society in India' (1959: 31).

[6] As is well-known, Marx owed this judgement about India to Hegel.

Thus for Marx, as for so many others since his time, including Indian intellectuals of various shades of opinion, the modernization of India had to be its westernization.

As has already been stated above, DP was intellectually and emotionally opposed to such a view about India's past and future, whether it came from Marx or from liberal bourgeois historians. He refused to be ashamed of or apologetic about India's past. The statement of his position was unambiguous (1945: 11):

> Our attitude is one of humility towards the given fund. But it is also an awareness of the need, the utter need, of recreating the given and making it flow. The given of India is very much in ourselves. And we want to make something worthwhile out of it. . . .

Indian history could not be made by outsiders: it had to be enacted by Indians. In this endeavour they had to be not only firm of purpose but also clear-headed. He wrote (1945: 46):

> Our sole interest is to write and to act Indian History. Action means making; it has a starting point—this specificity called India; or if that be too vague, this specificity of the contact between India and England or the West. Making involves changing, which in turn requires (*a*) a scientific study of the tendencies which make up this specificity, and (*b*) a deep understanding of the Crisis [which marks the beginning no less than the end of an epoch]. In all these matters, the Marxian method . . . is likely to be more useful than other methods. If it is not, it can be discarded. After all, the object survives.

'Specificity' and 'crisis' are the key words in this passage: the former points to the importance of the encounter of traditions and the latter to its consequences. When one speaks of tradition, or of 'Marxist specification', one means, in DP's words, 'the comparative obduracy of a culture-pattern'. He expected the Marxist approach to be grounded in the specificity of Indian history (1945: 45, 1946: 162ff.), as indeed Marx himself had done by focusing on capitalism, the dominant institution of Western society in his time. Marx, it will be said, was interested in precipitating the crisis of contradictory class interests in capitalist society (1945: 37). DP, too, was interested in movement, in the release of the arrested historical process, in the relation between tradition and modernity. He asked for a sociology which would 'show the way out of the social system by analysing the process of transformation' (1958: 240). This could be done by focusing first on tradition and only then on change.

The first task for us, therefore, is to study the social traditions to which we have been born and in which we have had our being. This task includes the study of the changes in traditions by internal and external pressures. The latter are mostly economic.... Unless the economic force is extraordinarily strong—and it is that only when the modes of production are altered—traditions survive by adjustments. The capacity for adjustment is the measure of the vitality of traditions. One can have a full measure of this vitality only by immediate experience. Thus it is that I give top priority to the understanding (in Dilthey's sense) of traditions even for the study of their changes. In other words, the study of Indian traditions ... should precede the socialist interpretations of changes in Indian traditions in terms of economic forces (1958: 232).

This brings us to the last phase of DP's work. Before I turn to it, however, I should mention that Louis Dumont has drawn our attention to an unresolved problem in DP's sociology. He points out that one's 'recognition of the absence of the individual in traditional India' obliges one to 'admit with others that India has no history' for 'history and the individual are inseparable'; it follows that 'Indian civilization [is] ... unhistorical by definition' (Dumont 1967b: 239). Viewed from this perspective, DP's impatience with the Marxist position is difficult to justify. In fact, it is rather surprising that, having emphasized the importance of the group as against the individual in the Indian tradition, and of religious values also, he should have opted for a Marxist solution to the problems of Indian historiography (see Dumont 1967b: 231) and for a view of India's future based on synthesis. He hovered between Indian tradition and Marxism and his adherence to Marxist solutions to intellectual and practical problems gained in salience in his later work which was also characterized by a heightened concern with tradition.

Modernization: Genuine or Spurious?

For DP the history of India was not the history of her particular form of class struggle because she had experienced none worth the name. The place of philosophy and religion was dominant in this history, and it was fundamentally a long-drawn exercise in cultural synthesis. For him 'Indian history was Indian culture' (1958: 123). India's recent woes, namely communal hatred and partition, had been the result of the arrested assimilation of Islamic values (ibid.: 163); he believed that 'history halts unless it is pushed' (ibid.: 39).

The national movement had generated much moral fervour but, DP complained, it had been anti-intellectual. Not only had there been much unthinking borrowing from the West, there had also emerged a hiatus between theory and practice as a result of which thought had become impoverished and action ineffectual. Given his concern for intellectual and artistic creativity, it is not surprising that he should have concluded: 'politics has ruined our culture' (1958: 190).

What was worse, there were no signs of this schism being healed in the years immediately after independence. When planning arrived as state policy in the early 1950s, DP expressed his concern, for instance in an important 1953 paper on Man and Plan in India (1958: 30–76), that a clear concept of the new man and a systematic design of the new society were nowhere in evidence. As the years passed by, he came to formulate a negative judgement about the endeavours to build a new India, and also diagnosed the cause of the rampant intellectual sloth. He said in 1955: 'I have seen how our progressive groups have failed in the field of intellect, and hence also in economic and political action, chiefly on account of their ignorance of and unrootedness in India's social reality' (1958:240).

The issue at stake was India's modernization. DP's essential stand on this was that there could be no genuine modernization through imitation. A people could not abandon their own cultural heritage and yet succeed in internalizing the historical experience of other peoples; they could only be ready to be taken over. He feared cultural imperialism more than any other. The only valid approach, according to him, was that which characterized the efforts of men like Rammohun Roy and Rabindranath Tagore, who tried to make 'the main currents of western thought and action . . . run through the Indian bed to remove its choking weeds in order that the ancient stream might flow' (1958: 33).

DP formulated this view of the dialectic between tradition and modernity several years before independence, in his study of Tagore published in 1943, in which he worte (1972: 50):

> The influence of the West upon Tagore was great . . . but it should not be exaggerated: it only collaborated with one vital strand of the traditional, the strand that Ram Mohan and Tagore's father . . . rewove for Tagore's generation. Now, all these traditional values Tagore was perpetually exploiting but never more than when he felt the need to expand, to rise, to go deeper, and be fresher. At each such stage in the evolution of his prose, poetry, drama, music and of his personality we find Tagore drawing

upon some basic reservoir of the soil, of the people, of the spirit and emerging with a capacity for larger investment.[7]

This crucial passage holds the key to DP's views on the nature and dynamics of modernization. It emerges as a historical process which is at once an expansion, an elevation, a deepening and a revitalization—in short, a larger investment—of traditional values and cultural patterns, and not a total departure from them, resulting from the interplay of the traditional and the modern. DP would have agreed with Michael Oakeshott, I think, that the principle of tradition 'is a principle of continuity' (1962: 128).[8] From this perspective, tradition is a condition of rather than an obstacle to modernization; it gives us the freedom to choose between alternatives and evolve a cultural pattern which cannot but be a synthesis of the old and the new. New values and institutions must have a soil in which to take root and from which to imbibe character. Modernity must therefore be defined in relation to, and not in denial of, tradition.[9] Conflict is only

[7] DP drew an interesting and significant contrast between Bankim Chandra Chatterjee and Rabindranath Tagore. He wrote (1972: 75–6):

[Bankim] was a path-finder and a first class intellect that had absorbed the then current thought of England. His grounding in Indian thought was weak at first; when it was surer . . . [it] ended in his plea for a neo-Hindu resurgence. Like Michael Madhusudan Dutta, Bankim the artist remained a divided being. Tagore was more lucky. *His saturation with Indian traditions was deeper; hence he could more easily assimilate a bigger dose of Western thought* (emphasis added).

[8] Marx, it will be recalled, had written (in 1853) of the 'melancholy' and the 'misery' of the Hindu arising out of the 'loss of his old world' and his separation from 'ancient traditions' (Marx and Engels 1959: 16). The task at hand was to make the vital currents flow. That this could be done by re-establishing meaningful links with the past would have been emphasized, however, only by an Indian such as DP. I suspect DP would have sympathized with Oakeshott's assertion that the changes a tradition 'undergoes are potential within it' (1962: 128).

[9] Many contemporary thinkers have expressed similar views. See, e.g., the motto of this essay taken from Popper (1963: 122). Or Schneider (1974: 205): 'Social life is meaningful; new meanings are established with reference to old meanings and grow out of them and must be made, in some degree, congruent with them; and exchange, whenever and wherever it occurs, must be articulated with the existing system of meanings.'

Shils puts it somewhat differently (1975b: 203–4):

One of the major problems which confronts us in the analysis of tradition is the fusion of originality and traditionality. T. S. Eliot's essay, 'Tradition and Individual Talent', in *The Sacred Wood*, said very little more than that these two elements coexist and that originality works within the framework of traditionality. It adds and modifies, while accepting much. In any case, even though it rejects or disregards much of what it confronts in the particular sphere of its own creation, it accepts very much of what is inherited in the context of the creation. It takes its point of departure from the 'given' and goes forward from there, correcting, improving, transforming.

One more example: Merleau-Ponty writes (1964: 59):

the intermediate stage in the dialectical triad: the movement is toward *coincidentia oppositorum*. Needless to emphasize, the foregoing argument is in accordance with the Marxist dialectic which sees relations as determined by one another and therefore bases a 'proper' understanding of them on such a relationship.

Synthesis of the opposites is not, however, a historical inevitability. It is not a gift given to a people unasked or merely for the asking: they must strive for it self-consciously, for 'Culture is an affair of total consciousness' (1958: 189), it is a 'dynamic social process, and not another name for traditionalism' (ibid.: 101–2). History for DP was a 'going concern' (1945: 19), and the value of the Marxist approach to the making of history lay in that it would help to generate 'historical conviction' (1958: 56), and thus act as a spur to fully awakened endeavour. The alternative to self-conscious choice-making is mindless imitation and loss of autonomy and, therefore, dehumanization, though he did not put it quite in these words.

Self-consciousness, then, is the form of modernization. Its content, one gathers from DP's writings in the 1950s, consists of nationalism, democracy, the utilization of science and technology for harnessing nature, planning for social and economic development, and the cultivation of rationality. The typical modern man is the engineer, social and technical (1958: 39–40). DP believed that these forces were becoming ascendant:

This is a bare historical fact. To transmute that fact into a value, the first requisite is to have active faith in the historicity of that fact.... The second requisite is social action . . . to push . . . consciously, deliberately, collectively, into the next historical phase. The value of Indian traditions lies in the ability of their conserving forces to put a brake on hasty passage. Adjustment is the end-product of the dialectical connection between the two. Meanwhile [there] is tension. And tension is not merely interesting as a subject of research; if it leads up to a higher stage, it is also desirable. The higher stage is where personality is integrated through a planned, socially directed, collective endeavour for historically understood ends, which means . . . a socialist order. Tensions will not cease there. It is not the peace of the grave. Only alienation from nature, work and man will stop in the arduous course of such high and strenuous endeavours (1958: 76).

It is thus that the world as soon as he has seen it, his first attempts at painting, and the whole past of painting all deliver up a *tradition* to the painter—that is, Husserl remarks, *the power to forget origins* and to give to the past not a survival, which is the hypocritical form of forgetfulness, but a new life, which is the noble form of memory.

In view of this clear expression of faith (it is that, not a demonstration), it is not surprising that he should have told Indian sociologists (in 1955) that their 'first task' was the study of 'social traditions' (1958: 232), and should have reminded them that traditions grow through conflict.

It is in the context of this emphasis on tradition that his specific recommendation for the study of Mahatma Gandhi's views on machines and technology, before going ahead with 'large scale technological development' (1958: 225), was made. It was no small matter that from the Gandhian perspective, which stressed the values of wantlessness, non-exploitation and non-possession, the very notions of economic development and under-development could be questioned (ibid.: 206). But this was perhaps only a gesture (a response to a poser), for DP maintained that Gandhi had failed to indicate how to absorb 'the new social forces which the West had released' (ibid.: 35); moreover, 'the type of new society enveloped in the vulgarised notion of Rama-rajya was not only non-historical but anti-historical' (ibid.: 38). But he was also convinced that Gandhian insistence on traditional values might help to save India from the kind of evils (for example, scientism and consumerism) to which the West had fallen prey (ibid.: 227).

The failure to clearly define the terms and rigorously examine the process of synthesis, already noted above, reappears here again and indeed repeatedly in his work. The resultant 'self-cancellation', as Gupta (1977) puts it, 'provided a certain honesty and a certain pathos to DP's sociology'. In fact, he himself recognized this when he described his life to A. K. Saran as 'a series of reluctances' (Saran 1962a: 169). Saran concludes: DP 'did not wish to face the dilemma entailed by a steadfast recognition of this truth', that the three world views—Vedanta, Western liberalism, Marxism—which all beckoned to him 'do not mix'.[10] One wonders what his autobiography would have been like.

Theories of Modernization

I hope to have shown in this necessarily brief presentation that, despite understandable differences in emphasis, there is on the whole a remarkable consistency in DP's views on the nature of modernization. Not that consistency is always a virtue, but in this case it happens to be so.

[10] It may be noted though that in his earlier writings DP had shown a greater wariness ragarding the possibility of combining Marxism with Hindu tradition. Referring to the 'forceful sanity' of the 'exchange of rights and obligations' on which Hindu society was organized, he had written (1932: 136): '. . . before Communism can be introduced, national memory will have to be smudged, and new habits acquired. *There is practically nothing in the traditions on which the new habits of living under an impersonal class-control can take root* (emphasis added).'

Genuine modernization, according to him, has to be distinguished from the spurious product and the clue lies in its historicity. The presentation of the argument is clear but it is not always thorough and complete, and may be attacked from more than one vantage point.

Professor Saran (1965), for instance, has rightly pointed out that DP does not subject the socialist order itself to analysis and takes its benign character on trust, that he fails to realize that a technology-oriented society cannot easily be non-exploitative and not anti-man, that the traditional and the modern world-views are rooted in different conceptions of time, that traditional ideas cannot be activated by human effort alone, that given our choice of development goals we cannot escape westernization, and so forth. It seems to me that DP's principal problem was that he let the obvious heuristic value of the dialectical approach overwhelm him and failed to probe deeply enough into the multidimensional and, indeed, dynamically integrated character of empirical reality. He fused the method and the datum.

I do want to suggest, however, that DP's approach has certain advantages compared to those others that are current in modernization studies. An examination of modernization theories in general is outside the scope of this essay; I will therefore make only a rather sweeping generalization about them. They seem to me to fall into two very broad categories. There are, first, what we may call the 'big bang' theories of modernization, according to which tradition and modernity are mutually exclusive, bipolar phenomena. This entails the further view that before one may change anything at all, one must change everything. The examples that come to mind are many, but Gunnar Myrdal's *Asian Drama* (1968) is notable. This view is, however, unfashionable now, and to that extent sociology has moved forward.

Secondly, there are what we may call the 'steady state' theories of modernization, according to which modernization is a gradual, piecemeal process, involving compartmentalization of life and living; it is not through displacement but juxtaposition that modernization proceeds. Examples are too numerous to be listed here (but see Singer 1972 and Singh 1973). As a description of empirical reality, the latter approach is perhaps adequate, but it creates a serious problem of understanding, for it in effect dispenses with all values except modernity, which is defined vaguely with reference to what has happened elsewhere—industrialization, bureaucratization, democratization, etc., and almost abandons holism.

By this latter view, one is committed to the completion of the

agenda of modernization, and hence the boredom, the weariness and
the frustration one sees signs of everywhere. The gap between the
'modernized' and the 'modernizing', it is obvious, will never be
closed. No wonder, then, that social scientists already speak of the
infinite transition—an endless pause—in which traditional societies
find themselves trapped. Moreover, both sociology and history
teach us, if they teach us anything at all, that there always is a residue,
that there always will be traditional and modern elements in the
cultural life of a people, at all times and in all places.

The virtue of a dialectical approach such as DP advocated would
seem to be that it reveals the spuriousness of some of the issues that
the other approaches give rise to. At the same time, it may well be
criticized as an evasion of other basic issues. I might add, though,
that it does provide us with a suggestive notion, one which we may
call *generative* tradition, and also a framework for the evaluation of
on-going processes. All this of course needs elaboration, but the present essay is not the place for such an undertaking. Suffice it to say,
the notion of *generative* tradition involves a conception of 'structural'
time more significantly than it does that of 'chronological' time.
'Structural' time implies, as many anthropologists have shown, a
working out of the potentialities of an institution. Institutions have a
duration in 'real' time, but this is the surface view; they also have a
deeper duration which is not readily perceived because of the transformations they undergo.

Concluding Remarks

To conclude: the task I set myself in this essay was to give an exploratory exposition of a selected aspect of D. P. Mukerji's sociological
writings, using as far as convenient his own words. I chose to
organize some of the available materials around the theme of 'tradition and modernity' because it occupied an important place in his
work and also because it survives as a major concern of contemporary
sociology. Taking DP's work as a whole, one soon discovers that his
concern with tradition and modernity, which became particularly
salient during the 1940s and remained so until the end, was in fact a
particular expression of a larger, and it would seem perennial, concern
of westernized Hindu intellectuals. This concern, manifested in a
variety of ways, and referred to by some critics as the apologetic patterns of the Hindu renaissance (see Bharati 1970), was with arguing
that India's intellectual and artistic achievements were in no way

inferior to those of the West. Hence the urge for a synthesis of Vedanta, Western liberalism and Marxism.

I have referred very briefly to DP's fascination for the Marxist method as also his insistence that he was not a Marxist. This needs a deeper examination than has been possible here. What is clear, however, is that he should not be claimed to be on this or that side of the fence without actually demonstrating such a stance. In this regard, his overwhelming emphasis on synthesis needs to be examined.

An equally important and difficult undertaking would be the elaboration and specification of his conception of the content of tradition. Whereas he establishes, convincingly I think, the relevance of tradition to modernity at the level of principle, he does not spell out its empirical content except in terms of general categories, such as those suggested by Giddings and already quoted above. One has the uncomfortable feeling that he himself operated more in terms of intuition and general knowledge than a deep study of the texts. A confrontation with tradition through fieldwork in the manner of the anthropologist, was, of course, ruled out by him, at least for himself. His tribute to G. S. Ghurye as the 'only Indian sociologist today', whilst others were 'sociologists in India' (1955: 238), is to be understood in this light. Also required is an examination of the general indifference of Indian sociologists to DP's plea for the study of tradition. Ramkrishna Mukerjee (1965) has a suggestive first essay on this problem, but much more needs to be done.[11]

---

[11] For a further discussion of D. P. Mukerji's views, see Chapter 2, pp. 31–3 and Chapter 6, p. 117. See also Chapter 11.

D. N. MAJUMDAR
ON THE DEVELOPMENT OF CULTURES

2

*With his expert knowledge of social relationships, the sociologist
can help predict, control and direct social change, and speed up'
social progress.*

D. N. MAJUMDAR

The Dynamics of Cultural Change

Dhirendra Nath Majumdar (1903–60) began his career as an anthropologist at Calcutta University, where he received his Master's degree in 1924 and was later awarded the coveted Premchand Roychand Scholarship. By the time he joined Lucknow University in 1928 (he stayed there the rest of his life) as a lecturer in 'primitive economics', he had already acquired a conception of the scope of anthropology as the comprehensive study of man from the biological and cultural points of view. From available accounts it seems that two influences were dominant in the Anthropology Department of Calcutta University during the years Majumdar was there. But before I proceed to describe these, it should be pointed out that I am concerned here only with cultural anthropology and not physical anthropology, though Majumdar made outstanding contributions in the latter field also.

First, there was the ethnographic tradition, recording of the customs and beliefs of tribes and castes, which had been initiated by the colonial government and cultivated by scholarly civil servants. In fact this tradition had had its beginnings in Bengal itself when, in 1807, Francis Buchanon was appointed by the Governor-General to undertake an

This essay is the first of the two D. N. Majumdar (Memorial) Lectures that I was privileged to deliver at Lucknow in January 1982 under the auspices of the Ethnographic and Folk-Culture Society. (The Society was founded by Majumdar and publishes *The Eastern Anthropologist*, of which he was the founder-editor.) The second lecture, 'Cultures of Development', was a critique of hegemonic theories of development. The two lectures with 'Concluding Remarks' were later published as *Culture and Development* by T. N. Madan, Delhi: Oxford University Press, 1983. I would like to express my gratitude to the Ethnographic and Folk-Culture Society for their many courtesies.

[1] For a brief account of Majumdar's life and work see Madan 1966a. See also Madan 1961a, 1961c, and 1968a.

ethnographic survey of 'the conditions of the inhabitants of Bengal and their religion' (Majumdar 1947: 40–1). People outside the government, including the intelligentsia, had also contributed to this stream of scholarly work of a descriptive factual nature.

Second, with the introduction of anthropology in the curricula of Calcutta University in 1920, a formal theoretical underpinning for ethnographic work had come to be provided by its being linked to theories of culture and social organization then prevalent in academic circles in the West, particularly in Britain. The concept of culture that appears to have been dominant was that of Tylor's celebrated formulation of it as 'that complex whole which includes knowledge, belief, art, law, morals, customs and any other capabilities and habits acquired by man as a member of society' (1871: 1). Also, the 'distributionist' and 'diffusionist' theories of Clark Wissler, W. H. R. Rivers and others seem to have appealed to many, including Majumdar, as these represented an advance upon the dogmatic unilinear evolutionist theories of the late nineteenth century. Nevertheless, a basic adherence to evolution as a historical process was never abandoned.

When we look at Majumdar's earliest cultural anthropological publications, what appears to be noteworthy in them is, among other things, his interest in the study of 'culture traits'. As far as I have been able to find out, the first three papers he wrote were published in 1923, all of them in *Man in India* (founded by S. C. Roy two years earlier), and dealt with 'the custom of burning human effigies', 'Kali nauch', and 'customs and taboos' connected with 'pregnancy and childbirth'. The data came from East Bengal (now Bangladesh) where Majumdar had been born and brought up. The concern with 'cultures' as 'wholes', which became conspicuous in his later work, is not prominent in these papers. Nor did he seem to be particularly interested in the phenomenon of social change.

But soon we find him writing about social change, particularly in situations of culture contact. This was to become, as I will try to show, a lifelong *interest*, and even more than that, a lifelong *concern*. The basic premise appears to have been that while some cultures grow or evolve, others stagnate and die. For the latter, contact with the former could become the engine of social change. In this regard, it is worth noting, Majumdar anticipated the formulation of the nature of the dynamics of culture change by Bronislaw Malinowski (1945), who regarded development as being a result of the impact of 'advanced' upon 'simple and passive' societies.

Majumdar was also perceptive enough to see that this process of development was not, however, an easy one. He felt that as an anthropologist he had to do something about the tensions, conflicts and burdens placed upon the weaker people, for the tribes in contact with caste Hindus seemed to be losers on all fronts—cultural, social, economic, psychological. He bothered about what he called 'the decline of the primitive tribes in India' (Majumdar 1936). The doctoral dissertation which he wrote at Cambridge University on the basis of fieldwork among the Hos of Singhbhum in Bihar dealt with the problems faced by a 'tribe in transition' (Majumdar 1937). The book also reveals the impact of the holistic approach of the functionalist paradigm as formulated by Malinowski, whose derivation of culture from social responses to biological and psychological needs held a particular fascination for Majumdar, as those who attended his lectures at Lucknow University in the 1940s and 1950s will remember well. This viewpoint also permeates his other writings of the period.

The teachings of Malinowski, whose famous seminar at the London School of Economics Majumdar attended when he was at Cambridge (1933–5), provided him with a framework which brought together all his interests and unified his theoretical perspectives. To quote one of his most considered statements on this subject:

> The emphasis of functional study has been on 'a culture' rather than on cultures. From this point of view the functional approach is surely significant. We have also been told that the functional approach is not anti-historical or anti-distributional, i.e. neither is it hostile to the study of the distribution nor to the reconstruction of the past in terms of evolution, history or diffusion . . . the integral approach of functionalism, therefore, puts the field anthropologist on an unimpeachable base, for he gets illumination on the totality of a culture and on the context of its linkages that must be understood before the traits are viewed in isolation. Besides, the methodology developed by the functional school, in respect of the study of primitive culture, helps in appraising the role of traits in a total cultural situation (1950: v.).

In the context of the present discussion, it is important that I locate, within the above broad framework, Majumdar's conception of the contact of cultures of unequal level of elaboration or growth and his view of the contribution that anthropology could make to easing the tensions inherent in such situations. The notion of unequal elaboration or growth of culture, explicitly an evolutionary one, was given precise definition by him. He wrote of the 'base' of a culture which he considered to be the resultant of the interaction of four crucial variables which, arranged in the 'order of importance', were Man, Area, Resources and Co-operation (MARC). 'Co-operation', he clarified, comprised the cultural responses to bio-psychological needs which are the essence of 'Man'. He also envisaged variability in the nature and magnitudes of these variables (see Majumdar 1950: xiiff.).

This late formulation had been anticipated at least ten years earlier, when he had written:

> The monographic method in amateur hands has invariably failed to separate the native warp from the foreign woof, and has failed also to evaluate the importance of the role of diffusion in culture progress. In India most of the tribal groups have come in contact with higher social groups and rites and customs introduced from highly organized societies have blended with those of a primitive or infantile character .... Analysis has shown how significant are the effects of such contacts, how social groups are adapting themselves to changed socio-economic conditions, and how mal-adaptation is leading to tribal extinction or absorption into more dynamic and vital cultures (1939: 1–2).

Two elements in the foregoing formulation seem noteworthy. First, there is an explicit acknowledgement of a gradation of cultures. Majumdar did not subscribe to any of the extravagant notions of 'culture relativism' which were made popular by certain American anthropologists, and which would invoke a contextual justification for all kinds of customs and practices. He referred to cultures as 'dominant' and 'decadent' without hesitation, and emphasized that 'decadent' cultures could hardly hope to survive except by 'surrendering their values and even identifying completely with the dominant culture' (1944: 219).

At the same time, Majumdar advocated an approach—and this is the second noteworthy point—to the tribal problem which was based on a concept of creative or generative adaptation: he was against wholesale cultural invasion from the outside but feared that, unless helped, weaker peoples would fail to withstand external pressures. For him Verrier Elwin's crusade in favour of leaving the tribes alone (see Elwin 1943) and G. S. Ghurye's counter-campaign to treat them as indistinguishable from backward Hindus (see Ghurye 1943), represented a Rousseauan romanticism on the one hand, and a political posture on the other, rather than the fruits of objective scientific inquiry. Optimistically, he discerned 'the avowed policy of the Indian Government' after independence, to be one of 'contact and understanding rather than laissez faire and segregation' (1951: 809). He further wrote:

> The two axioms of cultural rehabilitation should be: (1) we cannot be civilized unless everyone of us is civilized, and (2) every people, however primitive or civilized, has a right to its own way of life, and to the development of its own culture. To reconcile these two requires a complete grasp of the details, and a sympathetic understanding of the realities of tribal aims and aspirations (ibid.: 812)

Majumdar did not elaborate the strategy that he may have considered adequate for the purpose and it is rather curious that he should have considered it merely a matter of information about and understanding of tribal cultures. He posed no questions about the so-called civilized ways of life.

Majumdar had earlier enumerated the processes 'through which tribal cultures are usually transformed or modified'. These were: first, 'simple adoption'; secondly, 'acculturation' involving 'acceptance and adaptation'; and thirdly, 'social commensalism' or 'plural association' (1947: 161). Again, no questions about the desirability of the civilized ways of life were asked beyond their being regarded as available for adoption. Indicating his clear preference for 'acculturation', but at the same time acknowledging the risk of reaction or 'contra-acculturation', of which he himself recorded evidence among certain tribes, he wrote:

> What is needed is mutual respect and understanding, and where the dominant or ruling group has shown... respect and understanding, culture adjustment has been smooth and easy. It is I think possible for the tribes today to feel more secure and take greater share in the cultural progress of the country provided the attitude forced on the caste people by the numerical preponderance of the tribes and backward groups is not merely used for political expediency but as a sincere gesture towards a broad cultural movement seeking to absorb and assimilate the bulk of the primitive and backward substratum of population in the country. If the political leaders of the country fail to recognize the trends of political thought and aspirations surging in the minds of the newly conscious tribal groups and exterior castes, a possibility which, however, cannot be ruled out as the indication goes, the future of Indian culture must be viewed with misgivings (1947: 174–5).

This was written in the year of independence and yet there is a contemporary ring to some of these statements. Majumdar published his last book in the old style of ethnography—*The Affairs of a Tribe*—in 1950, and in it restated his position on the problems of acculturation and the notion of development of culture. He wrote:

The Hos are overwhelmed by the superiority of their neighbours.... When they adopt or imitate alien habits or ways of life, they find themselves cut off from their own tribesmen, but are not considered equal to those whom they imitate.... In some cases, this failure has developed an inferiority complex among a section of the tribal people, while many have fallen back on their own systems of beliefs, values and activities. A revivalism is manifest today among the advanced section of tribal population... [which] finds its natural outlet in the growth of tribal solidarity, in a political consciousness, which manifests itself in the *Adibasi* movement, a sub-nationalism, which is the result of contra-acculturation (314–15).

Majumdar concluded this book with a very clear statement of the notion of development of culture:

The past must be understood in the context of the present, and the present will stabilize the future if it can find its fulfilment in the moorings of the past. There was no golden age, there can be none in the future. Life is a process of adjustment and in its *unfolding*, it has thrown out individuals who are misfits and the latter have both helped and hindered cultural progress; the misfits are misfits in the context of a dynamic setting, and if only, the misfits could be fitted into the structure of life, the process that is life will continue to *unfold* itself, adjust and march on to man's destiny through an *integration and synthesis* that constitute the core of the dynamics of culture change and culture crises (ibid: 124, emphases added).

The emphasis on 'unfolding'—one presumes the reference is to the unfolding of the potentialities of a culture, its spontaneous development—and synthesis is interesting, but it would be far-fetched to read into it any deep ideological (Hegelian or Marxian) significance or interest in a macrotheory of social development. Majumdar was essentially a fieldworker, interested in attending to concrete problems like a 'clinician'. He derived his research interests from the realities of life around him rather than from any special concern with sociological or cultural anthropological theory.

The early 1950s saw the launching of the Community Development Programme in India (in 1952) and the commencement of planned development (in 1953). Majumdar's response to these initiatives was positive and in a sense dramatic. His numerous publications on the tribes of India had underscored his conviction that anthropology could offer useful knowledge and usable advice to the policy-maker, the administrator and the social worker. He reiterated this time and again in his lectures as well as in his publications. The changed situation in the early 1950s offered new challenges and he responded to them swiftly and energetically.

Anthropology and Sociology at Lucknow University (1950s)

At this point a brief digression on the climate of debate on development at Lucknow University in the early 1950s would seem to be
worthwhile. During these years the social science departments of the
university were notable alike for the calibre of their faculty and the
quality of their research activities. I will, however, confine my remarks
to three scholars only, namely Professors Radhakamal Mukerjee, D. P.
Mukerji and D. N. Majumdar.

Radhakamal Mukerjee's wide-ranging interests as economist,
sociologist and ecologist, and his abiding concern with the solution of
socio-economic problems and alleviating the sufferings of the poor
of this country—whether the farmer in the fields of Oudh and elsewhere or the Indian working class—are (or used to be) well known.
Just a year before independence his book *Planning the Countryside* (1946)
had been published. It contained his recommendations to the Maharaja
of Gwalior on the 'reconstruction' effort of that state. Earlier, he had
worked as Chairman of the Sub-Committee on the 'Aims and Purposes'
of the National Planning Committee set up by the Indian National
Congress. He had then evolved precise targets or norms for nutrition,
clothing, housing, leisure, literacy and health. But a deep sense of
distrust had entered his thinking about the possible course of events
in independent India. It is surprising how little he reacted to the inauguration of the development plans at the national and state levels.
His published work during the 1950s was more concerned with culture
history, philosophy of history, philosophy of science, religion and
symbolism rather than with socio-economic problems. But he did
express his fears in a long essay, significantly entitled *The Indian Scheme
of Life* (1951). He wrote at its very beginning:

> The modern philosophy of the secular state implies an exaggerated belief
> not merely in the all-sufficiency of economic goods, but also in the
> achievement or lapse of rightness in human relationships in the fields of
> economics and politics, of laws and institutions, rather than in the
> domain of religion. This is the same intellectual slant that underlies
> Western Socialism or Communism, concentrating on the equalization of
> the goods of life, oblivious of the relations of means and ends, lower and
> higher values, and understanding equality and freedom only from the
> economic and political view points (i–ii).

It is obvious that though Radhakamal Mukerjee accepted the *modern*
notion of a self-directed humanity, he was not wholly in tune with the
times. He had, in fact, never been a modernist, having always stressed

that the task of modern India was to seek a renewal of, rather than a break with, the past. Thus in an early and characteristic work, *Borderlands of Economics* (1925), he had written that nothing would be more detrimental to the economic progress of India than the destruction of the communal[2] background which he considered the expression of India's 'race temperament'. The great task of social reconstruction in the East was to renew and adapt the old and essential impulses and habits to the emerging complex and enlarged needs (ibid.: 85).

In fact in the very first book he wrote, namely *The Foundations of Indian Economics* (1916), he had confidently proclaimed that India would not adopt Western industrialism in its modern phase with its too exclusive adherence to the principle of division of labour, and that she would not divide society into a number of distinct groups or classes, with their divergent and even conflicting interests (p. 448).

D. P. Mukerji had a different view of the prospect of India after the attainment of independence.[3] Convinced of the creative role of tension and struggle, or class conflict, and of the state in our times, and of the importance of purposive leadership by men of high stature with a sense of the purposefulness of history, he warmly welcomed the dawn of the era of planning. At the same time, however, he gave expression to a sense of disquietude and foreboding.

In an essay titled 'Man and Plan in India' (1953) he affirmed that the 'real active element' of the socio-politico-economic situation in India in the 1950s was 'the Plan' (1958: 49). Agreeing with some of the 'assumptions' of the 'new social order' that was sought to be introduced—notably, the gradualness of change in the interest of harmony, the emphasis upon science and technology, the advisability of a mixed economy—he also sounded a sharp note of warning that without a holistic perspective—a philosophy of history—nothing of significance would be gained: mere affirmations would serve no useful purpose. He further wrote: 'The development, according to the Plan, is to be comprehensive. But little or no assumption is made in regard to the organization of patterns of values in the process of their evolution through the implementation of the Plan' (ibid.: 51).

He feared that enough attention had not been given by the planners to outlining clearly the nature of 'a new social order' and 'a new man', and also warned of a too narrow conception of implementation

[2] It may be noted here that the word 'communal' did not have in the 1920s the negative meaning it has acquired in discussions of South Asian societies since then.
[3] For discussions of D. P. Mukerji's work from two different points of view see Chapter 1 and Saran 1965. See also Saran 1959.

on the part of bureaucrats. He said: 'Those who composed the Plan
are highly educated people, competent, knowledgeable, scrupulously
honest and industrious . . .; still they do not seem to be of their Indian
earth, earthy; nor do they create the impression of being the agents of
mighty social forces' (1958: 53–4).

Mukerji went on to caution:

> The Plan is a beneficent social force, *an endogenous one*; but its implemen-
> tation may make it maleficent, even if we exclude the ugly possibilities of
> its being tied up so early in its career with foreign aid. The reported basis
> of this fear and uncertainty is our bureaucratic inefficiency, corruption
> and unimaginativeness. . . . [Worse still] the real defect of bureaucracy is
> that it feeds on itself . . . and thereby it removes itself from reality (ibid.:
> 54–5, emphasis added).

The real task, according to Mukerji, was 'to push on with the Plan
and to push it consciously, deliberately, collectively into the next
historical phase' (ibid.: 76), but without a total break with tradition.

Mukerji was torn between optimism and pessimism; and that was in
1953—the year in which the First Five-Year Plan was formally adopted.
In fact his doubts were deep-seated. In another paper (also published
in 1953), he had written, apropos Gandhi's insistence on the primacy
of values:

> From them [Gandhi's statements on values] one might also infer that the
> term 'under-developed economy', which is the excuse of technical assis-
> tance, was inappropriate in so far as it confused the coexistence of two diffe-
> rent value systems by placing them on the assembly line of historical
> development in which economic growth being the supreme value was sub-
> servient to and dependent only upon technological advance (1958: 206–7).

D. P. Mukerji's fears deepened as the years passed. In 1955 he
lamented that he had seen how India's progressive groups had failed
in the field of intellect, and hence also in economic and political action,
chiefly on account of unrootedness in India's social reality (1958: 240).[4]

---

[4] It is noteworthy that a similar judgement about rootlessness and lack of understanding should now be looked upon in China as the main cause of the poor results of
development efforts in that country.

> Why were the economic returns so poor and why was there such great waste in developing the
> national economy? These deficiencies were caused first of all by our expectations of easy suc-
> cess. The impetuosity in guiding ideology is to blame. In developing the productive forces, we
> one-sidedly sought high speed and high accumulation rates and hankered after large-scale cap-
> ital construction. In relations of production, we gave undue stress to the transition to a higher
> level of ownership of the means of production . . . . To trace these mistakes to their ideological
> soruce, apart from a one-sided understanding of the economic theories of Marxism, *they were
> rooted mainly in our insufficient understanding of China's reality* (Xian Zhen 1981: 14, emphasis added).

By 1959 he had almost totally lost faith in India's economists who were the experts of the planning process but regrettably, in Mukerji's opinion, 'Mostly busy with spinning cocoons of model-building, with formulating comparative or static models or a notional system that is neither here nor there', and in the process running the risk of contributing nothing significant and themselves becoming 'dehumanized' (1959: 71.).

The Study of Development: Problems and Processes

Returning to D. N. Majumdar, it is noteworthy that in his writings we find no sympathy either for Radhakamal Mukerjee's idealist speculations or for D. P. Mukerji's socialist aspirations for or fears about the future. As an anthropologist, he had always concerned himself with the 'here-and-now' of the peoples he had studied. It was precisely in this same spirit that he turned to the study of the problems of rural and urban development, and he did so with immense zest and confidence. Noting the long-lasting interest of economists in rural studies, but castigating them for a preoccupation with the perfection of techniques of quantitative analysis, and for a neglect of 'the cultural background' and 'the interrelation that exists between different sets of social phenomena', he too (like Mukerji) called for a holistic approach to the problems of development (Majumdar 1955: iii).

Majumdar's enthusiasm for a better future and confidence in the capability of social sciences to contribute to its making is best expressed in his own words. Thus:

> If social relations at any stage of development hinder or hamper the historical productive relations, that is the relationship of man to nature, the only way to avoid catastrophic cultural blow-up is to modify the existing social relations. Here comes the real role of a sociologist, for in this sense his discipline represents an instrument of social policy. With his expert knowledge of social relationships, the sociologist can help predict, control and direct social change and speed up social progress' (1956–7: 131)

Majumdar was obviously as confident of the usefulness of sociology as some of its European founding fathers. Accordingly, he pressed for an active association of sociologists and anthropologists with the planning process:

> Detailed knowledge of the dynamics of culture change in different communities, based on empirical investigations, can equip us to forestall resistances and solve many of the problems of personality adjustment and intergroup conflict which follow disequilibrating or induced changes. Association

of sociologists and anthropologists with the community development programme, at all levels—advisory, administrative and field execution—can help in safeguarding against possible pitfalls and insure the successful implementation of village development programmes (1956–7: 135).

Majumdar was not the man to wait for responses or invitations: he was a man of action. Characteristically, he initiated a number of studies on the problems and processes of planned development.

On the side of highlighting emerging problems, he focused attention on unemployment. Pinpointing social responsibility, he wrote:

> Unemployment is a curse, a tragedy, a challenge to society. In a welfare state, the social loss resulting therefrom is an intolerable enervation of society's vital lifeblood.... Without a guarantee of the right to work, democracy is devoid of its essential economic nucleus. Hence there is a clear shift of stress today from a vague concept of democracy to that of a planned social order the essential core of which is full utilization of human resources (1957: 1).

In his village studies Majumdar undertook to examine both selected problems calling for immediate relief, such as water scarcity in hillside villages in Jaunsar Bawar (Majumdar 1955: iii–xv)—showing in these the impact of some of the work of American anthropologists on the problems and processes of development—and the whole range of social relations in the setting of underdevelopment in the villages of south-eastern, central and north-western Uttar Pradesh. A persistent refrain in the conclusions he derived from these studies was that villagers were apathetic and immured in timeless inertia and, therefore, change had to be induced externally. Such intervention, he warned, would meet with resistance from powerful castes and communities if it led to the erosion of their privileges. Inter-group relations were the locus of both traditional power and authority and consequently of exploitation and stagnation. The attack on these relations with a view to changing them had to be multipronged and had to include the key factors of education and technological innovation. In the absence of such a broad-based strategy, the villagers would soon reduce development personnel to being, as he quoted some villagers near Lucknow telling him, '*tamasha-walas*' (entertainers) (1958: 343).

Majumdar identified several factors which impeded the ability of backward villages to benefit adequately by community development and other programmes. The villagers' past experience had made them generally distrustful of outsiders who often came pretending to be friends, but stayed only to exploit them and rob their habitat of its natural wealth. Government officials and agents had also been traditionally known to seek the villagers' submission and money (as taxes, levies or bribes) rather than their welfare. Within the village 'community' itself caste differentiation and factionalism militated against collective welfare and nourished the well-being of some at the cost of the many. Various kinds of cultural practices (e.g., group marriage in Jaunsar Bawar), religious beliefs, superstitions, etc. were seen by Majumdar as further obstacles to development (see 1962: 353–81).

Majumdar did not, however, consider villagers or tribesmen to be irrational or unchangeable: the issue was of right approach, of focusing on genuinely felt and not imputed needs, and of carrying conviction to them. In achieving this, Majumdar believed that the social scientist had much to offer in tribal, rural and urban settings. Thus, he concluded his book on Kanpur, the first city survey by an Indian anthropologist (published just a couple of months before his death at the height of his intellectual life) with the following exhortation: 'Our towns and cities are growing, our vigilance must not wane, sociologists must line up for social research and help the administration in its assigned task of building an urban population, socially aware and mentally conditioned for city life' (1960: 219).

Concluding Remarks

I have relied on Majumdar's published work to bring out both the continuity of interest and approach in it as also the responsiveness to changing social environment that it displays. He began in the 1920s among the tribes with a conception of *levels of culture* which entailed a notion of the historical *development of cultures*. By the time of the coming of independence he had refined this notion and formulated it as the concept of acculturation, which provided scope for both the retention of selected elements of traditional cultural heritage as also the adaptation and assimilation of new elements from other cultures. His evolutionary view of cultural development committed Majumdar to the notion of convergence of cultures (as a result of development). Modern Western culture, based on science and technology, was the model for him and he advocated interventionist social policy, backed by applied social science, to achieve modernization, but with due regard for the specific character of India's societies.

Modernization or social development and economic growth were seen by Majumdar as generally desirable and interrelated goals—as an unquestioned 'good'—with the clear implication that the country needed to develop in its villages and cities, in its homes and offices, a *culture of development*, i.e. a culture which would initiate, promote and sustain development. One was *not* to wait and watch for the 'unfolding' of the potentialities of a culture but to take charge of the process of innovation, not only to speed it up but also to give it a particular content and direction. Whatever stood in its way was to be eradicated. Since development had not been generated from within the traditional cultures, it had to be introduced into them from without.

Majumdar's views on the nature and processes of development might appear unduly uncritical today, but it should not be forgotten that he was a representative social scientist of his generation. Many more Indian social scientists shared Majumdar's confidence during the early years of planning than the anxieties of D. P. Mukerji or the dismay of Radhakamal Mukerjee. It should also be added that there are many social scientists today who hold the same views as Majumdar did on development and the role of the social sciences, though they are likely to state them in more sophisticated phraseology and with greater caution, being the wiser for the experience gained.[5] This is why it is worthwhile to have an exposition of his views (and of other intellectuals of his generation) in our effort to outline the course of the development of thinking on the problems and processes of modernization.

---

[5] As an example, I may cite the following observations of S. C. Dube:

Asian traditions are not unchanging. They have demonstrated great adaptability and resilience over time. Where the structure of opportunities was favourable the privileged section of the population took full advantage of it, and westernized itself in several areas of life. It was not slow to pick up the economic gains of modernization. If others also could not do the same the blame does not lie at the door of tradition. One has to look searchingly at the inner logic of the culture of poverty to explain the causes of their inability to adopt the new idiom of progress (1977: 83)

AN INTRODUCTION TO
M. N. SRINIVAS'S ŒUVRE

3

> *Though he still remains a member of his society, he [the sociologist studying his own society] is able to look at it to some extent as an outsider. His position is similar to that of a novelist who manages to observe his fellow man as well as to participate in the life around him.*

M. N. SRINIVAS

The village as the microcosm of Indian society and civilization emerged as a major intellectual preoccupation in sociological and social anthropological studies of India around the middle of the twentieth century. The division of labour between Indological studies of Hindu society by sociologists and fieldwork-based studies of tribal communities by anthropologists, which had generally characterized the work of the earlier generation of scholars, civil servants and others, almost disappeared rather rapidly. In this new intellectual venture, the work of M. N. Srinivas (b. 1916) came to occupy a unique place and enjoyed widespread influence. When David Mandelbaum's encyclopaedic survey of published materials on society in India came out in 1970, Srinivas, by then the acknowledged doyen of Indian anthropologists, expectedly was the most frequently cited author in its 700 pages (see Mandelbaum 1970).

I will recapitulate briefly in the first part of the present essay the content of Srinivas's published work up to the publication in 1976 of his *magnum opus, The Remembered Village,* and try to highlight what in retrospect seem to have been his most influential contributions. The intention, I would like to emphasize, is to describe Srinivas's earlier work so that his new book may be appraised in the light of what preceded it. In the second part of the essay, I will present a very

This essay was written in 1977 as the introduction to a review symposium on M. N. Srinivas's *The Remembered Village,* which was published as a special issue of *Contributions to Indian Sociology* (NS) (vol. 12, no. 1, 1978). I am grateful to Professor M. N. Srinivas for his help and understanding.

brief summary of the contents of *The Remembered Village* and follow
it up, in the last part, with a discussion of some of the observations
made by the participants in the review symposium.

Earlier Work

Srinivas's first two publications in 1942 included his book, *Marriage
and Family in Mysore*, and a short article with the interesting title, 'The
family versus the state'. The book had originally been written in 1938
as an M. A. dissertation at the University of Bombay at the suggestion
of Professor G. S. Ghurye. Srinivas dealt with Kannada-speaking
Hindu castes and based his description on data drawn from published
sources of various kinds, including compendia of ethnographic information, folklore, works of fiction, and on information obtained
through the personal questioning of 'many caste leaders on their beliefs
and rites' (1942a: 13). The reader is provided with an account of customs
relating to marriage, divorce, childbirth, interpersonal relations within
the family, kinship terminology, death ceremonies, etc.

It is obvious that *Marriage and Family* is modelled on the well-known
series of works of the colonial period on tribes and castes in various
parts of the country. The focus is on descriptive ethnography rather
than on sociological analysis. Thus, as Shah (1973: 267) has pointed
out, the book does not provide quantitative data, nor does it go into
the question of definitions (of marriage and the family which have
since attracted so much scholarly attention). Srinivas's own judgement
of the book is perhaps too severe: 'In retrospect . . . the book appears
immature and its style brash, and I was glad when it went out of print
in the 1950's' (Srinivas 1973: 134).

This early interest in marriage and kinship persisted in some of
Srinivas's later work but never again occupied a central place in it.
He published a paper on a joint family dispute in 1952 (Srinivas 1952a),
which was based on fieldwork in a south Karnataka village which he
called Rampura. The same year his book on the Coorgs came out
(Srinivas 1952b). Though it contains valuable data on the patrilineage
(*okka*) and the rituals associated with family life, including marriage,
the principal theme of the book is the relation of religion to the wider
social organization. Apart from one later piece on 'Indian marriages'
(Srinivas 1956b), Srinivas never again published anything on marriage,
kinship, or the family, except in relation to the status of women (see
footnote 6). The study of these subjects in India has not been, on the
whole, particularly influenced by his work.

It was *Religion and Society Among the Coorgs of South India* (1952b) that established Srinivas's leading position in Indianist studies. As Dumont and Pocock (1959: 9) pointed out, the book became 'a classic' within a few years of its publication. In it he produced a sophisticated sociological analysis of data collected earlier and first presented in his rather massive (900 typed pages) Ph.D. dissertation at the University of Bombay in 1944. Ghurye was again the supervisor, and it was apparently he who suggested to Srinivas to study the Coorgs (see Srinivas 1973: 137). The published version is, however, based on his second doctoral dissertation which he wrote at Oxford University under the supervision first of Radcliffe-Brown and then, after the latter's retirement in 1946, of Evans-Pritchard.

The strength of the Coorg book lies in its being firmly grounded in a clearly defined theoretical framework which happened to be essentially the one developed by Radcliffe-Brown who suggested the theme of the dissertation to Srinivas (see Srinivas 1973: 140). *Religion and Society* is a very lucid exposition of the complex interrelationship between ritual and the social order in Coorg society. It also deals at length and insightfully with the crucial notions of purity and pollution as also with the process of incorporation of non-Hindu communities and cults in the Hindu social order and way of life.

While the exposition of the interrelatedness of different aspects of society, made possible by the adoption of the functionalist paradigm, is the strength of the Coorg book, its weakness also stems from the same source. Religion is here reduced to ritual and is sought to be understood in terms of its function in the maintenance of the social order. It is obvious that Evans-Pritchard did not interfere with the development of Srinivas's thesis, for his own *Nuer Religion* (1956) was to be a very different kind of work, with its concern with meaning, rather than function, and with god, soul, sin and sacrifice—themes which Srinivas either omits altogether or just touches briefly. In fact, the treatment of religion in the Coorg book is highly specialized compared to even Nadel's *Nupe Religion* (1954) which is also, like Srinivas's book, a functionalist interpretation of the role (Nadel used the word 'competence') of religion in society, though influenced much more by Malinowski's teaching than Radcliffe-Brown's.

Characteristically, Srinivas himself has drawn attention to some of the limitations as well as the strong points of the Coorg book. He writes (1973: 141):

> As I looked at my material from the functionalist viewpoint, I found it falling into a pattern. The data was no longer unrelated and disorderly.

The different levels of reality were discernible as were the links between them. In retrospect, one of the troubles with my analysis was that every-thing was too neatly tied up leaving no loose ends. I must also add that the data was too thin for my analysis.

He also mentions the dogmatism and the narrowness of function-alism which obviously cramped his scope and style. *Religion and Society* remains a most noteworthy book, Srinivas's subsequent second thoughts notwithstanding; in fact, it is regarded by many readers as his best book so far.

The data which went into the making of the Coorg book were col-lected over a period of four years (1940–43). Ill-health, however, precluded continuous immersion in fieldwork and Srinivas had to resort to the technique of data-collection through 'short hit-and-run trips' (Srinivas 1973: 138). Obviously data of a quantitative nature either were not collected or, if collected, were not judged as relevant or useful to be included in the analysis presented in the book.

Srinivas has written that, earlier in his career, he had an interest in 'theory', and that Ghurye did not encourage it but insisted on his under-taking fieldwork (Srinivas 1973: 137). His stay at Oxford apparently enabled him to fulfil his interest in theory: it also aroused a new interest in fieldwork. What is more, Srinivas's appointment to the newly created lectureship in Indian sociology at the University of Oxford in 1948, enabled him to undertake intensive fieldwork in a peasant village stretched over almost a whole year. More about this later.

To return to the Coorg book, Srinivas introduced in it two related ideas which have indeed been very influential. He wrote about the 'spread' of Hinduism, categorizing it for analytical purposes into local, regional, peninsular, and all-India varieties. He stressed that these distinctions could be seen in their proper perspective only when the cohesive role of all-India 'Sanskritic' Hinduism and its central values was recognized. Related to this was the notion of 'Sanskritization' which Srinivas employed to describe the hoary process of the 'penet-ration' of Sanskritic values into the remotest parts of India. Imitation of the way of life of the 'topmost', twice-born castes was said to be the principal mechanism by which lower castes sought to raise their own social status. Curiously, Srinivas did not take up for consideration the phenomenon of the persistence of masses of Hindus of low or no status within the caste system. For him the most significant aspect of the history of the Coorgs, worthy of being recorded and discussed, was the history of their incorporation into the Hindu social order. A crucial observation in this regard is the following (Srinivas 1952b: 166): 'Splinter groups like Amma Coorgs are decades, if not centuries, in advance of their parent-groups: the former have solved their problem by Sanskritizing their customs entirely while the latter are more conservative.' This reads like the announcement of a new age. The notion of *yugantara* has, indeed, a perennial fascination for the Hindu mind. Srinivas has, moreover, noted that, in his initial preoccupation with tradition and Sanskritization, he failed to take notice of the parallel process of westernization (see Chapter 11). Actually he found the two processes linked in a 'dynamic relationship' (1966: 151).

Srinivas's interest in caste, which he called the 'structural basis' of Hinduism, turned out to be stronger than his interest in Hinduism in its totality. He never again did any work on religion though he wrote on Hinduism for *Encyclopaedia Britannica* (1958) and *The International Encyclopedia of the Social Sciences* (1968, with A. M. Shah). There is also an interesting essay (Srinivas 1974) in which he describes what being a Hindu means to him. It might also be noted here that, though there is a similarity of viewpoint between Max Weber's and Srinivas's delineation of the relationship between caste and Hinduism, there is no evidence that Srinivas has been influenced by Weber. This is rather curious for, among other things, Weber did mention at the beginning of his book the very process which Srinivas calls Sanskritization. Weber wrote of the advance of the barbarian 'by way of metempsychosis', further pointing out that his 'social status depends upon his way of life' (1958: 8).

As is well-known, Srinivas's name is associated above all with the notion of Sanskritization. He has written many times about it (e.g., see Srinivas 1956a, 1956c, 1958, 1966, 1967), refining it as he went along with his work, and it has been much written about by others. In fact, Sanskritization has become a word of common parlance in Indianist studies and has generated cognate words (not always elegant), such as Islamization and de-Sanskritization.

In focusing attention on the uneasy relationship between those who are born to high status and those less fortunate groups who aspire to rise higher in the caste system, Srinivas inevitably encountered situations of conflict. He conceptualized these in the notion of the 'dominant caste', first proposed in his early papers on the village of Rampura (see Srinivas 1951, 1955 and 1959). The concept has been discussed and applied to a great deal of work on social and political organization in India. Repudiating the charge that he had smuggled the idea of 'dominance' from African sociology, Srinivas points out that his fieldwork itself had impressed upon him that communities, such as the Coorgs and the Okkaligas, wielded considerable power at the local level and shared such social attributes as numerical preponderance, economic strength, and clean ritual status. He further noted that 'the dominant caste could be a local source of Sanskritization, or a barrier to its spread' (1966: 152).

A recent commentator, Suraj Bandyopadhyay, has pointed out that the two notions of Sanskritization and dominant caste, in fact, deal with the same phenomenon but from opposed vantage points, Sanskritization postulating gradual and peaceful status adjustment and dominant caste, perpetual conflict and non-accommodation. He suggests that many sociologists do not seem to be aware of this and are, therefore, unable to achieve 'a comprehensive understanding of the process' referred to by these two terms (Bandyopadhyay 1977: 121). This is a useful insight, but must not be allowed to obscure the fundamental distinction between culture and politics, i.e. between status and power, in the Indian context (see Chapter 4).

Srinivas's work on caste almost inevitably led him to the examination of an emergent dimension of the social situation in India, namely the linkage of caste to politics, administration, education, etc. He made this the subject of an important address which he delivered in 1957 in his capacity as the president of the anthropology and archaeology section of the Indian Science Congress. This seminal essay (Srinivas 1957), based on the work of several scholars and of selected newspaper reports, drew attention to the manipulation of the processes and institutions of democratic politics by caste lobbies generally and by dominant castes in particular. Responsive to the imperative need for the cultivation of national integration, he warned about the attendant pitfalls which included caste-exclusive loyalties as also a narrow view of nation building. He wrote in 1958 (see Srinivas 1962b: 110):

> There is no need, however, to be unduly frightened by the existence of 'divisions' in the country. It is true that a person does feel that he is a member of a particular caste, village, region, state and religion but these loyalties can represent a hierarchy of values and are not necessarily inconsistent with being a citizen of the Indian Republic.

The relevance of Srinivas's writings on caste and politics and related problems appeared during the 1950s, when political management emerged as a first concern of Indian leadership and voting in elections became a significant activity for millions of Indians. His ready willingness to write on these issues in professional journals as well as newspapers and widely circulated magazines and journals of opinion helped in the dissemination of his views. He thus came to be recognized as the outstanding authority on the sociology of India and on caste in modern India in particular.

About a dozen of these influential essays—dealing with such themes as caste and politics, the problem of Indian unity, the future of the caste system, Sanskritization, westernization, industrialization, etc.—were reproduced from various sources and published together in 1962 as *Caste in Modern India and Other Essays*, which was Srinivas's fourth major publication. It is also one of his most reprinted books. Earlier, he had authored with three colleagues a trend report on caste which came out in 1959.

Srinivas returned to the themes of contemporary politics and society in his Tagore memorial lectures delivered at Berkeley in the University of California in 1963 and published in 1966. *Social Change in Modern India* was an ambitious book inasmuch as he chose to tread well beyond familiar anthropological stamping grounds and discussed macro-level historical processes, though only of the recent past. Acknowledging what he called the 'need to see cultural and social processes in an all-India perspective' (ibid.: xiv), Srinivas proceeded to analyse selected data in terms of the notions of Sanskritization and westernization (see pp. 232–3 below), and added caste mobility and secularization to the discussion. He concluded with an expression of views on the study of his or her own society by the anthropologist.

His discussion of various nineteenth century happenings turns out to be, in effect, an evaluation of the forces set in motion by the confrontation of India with Western liberal values and Christianity. The point of departure is the caste system. The assessment of the outcome is, on the whole, favourable. The focus is on cultural processes, narrowly defined, and economic changes are barely mentioned. It is not therefore surprising that the views of Karl Marx and nationalist economic historians are not discussed (see Chapter 11).

Sanskritization, westernization, etc. had by the mid-sixties begun to appear rather familiar themes and Srinivas's promised monograph on Rampura village began to be eagerly awaited. He went to Palo Alto at the beginning of 1970 for what should have been the final phase of work on the book. His processed fieldnotes were, however, destroyed in a fire soon after, and preparatory work of two decades was suddenly lost. It was Sol Tax who suggested to Srinivas not to bother about this loss but to write a book about the village on the basis of his memory. He accepted the advice and the result is *The Remembered Village* (1976),[1] which is now acknowledged as the capstone of his *oeuvre*.

The Remembered Village

The idea of studying a multi-caste village, Srinivas informs us (p. 1), was planted in his mind by Radcliffe-Brown in 1945–6. Later, when the opportunity for fieldwork in India came after his appointment as Lecturer in Indian Sociology at Oxford, he came to his native Karnataka, then called Mysore (the initial 'M' in his name stands for Mysore), and embarked upon intensive fieldwork such as he had not done before. Chapter I of *RV* describes 'how it all began', and how the choice of the village was made more on sentimental rather than rational grounds. Chapter II introduces the reader to the village and describes the relationships which Srinivas was able to establish with the villagers. The advantages and disadvantages of his being a Mysore Brahman anthropologist and the successes and failures of his fieldwork are mentioned. His choice of friends, and some villagers' choice of him as their friend and patron, are also described. The next chapter is devoted to 'three important individuals': the headman; Kulle Gowda, Srinivas's fieldwork assistant and factotum; and Nadu Gowda, a rich elderly peasant leader.[2] The description of the relations of these men to other people in the village brings out some salient aspects of social and economic life in the village—for instance, the relations between a landowner and those villagers of other castes who are dependent upon him.

Chapter IV is devoted to 'the universe of agriculture', which Srinivas calls the 'dominant'(he obviously means the most important) activity in the village. Land, water, crops, animals and trees are discussed in terms of an overall agricultural complex. There are, of course, no hard quantitative data: these were consumed in the arson at Palo Alto. Economic activities are the bridge between the domestic and the extra-domestic domains. Moving into the household (Chapter V), Srinivas discusses the sexual division of labour and some other aspects

---

[1] Henceforward in this chapter, *The Remembered Village* is also briefly referred to as *RV*. Citations from the book are identified by page numbers only without the usual identification of the source by the year of its publication.

[2] These three men may be said to have comprised Srinivas's 'convoy'. I have used this term to designate those associates of a fieldworker who are more than informants, and help in providing orientation to the outsider journeying through their society (see Madan 1989: xxii, 270–3).

(conjugal and sexual) of the relations between adult men and women.

Relations between castes occupy the centre of the book in Chapter VI as they do of the discussion as a whole. It is almost as long as Chapter III which is the longest in the book. The reader who remembers Srinivas's earlier papers on Rampura will find himself on familiar ground. Harijans and Muslims are discussed along with the others. Srinivas, however, expresses regret over the paucity of his field data on these groups, and therefore of his memory of them. 'I realize only too clearly', he writes, 'that mine was a high caste view of village society' (p. 197). The ideas in terms of which the data are organized are social ranks and purity and pollution. He proceeds to describe what he calls the land-based hierarchy of classes (Chapter VII). The traditionally harmonious patron–client relationships and the interplay of factional interests form the substance of this chapter.

As elsewhere in India, technological change occupied a prominent place in the life of the people of Rampura soon after independence. Technological change, of course, went hand in hand with economic, political and cultural changes. These are discussed in Chapter VIII. In the midst of these changes there were abiding values, attitudes and behavioural patterns which together bestow on social relations any-where their most characteristic qualities. Chapter IX of the book is devoted to the explication of this theme under the headings of 'recip-rocity', 'hierarchy' (not in the Dumontian sense), 'face' (that is, hon-our), 'friendship and enmity', 'gossip', 'envy', and 'sense of humour'.

Religion is dealt with in Chapter X. Srinivas is not concerned with Sanskritic Hinduism here but religion as one encounters it in the every-day life of villagers. The kinds of deities and their characters, sectarian orders, belief in astrology, etc. are all described. Some religious ideas of the villagers are also discussed.

In the concluding chapter ('Farewell'), Srinivas writes of himself, as he does in the opening chapter, describing what fieldwork did to him and how the village and its people came to possess him, as it were, in some measure. Three short appendices, mainly on calendrical matters, and a glossary of Kannada terms follow.

Evaluation

The Remembered Village is a rather big book (about 350 pages), with a large aim. It attempts to present a comprehensive account of the village of Rampura in south Karnataka as also of the experience of fieldwork: it is not only an account of what the ethnographer saw and heard but also of what the seeing and hearing did to him. Srinivas's first two books, as I have described above, had specific themes: marriage and the family in the one case and religion and society in the other. The Coorg book also had a self-conscious theoretical load. *RV* has no sociological problem *per se* as its central concern and Srinivas apparently would like to assure the reader that he has no theoretical axe to grind. His explicitly stated intention, it may be repeated, is to write about Rampura and its people as he found them in 1948. Hence Srinivas writes about several aspects of village life—social structure, economy, culture, religion, social change, and so forth. One notices the neglect of marriage and the family. Perhaps more surprising is the fact that politics should not have been dealt with at any length, for it had been one of his important concerns as a sociologist during the 1950s and 60s. This is particularly noticeable because caste, the other major theme of Srinivas's sociological work, retains a central place in *RV*. Though the book is about the village, it is in fact pre-eminently about caste or, more specifically, about upper castes and the rural elite.

The question of the contents of the book is, of course, not important in itself. What is important is the fact that most of the contributors to the review symposium think that Srinivas has succeeded in evoking the totality of village life in his account of it, that he has been able to vividly capture the human element and convey the 'feel' of Rampura to the reader. This is in contrast to his earlier major works in which we encounter no human beings, only customs and rules of social intercourse, only status structures and role occupants. It is suggested that Srinivas has now been able to do this, despite the lack of detailed hard data, by recapitulating the impressions of his stay in the village and his memories of real people and real events. Scarlett Epstein, who also did her fieldwork in Karnataka and collected ample hard data, frankly confesses her failure where Srinivas has succeeded. Chie Nakane suggestively compares *RV* to a high-quality painting which, she writes, reveals more of the essence of a scene than does a photograph, by dramatizing certain elements in it. Sol Tax's tribute to *RV* (in the Foreword) as an ethnographic work which is also a work of art is echoed by most of the reviewers. Alan Beals calls it an ethnographic 'masterwork', and Epstein, a 'classic'.

But there are also questions asked and doubts expressed about the content and quality of the narrative and about the narrator's theoretical stance and method. Thus, it is asked whether Srinivas has unwittingly produced an account which is in some essential respects misleading if not untrue. Has he frozen what must have been changing? Has he treated as an isolate what could properly be understood only when related to the 'outside' world? Has he underemphasized some aspects of social life and potentially important trends of change? Is he unable to disentangle his sociology from an interest in caste at the cost of an imperative concern with class? A major reason for this to have happened, it is suggested, is Srinivas's theoretical stance, which the critics find conservative and perhaps incapable of coming to grips with the new and highly relevant questions of today. While one need not wear one's theoretical framework on one's sleeve, one may not take its adequacy for granted, or silence queries about it by taking it on trust. In short, what are the questions underlying Srinivas's questions? In contemporary jargon, what is his 'problematique'?

Srinivas's theory is judged by some reviewers to have been derived mainly from Radcliffe-Brown, with some elements taken from Redfield, perhaps. Others discern the influence of Evans-Pritchard. Owen Lynch describes Srinivas's theory as interpretive and reflexive and his approach phenomenological. According to him these are not only significant but welcome developments in Srinivas's work. The subject–object continuum à la phenomenology is explicitly denied by David Pocock who considers the positivist subject–object dichotomy a regrettable feature of *RV*. On the whole, the reviewers find Srinivas's range of interests and sympathies limited, and this accounts for the apparently holistic narrative not being after all comprehensive.[3]

Apart from what is not noticed, there is also the problem of Srinivas's reactions, intellectual and emotional, to what he did notice, inquire about and remember. Most of the reviewers draw particular attention to the fact that he often was surprised by things and happenings in Rampura which he as an Indian might have expected or taken for granted. This is, of course, the common experience of anthropologists everywhere, but then the object of his study was his own society. Were his reactions an effort, perhaps unconscious, to protect his own beliefs and his own concept of rationality? If so, Srinivas's alienation from traditional Hindu culture assumes salience as an element in his narrative.

In this regard, it has been suggested that, there is an unresolved struggle between the anthropologist and the basically sensible Indian in

[3] In a recent comment, André Béteille, who acknowledges Srinivas's influence upon him early in his career, observes: 'analytical rigour was not Srinivas's strong suit; his strength lay rather in his sensitive imagination and his unerring instinct for the ambiguities in a social situation, or what he called its "messiness"' (1991: 5).

Srinivas. Srinivas apparently operated in the village as any other anthropologist from outside the cultural region, if not India, might have done. The tools of his study and analysis, it has been pointed out, were those designed for the study of 'other cultures'. There is a sense in which he *was* an outsider in Rampura: an urban, 'England-returned' (to use this expressive phrase), highly educated Indian. Add to this his caste status of a Brahman, and you have a clue to the social distance and the cultural surprise that seem to have characterized his situation in the village. Nakane, however, asks whether a deliberate exercise of anthropological surprise (doubt) was at work; if this was so, then it may well be a worthwhile technique for those who want to study their own society.[4] But, one recalls, Srinivas himself had earlier emphasized the importance of empathy, rather than 'distantiation' (see Srinivas 1966: 156), in the work of any anthropologist.

Questions about the technique employed in the composition of *RV*, namely, a total or almost total reliance upon memory, thus become important. Once again there is a diversity of opinion on this issue. On the one hand, it is asserted that, the least significant thing about *RV* is that it is based on memory, because it is not a basically different kind of ethnography that Srinivas has now provided us with from what he had published earlier. On the other hand, it has been claimed that, the special flavour of the narrative is the result of the combination of the faculties of observation, reflection and recall. But, it is asked, has Srinivas's need to rely on the remembrance technique landed him in contradictions and resulted in unsatisfactory coverage of hard data? Mayer asks the more fundamental question: has Srinivas indeed written from memory? He could not have, suggests Mayer, because, he had maintained fieldnotes and had analysed and used them before the writing of *RV*. He also had his field diaries which he occasionally consulted to check the accuracy of what he had written.

It is indeed a pity that Srinivas does not take up this question himself, for it is important. British empiricists, whose influence on social anthropology has been very prominent, have a long tradition of concern with the problem of memory, going back at least to Hume; and, of course, there is the later interest of psychoanalysts in the related problems of remembering and forgetting. Fredrik Barth (1966) devised his own remarkable version of memory ethnography when he memorized the fieldnotes of his friend, Robert Pehrson, in an effort to capture the wholeness of Marri Baluch life. If only Srinivas had revealed to us

[4] For an elaboration of this point, see Chapter 6.

the kind of book he had embarked upon writing before the arsonists set fire to his study, one would have had some clue to the kind of filter his memory has been. The worry about the lack of hard data in *RV*—whatever this means—seems to me the less important issue: the nature and significance of what is in the book is certainly more crucial.

What Srinivas chose to include in *RV* is, of course, not to be entirely attributed to his theoretical framework or technique; the kind of audience he had in mind also must have played an important part in this. Was the book intended for the intelligent layman or the specialist or both? A statement about the book being intended for the layman notwithstanding (p. xv), Srinivas does not face this problem squarely. (The publisher's blurb says that *RV* 'ought to be essential reading for all those concerned with India and with peasant societies'.) Whichever the audience, can the fact of Srinivas being a sociologist, even though engaged in writing a book which is part ethnography and part autobiography, be ignored? He had written earlier (Srinivas 1966: 158): 'Unlike the novelist... the sociologist is primarily interested in a theoretical explanation of human and social behaviour, and in generalizations rather than the development of concrete particularizations.'

It seems that *RV* does not quite answer to the foregoing description nor does it really constitute a personal anthropology. The book has its outstanding portions—Chapter IX on 'The quality of social relations' by common consent; also the account of 'Three important men' in Chapter III. Each reader will doubtless choose some other parts of the book also as being of high quality and deep interest, depending upon his or her own interests. Complete agreement on this will understandably be difficult, as is illustrated by Epstein's and Ravindra Jain's satisfaction with the discussion of religion, and K. P. Gupta's and Beals's dissatisfaction with it.

The above merely indicates the kinds of questions which Srinivas's professional colleagues have raised and will raise about the innovative book that *RV* is. These are questions about theory, method and data. *RV* poses other questions, too, such as that of the ethics of sociological fieldwork among one's own people. One wishes Srinivas had attended to this question, particularly because ethical considerations cannot but have acted as a constraint on his putting down on paper many things that he must have remembered. If they did not, why not?[5]

A question that arises from the symposium is, why is there such a

[5] For Srinivas's response to the review symposium, see Srinivas 1978: 127–52.

diversity of opinion among Srinivas's professional colleagues about his book as is revealed in it? Difference of opinion is, of course, quite common in social science review literature, but it seems to be rather sharp in the present case. It is possible that what is most distinctive about *RV*, namely the author's intention to write a personal account of life in a village, also explains the range of reaction to it, for there is no standard yardstick to measure the success of such a work. *RV* is, perhaps, more like the first Mysore book than like the Coorg or the social change book: it is descriptive rather than analytical. Srinivas says so himself. But whereas *Family and Marriage* was a new kind of work when it came out in 1942, *RV* as an account of an Indian village, published in the mid-1970s, is not. Its distinctiveness is difficult to identify in terms of the story that Srinivas has to tell. His manner of telling it is where he excels.

The contributors to this symposium are sociologists or social anthropologists and, as Mayer has noted, their response to the book is bound to be of a different nature from that of the so-called 'intelligent layman'. The latter may well like to read Srinivas's *The Remembered Village* alongside such outstanding novels of rural life in Karnataka as Raja Rao's *Kanthapura* (1938) or U. R. Anantha Murthy's *Samskara* (1976).

Raja Rao portrays a village in the 1930s, much like Rampura, with its caste streets and temples, untouchables and Brahmans, folklore, belief and ritual, and the encroaching administrative, economic and political frontiers. It is, in fact, a remarkable novel which anticipated the concerns of social anthropologists as these took shape in the 1950s. The village of Kanthapura, however, emerges as significant not in itself but in terms of its relations with ancient traditions and with contemporary events beyond its mud walls. Anantha Murthy describes not so much a village and its institutions as a trapped human being struggling to discover himself and make his own choices. The focus apparently is on the local Brahman community, but their predicament has universal import. Some readers will, perhaps, say that *RV* belongs more with the novels of Srinivas's famous friend, R. K. Narayan. It has the same emphasis on character and on the scenic in everyday life, the same delectable sense of humour as in Narayan's well-loved novels and stories about life in Malgudi. And did not Srinivas tell us in his *Social Change in Modern India* that the sociologist who chooses to study his own society is rather like the novelist? Others too—Marcel Mauss, Edmund Leach, and Clifford

Geertz, to name only a few spanning three generations—have commented insightfully on the affinity between the crafts of the ethnographer and the novelist.

POSTSCRIPT

As it has turned out, Srinivas has not authored another book since *The Remembered Village* was published sixteen years ago; but he has written several major essays and addresses including his Huxley, Frazer, and J. P. Naik Lectures (Srinivas 1977, 1984a, 1984b). In these he has, besides providing further reflections on old themes (such as the nature of the caste system), turned to new subjects, most notably the persistence of stresses and strains in the changing position of women in India. He has also written about policy matters of national concern, such as nation building and the cultural dimensions of human fertility, and given his assessment of the meaning and significance of contemporary change. In his usual thoughtful manner Srinivas observes that Indians are today 'living in a revolution', although many of them do not seem to be aware of this crucial fact. He points out that the key elements of this revolution are 'adult franchise, protective discrimination and land reforms'. He warns that, although this revolution began non-violently, it is 'now entering an increasingly violent phase' (1986: 24). He has also written of science and technology in the context of rural development and briefly discussed secularism. But lack of sustained attention to the rhetorics of secularism, socialism and technology in his studies of social change is rather surprising. The interface of caste and politics in rural India has been his main interest, and this he has analysed insightfully.

Conveniently from the readers' point of view, most of these essays and addresses have been made available in three volumes (Srinivas 1987, 1989, 1992). And, almost predictably, Srinivas has given us a delightful short story, 'The Image Maker', which is about rural life in Karnataka and, of course, about human fate (Srinivas 1988). But why only one?[6]

---

[6] For a discussion of Srinivas's views on westernization, see pp. 226–7, 245.

LOUIS DUMONT AND
THE STUDY OF SOCIETY IN INDIA

4
>*India . . . teaches us hierarchy, and this is no little lesson.*
>
>*It should be obvious, in principle, that a Sociology of India lies at the confluence of Sociology and Indology.*
>
>LOUIS DUMONT

I
INTRODUCTION

Sometime in 1954, Louis Dumont (b. 1911) gave a lecture on marriage and kinship in South India at the University of Lucknow, where I had just begun my research and teaching career. I think he was on his way to Gorakhpur, where he later (1957–8) conducted extensive fieldwork in a multi-caste village. I had already seen his early papers on the subject of his talk. The first of these (incidentally also his first publication on India) had been published in *The Eastern Anthropologist*, which was edited by D. N. Majumdar at the Anthropology Department of the University. Two other articles had come out in *Man* in 1953 (see Louis Dumont's bibliography in Madan 1982b). Most of us at the Lucknow University had found these papers rather 'technical' and difficult to grasp. His lecture was helpful to some extent in making us appreciate what he was doing.

I was particularly interested because I was at that time contemplating a study of marriage, family and kinship among the Brahmans of rural Kashmir. My anthropological studies until then had been conducted under the guidance of D. N. Majumdar (see Chapter 2), who

While Part I of this chapter, and the postscript, have been newly written, Parts II and III are reproduced here from *Contributions to Indian Sociology* (NS), vols. 5 (1971) and 15 (1981) respectively. I owe thanks to André Béteille and Jit Singh Uberoi for their advice and help with the preparation of the review symposium of which Part II was the introduction.

was a functionalist, combining the perspectives of Bronislaw Malinowski and Ruth Benedict. My difficulties with Dumont's way of ethnographic analysis were, therefore, quite understandable, but this was not clear to me then. As is well known, A. R. Radcliffe-Brown himself was quite puzzled by what these two Frenchmen, Claude Lévi-Strauss and Louis Dumont, were doing to his favourite areas of intellectual concern, namely 'social structure' and 'systems of kinship and marriage'.

In the event, my fieldwork among the Pandits of rural Kashmir (1957–8), immediately preceded by six months of preparation in the Department of Anthropology at the Australian National University (an outpost of British social anthropology) was not at all influenced by Dumont's ideas (see Chapters 6 and 8). The books I carried with me to the field were the Nuer and Tallensi kinship books of E. E. Evans-Pritchard (1951a) and Meyer Fortes (1949) respectively, and Irawati Karve's *Kinship Organization in India* (1953).

In 1958, however, when the first issue of *Contributions to Indian Sociology* (1957) became available to me in Canberra, I was particularly attracted by the programmatic statement, 'For a Sociology of India'. Dumont (and co-author David Pocock) seemed to offer an approach to the study of Indian society which was refreshingly different from the prevailing Anglo-American perspectives. What appealed to me most was not only the acknowledgement that the people being studied might have points of view, but also, in fact more so, the affirmation that these points of view—'the principles that the people themselves give' (ibid.: 12)—must be taken seriously, and even treated as fruitful points of departure for anthropological inquiry. Dumont and Pocock had at the same time pointed out that the distinctiveness of the anthropologist's method lay in attempting to 'see things from within (as integrated in the society which he studies) and from without' (ibid.: 11–12), that is as 'collective representations' *as well as* 'social facts'. This way of putting things seemed to me to broaden the anthropological perspective most meaningfully and open new vistas of research. Actually one was only going back to Émile Durkheim, breaking away from a narrow exegesis of his views by British and American scholars.

The writing of my dissertation, however, proceeded (1958–9) independently of this awakening, mainly because my fieldwork had been guided by other ideas, but also because I was not clear about all the nuances of the new approach and the way they were interrelated. On my return to Lucknow in 1959, I found that *Contributions to*

Indian Sociology had arrived there, and while everybody else saw it as yet another serial publication, A. K. Saran (one of my former teachers) regarded it as offering a misleading perspective. His rejection of it was vehement and he gave expression to his views in an extended review of the fourth number of the periodical which he wrote at my invitation (see Saran 1962b: 53–68), focusing mainly on Dumont's essay on renunciation. Saran's criticisms touched different issues from those that concerned me, but were not wholly unrelated. During 1962–3, I was in London, at the School of Oriental and African Studies, and encountered yet another sharply critical response to Dumont's position from F. G. Bailey, in writing (see Bailey 1959), but much more strongly in the spoken word. Saran's and Bailey's positions were, however, diametrically opposed to each other.

Back in India (at the Karnatak University, Dharwar), I decided to write to Dumont directly about my doubts: I did so in 1964. He promptly responded by asking me to prepare an article on the subject for publication in *Contributions*. I prepared a short paper in 1965, and this was published in the last issue of the journal (see Madan 1966b), alongside an article of his own, which included a response to my queries as well as to Saran's criticisms (see Dumont 1966a). My main point had been this: 'I am not wholly satisfied with the Dumont–Pocock argument regarding the external point of view which they say the sociologist shares with the natural scientist. I am not sure that such a point of view exists . . . . If it did, it should have been possible for us to study social life through observation unaided by communication with the observed people' (Madan 1966b: 12). (Were I writing today, I would perhaps mention the phenomenological and hermeneutic approaches and even speak of fieldwork as 'communicative experience'.) I had clarified that 'when the sociologist allows "the principles that the people themselves give" to enter into his analysis and explanation he surrenders a truly external position' (ibid.). I had also wondered if the proposed approach did not carry the reliance on the texts—on Indology—as against what ordinary people say, too far (ibid.: 15).

In his response Dumont acknowledged that the approach he had proposed could be called 'positive-cum-subjective', but said that the viability of the external point of view could not possibly be doubted, given the ethnographic analyses that had been published in *Contributions*, in which the two perspectives (internal and external) had been effectively combined (Dumont 1966a: 22). He added: 'Duality, or tension is here the condition *sine qua non* of social anthropology or, if one likes, of sociology of a deeper kind' (ibid.: 23). I was not wholly convinced, and reiterated in a rejoinder that 'the *existence* of a body of literature [does not] settle the question of its *utility* or *epistemological status*' (Madan 1967: 90). I was, however, satisfied that Dumont had conceded that 'the implications' of their position 'should be more fully worked out' (Dumont 1966a: 22).[1]

The publication of the English edition of *Homo Hierarchicus* in 1970 seemed to offer an excellent opportunity for further discussion of the Dumontian approach and its substantive analytical results. Although the original French edition had come out three years earlier (see Dumont 1966b), it had remained inaccessible to all but a very few Indian readers. Accordingly, I thought it worthwhile to organize a review symposium on the book for publication in *Contributions*. Dumont readily gave his consent. (A similar request from Sol Tax, editor of *Current Anthropology*, reached Dumont after my suggestion, and he decided to advise against a second symposium.) Nearly all the scholars I invited to contribute reviews agreed. M. N. Srinivas, however, wrote that he was not ready with a considered response, and G. S. Ghurye did not reply.

Reproduced below as the second part of this Chapter is my commented summary of *Homo Hierarchicus* (Dumont found it quite dependable [see Dumont 1971: 58]), which appeared as the introduction to the review symposium in *Contributions to Indian Sociology* (NS) 5, 1971: 1–13. The article also highlighted some of the issues which were raised by the contributors to the symposium. As had been agreed, Dumont wrote an essay in which he clarified the notion of hierarchy and responded selectively to some of the points made by the other contributors

[1] Two points for record. (1) In the letter I wrote Dumont in 1964 (mentioned above), I also expressed regret that *Contributions* was going to cease publication and urged him to reconsider the decision. He obviously had received similar remonstrances from other colleagues. His reply to me was to ask why we did not take responsibility for a successor journal. A three-cornered correspondence and personal consultations followed in 1965, involving Dumont, Adrian Mayer and myself, and later F. G. Bailey and David Pocock also. *Contributions to Indian Sociology*, New Series, was thus launched in 1967, a year after the original periodical ceased publication.

(2) Nearly thirty years after the event, a careful Brazilian scholar has pointed out that I had misquoted A. K. Saran in my 1966 paper; that his statement (in his 1962 review of Dumont, cited above) had been that 'social reality *qua* social has no "outside"' and not, as I had written, 'social reality *qua* reality has no "outside"' (Pierano 1991: 325, fn.1). Regrettably, Dumont, though familiar with Saran's original text had relied on my quotation. The misquotation was, of course, not intentional, and I do not think it seriously misled him.

as well as by reviewers elsewhere (notably McKim Marriott) (see Dumont 1971: 58–81).

One of my own main observations was in line with my 1966 query about the problem of integrating the views from within and without. The particular form this had taken in *Homo Hierarchicus* was reflected in what I described as the unusual design of the book, with a main and a supplementary text, the former constructed theoretically and deductively, and the latter derived from empirical evidence available in Indian ethnography and constituting a considerable body of elucidatory notes. Ascertaining the fit between the model and the contemporary social reality seemed, I had written, to be only a secondary concern, resulting in the 'devaluation of the ethnographic datum' (Madan 1971: 4).

Responding to this point rather fleetingly, and in the specific context of contemporary social change, Dumont had observed that 'development' was not a 'social', but 'at bottom' an 'individualistic category', and hence it was not surprising that I was 'worried about the limited usefulness of the theory expressed in *Homo Hierarchicus* for the study of "contemporary change"' (Dumont 1971: 78).

Responding more directly in the Preface to the 'complete revised English edition' of *Homo Hierarchicus* (1980), he emphasized that, in his considered judgement, the textual duality, or unresolved tension, that I had detected, did not in fact exist: 'the "model" is given in order to account for "contemporary social reality" entirely in the perspective governed by social anthropology . . . . I state that I have always given the last word to observed reality . . . . I think this is confirmed by the fact that, when necessary, I have emphasized the difficulties the argument contains and the antinomies it draws near, so that critics who wish to stress them often need only to quote the text . . . . If one wishes, there is certainly devaluation in the sense that not all the empirical data are situated at the same level of ideology. The objection bears on the hierarchization of traits' (ibid.: xxii–iii).

The two responses read together have the merit of clarifying Dumont's position, but they also reinforce my suspicion that the relationship between the 'ideology' and the 'observed reality' is problematic. If observed reality indeed has the last word, then this seems to be so only in particular expressions of it, which are predetermined by the ideology. Put simply, this means that all that is observed is not equally significant. One would hardly want to disagree with that, nor with the principled stand that clearly stated criteria are needed to make the judgement. The problem lies with the manner in which a particular criterion emerges as self–certified, as it were, and of an all–encompassing character.

Dumont's relative lack of interest in on–going social change is an aspect of the same problem. I concede, however, that he, like any other scholar, had the right to decide on what to focus his attention. And he has stated it explicitly, in more than one place, that he considers the continuities in social life in India more significant than the changes.

It is obvious that such judgements about the empirical reality are derived from other judgements made at the level of 'first principles', which actually go beyond, and indeed confront, the principles that the people being studied themselves enunciate. Dumont acknowledged this encounter of ideologies later in a major statement on the subject. Taking note of the increasing attention being paid by anthropologists to ideas, values, and ideologies, he called for, 'by way of complementarity', 'reflection on the ideology of the anthropologist himself; in the double sense of the ideology of his speciality and that of the surrounding society' (1986b: 203). I guess this would be called the cultivation of 'reflexivity' in today's jargon (see Chapter 8). Max Weber, of course, anticipated all of this, but that is another story.

Part Three of the Chapter is an abridgement of the essay 'For a Sociology of India' (Madan 1982a), which appeared as the epilogue in the volume that I put together to felicitate Dumont on his seventieth birthday in 1981, and to mark the twenty–fifth anniversary of the founding of *Contributions to Indian Sociology* in 1957. The Festshrift was released early in 1982 as volume 15 (1981) of *Contributions* and as a book, *Way of Life: King, Householder, Renouncer: Essays in Honour of Louis Dumont* (Madan 1982b), which was published in both Delhi and Paris. The contributors had been invited to turn attention to Dumont's work in the specific context of the Hindu (Brahmanical) notions of 'goal–oriented action' (*puruṣārtha*) and 'the good life'. The result had been a very rich volume of essays covering a variety of themes from several disciplinary perspectives. In the epilogue I had tried to contextually locate Dumont's contributions to the making of the sociology of India. I had also highlighted the issues which the contributors had raised in relation to his work, acknowledging its seminal influence. Given the nature of the book, which was a tribute to Louis Dumont's role as an outstanding pathfinder, no response had been solicited from him, though it included an edited version of a conversation between him and Jean-Claude Galey bearing on different aspects of his professional life (see ibid.: 13–22).

II

ON THE NATURE OF CASTE IN INDIA

Homo Hierarchicus: *General Principles*

Louis Dumont's credentials as an Indianist are of an exceptionally high order. He is a scholar of international renown who is equally at home in the domains of sociology, social anthropology, and Indology. The subjects on which he has written have an impressive range and include Hinduism, caste, kinship, marriage, kingship in ancient India, and social–political movements in modern India. His *magnum opus, Homo Hierarchicus,*[1] is an unusual work in its conception, design and execution. It is deserving of our most serious study.

  The task that Dumont set himself is succinctly announced in the subtitle of the book: an inquiry into 'the caste system and its implications'.[2] The first question that will, therefore, occur to the reader is: How does Dumont define caste? Definitions, which should constitute part of the conclusions of a scientific inquiry, by necessity have to be its starting point as well. This fact often is at the root of considerable confusion as all kinds of *a priori* assumptions creep into a chosen definition which influences the course of inquiry and almost predetermines its conclusions. One of the refrains of Dumont's book is that the Western scholars' definition of caste as a type of social stratification

---

[1] *Homo Hierarchicus: Essai sur le système des castes* (445 pages) was originally written in French and published by Gallimard of Paris in 1966. An English translation by Mark Sainsbury, under the title of *Homo Hierarchicus: The Caste System and its Implications* (xxii + 386 pages), was published in 1970 in the USA and in England by the University of Chicago Press and Weidenfeld and Nicolson respectively. It was published in India in 1971 by Vikas Publications of Delhi.

  The first draft of the translation was revised by Dumont. We are therefore assured of its faithfulness to the original text. The English version differs from the original work only inasmuch as three of the four essays forming the Appendices of the latter have been omitted and a new Preface has been added. All these essays were originally published in *Contributions to Indian Sociology* (1957–66). The three omitted pieces were included in a collection of the author's essays, *Religion, Politics and History in India* (1970), and in the complete English edition of *Homo Hierarchicus* (1980).

[2] Dumont writes in the Preface to the English edition that its subtitle is what he had chosen for the original work, but that it had been abandoned on the French publisher's insistence who found it 'too technical' (xi).

is ethnocentric. They must therefore liberate themselves from their preconceived ideas (such as egalitarianism, individualism, the pre-eminence of politics and economics in society) by which they are trapped. Caste, which undoubtedly stands for 'inequality', in theory as well as in practice, should not be interpreted as a notion which is the opposite of 'equality', and therefore an anomaly or, worse, a per-version. The inequality of the caste system is a special type of inequality, and the sociologist's principal task is to lay bare its nature. Let us see how Dumont does this.

Dumont writes in the Preface to the French edition: 'In a work of this nature, everything depends in the last analysis on the theoretical orientation. On this point it is not enough to say that I owe everything, or almost everything, to the French tradition of sociology. For not only has it nurtured me, my ambition is to extend it' (xv–xvi).[3] Suffice it to point out here that it is the intellectualist or idealist orientation in this tradition which is the dominant element in Dumont's conception of the office of sociology: sociologists should concern themselves with forms or essences: they must penetrate the facade of observable behaviour to get at the 'ideas and values' which the people being studied themselves assume, recognize and express

> the ideas which they [the people] express are related to each other by more fundamental ideas *even though these are unexpressed*. Fundamental ideas literally 'go without saying', and have no need to be distinct, that is tradition. Only their corollaries are explicit. The caste system for example appears as a perfectly coherent theory once one adds the necessary but implicit links to the principles that the people themselves give (1957a: 12, reprinted in 1970b: 7).

Dumont has consistently put forward this point of view for quite some time now; in the present work we find its most extended appli-cation. Needless to emphasize here, the search for latent, underlying structues is a first principle of the methodology of structuralism.

The French (and German?) sociological tradition leads Dumont to stress the role of ideology in moulding human behaviour and, there-fore, to seek to bring together sociology and Indology. Following Bouglé, one of the French masters, he chooses the Hindu notion of the fundamental opposition between the pure and the impure as his starting point for an understanding of the caste system. Bouglé, at the beginning of this century, had defined the caste system as consisting

---

[3] Page numbers in parenthesis, without reference to their source, throughout this chapter refer to the English edition of *Homo Hierarchicus*.

of hierarchically arranged hereditary groups, separated from each
other in certain respects (caste endogamy, restrictions on eating
together and on physical contact), but interdependent in others (traditional division of labour). Dumont stresses the importance of recognizing these three features, or 'principles', as mutually entailed, resting
on 'one fundamental conception', for the atomization into simple
elements is the student's need and not a characteristic of the system
itself. What we need in order to transcend the distinctions we make is
'a single true principle'. Such a principle, Dumont maintains, is the
opposition of the pure and the impure. 'This opposition underlies
hierarchy, which is the superiority of the pure to the impure, underlies
separation because the pure and the impure must be kept separate,
and underlies the division of labour because pure and impure occupations must likewise be kept separate. *The whole is founded on the
necessary and hierarchical coexistence of the two opposites*' (43).[4]

Hierarchy, defined as the superiority of the pure over the impure,
then, is the 'keystone' in Dumont's model of the caste system. It is of
the greatest importance to realize at once that, as employed by him,
the notion 'is quite independent of natural inequalities or the distribution of power' (20). It is *'the principle by which the elements of a
whole are ranked in relation to the whole*, it being understood that in the
majority of societies it is religion which provides the view of the
whole, and that the ranking will thus be religious in nature' (66). In
other words, hierarchy is the relationship between 'that which encompasses and that which is encompassed' (xii). Such a perspective helps
us to obtain a holistic view of the system and to overcome the dualism
of opposition.

Dumont's starting point—his definition of caste—is clearly stated.
The questions which arise next are: What does he do with it? Where
does he proceed from it and how?

Dumont's concern in the present work is with 'the traditional
social organization of India from the point of view of theoretical
comparison' (xv). He sees his task as the construction of a model of
the traditional caste system, of an ideal type. He is concerned only
secondarily with ascertaining the 'fit' between it and contemporary
social reality. His construction of the model does not proceed in the

---

[4] Among Indian students of the caste system writing in English, Ketkar probably
was the first to emphasize the notion of purity-pollution. He called it 'the chief principle on which the entire system depends . . . the pivot on which the entire system turns'
(1909: 121–2). He also distinguished caste gradation from socio-economic ranking.
And his authority was Manu.

manner of the chronology-oriented historian, either. In fact, Dumont declares at the very outset that he has 'not set out to provide a *history* of the caste system' (xix), though he employs historical data in his analysis. His method is that of a theorist: he begins with a key idea and then proceeds deductively and dialectically, working out its implications step by step. He calls his work an 'experiment' (xiii): if the reader remembers this, he will appreciate better what Dumont does in the book and the manner in which he does it. Dumont's regret seems to be that 'the work as a whole remains semi-deductive, which is hardly surprising in the present state of the social sciences' (xix).

An important problem that arises in the context of Dumont's method is his use of ethnographical materials. He does this in two distinct ways; one might say he employs it at two different levels. Having declared his foremost concern to be with ideology, i.e. with 'a system of ideas and values' (36), he hastens to caution that 'ideology is not everything' (37). Ideology will not *explain* everything, though it encompasses the whole of social reality; nor does observation of actual behaviour *reveal* everything. There remains a 'residue' (not necessarily of inferior ontological status) which is deduced from a 'confrontation of ideology with observation' (77). In the main text of the book ethnographical materials are employed in such a confrontation—but more about this later.

At another level, Dumont uses ethnographical data to elucidate, elaborate or qualify various aspects of the main argument. They are presented in the form of notes which cover 83 pages (set in thinner type than the main text). The bibliographical references cited in the notes come to about 400 items. The notes are in the nature of a supplementary work, as it were. It was this feature of the book which I had in mind when I described it above as being unusual in design.[5]

Homo Hierarchicus: *A Summary*

I have so far made an attempt briefly to describe the scope of Dumont's work and the methodology employed by him. I will now give a chapter-wise synopsis of the contents of the book to show how he constructs his argument.

The introductory chapter, we are told, was written with the French reader in mind, to pinpoint for him why the understanding of caste should be of interest to him, given his devotion to the values of

[5] One may contrast Dumont's use of ethnographical materials with Mandelbaum's in his recent work (1970) in which he tries to construct an account of continuity and change in society in India *on the basis* of such materials.

egalitarianism and individualism. The caste system teaches us a fundamental social principle, namely hierarchy (2). And we can fully understand equality only after we have contrasted it with the opposite notion,
which should be hierarchy and not inequality. Hierarchy is an indispensable element of social life everywhere, but it is in India, where it
is explicitly affirmed, that it is best studied.

Chapters 1, 2 and 3 deal with the concepts employed in the work
and outline the ideology of caste. Dumont begins with a critique of
the Western scholars' ethnocentric conceptions of caste during the
19th and 20th centuries, and also complains of the pernicious separation between the so-called textual and contextual studies. The
notions of 'system' and 'structure' are then introduced: 'the caste
system is above all a system of ideas and values, a formal, comprehensible, rational system, a system in the intellectual sense of the term . . . .
Our first task is to grasp this intellectual system, this ideology' (35).
Castes, we are further told, are mutually related through 'a system
of oppositions, a structure' (39), i.e. in terms of the opposition between the pure and the impure. A discussion of purity-pollution
follows.

Chapter 3 deals with hierarchy and the theory of *varṇa*. It is a most
crucial discussion and focuses on the differentiation (disjunction) of
status and power and the subordination of the king to the priest in
Hindu society. Hierarchy is said to involve gradation, but is asserted
to be distinct from both power and authority. It is 'religious ranking'
and classifies 'things' and 'beings' according to their 'degree of dignity'
(65).[6] It is an all-embracing, comprehensive concept. Hierarchy and
the scheme of *varnas* are found to be in consonance with each other,
as are *varna* and *jati*. In fact, hierarchy encompasses both the *varna*
divisions and the caste system. What remains problematic, however,
is the connection of hierarchy with power, for 'hierarchy cannot give
a place to power as such, without contradicting its own principle.
Therefore, it must give a place to power without saying so, and it is
obliged to close its eyes to this point on pain of destroying itself' (77).
At this point, Dumont undertakes a somewhat detailed examination
of ethnographical evidence (Risely, Mayer and Marriott) to examine the
interaction between purity and power in 'actual situations'. He concludes that though both 'interaction' and 'attributions' (as distinguished

---

[6] It may be of some interest to recall that Durkheim associated hierarchy with sacredness and dignity. He wrote of '. . . the hierarchy of things [wherein the sacred
objects] are naturally considered superior in dignity and power to profane things'
(1964a: 37).

by Marriott) are present in such situations, the ideological orientation prevails.

Having introduced the ideology, Dumont proceeds to consider aspects of behaviour within and between castes in terms of it. Chapter 4 shows that the traditional division of labour (the *jajmani* system) is based on religious values rather than on economic logic. It does not, however, account for all economic transactions, and Dumont admits this. Chapter 5 considers the regulation of marriage (endogamy, isogamy, hypergamy) in terms of the key concept of hierarchy. Chapter 6 carries the argument further to cover rules concerning contact, untouchability, food and vegetarianism. The opposition between the pure and the impure emerges clearly and convincingly in these three chapters.

Chapter 7 deals with power and territory and Chapter 8 with justice and authority. It is here that the confrontation of the ideology with observed social reality is most prominent: 'in conformity with our method, we shall now begin to set out what is actually encountered in caste society while not figuring directly in the ideology' (152). We are now brought face to face with territory, power, social dominance, and ownership of wealth, and their mutual relationship. These are said to be questions of fact and not at all of theory. In fact, in terms of the theory, they enter 'surreptitiously' on the scene: power pretends to be the equal of status (153). Dominant caste, factions and economics also are discussed in this very framework. The final conclusion expectedly is: 'just as religion in a way encompasses politics, so politics encompasses economics within itself. The difference is that the politico–economic domain is separated, named, in a subordinate position as against religion, whilst economics remains undifferentiated within politics' (165).

The results of the 'experiment' are not yet complete, however. Chapter 8 passes on (from power) to authority. Ethnographical data on caste government from Uttar Pradesh are examined. Such matters as the source of authority, the village *panchayat*, the caste assembly, caste jurisdiction, and excommunication are discussed. Here also Dumont makes a major concession in favour of ethnographical evidence as against ideology. To understand the exercise of authority, the principle of hierarchy is held to be applicable but incomplete: it is 'completed by dominance' (183).

The problems discussed in Chapters 7 and 8 are described as difficult and controversial and are said to

hinge round a simple dilemma. Either power must be accommodated within the theory of caste, as here, or else the theory of caste must be brought under the notion of power and 'politico-economic' relations .... It is a matter of approach.... The fact remains that the empirical approach [which highlights politics and economics] is a misconstruction of Indian civilization: it amounts to assimilating *dharma* to *artha* . . . (308).

The main argument of Dumont's essay ends with Chapter 8. Chapter 9 deals with renunciation and sects—the opposites of the notions of 'collective man' and caste. An examination of these is a methodological necessity (device) for Dumont, for he seeks an understanding of India (and of Western society) through a dialectical process, through the juxtaposition of logically opposite cultural types. He writes:

> It may be doubted whether the caste system could have existed and endured independently of its contradictory, renunciation. The point is important for comparison with the West: we are not dealing with a solid opposition, as if in one case there was nothing but the individual, in the other nothing but collective man. For India has both distributed in a particular way (186).

This is a most important conclusion: the fundamental structural elements of these two (all?) societies are the same: highly significant differences between them arise out of the different patterns of relationship between the elements, however.

Chapter 10 takes up the problem of comparison: 'are there castes among non-Hindus and outside India' (201)? Given Dumont's emphasis upon ideology and upon hierarchy, it is not surprising to read: 'One is therefore led to see the caste system as an Indian institution having its full coherence and vitality in the Hindu environment, but continuing in existence, in more or less attenuated forms, in groups adhering to other religions' (210). Enlarging the scope of comparison, Dumont suggests that caste should be deemed to be present *only* where the disjunction between status and power is present and where castes exhaust the entire society (214–15).

In Chapter 11 comparison is continued, but in temporal, rather than spatial, terms. In other words, Dumont takes up the problem of change: 'What is the caste system becoming nowadays?' (217). The tone of the whole discussion is set by his statement made at the very outset that contemporary literature 'exaggerates' change. 'One thing is certain: the society as an overall framework has not changed ... there has been change *in* the society and not *of* the society' (218). And again:

'Given our way of thinking, we must face the fact that the anticipated links between technico-economic change and social change did not operate, and that caste society managed to digest what was thought [by Marx, among others] must make it burst asunder' (218).

In Dumont's view, the only significant change that does seem to have taken place is that the traditional interdependence of castes has been replaced by 'a universe of impenetrable blocks, self-sufficient, essentially identical and in competition with one another' (222). Dumont calls this 'the substantialization of caste'. An inventory of sources of change in the caste system lists juridical and political changes, social–religious reform, westernization, growth of modern professions, urbanization, spatial mobility, and the growth of market economy. But, despite all these factors making for change, the most ubiquitous and general form that change has taken in contemporary times is one of a 'mixture', or 'combination', of traditional and modern features (228–31).

Dumont concludes by asserting that hierarchy is 'a universal necessity' and that, if it is not formally recognized in a society, it may assert itself in a pathological form (e.g., racism). It is, therefore, of the greatest importance for Western man to endeavour to study and understand a social system in which hierarchy is recognized, and, in fact, accorded the status of a first principle. That is why the book is offered to the French public.

The Appendix contains Dumont's well-known essay, 'Caste, Racism, and "Stratification"', first published in 1960. It presents all the principal ideas elaborated in *Homo Hierarchicus* and should help the reader to recapitulate the argument.[7]

Commentary and Criticism

Homo Hierarchicus is a most impressive achievement and shall long remain a basic work for the students of Indian societies. Dumont's view of caste stands a long way off from that of Henry Summer Maine, one of the founding fathers of comparative sociology, who, writing about a hundred years ago, condemned it as 'the most disastrous and blighting of all human institutions' (1917: 11). Not that Dumont is interested in defending caste; he does regard it worthy of serious study, however, if only to better understand that Western society itself which Maine and his contemporaries regarded as the acme of human history.

[7] For a more detailed summary in English, see Boel 1968.

To what extent Dumont is successful in the latter enterprise—i.e., in his effort to understand *Homo aequalis* in terms of the opposite type of *Homo hierarchicus*—remains to be seen. It is even more difficult for an Indian to judge whether the Western reader—the Frenchman—to whom Dumont says the present work is addressed, is going to have a better appreciation of his own culture and society as a result of reading it. It may well be argued that the intellectualist vision is but a mirage for the empiricist—that those who unremittingly pursue political and economic *interests* are unlikely to find a sociology of *values* the most useful of analytical frameworks. Such speculation is not very relevant right now [in 1971], however. *Homo Hierarchicus* is a work complete in itself and must be judged as such.

What distinguishes this work from the usual social anthropological discussions of caste is that it does not proceed from fieldwork to a model of how the system works. Instead it begins with a cardinal explanatory principle—hierarchy—and boldly sets out to build a model thereon, maintaining throughout the position that theory or ideology overrides and encompasses ethnography. A conscious and single-minded preoccupation with the ideology of complementarity and separation leads Dumont to ask fundamental questions about Hindu society and about the structuralist method. Most contributors to the review symposium (see *Contributions to Indian Sociology* (NS) 5 (1971: 13–81)[8] have noted this (as have others writing elsewhere). In fact, Leach rightly asserts that it is his concern with basic issues which makes Dumont 'one of the most important sociological thinkers of his generation.'

The same preoccupation and the consequent devaluation of the ethnographic datum also bothers some of Dumont's critics most. They complain of his cavalier attitude to empirical evidence. Berreman's comment is a forceful statement of such criticism. He accuses Dumont of presenting a 'distorted image' of the caste system based upon 'limited, biased, albeit scholarly, sources of evidence'.

Fürer-Haimendorf is by no means critical, as Berreman is, but he too regrets that Dumont did not spread his net wide enough so as to examine non-Hindu tribal societies. Such an exercise would have sharpened Dumont's analytical categories, he thinks. It would have released him from his preoccupation with the pure–impure dichotomy

---

[8] The contributors were: G. D. Berreman, Veena Das and J. P. S. Uberoi, C. von Fürer-Haimendorf, J. C. Heesterman, D. Kantowsky, R. S. Khare, E. R. Leach, and Milton Singer.

and brought him face to face with situations where status has other bases such as 'sacredness'. He fails to appreciate that Dumont is concerned with Hindu society and not with a general theory of status ranking.

The question, it seems to me, is not whether Dumont *himself* has taken note of this or that piece of ethnography. Such a question could perhaps be addressed to Mandelbaum (1970). Not only has Dumont drawn on and cited quite a massive body of Indological and ethnographical literature, but such an approach to the assessment of the value of a model is also wholly erroneous. As Leach puts it, his argument is 'autonomous' of the 'hard facts of the case'. Conceptual models are neither real nor intended to be replicas of reality. We choose some initial conditions upon which to build a model obviously not with a view to falsify ethnographic reality but in order to simplify it—overcome its complexity—by introducing a particular kind of order into it. Models, therefore, are not to be judged as true or false but as possessing more or less explanatory power. The important question then is: Are Dumont's categories of analysis so narrow that they fail to explain crucial issues in relation to the caste system—be these religious or politico-economic in nature—that have been highlighted by research workers? Khare makes the most general point in this connection. He acclaims Dumont's 'originality and brilliance' but suggests that 'the axioms that the author may tend to accept as "proven" under his scheme need to be continuously tested against new data.' He believes that better models emerge through 'a process of approximation'.

Das and Uberoi, and Heesterman also, acknowledge the importance of Dumont's work but they express their doubts about the adequacy of his use of the structuralist approach and, therefore, of his model. Das and Uberoi would like the pure–impure dichotomy to be replaced by the more inclusive opposition between the sacred and the non-sacred. In this they, of course, follow Durkheim who maintained that, 'In all the history of human thought there exists no other example of two categories of things so profoundly differentiated or so radically opposed to one another (as the sacred and the profane)' (1964a: 38). A model built on the opposition between the sacred and the non-sacred will shed light on a larger area of the ethnographic map, they suggest. They further argue that the notion of hierarchy needs to be supplemented by that of reciprocity and equality at the level of the mutual relations among the non-clean castes themselves. This suggestion is problematic, however: do we have one caste system or two? If one, then how can the use of two mutually exclusive principles of organization—hierarchy and equality—be defended? In other words, what is the relation between the two principles?

Heesterman maintains that the *brahman-kṣatra* relationship, all-important in Dumont's model, cannot be fully grasped in terms of complementarity alone: the notion of contradiction is also required and on an equal footing. He points out that Dumont hints at this but does not develop the argument, as he should have, for 'contradiction is at the core of all civilization' (see Heesterman 1985).

The *brahman-kṣatra* relationship is, in fact, one of the most crucial structural elements in Dumont's model of the caste system. He defines caste in terms of it: 'We shall say that there is caste only where this characteristic [the disjunction between *brahman* and *kṣatra*, i.e. between status and power] is present, and we shall request that any society lacking this characteristic, even if it is made up of closed status groups, be classified under another label' (214). Two issues arise from this stand: (1) Is the disjunction between status and power 'oversharp' (Singer) or 'false' (Berreman, Kantowsky)? (2) What is the import of Berreman's complaint that Dumont is against 'cross-cultural comparisons of caste organization'?

The notion of disjunction between status and power—the subordination of the latter to the former—does indeed create difficulties. I do not see, however, how one can call such a distinction false (or true) at the level at which Dumont employs it. Moreover, he is aware of the difficulties and devises his methodology of confronting ideology with observation—or, as Khare points out, of combining the attributional and interactional approaches—to deal with it. The approach is ingenious but the results are not wholly satisfactory. Dumont criticizes Bailey's model in which there is 'a high degree of coincidence between politico-economic rank and the ritual ranking of caste' (Bailey 1957: 266). He points out that when Bailey finds this congruence disappear at the two extremes of the hierarchy, he explains it away as 'a peculiar rigidity in the system of caste' in the middle rungs of which 'ritual rank tends to follow . . . economic rank' (ibid.: 266–7). Dumont emphasizes the expression 'peculiar rigidity' and calls it 'delightful' (76)!

If Bailey fails to make full allowance for status, does Dumont fare much better with power? He writes: '. . . power, devalued to the advantage of status at the overall level, *surreptitiously makes itself the equal of status in the interstitial levels*' (153, emphasis added). This is very well put, but I find an uncomfortable similarity between Bailey's and Dumont's predicaments. The 'peculiar rigidity' of the two extremes of the hierarchy in Bailey's model is matched by the 'surreptitious' entry of power into the middle rungs of Dumont's model.

Even so, the chief virtue of Dumont's exercise lies exactly in that he holds up for public view, as it were, the potentialities and limitations of his view of caste and of his methodology. If his critics are able to highlight the limitations, they are enabled to do so better because of his intensive inquiry. To that extent even they are in his debt. As for himself, Dumont believes that his choice of hierarchy as the cardinal explanatory principle was 'a good one and enabled us to test the consistency of the system' (212).

As for Dumont's emphasis upon the *specificity* of the Hindu caste system, and Berreman's criticism of this position, I personally stand behind the former. Dumont preserves the system by 'typifying' it and does not dissolve or neglect it by 'classifying' it (in this connection see also Dumont 1967a: 31ff.). His approach seems to me to be the truely sociological one, seeking the understanding of *particular* phenomena through the use of *general* concepts. Berreman's criticism of Dumont is based on too narrow a definition of the aims of the comparative method. How does Dumont arrive at the specificity of the Hindu caste system except through comparison which, however, stresses differences (particularities) as well as similarities between societies in terms of their underlying structural principles (see Dumont and Pocock 1960: 86–9)?[9] Further, does not Dumont's aim of employing a sociology of India to constitute 'an adequate idea of mankind' (1957a: 9) represent his commitment to the comparative method? One need hardly add that the present work begins and concludes with an avowal of this method when Dumont proclaims the relevance of an understanding of *Homo hierarchicus* for the study of *Homo aequalis*. Moreover, as Berreman himself points out, Dumont employs the tools and insights of European philosophy and sociology in his study of caste in India, and comparison is implied in this attempt.

Finally, we come to the important question of social change discussed by Dumont in the last chapter of his book. There seems to be

---

[9] Though it is true that Dumont derives his concepts from European sources, yet some of them are less alien to Hindu thought than may be readily imagined. Thus, the notion of 'pairs of opposites' is present in ancient Hindu literature as an instrument of argument. In fact, we find in the *Bhagavadgītā* (chapter, 2, verse 45), the exhortation that for true knowledge to be attained it is necessary for one to transcend the limitations of thought based on *dvanda*, i.e. pairs of opposites.

general agreement that one of the most urgent problems in Indian
sociology today is to achieve an understanding of modernization,
meaning by that much defined term, *inter alia*, the process of adaptation by which traditional institutions take on new functions and thus
undergo transformations in their meaning. Two reviewers, Kantowsky
and Singer, touch upon this problem. Both agree that Dumont does
not concern himself much with contemporary social change. But while
Kantowsky, reaches a pessimistic conclusion regarding the success of
sponsored social change in India on the basis of his reading of *Homo
Hierarchicus*, Singer feels that Dumont provides us with some fundamental insights which should make for optimism.

Kantowsky finds evidence of much greater social change in his
own fieldwork than Dumont concedes in his book. Similarly, Singer
suggests that Dumont overstresses stability of the caste system to the
point of equating it with stagnation. The merit of Dumont's model,
according to Singer, lies in the fact that it identifies a locus of
change—*artha*, the politico-economic domain—just as it identifies
the locus of stability—*dharma*.

My own chief problem lies right here. Dumont constructs a
model of traditional Hindu society. It is to be presumed that this
structure evolved over time. It is not clear, however, at what time
Dumont believes the crucial structural elements of the caste system,
as presented by him, to have crystallized. The best guess I can make
is that this happend before the arrival of the Muslim king on the
scene. His manner of citing literature is not very helpful in this respect.
More importantly, it seems that once the crystallization took place,
all further change was ruled out. Dumont seems to argue in the manner
of Plato that all change is illusory because reality is eternal and timeless.[10] Is it not Dumont's preconceptions, then, which make him
play down the element of change? He writes: 'a form of organization
does not change, it is replaced by another; a structure is present or
absent, it does not change' (219). This makes me uneasy, given the
definition of modernization I adopted above. It seems to me that
Singer overlooks this problem in Dumont's book.

[10] As already noted, Dumont acknowledges his primary indebtedness to the French
tradition in sociology. For one interested in tracing the lineage of his ideas beyond France,
the influence of the German idealists (particularly Hegel) and of the great Greek philosophers is obvious. Plato has just been mentioned. Dumont himself quotes Aristotle
(337) on the same theme and almost to the same effect. His intellectualism could be
traced as far back as Socrates who, we are told, maintained that thought is best when
the mind is gathered into itself.

It is true that, as Singer points out, the politico-economic domain in Dumont's model is more susceptible to change than status. But it seems reasonable to argue that such change is devalued in Dumont's model precisely because of its location. This may be unexceptionable when we have the traditional society in mind. But if the model prevents us from coming to grips with ongoing change, one has reason to worry. Today politicization and economic development have become the principal driving forces of social change not only in India but in most developing societies. Dumont's model would seem to ill-equip one for their study,[11] for he prejudges the outcome of the encounter.

III
FOR A SOCIOLOGY OF VALUES

Preoccupation with Caste

In the last several decades the contributions of an international community of scholars to the sociology and social anthropology of India have been impressive in both their scope and seriousness of purpose. Within the limitations that have been imposed by the state of the art and several other considerations—not all of which have been academic in nature—the achievements have been considerable. One of the positive characteristics of such an international enterprise should have been the widening of perceptions through the cross fertilization of ideas from different cultural backgrounds. Unfortunately this has not happened, at least not in the fullest measure. Indian sociologists have been the products of Western universities or their outposts in India and have remained rootless, being strangers equally to the Indian and the Western philosophical traditions. The need for a synthesis of the philosophical presuppositions of 'social science' has been voiced by some scholars, but no significant advances have been made mainly because the questions have not been posed properly: in fact, it is not easy to do so.

[11] It may be noted here that a contemporary and compatriot of Dumont, the economist Bettelheim (1968: 39–42, 95–100), has written optimistically about the breakdown of the caste system as agrarian reform and industrialization proceed apace. On the role of the politics of modernization, see Kothari 1970 and Rudolph and Rudolph 1967. Kothari opens his book almost dramatically thus: 'If "modernization" is the central tendency of our times, it is "politicization" that provides its driving force' (ibid.: 1).

So far as non-Indian sociologists are concerned, the majority of them have come from the UK and the USA and their contributions have been characterized expectedly by an overweening accent on empiricism. Their manner of the definition of problems and delineation of concepts and methods has had a deep influence on the work of Indian sociologists. It is noteworthy that the only non-Indian Asian sociologist of high stature who contributed to the sociological studies of India during this period, namely Chie Nakane of Japan, has also worked within the empirical tradition.

The dominant paradigms—structural functionalism and Marxism—contributed to a constriction of perspectives so that the sociology of India became in effect the study of village and tribal communities, of caste and kinship. 'Three things are absolutely necessary for the understanding of any cultural phenomenon in India', wrote Irawati Karve: 'These are the configuration of linguistic regions, the institution of caste and the family organization' (1953: 1). It was, however, caste which received the most attention because, perhaps, as G. S. Ghurye pointed out half a century ago, the foreigners (Westerners) found it not only strange but also ubiquitous in India (1932: 1).[12] By the early 1950s we find Majumdar complaining that society in India had been reduced to the caste system (1955: vi). So much so that when a book on kinship and the family among the Kashmiri Pandits was published in the mid-sixties (Madan 1965), a reviewer exclaimed: 'At last a book about Indian family and kinship which is not about caste' (Benedict 1966: 584)! Surely, there was work done on social and peasant movements, politics, cities, sadhus, and other subjects but these were the frills of the corpus. The only two major works from a Marxist point of view were, one, a study of the social background of Indian nationalism (Desai 1948), reprinted many times, and the other a work on the

[12] It is perhaps worth noting here that two years before Ghurye's book was published as a volume in 'The History of Civilization', edited by C. K. Ogden, another (in fact, the only other) work by an Indian scholar in this series, viz. N. K. Sidhanta's *The Heroic Age of India: A Comparative Study* (1929) had come out. A scholarly work based mainly on the *Mahābhārata*, and written from a cross-cultural perspective, it contained much material, including two chapters on 'society in the heroic age of India', which might have interested the student of Indian sociology. This did not happen. In fact, given the prevailing climate of opinion, it is perhaps not surprising that the book should have escaped the attention of Indian sociologists. Even so erudite a scholar as Irawati Karve, who herself wrote a book on the *Mahābhārata* (Karve 1974), and had earlier written on kinship usages as depicted in the epic (Karve 1953), does not seem to have been aware of it. Sidhanta was, of course, neither an Indologist nor a sociologist, but a professor of English literature; even so his book was an outstanding study when it appeared and retains its interest despite its outdated anthropological concerns.

rise and fall of the East India Company (Mukherjee 1958a). Both books were products of library research and concerned with the colonial period. Mukherjee was also involved in survey research and fieldwork and the focus of his interest was the villages of Bengal (Mukherjee 1957 and 1958b).

The preoccupation with caste in fieldwork was all to the good in as much as it focused the attention of the student on what was most distinctive about social structure in India: but the approach was extremely narrow. What began as a wholesome concern with the facts on the ground and a respect for the observable datum did, however, result soon in reducing Indian villagers into interacting pawns on the sociocultural chessboard, being moved hither and thither by 'fate', as they were said to believe, or by their 'interests', as the sociologists said they had discovered. Srinivas drew attention to the imperative need to move from the 'book-view' to the 'field-view' of Indian social reality and stressed the deepening of understanding achieved thereby (1962b: 63–9 *et passim*). Marriott evaluated the relative advantages of the attributional and interactional theories of caste, coming down quite explicitly on the side of a transactional view of intercaste relations (1959: 92–107, 1968: 133–71). Empiricism had indeed helped in establishing the data base of the sociology of India, but the datum was defined too narrowly to the near exclusion of ideas: the separation between 'fact' and 'value'—a hallmark of positivism— came to leave a deep imprint on the sociology of India. Mukherjee (1977, 1979) has written about these developments at length and I draw attention to his important and informative survey here, though our viewpoints diverge on several fundamental issues as do our assessments of major trends. The most notable summing up of the results of this empiricist tradition in the sociology of India was Mandelbaum's monumental two-volume *opus, Society in India* (1970). It brought out clearly the strength and the weakness of the dominant tendencies in the sociology of India during the 1950s and 1960s (see Madan 1972b: 754–7). [13]

Holistic Perspectives

An overwhelming preoccupation with caste and the understanding of it in terms of systemic models of interaction was, then, the distinctive contribution of sociologists to the understanding of Indian society during the first two decades of the present half of the century. Indian

[13] Since this essay was written (in 1951), another useful survey of research in the fields of sociology and social anthropology has been written by Yogendra Singh (1986).

society and culture had been, however, reflected upon and written about earlier in the century, and for longer than that, by scholars trained in Western methods of research and study. These earlier scholars had retained the traditional comprehensive viewpoint of the sociocultural reality which looked upon caste or *varṇa* as an element in a complex whole called the *varṇasrama* dharma, or the appropriate *way of life*, based on the organization of society in terms of the four social divisions called the *varṇa* and the ordering of individual lives in terms of the four life-stages called the *āśrama*. An overarching ideological framework for the individual and social dimensions of life was provided by the concept of the four goals of life called the *puruṣartha* and the notion of moral obligations entailing the five sacrifices or the *pancamahayajna*. Thus, one finds this comprehensive theory of society not only in the *Manusmṛti* (see Bühler 1886), but also in such widely read and influential contemporary expositions as Radhakrishnan's *The Hindu View of Life* (1927). I am not concerned in this essay with the criticism that this and similar expositions were written for Western audiences and contained oversimplifications and even distortions in order to present Hinduism in a form in which it would appear respectable in the West. The criticism is perhaps fair, but Indian sociologists have gradually turned away from such studies, and that is what is relevant here.

Radhakrishnan wrote: 'While the individual and social sides of karma are inseparably intertwined, the theory of varṇa or caste emphasizes the social aspect, and that of āśrama or stages of life, the individual aspect' (1927: 82). As for the notion of puruṣartha, he wrote: 'It binds together the kingdoms of earth and heaven' (ibid.: 79). It might also be recalled that a keen though prejudiced observer of the Hindu way of life in the nineteenth century, the Abbé Dubois, devoted more than half of his book on customs and manners to the entailments of the āśramas (1959: 160–541).

Right at the beginning of formal sociological studies of India, Thoothi, a Parsi scholar, wrote a doctoral dissertation at Oxford University in the early 1920s on what he called 'the methods of investigation of social life', with specific reference to Hindu society. He began his study with a discussion of the four puruṣārthas. In this early classic, now hardly remembered or read by anyone, Thoothi wrote that dharma, 'or the fundamental principles that govern life' in Hindu society, may be studied in terms of the concepts enunciated in the ancient texts. Of these the most notable, according to him, were *mārga* ('the way'), *mata* ('the doctrine that justifies the way') and *sampradāya* ('which combines a way and its doctrines in terms of a sect or following') (1935: 64). From these first principles he proceeded to consider social organization among the Vaishnavas of Gujarat in terms of varṇa, *gnyāti (jāti)*, *gotra* and *kula* as also their economic organization (the village community, trade guilds, towns and cities), and their literature, drama and fine arts—a splendidly holistic effort.

Subsequently, Prabhu (1954), a student of Thoothi and a social psychologist, also made an attempt to present the design of Hindu social organization in terms of the ideals of varṇāśrama dharma which, he wrote, provided the 'corner-stones' of society; further, he maintained that the working of this society was impossible to understand without taking into view the notion of puruṣārtha.

This brings us to the 1950s and the inauguration of the phase of modern sociological studies with which I am concerned here. Radhakamal Mukerjee, the doyen among Indian sociologists at that time, wrote an essay in which all the above notions are presented as a single integrated scheme of life. He observed: 'The entire scheme of duties and obligations of strata and stages of life (varṇasrama dharma) rests on a proper scaling of values of life (puruṣārtha)' (1951: 31).

The 1950s brought about the change of intellectual climate which I mentioned above, resulting in a turning away from and even the devaluation of ideas and ideologies as misleading rationalizations or as irrelevant linguistic survivals—in either case a dangerous trap—or as simply non-existent. The baby had indeed been thrown away with the bath water: to change the metaphor, a much needed cleansing operation ended up as amputation and mutilation. By 1961, Karve (1905–1970), who was perhaps the most erudite Indian cultural anthropologist of her generation, wrote a book entitled *Hindu Society—An Interpretation*, which was about jātis and varṇas and very little else.

Louis Dumont's Civilizational Perspective

The importance of the contributions of Louis Dumont to the sociology of India is best understood when seen in the light of the situation that was developing in the middle of the century, which I have outlined above. It is important to recall that when he came to India, he was already a mature scholar who had worked intensively at the Musée des Arts et Traditions Populaires in Paris (the nature of this museum was by no means an unimportant fact or influence), written a detailed study of Tarascon, a French folk festival, studied Sanskrit, and come into close contact with Claude Lévi-Strauss who had shown him the

Indian chapters of his *opus* on kinship. All this comes out in the transcript of Dumont's conversation with Jean-Claude Galey (see Madan 1982b: 13–22). A deep concern for ethnographic detail about social structure, collected and organized in terms of a general theory, informed his fieldwork among the Pramalai Kallar of Tamilnadu and has, in fact, characterized everything that he has written on India. Those critics who complain of Dumont's 'intellectualism' or his preoccupation with 'rationalism' do so in utter disregard of the magnitude of his contributions to the ethnography of Tamilnadu: needless to emphasize, all good ethnography has got to be local. Establishing himself firmly in the intensive study of a subcaste, he moved outwards into a consideration of the nature of marriage and kinship in South India. He then came to grips with certain major themes—kingship, individualism, renunciation—of the classical literature. Dumont is perhaps the only sociologist writing on India after 1950, who has written about the *Arthaśāstra* seriously and purposefully. The texts did not, however, become an exclusive preoccupation and he evinced keen interest in contemporary events of great historical importance —notably nationalism and communalism—and in the nature of village communities and the changes sought to be introduced into them. A fitting capstone of this body of rich and stimulating scholarly work was, of course, *Homo Hierarchicus* (1966b).

The vantage point from which Dumont viewed Hindu society and culture as also contemporary India was *civilizational* rather than *societal* and entailed both holism and comparison. He enunciated the essential elements of his approach in his inaugural lecture at the École Pratique des Hautes Études (6th Section) in 1955, which was later published in an abridged and revised English version (prepared jointly with David Pocock), under the title 'For a sociology of India', in the first number of *Contributions to Indian Sociology* (1957). It was stated at the very outset of this seminal essay that '*a sociology of India lies at the point of confluence of Sociology and Indology*' (Dumont and Pocock 1957: 7, emphasis added). Such an interdisciplinary approach was seen by the authors as a 'necessity' which was imposed upon the student 'by experience'. The unified (integrated) approach would lead one to an apprehension of the unity of India (or Indian civilization) in the midst of the dazzle of diversity of custom; and this unity would be found 'above all in ideas and values'. 'The moment we get from haphazard notes to exhaustive, intensive study, and from isolated features to *sets of relations between features*, the empirical diversity recedes in the background, and an almost monotonous similarity springs forth' (ibid.: 10).

Distinguishing (*but not separating*) the dimensions of 'fact' and 'value' of the social reality under study, and stressing the importance of combining empiricism and rationalism to grasp it, Dumont maintained: 'first we must describe the common values and take care not to mix up facts of "representations" with facts of behaviour . . . *we must learn from the people themselves which modes of thinking we have the right to apply and which we should reject*' (ibid.: 11, emphasis added). Needless to add, this is no easy task and calls for most highly cultivated faculties of inquiry and judgement. Dumont himself recognized this: 'We have come to realize since Durkheim that social facts are and are not *things* . . . and their definition is established with more difficulty than he imagined. But modern social anthropology has made a serious contribution to their definition in its insistence that the observer sees things from within (as integrated in the society which he studies) and from without' (ibid.: 11–12).[14]

The recognition of the crucial significance of the dual viewpoint led Dumont to consider the dialectics of Hindu social life: alongside of caste, anti-caste or sect would have to be studied; alongside of kinship, marriage; alongside of and worldly obligations, renunciation would have to be accorded its due place of importance; alongside of the status of the Brahman, the power of the king would have to be recognized as an element within the social system; and so on. Dumont did exactly this in the many essays which appeared over a decade (1957–66) in the pages of *Contributions to Indian Sociology*, paving the way for *Homo Hierarchicus*. In some of these essays Dumont related jāti and varna to āśrama and puruṣārtha.

Reactions to the Dumontian Approach

The approach proposed by Dumont (in collaboration with Pocock) provoked, almost immediately, both positive interest and negative reactions. Bailey feared that such a culturological approach would destroy rather than contribute to the sociological understanding of India (1959: 88–101). Saran considered the approach to be nothing new but, in fact, an off-shoot of positivism, and denied the validity

---

[14] Dumont returned to this theme ten years later. Cf., for instance: '. . . . we slowly progress in scientific understanding because different cultures can be made to communicate within a single man's experience. Duality, or tension, is here the condition *sine qua non* of social anthropology or, if one likes, of sociology of a deeper kind' (1966a: 23).

of the external viewpoint (1962b: 53–68). Between these two extremes of the negative response there were other expressions of qualified support or criticism such as that of Imtiaz Ahmad, who maintained that the making of a sociology of India would remain incomplete until a methodology was evolved whereby it could be made to take into account non-Hindu cultures and societies as well as the Hindu (1972: 172–8).

It is rather curious that while two sharply worded critical reactions—those of Bailey and Saran—appeared in print in quick succession, the positive responses remained largely unvoiced. There can be no doubt, however, that the impact of the approach proposed by Dumont was felt widely and came to influence the work of a large number of sociologists, social anthropologists and other Indianists in India and abroad. What is more noteworthy is the fact that this widespread influence has survived over a quarter of a century, as is witnessed by the nationalities and academic disciplines of the contributors to *Way of Life*, the Indian Festschrift in his honour (see Madan 1982b), who include Dumont's near contemporaries and scholars of two succeeding generations. [15]

It is not suggested here that criticism has waned and acceptance become general; the measure of influence is seen rather by the manner in which most contributors to the field of the sociology of India have found it imperative to define their own respective positions on various problems—be it caste, kinship or power—in relation to Dumont's. This is particularly true of the younger scholars, but not only of them. In fact, it would seem that some of the more recent studies on India done under the combined influence of Dumont's work and that of the 'culture analysts' (notably David Schneider) has caused Dumont some disquiet (see Dumont 1980: xxxivff.).

Puruṣārtha *Revisited*

While for Dumont himself the question of a gap between his approach to the laying of the theoretical foundations of the sociology of India and the understanding of particular socio-cultural institutions does not obviously arise, it would seem that many of the scholars influenced by him have defined their specific research problems in relation to his ethnographic works without accepting his theoretical position explicitly, or rejecting it: the general considerations have remained

[15] The contributors are: Madeleine Biardeau, Veena Das, Jean-Claude Galey, Ramchandra Gandhi, J. C. Heesterman, Ronald Inden, T. N. Madan, Charles Malamoud, Frédérique Marglin, A. C. Mayer, Ralph Nicholas, J. P. Parry, D. F. Pocock, Tom Selwyn, K. J. Shah, S. J. Tambiah, and Romila Thapar.

submerged, as it were. Moreover, research in some problem areas has been influenced more than in others, partly because of the subject-specific emphases of his own work. Thus it is in the work on caste, kinship and marriage that his influence is most discernible. His essay on renunciation also has been very influential and not among sociologists alone. Some other significant themes on which he has written insightfully though not at length—for example, the problematic character of individualism or nationalism—have not regrettably had the same degree of impact. The preoccupation of the sociology of India with caste and kinship within the earlier empiricist tradition is partly responsible for this. It is, however, important that the relatively neglected problems too are studied. The scope of such studies is immense as is borne out by the contributions comprising the Indian Festschrift. Here sociology, Indology and philosophy came together in a collective endeavour to explore the Hindu way of life in terms of puruṣārtha and āśrama; and the exploration became an invitation for further work.

The essays in *Way of Life* have thrown up several interesting issues and underscored certain perspectives, some of which may be briefly mentioned here. Thus, at the very outset, there is Charles Malamoud's contention that the introduction of the concept of hierarchy (in the special sense in which Dumont has used it) into the study of Indian society leads one to perceive the need for a 'revolving hierarchy' because the puruṣārthas are multiple and the 'best' among them is difficult to establish on the basis of the texts; for these represent multiple points of view. Both he and K. J. Shah emphasize not merely the complementarity of the puruṣārthas but also, at a deeper level, the primacy of the whole over the parts. The holistic point of view may not be secured by elevating any one puruṣārtha to a level above the others and inclusive of them. This is an issue of fundamental importance and calls for further examination. It is important, however, to recognize that the monistic perspective which is recommended by some scholars does not settle the issue but only makes it more complex.

The essays deal with ideological issues and are primarily concerned with Brahmanical thought. This thought, Madeleine Biardeau and Stanley Tambiah have pointed out in their respective papers, is hierarchical and comprehensive in its scope. The welfare of all is what, according to Biardeau, is the central ideal enshrined in the *Mahābhārata*, but the manner in which a social group or actor may contribute to it is variable. The king's means to the achieving of this end is through the pursuit of *artha* and ultimately through waging of

war which constitutes his mode of renunciation. The Brahman's life
design has got to be different. This is once again the same issue of multiple points of view which Malamoud raises and to the understanding of
which Ron Inden's, Frédérique Marglin's and Adrian Mayer's essays
make contributions. The king does not stand in isolation but is en-
meshed in a cosmo-moral configuration which links him to gods, to
the priest, to his subjects, and to other kings, and in which the wielding
of power is meaningful at least partly in terms of the obligation to
'serve' the people. In short, there are no gods, no kings, no priests and
no subjects, but only relations and the relations between relations—a
perspective Dumont has emphasized repeatedly in his own writings.

In the context of kingship as an expression of power, Marglin contributes significantly to a promising area of research. She maintains
that royal power, which (following Dumont) she distinguishes from
status, belongs to the realm of 'auspiciousness' rather than to that of
'purity' and is in this respect homologous to 'female power'. The
categories of 'auspiciousness' and 'inauspiciousness' are not, of
course, new in the sociology of India but their systematic treatment
is only just beginning and promises rich rewards, not only in the
domain of kingship and the analysis of power generally, but also in
the field of kinship (see Madan 1987 and 1991; Parry 1991).

The holistic perspective may appear in a dramatized form in the
concept of kingship or power, but it is equally essential to the understanding of the lowliest of householders. Oppositions which com-
partmentalize social reality are a trap which the householder and the
sociologist, who seeks to study him, both have to avoid assiduously.
Veena Das demonstrates how the lineage of Raghu was finally saved
from extinction by Sita's renunciation which was her manner of expression of not only maternal love (which is obvious) but also conjugal
love—her mode of *kāma*. Being born, growing up, procreating,
dying and relating to the dead—which constitute the life cycle—are,
Ralph Nicholas and Johnny Parry show, processes and not isolated
events: moreover they are not mere biological processes but cosmo-
moral ones. This is affirmed in both ideology and practice. The
Kashmiri Pandit householder seeks to assimilate the love of man for
fellow human beings and his pursuit of dharma, artha and kāma, and
indeed of *mokṣa*, to the love of god. As I show in my essay, for him
being a householder does constitute a variety of renunciation.

The householder is not the supreme 'enjoyer' which, Inden points
out, the king is, and *aiśvarya* is not for him. Nevertheless, both Indological

and ethnographical studies point to the centrality of the life of the householder in the Hindu scheme of things. The entire cosmos seems to rest on him and his adherence to the dharma appropriate to his āśrama. The importance of sentiments, ideas and values in the way of life of the householder would seem hardly to require emphasis and yet it has received very limited attention from sociologists. We know much more about the details of interpersonal relations in the Hindu household or family than we do about the meaningfulness of these to the actors themselves—such has been the hold of behaviourism over our studies. This is not to deny the importance of the detailed ethnography on the subject that has been accumulated, but only to point to the relative neglect of the ideological dimension. It may have intruded in our studies; the point is to include it explicitly.

Apropos the householder, Dumont has drawn attention to a crucial tension that lies at the very core of the ideology of puruṣārtha: while renunciation is called by him a universal language of the Indic world, he has also pointed out that a subdued hostility to renunciation is clearly discernible in this world. The renouncer's way of life is not only a repudiation of the way of life of the man–in–the–world but is, at the same time, a rejuvenation of it through the construction of an alternative, and even the creation of new values. This relationship is indeed both crucial and complex and Jan Heesterman, Stanley Tambiah and Romila Thapar highlight it in their essays. A kind of 'archaeology' of puruṣārtha and a general tendency in Indic thought to hierarchize is revealed in these three contributions.

While Tambiah points to the manner in which the Buddhist renouncer creates a new community, at another level from that on which he has turned his back, Heesterman raises the issue of the origins of the renouncer or wanderer. In this connection, he asks whether Dumont goes far enough, first in emphasizing the opposition between the man–in–the world and the renouncer and, then, in attempting to resolve it. Dumont has written of the 'dialogue' between the two, even of 'dichotomy', and drawn attention to the creative character of the encounter. While Thapar thinks that this binary opposition is best viewed not in terms of the 'theory' of āśramas but of the 'content' of each āśrama, Heesterman is of the opinion that the real nature of the relationship in question is one of 'insoluble conflict' and suggests that the synchronic approach, which is the approach of sociology, is not adequate to handle the problem. He writes that the institution of renunciation arose 'orthogenetically within the Vedic tradition as a result of the inner logic of that tradition'. The worldly householder and the ascetic wanderer are united in the Vedic sacrifice. Here, it seems, is a major opportunity for further dialogue between the Indologist and the sociologist (see Heesterman 1985).

Concluding Remarks

The sociology of India is not an edifice to be completed tomorrow, as it were. Nor is the plea for theoretical clarity an endeavour to foreclose constructive controversy and meaningful discussion.[16] A mindless drift would, however, amount to wanton disregard of the responsibilities of the pursuit of scholarship. The sociology of India moves forward dialectically, deepening our understanding of aspects or parts of the socio-cultural reality in relation to the whole. The whole is not, however, a static datum as the relations between it and the parts and between the parts themselves keep changing. The definition of the relationship of the parts and the whole is derived from one's theoretical standpoint.

The multiplicity of such standpoints happens to be a fact and not unwelcome in principle, but care is needed to ensure that it does not degenerate into confusion—that 'most hopeless condition of atomization' about which Dumont and Pocock (1960: 82) had cautioned us. Dumont has stressed in his conversation with Galey (see Madan 1982b: 13–22) the importance of viewing our work in terms of what he calls 'common endeavour' or 'collective orientation' in the context of which alone individual contributions become meaningful. We have, then, this problem of 'communication'—or gap in communication—among those who are contributors to the sociology of India. It will not be solved by evasion or exclusion: the former attitude leads to solipsism and the latter to the opposition of one viewpoint as a critique of another without anybody modifying his or her own position. The establishment of a common ground for discussion, therefore, remains as important a task now as it has been in the past and as difficult as Dumont says he found it. His contribution to this effort has been by no means anything less than monumental.

---

[16] Many scholars are, in fact, concerned explicitly with proposing certain objectives and paths for future research, bringing out into the open the importance of the diversities of theoretical perspective and the influence these have on the choice of themes for research. See, for example, Saberwal 1980.

POSTCRIPT

In the twelve years since the publication of the second edition of *Homo Hierarchicus* (1980), Louis Dumont's work on India continues to attract appreciative as well as critical attention, notwithstanding the fact that he himself has withdrawn completely from Indianist studies. Only once in these twelve years he has alluded to his Indian work in the course of a rejoinder (see Dumont 1987). *Homo Hierarchicus* (the revised Chicago 1980 and the second Indian 1988 editions) is still in print. Available in several European languages, though not in any Indian language, its status as a major classic of social anthropological literature stands well established. As for the absence of an Indian language translation, the reason appears to be twofold. First, the kind of readership that would be attracted to it is used to reading and writing in English. Secondly, and more curiously, notwithstanding an early, laudatory and perceptive review by N. K. Bose (1971),[17] and the fact that M. N. Srinivas made a critical assessment of the ideas contained in it the subject of his Frazer Lecture (see Srinivas 1984a), the book has not been found readily accessible by Indian sociologists and social anthropologists generally: reportedly they find the method of analysis abstract and the writing dense.[18] At the same time, and as one would have expected, *Homo Hierarchicus* has received serious attention from many able scholars in the fields of sociology, history and political science. A noted economist and Marxist

[17] Bose wrote: 'Among books of an interpretative nature on the caste system, the book under review is apparently one of the best that has appeared in recent years. ... We believe that, for several years to come, Dumont's book will remain as one of the most penetrating and stimulating books written on the caste system'. After drawing attention to what he considered a 'historical inaccuracy' in the book, Bose concluded by 'registering our unqualified appreciation of the work which Louis Dumont has produced' (1971: 405–10).

[18] It is regrettable that the English translation of Dumont's main ethnographic work on India, *Une sous-caste de l'Inde du sud* (1957c), took very long in becoming available (see Dumont 1986a). (For the sake of record, I should note that translation ultimately became possible, thanks to the positive response of M. Clemens Heller, then the Administreteur Adjoint of the Maison des Sciences de l'Homme, to my proposal in 1978 that this should be done. Later M. Gilles d'Humiers at the French Embassy and Mr Ravi Dayal at the Oxford University Press in New Delhi did the rest to make publication possible.) Many Indian readers would not have found *Homo Hierarchicus* as abstruse as they seem to have, had they read the ethnographic *opus* earlier. The monograph *Hierarchy and Marriage Alliance in South Indian Kinship* (1957b), of course, became available quite early, but lack of familiarity with the structuralist approach was an obstacle. It did, however, become required reading in advanced courses on marriage and kinship at Delhi University and elsewhere.

intellectual, Arun Bose, has written a thoughtful commentary on it
(see Bose 1989: 86–103 *et passim*).

   The criticisms that *Homo Hierarchicus* has attracted in India and
abroad (mostly abroad) concern a wide range of issues, but this is not
the place or occasion for details. I will therefore mention only a few
of these issues by way of illustration. First, there is the question of
the presence or absence of the individual, ideologically acknowledged
and not merely empirically present, in Indian tradition. This leads
to the second issue: Is Dumont's emphasis on ideology excessive?
Does ideology, in fact, yield ground to observed reality if the latter is
contrary to it? In what circumstances does this happen? Thirdly, while
Dumont has written insightfully on some aspects of modern Indian history (the response to the West; the uneasy relationship between
nationalism and communalism), does he remain confined within this
historical period? In other words, is he insufficiently attentive to
medieval India and to post-independence India? Fourthly, does
Dumont's method result in ethnographic variation being too readily
relegated to the domain of the anomalous? Finally, and at a more general
level, is the relationship between individualism and equality more
complex than his analysis allows? What seems remarkable to me is
that Dumont's Indian *œuvre* continues to generate such significant
questions and stimulate research. As one of his very recent critics has
written, 'despite... criticisms, the appeal of Dumont's interpretations
seems to continue to grow and his book, *Homo Hierarchicus* . . . is
undoubtedly the single most widely read treatise on India today'
(Mines 1992: 131 n2).

IMAGES OF INDIA
IN AMERICAN ANTHROPOLOGY

5

Passage to more than India . . .
Passage to you, you shores, ye aged fierce enigmas!

WALT WHITMAN

Images consult one another,
a conscience-stricken jury,
and come slowly to a sentence.

A. K. RAMANUJAN

In this chapter I will discuss selected images or representations of Indian society (to be precise, of Hindu society) in the work of American cultural anthropologists. I use the word 'representations' to mean ethnographic statements that are intended by those who make them to convey not only information but also, explicitly or implicitly, opinions or judgements. I believe that rhetoric is an inescapable component of the act of representation. I do not mean to suggest that we cannot make a longer list of such anthropological representations of Hindu India or that the images that I discuss do not overlap. My selection is consciously arbitrary, describing what has seemed significant to me, and my procedure is illustrative rather than exhaustive. I am also conscious of the fact that it would perhaps be more meaningful to write of anthropological representations *per se* rather than of the images constructed by American, British, or French anthropologists. Doing so would have, however, necessitated detailed discussion, well beyond the intended scope of this essay. I will return to this issue in the concluding remarks.

Written in 1984, this essay was presented the following year at a conference at Harvard organized by Nathan and Sulochana Glazer. I am beholden to the Glazers for their helpful comments and many courtesies. I am also indebted to Val Daniel, Ron Inden, Charles Keyes, Dave Plath, Susanne Rudolph, Satish Saberwal, and Jit Uberoi for their criticisms and suggestions. The essay is reproduced here from *Conflicting Images: India and the United States*, edited by Sulochana R. Glazer and Nathan Glazer, Glenn Dale, MD: Riverdale, 1990.

Anthropologists are of course the modern West's very own experts on 'other', non-Occidental, cultures. Nevertheless it may well be asserted that these pedlars of 'otherness' are hardly so influential as to affect relations between nations through the images they fashion of them. Such an objection does not concern me here: within the narrow groves of academe anthropologists have indeed influenced the work of fellow social scientists (of historians, political scientists, jurists, psychologists, and occasionally even economists) just as they themselves have been influenced to varying extents by these others. Some of the weight of social science knowledge, light though it might be, does make scratches on the minds of opinion-makers.

When Mrs Eleanor Roosevelt observed in 1953 that it would be necessary to educate and re-educate the renunciation-loving Indians to cultivate an aptitude for hard work and an interest in material gain, if the efforts of their leaders to improve their living conditions were to succeed (see Roosevelt 1953), she was echoing the prevailing opinion of social scientists generally. Experts such as the well-known Eugene Staley (1954) (he wore several hats including that of an economist) or, for that matter, Arnold Toynbee (1956) (who would know better about human fate?) were saying during those heady days that they could already see signs of the Hindu Rip van Winkle waking up from his age-long slumber, and of this-worldliness emerging among Indians. McKim Marriott, then a young anthropologist, joined hands with some fellow Americans to produce a book on community development in India (see Mayer *et al.* 1958).

Those were the days of bright-eyed hope or, perhaps, innocence. Everybody believed then that India had begun well to build a path for her passage to modernity. A hundred years earlier some New England 'transcendentalists' had looked to India for her traditional wisdom—an interest which was immortalized by Walt Whitman in his poem 'Passage to India'. There were others less mystically minded or poetically gifted than Whitman, Thoreau, and Emerson who turned to India for more practical concerns (see Singer 1972: 21–6).

The first American scholar to become so interested in India was Lewis Henry Morgan (1818–81), one of the founding fathers of cultural anthropology. His worldwide search for kinship terminologies, which he thought would help him reconstruct the evolutionary sequence of forms of human social organization, yielded him some crucial linguistic data from Tamil society: these data fascinated him because they were similar to the corresponding material he had gathered from the Iroquois Indians. Surely, Morgan speculated, such evidence pointed to the possible Asiatic origin of American Indians. An image was sought to be shaped of Tamil Indians as the cousins or living ancestors of the so-called Red Indians, who were the 'others' to the white settlers. Particular peoples, however, mattered less to Morgan than the natural history of social organizational forms. Information about 'Indians' of all climes was merely the raw material for the construction of theories of unilinear evolution. Eventually, however, Morgan failed to substantiate his theory of the Asiatic origin of American Indians (see Trautman 1981: 62–72).

Three-quarters of a century had to pass before another major figure in American anthropology would turn his attention to India in a big way. In fact two of them did so and in somewhat similar fashion. Alfred Louis Kroeber (1876–1960) and Ralph Linton (1893–1953) took time off to read, reflect, and write about India in their worldwide surveys of human culture and creativity. Anthropologists are typically fieldworkers but neither of these two scholars ever visited India, certainly not for fieldwork. We will not hold this against them but concentrate on a delineation of the images of India which they presented. These are of interest inasmuch as they anticipate the paleocentric or futuristic images of India which have since emerged clearly from the work of India specialists among American anthropologists.

Yesterday's India: A Stagnant Culture

Turning to Kroeber, then, the first detailed assessment of Indian (Hindu, Buddhist, Jain) civilizations by an American anthropologist is to be found in his monumental work, *Configurations of Culture Growth*, completed in 1938 but published only in 1944. He was at that time the undisputed doyen of American anthropologists and a scholar of international repute. He had set himself the task of investigating the curious phenomenon of cultures attaining their highest level of achievement 'spasmodically', 'especially in their intellectual and aesthetic aspects, but also in more material and practical aspects'. Kroeber sought to discern 'configurations in time, space, and the degree of achievement'. 'In tracing the historic configurations of growth of patterns of higher culture', he 'used as chief evidence the products of individuals recognized as superior' (Kroeber 1944: 5–7). The areas of creativity he examined were philosophy, science, philology, sculpture, painting, literature, drama, and music; the cultures explored included Greek, Christian, Arab-Muslim, Occidental, Chinese, and Indian.

So far as Indian culture was concerned, given Kroeber's concern for dates and periodization, he was driven to desperation: 'the Hindus are notorious for having developed a great civilization without historical sense (ibid.: 62). He repeatedly deplored the Hindu indifference to time. That apart, what are his major conclusions? What is the image he constructs? Except in the field of music, about which he is understandably silent (Ravi Shankar and Ali Akbar Khan were two unknown teenagers then!), he credits India with high achievements in all the chosen fields, particularly in philology. But he had his doubts about science: 'a given mathematical achievement, if original, may argue creativeness of a high order, but if imported from the Greeks, nothing more than a degree of intellectual receptiveness' (ibid.: 179)

A characteristic judgement is about Indian sculpture, which is said to have reached its highest point during the Gupta period. 'This is not the art which makes a strong impress at first sight. It lacks architectural setting and the weight of masses. It is unrelieved by Mediterranean strains, is sufficiently Indian—with occasional animal-headed and multiple-armed figures—to seem very strange, yet lacks the shock of overwhelming barbaric exaggeration' (ibid.: 257). This is a downright Eurocentric judgement, but honestly delivered. Nor does he omit to comment upon 'self-centred and resistive' Brahminism which, unleavened by Buddhism, would have soon 'atrophied into sterility' (ibid.: 685).

Taking an overall view, however, he finds evidence for great historic growth in Indian culture spread over one thousand years—from AD 100 to 900—a duration unparalleled heretofore in any other culture. All this is very good and gratifying; but it is what follows to which I want to draw attention: 'Since 1200, little of a very high cultural order has been accomplished by India. There are Moghul-Rajput painting and vernacular poetry, the latter, especially in Hindi, both culminating around 1600. But neither of these growths can pretend to genuine first rank of value by worldwide standards' (ibid.: 684). In short, Kroeber's image is of a culture distant in both space and time, pronounced stagnant if not dead for a thousand years. In its efflorescent past, Indian culture was exotic; in its withered present, it is empty handed despite its many hands.[1]

Linton was no Kroeber but he helps us to round off this representation of India as a stagnant society by bringing in future possibilities. If

[1] Although Kroeber's views on India are reminiscent of Hegel's in many respects, yet *The Philosophy of History* is not included in the bibliography. See Hegel 1956: 139–72.

nothing else, the march of events in India made it imperative that he do so. His *Tree of Culture* came out posthumously in 1955, although he had more or less finished writing it when he died in 1953. By then India was a free nation at the threshold of modernization. The tree of the title of the book is the banyan tree of the tropics, a jungle of a tree, as it were: its growth and proliferation are traceable to the parent trunk. So, for Linton, all cultures must be studied from their prehistoric origins onwards. This is what he does in the case of India, beginning with the paleolithic age and ending with the consequences of British colonial rule.

Linton is much impressed by the complexities and diversities (environmental, racial, linguistic, subcultural) of India and the depth of its roots in time. India has been deprived of continental status, he complains, by the parochialism of outsiders. He proceeds to construct an image in rather familiar terms; hoary antiquity, Brahminic 'asceticism', Buddhist 'negativism', Muslim 'dynamism', British 'modernism', and so on, including, of course, village self-government, the caste system, and the joint family. 'Indian culture was characterized by an extreme development of ascribed status and role which made it the most static and the most perfectly integrated culture so far developed'. Not only *antiquity* but *staticity* too is emphasized. Further, it is asserted that: 'The caste system is excellently adapted to keeping a highly complex but static culture functioning successfully. Caste has become a basic pattern of Indian life and most new social elements are interpreted and adjusted in its terms' (Linton 1955: 517). Indian culture had, perhaps, a perverse dynamism of its own, since it had been able to absorb innovations: it was not totally quiescent. Linton does not, however, say so.

Then came the encounter with the West, and Linton observes: 'British colonial rule in India, among other things, dealt a body–blow to the autonomy and self-containment of the village and further fractured the caste system. Today in independent India other significant forms of social relationships are in the process of drastic reform. Through the enactment of new laws, changes are now taking place in caste relationships, land ownership, and in the structure of the joint family' (ibid.: 518–19). This is a point of view which many Indian sociologists and social anthropologists also espoused during the 1950s and the 1960s.

For Kroeber and Linton, India is along with China (and Japan) the Orient. It is not like the West. Indian culture is exotic if not mysterious, static if not dead. Occidental influences have worked upon it and, according to Linton, are bringing it into the modern world. Kroeber (like Toynbee) saw no future for Indian culture as traditional Indian culture; Linton (like Marx) hoped that British colonialism had brought India into the mainstream of world history and her own leaders were carrying on with the good work.

Anthropological images are typically the handiwork of footloose fieldworkers, and Kroeber and Linton did not engage in field research in India. The American anthropologist who led the way to fieldwork in India was David Mandelbaum (1911–87).[2] M. N. Srinivas has often referred to fieldwork-based ethnography, in contrast to textual Indological studies, as 'the worm's eye view' of a society: but it turns out that there is no single representation of India resulting from such efforts, for anthropologists, unlike worms, have points of view that are complementary in some respects and contradictory in others. In any case, if we subscribe to cultural pluralism, it is only reasonable that we also allow a diversity of approach to the study of culture.

Eternal India: Continuity and Change

For a delineation of such images, Mandelbaum's two-volume magnum opus, *Society in India* (1970), is our best guide to start with. He began fieldwork in 1937 in the Nilgiri Hills among the Kota, a so-called tribal community, and published excellent ethnographic accounts of them and their relations with neighbouring groups. But, he says, the idea of writing a general work on society in India occurred to him right at the commencement of his Indian researches. 'Like other students of the people of India, I was struck by the great diversity among them and yet I could sense the common qualities of society and civilization which they shared' (1970: viii). Unity in diversity, then, rather than rank pluralism is the key to Mandlebaum's grass-roots image of India.

It is an image of our times, for Mandelbaum's data come from about 700 works—books, monographs, articles, and dissertations, many of them authored by American anthropologists—published mostly during the 1950s and the 1960s. Here we have Anglo-Saxon empiricism at its detailed best. The image that emerges is contextual,

[2] It may be noted here that the Americans who pioneered the intensive study of village communities in India were William and Charlotte Wiser, members of the American Presbyterian Mission, who took up residence in a north Indian village in 1925 and published their book *Behind Mud Walls*, long acclaimed as a classic, five years later (see Wiser and Wiser 1963). William Wiser later received a doctorate in anthropology for his influential ethnography of intercaste relations, *Hindu Jajmani System* (1936).

constructed brick by brick, as it were, drawn from village India. Its building blocks are the family, the lineage, the *jati* (i.e. caste as commonly understood, but Mandelbaum wisely avoids this confusing word, except as an adjective, because of its several referents), and the village community. Beyond the village, and encompassing it, is that abstract reality called the Indian civilization. On the horizon loom the forces of modernization. The key notion of a 'social system', as developed in functionalist sociology and anthropology, holds the data together and accounts for the well-defined profile of the image. It is the 'underlying premise of the analysis' (ibid.: 6).

Mandelbaum's India is a going concern and it is stable, not static. The systemic character of the image is seen to reflect the nature of the social reality itself. Change is identified as a familiar and recurrent process within Indian society though essentially subordinate to structural continuity. Its typical manifestations are said to be mobility and adaptation within the caste system and, nowadays, politicization. Urbanization, industrialization, and secularization are obviously judged as weaker forces for they are not discussed in any detail.

Mandelbaum concludes: 'The systemic changes that are in view do not point directly toward an unstratified society but toward fewer and more homogeneous social groups' (ibid.: 634) Further, 'People throughout India commonly keep to traditional social patterns while adapting them to modern circumstances. Abstract ideals are most readily revised: fundamental motifs of cognition and motivation seem little altered and are evident in the newer arenas of competition' (ibid.: 655). Thus, 'a person's role as citizen and voter has become attached to his role as jati member' (ibid.: 657). And finally: 'A new phase of social development may well follow the rise of industry and the great improvements in agricultural technology. Both are still in beginning states' (ibid.: 658).

Modernization is thus seen as a gradual and cumulative process of juxtaposition rather than displacement. To unity in diversity we must then add another critical strand of this view of India: structural stability in the midst of myriad changes. Nothing significant really changes: change in eternal India, one might say, is *maya*, mere illusion.

This grass-roots view would, perhaps, find the most supporters among the ranks of American anthropologists who have worked on India in the last four decades (since India's independence). Most of them would by the very nature of their work (consisting of synchronic studies of social institutions and situations) have little interest in whether the Hindus have had a history or only a past; at the same time they would refuse to accept the view that India's future is her past, that she is incapable of change though she may not be ripe for revolution. Mandelbaum's emphasis upon politicization as a critical agency of social change is noteworthy in this context. It is important to note that, according to this view, the future of India is in the grip of impersonal institutions and processes and hardly in the hands of Indians themselves. They never have and perhaps never will make their own history [see Inden 1986].

Democracy obviously is a cardinal value deeply cherished by Americans, and American anthropologists have argued that traditional institutions such as caste can themselves become, through an adaptive process, the vehicles of the modern processes of democratization, urbanization and industrialization (see e.g. Gould 1963). Political scientists have provided detailed support to the thesis that the newly introduced democratic institutions can flourish in village India, though in the process they undergo a certain narrowing, but then, the traditional institutions also get loosened up in the process (see Rudolph and Rudolph 1967). It is not mere coincidence that the American social scientists who have been most attracted to India have been anthropologists, political scientists, and historians, and not economists, sociologists, or psychologists. India is interesting because it is different, in terms of its culture, social organization, and long duration, though it is also contemporaneously similar, given the massive experiment in democracy upon which its leaders have embarked.

To make sense of the masses of concrete grass-roots level empirical data—that is, to be able to construct a representation on their basis— one needs to anchor these data in something stable and, perhaps, abstract—in an inner *élan*. Mandelbaum fleetingly invokes the ideological background, the high civilizational backdrop. It is in the work of those influenced by Robert Redfield and Milton Singer that we encounter a view of the grass-roots reality from above, as it were, without losing hold of these roots, however. To return to Srinivas's metaphor, it is not the bird's eye-view, or the worm's, that we need, but a two-sided view, from above and from below, so that a richer image, filled out rather than flat, may be constructed.

This composite view locates everyday life at the conjunction of what Robert Redfield (1897–1958), drawing upon his field studies of local communities in Mexico and his wide knowledge of ethnographic literature generally, called the Great and Little Traditions (see

Redfield 1956: 70ff., 87–101). The Indian village is not understood best by treating it *as if* it were an isolate—the anthropologist's most highly favoured island community—because it is not such an isolate. It is representative of Indian civilization and a microcosm of it. Moreover, the village community is not a passive carrier of some things handed down to it from above, but in fact actively contributes over time to the making and enriching of the Great Tradition itself. McKim Marriott called these processes 'parochialization' (the downward process) and 'universalization' (the upward process) respectively. Through the application of such a civilizational approach, the inner dynamics of Indian culture turns out to be more complex and rich, I suppose, than what one learns from the systemic approach, namely the adaptive nature of social institutions. As Marriott puts it, 'A focus upon the small half-world of the village and a perspective upon the universe of Indian civilization thus remain mutually indispensable for whole understanding, whether of Hinduism or of the traditional forms of India's social structure' (1955: 218).

To employ the terms used by Milton Singer (b. 1912), a valid view of Indian culture and social reality is possible only when text and context are combined. He writes: 'In this kind of inquiry, the cleavage between the contextual and textual approaches will be progressively closed as the texts of different kinds—written, seen, and heard—come to be regarded as the media of cultural transmission cultivated by intellectuals, modern as well as traditional, to link different groups of people into a single and differentiated network of communication' (1972: 50).

While stressing the traditional roots of contemporary Hindu cultural performances, Singer often brings in American notions and perspectives: the composite view from above and below also becomes the view from within and without. Thus, he writes that the devotional movement in the city of Madras has become 'ecumenical', and 'an expression of democratic aspirations within Hinduism' (ibid.: 158). The images of India seem to appear in sharper focus when they are thus viewed in terms of the categories of Western culture. This is not simple comparison: it is translation, or, as Singer would now have it, an exercise in semiotics.

Such comparisons notwithstanding, Singer's basic emphasis is upon cultural specificity, upon the traditional roots of modern India. Like Mandelbaum he too emphasizes continuity: social change is not an abandonment of tradition but rather its forward movement. A radical break is denied but significant change is admitted: 'As India takes the path of modern nationalism, it will undoubtedly become less fascinating to the rest of the world, but it will also become less of an "image" and more of a reality in that world' (ibid.: 36). For significant changes to fructify, however, it is imperative that legitimacy be bestowed on them: 'In the long run cosmic time perspective of Hindu cosmology, innovations and adjustments may look like the ephemeral appearances of an absolute reality, or the recurrent disorders of a Kali age. In the short run perspective of human life and culture history, however, the changes are very real and progressive even to a devout Hindu. To traditionalize them is to seek legitimacy and meaning for them in an accepted world view and value system' (ibid.: 412).

Singer's recent reliance upon Peircean semiotics has led him to stress even more the composite character of the image. He maintains that the 'activities of reinterpreting and restructuring old signs and symbols of Indian identity are the activities of growing and changing selves, whose identities are reaching out to the future as well as the past, to the foreign as well as the native. These Indians are trying to become *that* by "seeing everything in the self and the self in everything"' (1984:187).

This may appear a very Brahminical view of things, and so it is. But many American anthropologists just will not have it thus: they consider it their professional obligation to penetrate Brahminical facades to see the Indian social reality in its true colours, 'upside down', 'bottom up', or simply demystified.

Tomorrow's India: The View from 'Below'

The proponents of the 'upside down' or 'bottom up' view (the phrases are Joan Mencher's) seek to construct an image of Indian society as they think it should be done, standing on its feet. They maintain that this can be done only when we look at the caste system (which is regarded as the typical form of social organization in India) from the point of view of the exploited multitudes: after all every seventh Indian belongs to a low and often untouchable caste. Mencher writes: 'The traditional view of Indian social structure . . . assumes that hierarchy is accepted by all as an inevitable part of human existence. It assumes that each person accepts his niche and his relationship to others above and below him and believes that he is in that position because of his actions in former lives. . . . [But] this is a distortion of reality since it represents a onesided view of social processes, a view which is essentially from the top down' (1975: 114–15).

Such a top-down view is said to have 'masked' the prevailing socio-economic differences, drawn a curtain on economic exploitation, and prevented 'the formation of social classes with any commonality of interest or unity of purpose' (1974: 469). Without a radical social transformation, which might replace non-antagonistic castes by antagonistic classes, the poor will never become organized in defence of their interests and against their oppressors. The caste system is thus, like systems of social stratification elsewhere, a promoter of the interests of the ruling classes. Moreover, contrary to the widely held view, the caste ideology justifying unequal access to economic resources and political power is not accepted by the lowest and most exploited castes. The germs of class conflict are, therefore, very much present in the body social.

Kathleen Gough has asserted that the alleged conservatism of the Indian peasant is not much in evidence today and has perhaps 'never been an accurate assessment of the lower castes, whose customs are more flexible than those of orthodox high caste Hindus and who have nothing to lose by change'. Further, Gough maintains that when progressive political parties go to the countryside with radical programmes based on the values of 'equality and brotherhood', they are welcome because these values are 'dear' to the peasants, who have 'for centuries . . . practised them quite fanatically within their castes' (1973: 243). The point, according to these authors, then, is to represent social reality with a view not only to understanding it but also, and more importantly, changing it. Gerald Berreman (1981), sees this issue in terms of what he considers 'the social responsibility of the anthropologist' and, in fact, the 'moral accountability of anthropology'.

Berreman has argued that, contrary to the rather benign forces of consensus and organic solidarity, Indian society is held together by power, concentrated in certain privileged groups. Consensus, instead of being the basis of the caste system, is in fact a threat to hierarchical pluralism, its essential ingredient. 'The human meaning of caste for those who live it is power and vulnerability, privilege and oppression, honour and denigration, plenty and want, reward and deprivation, security, and anxiety' (1979: 159). The ability of such a social organization, Berreman concludes, 'to withstand universal education, mass media, equalitarian ideologies . . . is doubtful' (ibid.: 113). In other words, the 'two thousand years of struggle' are at long last reaching their fulfilment—or were seen thus in the early 1970s. Some of the changes that have occurred since then—for example, a people's movement in north India (where Berreman has done his fieldwork) against deforestation and exploitation of hill people by forest contractors, moneylenders, and others (see Guha 1989)—have strengthened the democratic and egalitarian forces while the development strategies of the dominant classes have failed to do so.

A significant feature about this view of Indian society is the insistence of its proponents that there is nothing impenetrably unique about the caste system. Thus, for Berreman, it is perfectly meaningful and legitimate to view race relations in the southern United States in terms of the caste system. In the process the latter itself is demystified and seen for what it really is—just another expression of socioeconomic exploitation. 'A comparison of the realities of caste attitudes and interaction in India and the United States suggests that no group of people is content to be low in a caste hierarchy—to live a life of inherited deprivation and subjection—regardless of the rationalizations offered them by their superiors or constructed by themselves' (1960: 127). It is change, then, not continuity, which should be the social scientist's first concern as it is the people's.

If the comparativists in their quest for cross-cultural similarities—for the sociological hard core—considered cultural relativism of the traditional variety an erroneous and spent force, they had not reckoned with the emergence of cognitive anthropology and ethnosociology as major theoretical thrusts in American anthropology during the 1970s and the 1980s. With it has emerged yet another image and the plea for yet another view of Indian culture. This may be called the 'view from "within".'

Another India: The View from 'Within'

Here 'cognitivists' have led the way, emphasizing that the way to an understanding of Indian culture and society lies through an understanding of the Indians' basic cognitive orientations, or ways of perceiving the universe. Native categories of thought are the foundation on which to build, but an outsider may never really enter into this alien world.

Thus, Stephen Tyler contends that 'India as it is known to those who live there remains as fabulous and mysterious to me as it must have to those first Europeans who visited it in the fifteenth century.' It is therefore hardly surprising that he writes, on the one hand, that

'Indians are among the world's few truly civilized people' and, on the other, that they are expert at 'double think', uncritically eclectic, legalistic, delighting in interminable hair splitting, self–righteous, and so on (1973: 2). But, then, this is all a question of viewpoint, of cognitive orientation: 'Indians see Westerners as calculating, closed, insincere, lacking in warmth, incapable of appreciating the mul-tilayered realities of social life, and Westerners see Indians as guileful, shifting, dishonest, and incapable of holding on to a unified one-dimensional reality' (ibid.: 6).

How do Indians see themselves? Having said at the very outset that he will never know, Tyler still heroically, ventures an answer. The Indian in his role as master—and every Indian is master of some just as he is a servant of others, which is what social rank is all about—'is supposed to be like a father. . . . He must be like an *avatara* . . . or an ascetic. . . . He must be deadly serious, dispassionate, and chaste, living in a sort of militant monasticism, his human qualities entirely eschewed. Finally, he should manifest a personal unap-proachability and, if possible, wear a uniform of some sort' (ibid.: 5).

Where Berreman sees mutual hostility, Tyler sees a smooth 'com-petence in social relations'; while the former detects in power an instrument of exploitation, the latter sees in it the 'paternalism of noblesse oblige'; what to the former are 'two thousand years of struggle' are to the latter 'two thousand years of life without privacy', in which 'the moment of dissent or the sense of contradiction is always pushed further and further back, rather than brought to the surface' (ibid.: 2–3). It may be noted here that, despite their strikingly contrasting views, Berreman and Tyler both are in agreement on one important point: they detect an absence of historical development in Hindu society, an absence of a sense of time in Hindu culture. Not surprisingly, Tyler writes (in the Preface) that 'there are many Indias' and that his own 'is the India of scholarly imagination'. We are all image-makers, according to our author, and therefore re-presentations are, I guess, real—perhaps the only reality. In other words, it is not reality as such that matters (presuming that it is knowable) but the perspective one adopts for its study. Surely this is carrying scholarly imagination too far.

Taking leave of Tyler, let me move on to McKim Marriott (b. 1924). I do so with a sense of trepidation, for Marriott's position is still evolving—I dare not say it is 'fluid'—and one fears one may mis-represent it. If misrepresentation does enter into what follows, it is here in spite of my efforts and not because of them. Needless to emphasize, my intention is to present a brief outline of Marriott's point of view and not to attempt a detailed critical exposition of it.

The point of departure for Marriott's enterprise of the last two decades or so to construct a distinctive and what he obviously considers a superior approach to the study of Hindu society, has been 'the axiom that the pervasive indigenous assumptions of any society . . . provide bases on which an anthropologist may construct his models of cultural behaviour in that society' (1976a: 109). It would seem that such assumptions, being pervasive, are available in local knowledge (preserved in oral traditions) no less than in diverse textual sources. May be in the former one finds only syntactic traces of the assumptions, but one finds them all right. Truly, then, as O'Flaherty (1984) has reminded us, in India, to look into Krishna's mouth is to look at the universe. The small half-world of the village is now, it seems, in a different relationship to the universe of Indian civilization.

The importance attached to indigenous cognitive categories and the interpretation of behaviour in terms of them recalls to one's mind the approach to the sociology of India advocated by Louis Dumont during the 1950s (see Chapter 4). Marriott acknowledges this explicitly (see Marriott 1976b: 190), but he disapproves of what he considers the abandonment by Dumont in his *Homo Hierarchicus* (1970a) of South Asian categories of thought. The synthesis that Dumont produced in this book is decried by Marriott as being European (idealist, intellectualist) rather than South Asian in inspiration. Thus, while he agrees with Dumont that the individual (and individualism) are alien categories of thought in South Asia, the reasons he gives are quite different.

Repudiating the dichotomous classification of societies as holist or individualist, he invokes the notions of the divisibility, transformability, and transmissibility of the person: there are no bounded individuals in South Asian thinking but only free-flowing 'particles' and 'dividuals'. Hindu cognitive categories are said to be based on 'biological substantialism', characterized by a 'systemic monism and particularism', and expressed through highly elaborated 'transactional thinking'. An image of Hindu society is thus presented in which 'dividual actors' engage in 'substantial action' guided by 'four elemental [transactional] codes'. 'Since this transactional model attempts to follow Hindu cognitions of monism, particularism, and dividualism, it necessarily ignores some assumptions as to ultimate

dualities that are explicit or implicit in the Western sociological tradition' (1976a: 137).[3]

The issue, then, is of the unsuitability of a culturally rooted Western social science for the understanding of South Asian cognitive-
cum-action systems. Similarly, Hindu categories of thought would
be no good, if not a hindrance, in our efforts to understand Japanese
society. Marriott advocates a retreat into society's own thought
structure as a methodological device: the ultimate aim is a higher
level dialogic anthropology of human culture. Such a hermeneutic
bridge may not, however, be properly constructed of the categories
of thought peculiar to a particular culture; their universal applicability
may not be simply assumed. Aristotelian logic is Greek; it is not
Hindu or universal.

In a public (1985) statement, Marriott argued that, in the West, the
world or society is made up of bounded individuals, who are conceived in terms of equivalence relations of *reflexivity* (the individual is equal to himself, self-sufficient), *symmetry* (one person is
equal to another), and *transitivity* (all are equal to one another).[4] It is a
world marked by consistency, regularity, and integration. But
South Asians reverse all this: theirs is a world of non-equivalence and
nothing stays the same very long: it is a world in constant flux and
the metaphors that describe it best are liquid metaphors. Thus, whether
one thinks of the elements (fire, water, air), or the Ayurvedic humors
(*kapha, pitta, vāyu*), or the essences (*guṇa*) of Sāṁkhya philosophy
(*sattva, rajas, tamas*), we are confronted with fluid signs. Such fluid
signs highlight the Hindu thought structure but they do not exhaust
it: after all *saṃsāra* has its stable points. With fluidity go 'openness' (as
against 'boundedness'), asymmetry, and instability. Even the key
notion of code-substance or substance-code (exemplified by, for
instance, the ties of marriage and blood or the ingestion of food) is
permeable, divisible, and transmissible. Time as flux emerges as a

[3] Indian readers are apt to misunderstand the precise connotation of the term
'monism' as employed by Marriott. In a conversation with me in 1987 he denied special interest in the use of this term in the context of theology and in the manner of
Shankara's *advaita* philosophy. Instead of the man–god relationship, it is the more
mundane contexts that Marriott has in mind: for example, the materialism–idealism
dichotomy, in our knowledge of the external world.

[4] Marriott, 'Anthropology in South Asian 3-D.' Lecture delivered at the University
of Chicago, April 15, 1985. Audio-tape. I am grateful to Joan Erdman for making this
tape available to me. I have found the lecture one of the more lucid expositions of Marriott's evolving viewpoint. Apart from this lecture and some published papers, I
have also drawn from my notes of the long discussion I had with Marriott in Chicago
in April 1987.

critical element of all social relations and therefore of all social situations: no wonder, Marriott points out, that the most widely read book
in South Asia is the almanac.

   This is the view from within, or the manifest view, according to
Marriott. It is, however, by no means complete. It is this realization
which has persuaded Marriott to experiment with a three–dimensional
representation of Hindu society. In doing so, he maintains, he is only
following the Hindus themselves. Those Indian social scientists who
may not recognize such a basic pluralistic perspective as their own,
have, Marriott may be expected to say, only their modernism and
training as social scientists to blame for their alienation. Thus, 'it
does not seem to be Vyāsa or the Hindu grammarians, but Marx or
F. G. Bailey who teaches the separation of "ideology" from material
reality; not Manu, but Max Weber who instructs in the distinction
between "status" and "power"; not Caraka who defines "purity" as
separation from the organic aspect of man, but Durkheim or Albert
Schweitzer' (1976b: 193). The Indian social scientist is thus ironically held
captive in a double bind; those who would free him from bondage to
Western social science are also Western social scientists (see Chapter 8).

Concluding Remarks

· Although I call them 'American' representations, the approaches
described above could surely be broadly designated as representations
of India in Western anthropology or, simply, anthropological images
of India. They would find echoes in the work of British anthropologists,
but that work is more strongly rooted in local settings: particular tribes,
castes, or communities rather than civilizational wholes emerge as the
focus of interest. The colonial origin of the British ethnographic enterprise in India (and elsewhere), and the concern with effective administration that it entailed, explains this preoccupation with local societal
forms and problems, an orientation further strengthened during the
heyday of functionalist anthropology. The French holistic perspective,
derived from Marcel Mauss and best expressed in Indianist studies in
the convergence of Indology and sociology that has been the proclaimed
foundation of Louis Dumont's *oeuvre* (see Chapter 4), may have inspired
Marriott's ongoing studies but it does not account for its content or
character. In short, the work of American anthropologists on India
forms a corpus having certain distinctive characteristics.

   Quite anti-climactically, these American representations like all
anthropological images, are a product of the homogenizing gaze of

modern man, emphasizing 'otherness'. By focusing on caste, which had already become well established in Western discourse as India's most distinctive social institution—Ghurye pointed this out in 1932 in the opening sentence of his classic work on the subject (see Ghurye 1969: 1)—American anthropologists found it easy to emphasize cultural difference.

It is only when he focuses on cultural difference that modern man is able to assert his role as modernizer. Not all anthropologists, however, look upon their academic work in such activist terms. Thus the representations offered by those who have adopted what I have called 'the view from above' not only stress otherness in terms of social and cultural specificities but they also express clearly a certain fascination for them. These specificities are not, however, considered unchangeable or intellectually inaccessible to outsiders. In fact, cognitive categories derived from modern American culture are occasionally found helpful in making sense of what is happening in India today. Given their evolutionist leanings, these scholars have taken India's modernization for granted, although they do not apparently advocate an interventionist role for the anthropologist.

Such a subdued perspective on otherness is not, however, shared by those who advocate 'the view from below'. For them representing entails intervening with a view to promoting 'social equality' and 'justice' which they consider universally valid values. Marxian or Rawlsian justifications of these Western notions are obviously considered adequate. As already stated, they consider traditional Hindu social organization highly inequitous and exploitative of the poor, and the associated cultural traditions are seen by them as a thinly veiled justification of the existing social order or, simply, mystification. Otherness is not viewed here as something that may be preserved but rather as something that must be abolished, and the anthropologist should contribute to this task.

In contrast, the so-called 'view from within' comes close to being a statement of cultural uniqueness, and thus emphasizes otherness most of all. It is also suggested that the confrontation with otherness—the encounter of cultures—will in the long run lead to the widening of the intellectual horizons of the observers no less than those of the observed. Otherness is here accepted, I presume, as a pregnant social fact; it is to be studied with care—not to be just extolled or excoriated—so that intercultural communication may be established.

A particularly noteworthy feature of all four representations of otherness is what has been called 'allochronism', that is the denial of coevalness between the anthropologist and the people he studies (see Fabian 1983: 25–35 *et passim*). To say that the Hindus live elsewhere in space—in the far away East Indies—or that they have different customs or practices or institutions would be rather banal: to say that they live in another time, however, does seem to be more significant as a sign of otherness. Let me elaborate on this point.

For Kroeber, India's contributions to the cultural history of mankind ended a thousand years ago: her *creative* time (as against mere duration) was in the past. In contrast, Berreman (and others with a similar point of view) would suggest that India's *real* time—the time of hope and creativity and not merely struggle for her downtrodden millions—lies in the future. The future of America and India may be similar, one hopes, though the present is significantly different.

Linton, Mandelbaum, and Singer all emphasize continuity in a manner that must set Indians apart from Americans. For Linton, Indian culture stretches so far back in time that it has fossilized and appears as archaic and exotic as the banyan tree. For Mandelbaum and Singer India seems almost to stand outside time as it is understood and experienced in the West and by modern man generally. Continuity dominates change, suggests Mandelbaum; it is tradition which modernizes itself, says Singer. Continuity and tradition are the significant historical phenomena, not change and modernity.

Marriott places time at the very centre of the world of Hindu conceptual thought and experience; it is not, however, linear time as known in the West but *cyclical, fluid* time. This makes the Hindu cultural universe and Hindu mentality critically different from those of the Americans though not impenetrable. In short, whether in terms of the conceptions of time, or of the nature of human nature, custom, or society, the images emphasize otherness.

Edward Said (1978), Fabian (1983), Inden (1986), and others have pointed out that the relationship between the observer and the observed as embodied in Orientalist literature and in anthropology generally spelled hegemony and inequality between peoples. Western knowledge about others was considered, *ipso facto*, superior to their knowledge about themselves, and this is now being rightly questioned. There is an element of 'allochronistic dismissal' in the images of India shaped by Kroeber and by Berreman—the grounds for 'dismissal' are, of course, not the same in the two cases—but it seems to be no part *consciously* of the other representations described here. In these other cases the intended emphasis upon otherness is more a discursive than a political act. As Boon puts it, 'A culture can materialize only in counter-distinction to another culture (1982: ix). Moreover, it is from the consideration of the otherness of particular cultures, from the anthropologist's point of view, that the unity of mankind, which has remained a basic philosophical postulate of the anthropological discourse from its very beginning, from Morgan and Tylor to Lévi-Strauss and Dumont, can be transformed from an abstract into a concrete notion. The problem here is the gap between the representations fashioned by a particular ethnographer and cultural anthropology as a discourse: does the latter breathe through the former independent of the intentions of the author? If so, do those of us who do anthropology at home become collaborators of our own oppressors, letting them steal our senses and hold our minds captive? This could be so but need not be so. I do not accept the notion of inevitability in this context.[5]

The anthropologist who would study his own society (as I have) must also try to so distance himself from the familiar that it appears as the other: he must hope to be surprised, and if he is, only then may he achieve new and deeper understandings. The true significance of otherness, of the prodigious stranger, lies in the possibility of the mutual interpretation of cultures (see Chapters 7 and 8). Significantly, it is Marriott among the image-makers considered here who emphasizes this point most explicitly. In the post-colonial world, anthropology should, I think, become a mode of self-reflection without spawning many insular autologies. American anthropologists should know better than most the philosophical infirmities of the notion of cultural relativism and its potential for political mischief.

Cultural difference does not entail conflict nor does it mean unbridgeable distance but, if those concerned are not careful, it could shape into hegemony. This after all has been the history of East–West cultural relations. Today anthropology does not have to be an expression of

---

[5] I realize my formulation on this point is open to serious objections. First, it could well be argued that dismissal could be achieved by appreciation as well as by depreciation: the strategy is the same, namely exclusion. Secondly, my emphasis upon intentionality might be considered misplaced but I am not easily convinced of that for I do not believe in guilt by association. Thirdly, and most seriously, it could be maintained that the proclamation of the unity of mankind in the colonial age by specialists who served or promoted the interests of the exploiters, while stigmatizing the exploited as primitive savages, enigmatic Orientals, or whatever, only underscored the duplicity of anthropology. An easy defence is perhaps not available so far as past practice is concerned, but surely the position is different today, the most significant difference being that anthropologists have turned to the study of their own societies including Western society. The issue calls for vigorous debate rather than name-calling.

guilt feelings nor does the anthropologist have to be 'an amputated man', as Lévi-Strauss (1963b: 58) once put it, which is not to belittle the difficulties that attend intercultural communication and its conceptualization. I doubt we have yet developed an adequate language for it.

The acknowledgement of the hermeneutic possibility as the true significance of the emphasis upon otherness in the representations of India in American cultural anthropology still leaves open the question of their epistemological status. This is a serious matter. The temptation to hold up one image as true and reject the others as false must be resisted as it has no objective basis. Such a tendency is, however, general; it is more or less discernible in the views of all the anthropologists whose work I have examined here. They invoke the authority of having been there and/or having studied the relevant texts. For them cultures have existential reality and our knowledge of them can only be based on empirical investigations. In this sense they are all positivists, Marriott no less than Berreman or Mandelbaum.

Speaking as an Indian, it seems to me that all the representations are indeed grounded in empirical reality and what distinguishes them from one another is the perspective of each.[6] They are all representations of the 'reality' from particular points of view; they are not natural depictions or mirror images. 'Ethnographic truths are thus inherently *partial*—committed and incomplete' (Clifford 1986a: 7). This does not mean though that someone has to piece them together and render them

6 It may be of interest to note the influence of Indian scholars or its absence on the American anthropologists discussed. Kroeber relied upon Western scholars only for his knowledge of India: the only South Asian scholar he included in his bibliography was the Sri Lankan art historian, Ananda Coomaraswamy. He did, however, read the work of Indian historians on Cambodia. Although Indians are more noticeable in Linton's bibliography, they are by no means prominent. One must add, however, that during the 1930s and 1940s, books by Indian scholars may not have been readily accessible to American scholars. The situation changes considerably when we come to Mandelbaum who relied rather heavily on the work of Indian anthropologists in constructing his synthesis: well over one-third of his references are to works by Indian authors. There is hardly any major work relevant to his themes that is not cited by him. Singer's work has been deeply influenced by M. N. Srinivas and by the Sanskritist V. Raghavan. Mencher obviously owes several of her insights to André Béteille, and cites many other Indian authors, as do Berreman and Tyler. Marriott not only draws upon contemporary social science literature emanating from India but also cites traditional texts such as the *Manusmriti* and *Charakasmhita*. While the complicity of Indian scholars in the shaping of the images of India by American anthropologists has definitely increased over time, their contribution is generally as purveyors of ethnographic information rather than as originators of new perspectives. This is nothing new, for anthropologists have generally given ethnographic substance to images that are already in existence.

complete. Their utility lies in their being what they are and in their *mutual contestation*. The assessment of the truth value of anthropological images thus turns out to be not merely a question of information about the present situation (Mandelbaum), of historical roots (Singer), or of future possibilities (Berreman), but also a debate about appropriate perspectives (Marriott). Such debates are, of course, notoriously inconclusive. One clear guideline though is that the perspective which enables us to understand more of the facts on the ground economically and in an internally consistent manner, and does not claim exclusiveness, is to be preferred to those that lack coherence and lay claims to monopoly over truth.

Judged by such a criterion, I find Marriott's project the most ambitious but also very problematic. I feel uncomfortable about the manner in which intuitive insights appear to be elevated by him to the status of first principles to which empirical data are then subordinated. Rhetoric seems to override evidence, at any rate at the present stage of the Chicago project. The resultant merger of ideology and observed behaviour, unrelieved by a notion of levels, is unsatisfactory. Also, a well articulated theoretical back-up is required to overcome the feeling of a rampant eclecticism characterizing the manner in which ideas from different kinds of discourse—e.g. medicine (*āyurveda*), philosophy (*sāmkhya*) and astrology (*jyotisha*)—are combined in furtherance of a monistic perspective, which many Hindus would repudiate unless adequately qualified. The cognitive categories so derived are invested with an internal consistency and durability which are not convincing (see Barnett *et al* 1976: 627–46). Altogether Marriott's view of culture is far too static. It is so in spite of his emphasis upon fluidity as a key concept in Hindu culture. His approach, which has by now found quite a few followers among American anthropologists, may, I fear, result in cultural stereotyping of the kind associated with Orientalism. This is not, I know, Marriott's intention, but it could be an unintended consequence of his teaching.

As for the other two fieldwork-based approaches discussed in this essay, 'the view from above' and 'the view from below', they share their epistemological stance and are quite familiar as mainstream American cultural anthropology. Their strengths and shortcomings too are familiar. By virtue of their empiricist epistemology, they are appropriately attentive to what they consider fully observable reality, but in effect they are too heavily behaviouristic. This importance of ideas is, however, receiving recognition increasingly. The problem appears to be how to establish a dialectical relationship between ideas and behaviour (or interests) in anthropological discourse. This is more easily stated than done. Moreover, the explicit activist orientation of 'the view from below' will be resisted by those who, though not against social change, do not believe (as I do not) that ethically or politically commanding directives issue directly from social science knowledge: they rather originate in one's ethical or political convictions.

In sum, anthropological representations, their claims to holism notwithstanding, express particular visions of reality. Far from being their weakness, this is, I think, their strength. An absolute truth value may not be claimed for any one of them. This does not mean that they are all equally useful: the criteria of correspondence, coherence, and parsimony should apply. Any claims to the contrary will only land us in a Kafkaesque situation of the kind where people lose faith in the notion of Time because different clocks in the house show the hour variously.

POSTSCRIPT

Since the above essay was written (in 1985–6), McKim Marriott has published two articles elaborating and clarifying his position (through a careful combination of text, tables and graphs, see Marriott 1989, 1991). His own articles should be read together with the ethnographic analyses deeply influenced or partly inspired by his ideas (see Marriott 1990). These publications are readily available and I will not attempt to summarize them. I will rather confine myself to highlighting some aspects of the theoretical argument and offering a couple of comments.

Marriott regards the efforts of himself and his collaborators in the construction of an ethnosociology of India as 'a project' of 'vast design'. He estimates that, in 1991, the project (begun in 1976? or a few years earlier?) was 'about half way to its initial exploratory goals' (Marriott 1991: 299 n9). This means that what we now have, even though in print, is still a provisional formulation, and changes (alterations, elaborations) are to be expected. Such changes have already taken place in the initial phase of the research. Thus the earlier emphasis on monism has now been overtaken by a Sankhyan triplicity, but duality seemingly remains an anathema. Pentads seem to be on the way.

To remind ourselves, what exactly is the project? It simply is the urgency of our being able to recognize that the social sciences used in India today have developed from thought about Western rather than Indian cultural realities. Their claims to 'universal applicability' must, therefore, be judged to be pretentious. In fact, because of their origins, they 'cannot deal with the questions to which many Indian institutions are answers.' Alongside of the ethnosocial sciences that today dominate the world, the call is given to erect Indian (and other) ethnosocial sciences (see Marriott 1989). This is indeed a very interesting endeavour.

The way to go about doing this is said to be through the identification of a culture's 'natural categories' which are then to be used to construct 'a general system of concepts'. In other words, the recommendation is 'to synthesize a theoretical system' (ibid.: 5). Thus far the objective does not seem all that different from Louis Dumont's efforts to bring sociology and Indology together in fruitful intercourse.

The distinctiveness of the project becomes apparent with the presentation of the materials for Hindu ethnosocial sciences. They are said to be plentiful (a case of *embarras de richesses*, I guess), but detailed illustration is limited to the elements (*bhūta*) of Hindu cosmology, the humours (*doṣa*) of Hindu medicine, the strands (*guṇa*) of Hindu metaphysics, and the human aims (*puruṣārtha*) of Hindu moral philosophy (ibid.: 7). This range of physical, biological and social concepts is said to be united in 'common conceptual denominators' of metaconceptual kinds, such as 'relationships' and 'processes', which must be identified. Moreover, none of the four chosen categories consists of less than three 'components': '*three appears to be the irreducible number of properties or components with which Hindus will comfortably think about human affairs*' (ibid.: 8, emphasis added).

This frankly magisterial verdict may leave some Hindus gasping, but it yields 'the constituent cube' of Marriott's analysis. Its six surfaces, or faces, stand for three pairs (the return of the repressed?) of processes, namely mixing–unmixing, unmarking–marking, and unmatching–matching (that is the order in which Marriott presents them). Its dimensions of breadth, depth and height stand for the properties of nontransitivity, nonreflexivity and nonsymmetry (mentioned above, p. 99). In the property-space thus generated one tries to locate, through three–dimensional graphing, the materials from Hindu texts and from observed Hindu behaviour that appear to be available in abundance. Marriott, of course, provides helpful glosses for all these unfamiliar terms, and his collaborators try out the cube on their data, or is it the other way round?

D. P. Mukerji at the first Indian Sociological Conference in Dehra Dun (1955).

Louis Dumont
Photograph by Jacques Robert, N. R. F. (*c*.1980).

D. N. Majumdar in his office at the University of Lucknow (*c.* 1958).

Milton Singer (with the author, on the left) in Chicago.
Photograph by Joan Erdman (1985).

Radhakamal Mukerjee
after his retirement in
Lucknow. Photograph
by Shankar Srivastava
(*c*.1956).

M. N. Srinivas

PART TWO

In Search of a Path:
A PERSONAL ACCOUNT

FIELDWORK
COMPARISON
REFLEXIVITY

RURAL KASHMIR
BANGLADESH
INDIA, JAPAN

And what there is to conquer
By strength and submission, has already been discovered
Once or twice, or several times, by men whom we cannot hope
To emulate . . . .
For us, there is only the trying. The rest is not our business.

T. S. ELIOT

On Living Intimately
with Strangers

6

Mine is the thought of him who is lost in his own country, of the alien in his own nation, of the solitary among his own kinsfolk and friends.

KAHLIL GIBRAN

This essay is intentionally personal in mood. Drawing on my own experience, I hope to be able to demonstrate the importance of the element of subjectivity in social anthropological research in general and in fieldwork in particular. The choice of a theme or problem, of a theoretical framework, and of a strategy of data collection, are all influenced by the prejudices and predilections—some of them subliminal—of the individual researcher and of his peers and mentors. The influence of one's fellow researchers can be particularly overpowering if one is placed with a group of scholars who have come to constitute a 'school', or if one's adviser happens to be a person of towering stature. Thus, the development of anthropological research along different lines at some major universities in England and in the USA is too well known to need more than a mention here.

In other words, themes for social anthropological and sociological research are not naturally given, in the manner of the structures and processes which are the subject matter of natural and physical sciences; nor are the methods of social research as precisely laid down as those that one practises in the aseptic atmosphere of a laboratory. The problems of social science are, I suggest, constituted *in part* by ourselves: our personality enters in a big way into what we choose to study, and, even more so, into the course that our fieldwork runs and the results that flow from it. The contrasting pictures of the village

Written in 1974, this essay owes its origin to a number of conversations I then had with André Béteille. It was published in *Encounter and Experience: Personal Accounts of Fieldwork*, edited by André Béteille and T. N. Madan, New Delhi: Vikas, 1975. I owe warm thanks to Leela and S. C. Dube, Satish Saberwal, and Jit Singh Uberoi for their comments on an earlier draft of this paper.

of Tepoztlan in Mexico given us by Redfield (1930) and by Lewis (1951) are well known. Whereas some of the differences between these two accounts must be attributed to the long interval between the two spells of fieldwork, and to the more sophisticated techniques Lewis was able to employ, it is reasonable to conclude that the personality differences of the two anthropologists, widely known to their colleagues, also played a crucial role. Both of them thought so too (Lewis 1951: 428–9 and Redfield 1955: 133–5).

It is not my intention to deny the existence of intersubjectivity in social research. Surely, no researcher would fail to encounter the element of hierarchy in a Hindu village anywhere in India. The theoretical constructs he employs to interpret hard ethnographical data on caste are, however, a different matter: compare, for example, the contrasting frameworks outlined in Dumont (1961) and in Bailey (1963).

It may also not be denied that anthropologists have at their command a well developed and sophisticated repertoire of fieldwork methods, discussed in, for example, the excellent volumes edited by Epstein (1967) and Freilich (1970). Besides, there are handbooks, such as the well-known (though old fashioned and at places misleading) *Notes and Queries on Anthropology* (see R A I 1951), 'check lists' of topics (Murdock *et al.* 1950), and gadgets like the camera, the tape recorder, and—the latest of the wonders—the videotape. All these aids make fieldwork today very much more of an objective 'scientific' enterprise than it probably was fifty years ago.

The point I am trying to make is that, no matter how thorough an anthropologist's formal training and preparation for research, it is his encounter with the fieldwork situation and his handling of it that ultimately determines the outcome of his efforts. Fieldwork at times unfolds problems which are either not genuine or which the anthropologist is not prepared to tackle because of their being totally unanticipated. Such situations must be squarely faced and the temptation to brush them off resisted. Some of these problems may well be crucial to one's preconceived categories being unmasked and to one's understanding of the society and culture under study. The researcher must devise, if necessary, on-the-spot strategies to come to grips with such unforeseen challenges of fieldwork. In the measure of his success in doing so lies the intellectual fascination and joy of research.

Ethnographers and Natives

My first impressions of the nature of social anthropological fieldwork were formed through contact with the anthropologist D. N. Majumdar and the sociologist D. P. Mukerji at Lucknow University, where I read for my master's degree in 1949–51. Majumdar was a functionalist, and admirer of Malinowski, whose famous seminar he had attended in the mid-thirties, and of Ruth Benedict. To introduce anthropology to us, he gave a course of lectures on 'primitive societies'. His own fieldwork till then had been among the so-called tribal peoples of Bihar and Uttar Pradesh. It was obvious from his teaching and research that anthropology was for him the study of cultures other than one's own: it was concerned with the remote and the unfamiliar. Fieldwork was no picnic but an exacting task, judged by its precious fruit: knowledge and understanding of the diversity of human cultures, of the many ways in which people affirm their humanity (see Chapter 2).

D. P. Mukerji, a powerful influence on the thinking of many of his students, held out to us a somewhat different image of anthropology: a kind of foil to display the riches of sociology. He deplored the narrowness of anthropologists' concerns and the preoccupation in their fieldwork with the minutiae of a people's daily life. He hailed anthropology as a 'shock absorber', and pleaded for the recognition of its higher relevance to cultural reconstruction. It followed, DP taught us, that anthropologists must study history and philosophy and give up their wrong-headed posture of value neutrality. He maintained that the promise of anthropology had been glimpsed in the work of Boas, Benedict, Malinowski—the only book by an anthropologist that he discussed with us at length was Malinowski's *Freedom and Civilization* (1947)—and above all Kroeber, but that it had remained largely unrealized (see Mukerji 1958: 258–69). Majumdar's view of anthropology as a 'field science' was supplemented by Mukerji's humanistic vision of it, and though the latter attracted me more, I was also fascinated, notionally, by the study of the strange and the exotic (see Chapter 1).

In 1951 Majumdar offered me a scholarship for research. Acutely conscious of my awkwardness in dealing with strangers, and attracted by Mukerji's plea for 'theoretical concerns', I inquired of Majumdar if fieldwork in a tribal area would be an essential requirement. He said that it was not for the limited purpose of a doctoral dissertation, but that I could not hope to make a professional career out of anthropology without it. There was no escape, but the difficult day of fieldwork had been postponed. Accordingly, I registered as a Ph.D. student with Majumdar and commenced work on the problem of 'rehabilitation of Indian tribes'. The data were to be drawn from published sources.

About a year later, I joined a group of MA students who were being taken to Ranchi for a two-week field trip as part of their studies. It was a depressing, and even traumatic, experience. Not that the Oraons turned out to be culturally very different from the Hindu villagers of the same area, or that we encountered any savagery at their hands; what upset me was our own behaviour. Everybody was asking the people questions about their most intimate relationships and fondest beliefs, without any regard for their feelings or convenience. My shyness crippled me, and the only thing I could do adequately was to photograph an Oraon cremation, without first seeking anybody's permission to do so. As we came away, I had the uncomfortable feeling that there was something indecent about such field trips. A year-long stay in the field by a single anthropologist would be, I thought, far from the kind of 'assault' in which we had been engaged. Nevertheless, a strong feeling that anthropological fieldwork was in a certain sense degrading to the unwilling subject of observation by a stranger took firm hold of me. This feeling was, most probably, a kind of cover for my own fear of strangers and temperamental inadequacy as a fieldworker. Gradually, almost imperceptibly, it occurred to me that a solution to the problem perhaps lay in studying my own community, the Kashmiri Pandits, though not my own kindred or the neighbourhood where I had grown up in the city of Srinagar (in Kashmir). It is clear to me now, though it was not then, that I was transforming the familiar into the unfamiliar by the decision to relate to it as an anthropologist.

During the following summer (1953), I collected some information on the Pandit kinship terminology, and gave a paper based on it to Majumdar, suggesting to him that I might eventually study a village in Kashmir. He published the essay in *The Eastern Anthropologist* (Madan 1953), but did not particularly discuss with me my proposal about fieldwork.

Early in 1954, S. F. Nadel visited Lucknow. I took the opportunity to discuss my problem with him. He told me that he could see no objection to an Indian studying aspects of his caste or community of birth. He stressed the importance of training in formal anthropological research which, he thought, should help one to overcome the limitations of subjective bias. He also emphasized the importance and advantages of a good command over the 'native tongue' to anthropological research, particularly in the study of kinship and religion, and pointed out that being a native speaker would give one a headstart in fieldwork.[1]

Soon after I discontinued work on my dissertation on the problems of Indian tribes. Majumdar, who had by then himself initiated a research project in a village near Lucknow (Majumdar 1958), agreed that I should make a study of Kashmiri Pandits when a suitable opportunity arose. On his and Nadel's advice I submitted a research proposal to the Australian National University (ANU) for the study of 'kinship values' among the Pandits of rural Kashmir, and was awarded a research scholarship. I could never find out what exactly Nadel thought of my proposal, for he died early in 1956, before my arrival in Canberra. I had been apprehensive that he might not approve of the theme I had suggested: there was no evidence in his own published work of such an interest. My confidence had been somewhat shaken by another teacher, A. K. Saran, a stern critic of positivism, who summarily rejected the idea of a study of values through fieldwork. I was, however, optimistic that he could be answered.

Beliefs and Rituals

After my arrival in Canberra, the first person to discuss my proposal with me at considerable length was Edmund Leach, who was on a short visit to the ANU. He told me that, given his structural-functional approach, my proposal worried him. He thought that it would be a serious mistake for me to get involved in such a vague and difficult-to-handle theme as 'values'. What mattered most in peasant kinship systems in South Asia, he said, was the ownership and inheritance of property, the disputes that arose over it between the children of different mothers in an extended family, and the manner in which these were resolved. He advised me to collect case studies and subject them to analysis—so that the existence of norms may be demonstrated—and to avoid getting bogged down in an ideal, value-governed, mythical state of existence.

Leach thus raised doubts about the study of kinship values, as had Saran before him, but for almost the opposite reasons. His advice, as

[1] For his views on the importance of language competence in fieldwork, see Nadel 1951: 39–48. This impressive book had come into our hands a couple of years earlier and seemed to me to do some of the things that D. P. Mukerji used to ask for in his lectures. I had not found it an easy book to read, particularly its later portion; there was something cloying about its prolixity and forbidding about its psychology—at least for me. I was, nevertheless, much influenced by it.

I understood it, was to lay aside the people's notions of ideal behaviour and to adopt a statistical concept of customary or normative behaviour: to study people's behaviour itself rather than their ideas about it. One could trace this distrust in what people say or affirm to the many excellent demonstrations of the gap between word and deed that exists in ethnographical literature, beginning with Malinowski's monographs on the Trobriand Islanders. He had emphasized that the all-important *'inponderabilia of actual life'* cannot be grasped except through their intensive observation (1922: 18).

In other words, Leach exhorted me to concentrate on what one might call (invoking Robertson Smith's celebrated distinction) 'rituals' rather than 'beliefs'. Though rather depressed by his almost total rejection of the proposed focus of my research, I was much relieved that he had not objected to my studying the *Pandit* kinship system. In fact, he advised me to write down whatever I thought I knew about the subject, and then proceed to check it against field data and thus develop my research. I decided to accept his advice and not insist on a primary focus on values.[2]

Looking back today at the course of my studies, I think Leach's advice was of help to me in my fieldwork, though his distrust of the study of values underlying interkin relations was exaggerated. A primary concern with values was something I was not equipped to study at that time. It was therefore the right thing to have done to concentrate on observable behaviour. I do not mean to suggest that values and ideas thus got dropped out; they never do, at least in the study of kinship, as I was to realize later. But more about this in the last section of this essay.

During the next six months I was engaged in preparing for fieldwork. Of my two advisers, Derek Freeman strongly reinforced Leach's advice, stressing the importance of studying the structure of social relationships in terms of concrete rights and obligations. His own exemplary researches on the Iban had been characterized by a wealth of quantitative and qualitative data (Freeman 1970). W. E. H. Stanner drew my attention to the human aspects of fieldwork, and

---

[2] It may be of interest to recall here that Leach was at this time doing fieldwork in Sri Lanka. In the book based on it he was to write later on: (i) 'It is my thesis that jural rules and statistical norms should be treated as separate frames of reference, but *the former should always be considered secondary to the latter'* (1961: 9, emphasis added). (ii) '. . . I want to insist that kinship systems have *no reality at all* except in relation to land and property. What social anthropologists call kinship structure is *just a way of talking* about property relations which can also be talked about in other ways' (ibid.: 305, emphasis added).

insisted that, in the end, it could really never be learnt; it could only be experienced.

At that time (1956) no major fieldwork-based study of Hindu kinship, other than Irawati Karve's general work (1953), was available. Inevitably, I fell back upon the many excellent books on kinship among the peoples of Africa, South-East Asia, and the Pacific. I also read several works on fieldwork methods. A conclusion which I drew from my studies was that, in my proposed study of kinship among Kashmiri Pandits, the sociological census and the genealogical method were going to be of great help and importance to me.[3] I saw Freeman's sociological census of the Iban and also several genealogies he had made. I was much impressed by the rich information, spanning generations and embracing several longhouses and settlements, that had been neatly compressed into each such chart. It was then that I decided that one of my major fieldwork tasks would be the collection and interpretation of genealogies as charters for social action and as a record of events that had actually occurred.

The process of my adulthood socialization into social science research which had begun at Lucknow University was, in a sense, completed at the ANU. I left Canberra fairly clear in my mind—or so I thought—regarding the scope of my research among the Pandits and the manner in which it was to be conducted. That kinship was a major framework in terms of which the Pandits organized their social life had been a well-grounded impression. My own experience had been limited, however, by the fact that I had grown up in an urban neighbourhood in which only one other household was related to ours by ties of kinship, but did not belong to the same family as we did. When I look back today on the choice of kinship as my principal concern, I think religion would have provided an equally valuable point of entry into the culture and society of the Pandits. It would have perhaps led me more directly to the study of values. I am, however, unable to explain now my early decision in this regard.

The Private and the Public

My arrival in the village of Utrassu-Umanagri (see Madan 1965) did not create a commotion, and this was precisely what I had hoped for. I was not a total stranger inasmuch as I was a Kashmiri. There were several outsiders already resident in the village: two Pandit teachers (one of them, like me, belonged to Srinagar), one Pandit *patwari*

---

[3] Cf. Rivers (1924: 53): 'I define *kinship* . . . as relationship which is determined, and can be described, by means of genealogies.'

(keeper of land ownership and revenue records), and a few Muslims. They were living in different houses, each as a tenant or as a guest. Some had their families with them. I too rented half of a house belonging to a Pandit widow and took up residence in it.

Apart from my landlady and half a dozen Pandit and Muslim men, no adult took much notice of me during the first few days. My statement that I wanted to live for a year in the village to collect authentic materials for a book about the Pandits was readily accepted by them. The Muslims thought of me as just another Pandit who would need goods and services from them. In fact, the first two persons in the village with whom I entered into a long-term formal relationship were my Pandit landlady and a Muslim milkman who agreed to supply me milk and yoghourt and to work for me as my water carrier.[4]

During the first couple of weeks of fieldwork my only fruitful contacts were with teenage children, mostly boys, who were lured by my big battery-operated radio. There was only one other such radio in the village but none in the hamlet of Umanagri where 'my' house was located. (The transistor had yet to make its appearance.) My young informants were very enthusiastic and co-operative and greatly appreciated my confidence in them. It took me time to realize the full import of this relationship: in Pandit society the cleavage between age-groups is quite sharp, and it is unusual for children to be taken seriously by adults, even when they are entrusted with certain chores. This is why they were appreciative of my attitude towards them and, in return, helpful to me. With their assistance I prepared a list of households. This was the beginning of my census of the village. I found these young informants invariably truthful and maintained my contacts with them throughout my stay in the field.

My next step was to make calls and to explain to the people my research interests in some detail. It soon became clear to me that though the people themselves are very intimately involved and interested in their own kinship system—in the ideals and moral values they affirm as well as in the daily events of domestic life—there was a hiatus between their interests and mine. For them these events, and the relations between kinsfolk, carried a heavy emotional load and clearly belonged to the realm of private life. It was obvious to them, and to me, that my inquiries would destroy the prized privacy of domestic life by rendering it public.

[4] For an analysis of traditional Pandit–Muslim relations in rural Kashmir, see Chapter 9. It may be noted here that my interest in the Muslims was aroused only after several months of stay in the village.

I tried to overcome this problem by pointing out to them that my interest—in *particular* events and relationships—was solely for the purpose of writing a *general* account of the Pandit kinship system, and that I could solemnly promise not to embarrass any household or family by exposing their privacy and secrets. Somewhat reassured, they still declined to answer specific questions. I found myself constrained to dwell on the general, such as rules of behaviour, customary obligations and rights, and so on. This bothered me: my decision had been to arrive at general statements through the collection of concrete data about specific events. This was the first of the many trials of my fieldwork.

Fortunately for me the problem solved itself. I found that the Pandits soon tired of discussing general rules, and themselves brought in concrete illustrative material from their own and one another's families. I took my cue and carefully avoided direct questions of a delicate nature about an informant's own family or household, and let him lead me to them. It was thus that the data I so badly needed started coming in, meagrely at first, with the informant exercising a fair degree of control over what he was revealing, but in ample measure and more freely as time passed.

A Pandit has the most intense relations of love and hatred with his own kinsfolk. His life is inextricably involved in the affairs of his household: a ritual for the manes, his son's initiation, his daughter's wedding. As already stated, my informants found my interest in such events in general less irksome than my curiosity about particular households; they also found it less understandable. Why should one spend one's time inquiring about the domestic life of others when the responsibilities to one's own family would teach one everything that there was to know? My interests must have seemed rather idle, if not odd, to them. Quite early during my fieldwork I was advised by some of the people I had come to know to get in touch with a particular villager, Sarvanand Pandit by name; the implication, perhaps, was that I should leave the others alone. As I have said in my book (1965: 243–4), I met my *rara avis* in him.

Sarvanand turned out to be a bachelor in his early fifties, a scion of one of the most respected and rich families of the village. He was literate, like most other Pandit men, and had also attended a commercial-art school at Srinagar for some time. He had never worked for a living, however. He did not have to as he was a landowner. Being unmarried, he had no family of his own, but his step-mother, step-brother, and the latter's wife and child, were living with him.

Sarvanand was an intelligent but a lonely and shy man. He had the natural gift of a prodigious memory and had applied it to an interest in the domestic affairs of the Pandits of the village, some of them constituting his own kindred. He was well informed about the 200-year-old history of the hamlet of Umanagri and of the origins of the different Pandit families of the village. He had even kept a written record of some particularly notable events in the village during his own lifetime. His fellow villagers thought that he was a rather eccentric person: not having a family of his own, he yet was almost obsessively interested in other people's domestic affairs. Denied the opportunity of involvement in intimate relationships and events, he had developed, it seemed to me, an interest in them generally.

It was obvious to me that Sarvanand was some kind of a born ethnographer. Inevitably, we became friends. For him, his discovery of the role of ethnographer was a deeply appreciated vindication of a lifelong interest. For me, my meeting with him was one of the real satisfactions and joys of my fieldwork in Kashmir. I had found in him the key informant that the ethnographer invariably seeks and cultivates (Casagrande 1960). The opposition between the public and the private, the general and the particular, got resolved in his person. He was a source of information about the private and appreciated the legitimacy of making it public. Our dialogues soon developed into group discussions as more and more Pandits assumed the role of informant. The way to this satisfactory situation had led, as I have described, through a period of trial, which had luckily been short. The Pandits' reluctance to talk about their family lives was gradually overcome. Sarvanand remained a principal informant throughout my fieldwork, for he knew so much; but even he did not have the answers to all my questions. Limitations of space preclude my giving many examples: I will discuss just one major problem to which I had to find my own solution.

Kinsfolk and Strangers

By the time I completed my census of the village, I had talked with practically all the adult men among the 522 Pandits, many children, and with some women. I never was able to meet with all the women but only young girls and relatively old women. Pandit etiquette ruled out any but the most restricted contact between nubile girls and young married women on the one hand and an adult male stranger on the other. This limitation was never overcome and undoubtedly affected the quality of the material I was able to obtain, but imposed no limitations on the quantitative dimensions of the census I had taken.[5]

In about three months after the commencement of fieldwork, I was ready to employ the genealogical method of investigation to the Pandit kinship system (see Rivers 1900 and 1910). As stated above, I had great expectations of its potentialities. My enthusiasm suffered an immediate set-back when I found that the Pandits were singularly lacking in an interest in the subject of pedigrees.[6] This came to me as a surprise for two reasons. I had already become aware of the strong patrilineal ideology in Pandit society and this had made me expect that pedigrees would be an important item in its cultural kitbag. Moreover, given the fact that the Pandits have a tradition of literary achievement—hence their name—and almost all men are literate, I had expected that some families might even be in possession of written pedigrees. I was obviously mistaken: there was not a single household which had such records.

The only written materials bearing upon pedigrees that were mentioned to me were the registers (*bahī*) of the ritual functionaries, called Pandas, at the nearby pilgrim town of Mattan, about thirteen kilometres from Utrassu-Umanagri. Two households of the village had marriage ties with these Pandas,[7] and through their help I was able to examine some registers. These interesting documents, the valued possessions of Panda households, contain the record of their clientele (*yajamān*). Every three years, during the Brahmanical leap year, Hindu pilgrims from all over Kashmir and north India, and from even remoter areas, flock to the holy springs and streams of Mattan to offer oblations to their manes. To perform the ritual (*shrāddha*), a man needs the services of a Panda, who also looks after the visitor's requirements of food and shelter, all in exchange for the traditional 'fee' (*dakshinā*).

As soon as a pilgrim arrives, he is subjected to a volley of questions regarding his family and *gotra* names, places of ancestral and present

[5] The problem seems to be both general and persistent. Vatuk, who did fieldwork in two city wards in north India in 1966–7, writes: 'Because I was in a society where considerable segregation of the sexes is customary I obtained most of my data from talking to women and observing their activities' (1972: 203).

[6] I have followed here the useful distinction between pedigrees and genealogies made by Barnes (1967: 103). 'I propose to extend the practice of many genealogists... by using the world "pedigree" for a genealogical statement made orally, diagrammatically, or in writing by an actor or informant.... By "genealogy", in the concrete sense, I mean a genealogical statement made by an ethnographer as a part of his field record or of its analysis.'

[7] The Pandas are a small specialist group who marry among themselves and also with other Pandits. See Madan 1965: 22–9.

residence, and so on. Each register establishes the claim of a particular Panda household to all the patron-clients from certain specified areas. Employing a method of indices, the register is read at a particular page, which gives the dates and other details of earlier visits by the same pilgrim or his agnatic kinsmen, dead or alive. The claim established, the details of the present visit are entered in the register, including the names of the visitor's close kin and companions, for future reference. Distinguished visitors are accorded the privilege of making the entries in their own hand.

The registers in the possession of the Panda households contain information about others, including non-Kashmiris, but not about themselves. Moreover, they do not contain enough data for the construction of genealogies. Women are rarely mentioned, and even the records about men are scattered as the registers are divided at the time of a household partition, the clientele being treated as property. Duplicate or incomplete entries, similarity of names, and other sources of confusion are not rare. I saw the Pandas fight among themselves, brandishing the registers, covered in crimson cloth, seeking to establish claim over a visitor, while he helplessly awaited the outcome of the wrangle!

In the circumstances it seemed as though I would have to assume the role and responsibility of a genealogist, and write down on paper what surely the Pandits had stored in their memories. I was again disappointed: they seemed to remember very little. Even with goading from the well-informed Sarvanand, few Pandits remembered much about their kinsfolk and affines beyond three ascendant generations and two degrees of cousinship, unless the relatives were their co-villagers. Few informants remembered the names of even their lineal ancestors beyond about four or five generations. Any information about collateral kin was very difficult to obtain. Informants would quickly lose interest in the subject and plead their ignorance. The most detailed genealogy that I was able to construct had a depth of seven ascendant generations, but it was very inadequate in its collateral spread even at lower levels. Female agnates often constitute full stops: one might call them the chopped–off branches of the lanky genealogical tree.[8] Information about the natal relatives of incoming wives turns out to be even more limited.

In view of the importance that had been placed on the 'genealogical method' in the course of my preparatory studies at Canberra, I

[8] A Kashmiri proverb says: 'Born a daughter in the family, I grew up to become an aunt, a grandaunt and, then, a stranger.'

was much harassed by the situation unfolded by fieldwork. I was fairly confident that information was not being held back from me, but that only increased my puzzlement.[9]

The problem that faced me was this. The Pandits apparently were aware that written pedigrees were useful documents, but their utility obviously lay in their being concerned, not with one's kinsfolk, but with strangers, namely the pilgrims who came to perform rituals for their manes. For a Panda the pedigrees in his possession were his guarantee of legitimate income. My own expectation had been that it would be one's own pedigree that would be judged as a valuable document. Once again, there was a lack of consonance between my definition of the situation and the people's conception of it. And my informants certainly could not help me in my predicament for they would not acknowledge its validity. I was on my own.

If the Pandits are lacking in an interest in pedigrees, I argued, how do they find their way about in matters in which such knowledge would have served as a guide![10] It seemed to me that the principal utility of a pedigree to the people themselves would lie in the location of one's kinsfolk in social space, and in their categorization for various purposes, notably: (1) avoidance of breaches of the rule prohibiting marriage between people related by blood; and (2) observation of a period of pollution, and the attendant restraints, following births and deaths among one's patrilineal kin. Less importantly, perhaps, pedigrees would guide one's conduct in cases of conflict among one's kinsfolk, some of whom might be more distant than others and, therefore, less deserving of support.

A relatively easy clue to the situation seemed to be offered by the nature and significance of *gotra* names among the Pandits. As I have discussed elsewhere (Madan 1962a), though not all persons bearing the same *gotra* name are agnatically related, patrilineal kin invariably have the same *gotra* name. Their patrilineal ideology makes the Pandits very anxious about even an unwitting breach of the rule prohibiting

---

[9] Later publications (Mayer 1960: 203 and Dumont 1966c: 104–5) attest to the widespread lack of interest in pedigrees among the Hindus of north India, other than Rajputs perhaps.

[10] See Barnes (1967: 103): 'The genealogy conforms to the logic of the system, and in analysis we use genealogies collected in the field along with other evidence to infer the properties of the kinship system generating them. In this sense the genealogy is an analytical tool used by those who study kinship. But in another sense it is a tool used by the actors who operate, and not merely observe, kinship systems.'

marriage between agnates with a common ancestor in the seventh or a lower generation. The rule of *gotra* exogamy takes care of this proscription with economy of effort and with certainty. Obviously, it is so much easier to remember one's *gotra* name even when it is a mouthful, such as Deva-Vatsa-Upamanya-Laugakhya, than to memorize or keep a record of one's pedigree.

Gotra exogamy, then, takes care of one's agnates, negatively, in respect of marriages that must not take place. How about the obligation to avoid marriage with non-agnatic cognates? Though the prohibited degrees in respect of them, according to the Dharmashāstra, are narrower, than in the case of agnates, by two ascendant generations, even so a large number of people scattered over many villages are involved. In practice, the Pandits seem to follow a simple procedure: ideally, a man should not take a *known* kinswoman as his wife. All his female relatives in his own and adjacent villages are thus excluded from the category of potential spouses. The closeness or otherwise of cousinship is simply not reckoned. A man may however take as his wife any woman, resident in a distant village, who is separated from him by more than two degrees of cousinship, though he really ought not to do so. Half a dozen such cases of marriage were cited to me. Pandit practice in this respect accords well with their kinship terminology in which specification is abandoned after two degrees of cousinship and the blanket terms of *piter* (agnates) and *ashnav* (non-agnatic cognates) are employed (see Madan 1963). In other words, beyond two degrees of cousinship, it is vicinage rather than genealogical connection which emerges as the deciding factor in settling marriages. I believe this to be a most important underlying principle of the Pandit kinship system.

In respect of the observation of pollution, my inquiries of actual practice as against the rules, once again revealed the importance of vicinage. It is obligatory that, in the event of a birth or death, all one's agnates falling within the innermost circles of brothers and of first and second cousins must be informed, wherever they are at the time. For the recipient of the message, pollution begins from the moment he hears of it. In case of remoter agnates, no messages may be sent if they are not one's co-villagers or living in an adjacent village.

My bewilderment and anxiety about the Pandits' indifference to pedigrees led me to appreciate fully the importance of vicinage in their kinship system. It became clear to me that, beyond certain limits, kinship is spatially validated. One might even say that, what the Pandits do not store in memory, they mark on the ground. By compressing and coding a substantial part of knowledge about kinship ties in spatial terms, they have devised a cultural means of easy and efficient information management.

The conflict between the Pandits' conception of pedigrees and mine was resolved through my discovery of the definition and importance of social space in their culture. I had arrived at this conclusion by imputing to pedigrees certain functions which I thought they ought to perform. In other words, I was trying to step completely outside the culture, as it were, and look upon it with the uncomprehending eyes of an observer. This act of 'desocialization' became a fruitful heuristic device for me to attain understanding of Pandit culture, in a way, to achieve 'resocialization' into the society of my birth.

Conclusion—Outsiders and Insiders

The purpose of social anthropological research is generally defined as the study and understanding of social behaviour in diverse ecological and cultural settings. Traditionally, such research has been a pursuit of Western scholars outside their own 'natural habitat' and ha^ understandably been defined as the study of 'other cultures', 'natives', or 'alien peoples'. Twentieth century anthropology has prided itself on its emancipation from the ethnocentrism of earlier days; it has sworn by different degrees and shades of cultural relativism and functionalism. Its chosen task has been to make sense of 'strange' ways of thought and living by laying bare their underlying rationality or situational logic (Gellner 1963 and Jarvie 1964).

The only recognized and trusted procedure adequate to the above task has been *fieldwork*: the intensive observation and recording of the flow of events 'out there' in the field, be it the Amazonian jungles, African deserts, New Guinea highlands, or wherever. Fieldwork has been now accepted as an indispensable *rite de passage* in the making of a modern anthropologist for whom the rich book-lined study of an aristocratic home, or the comfortable sun-shaded deck chair of an expeditionary boat in the tropics, is no longer good enough as a vantage point.

Observations made in the field are supplemented by intensive, though generally informal, questioning of the people under study as regards the purpose and meaning of what they do. The medium of communication is ideally the native tongue. A well-defined theme, and probably a set of hypotheses, are expected to provide the crystallizing points round which data collection will be organized. A theory of social behaviour or action, derived from the corpus of social science, finally guides the interpretation of the data when the fieldworker is back home (Evans–Pritchard 1951b: 64–85).

Fieldwork as described above may well be described as the act, or feat, of *living intimately with strangers*. It is the dualism inherent in this situation which yields understanding. The anthropologist is an outsider trying to become enough of an insider to understand what the insiders do and how they make sense of it. As Pehrson put it to his informants, 'I want to become a Lapp so that my people may learn something of your people' (1957: iv): a statement hard to improve upon. In more formal phraseology, the anthropologist looks upon his subjects, and their actions and beliefs, 'from without' and 'from within' (Dumont and Pocock 1960: 84; see also Chapter 4). The balance between the two competing yet complementary points of view must be maintained: the researcher must steer clear of the Scylla of ignoring the native point of view and the Charybdis of 'going native'.

Disregard of the native point of view seems to me to be the greater of the two dangers. The number of scholars who gave up anthropology to mingle with the natives must be very small. The best known case is, probably, of the German scholar who went to study Indians in the Amazonian jungles and never returned. He took the partly native name of Curt Nimuendaju. Even he did not, however, completely forsake his earlier lifestyle. Frank Cushing, the celebrated student of the Zuni Indians, has left behind his fieldwork data which he would not publish because of his emotional identification with the people; but he never became a Zuni (Paul 1953: 435; Baldus 1946). In India, Verrier Elwin became very close indeed to the tribal people, married among them, and became an Indian citizen . He too never quite ceased to be the Englishman that he was (Elwin 1964).

The phrase 'participant observation', generally applied to anthropological fieldwork, creates a misleading impression about the researcher's capacity for a special effort of empathy. Many scholars have, I think, overrated both its desirability and possibility (Evans–Pritchard 1951b: 75–85 and, for a more detailed discussion, Whyte 1953: 279–360). The fear about the danger of being swallowed up by the 'native' culture—at least being misled by indigenous categories of thought—is a result of the foregoing misconception. In fact, participant observation poses challenges of a different kind: it involves deliberate role playing and what has been called 'impression management'. The parties involved in the encounter know this, judging by the manner in which roles are adjusted and altered on either side (Berreman 1962).

If full participant observation is neither necessary nor possible, so is a *wholly* external point of view a chimera. An overweening emphasis on externally observable behaviour, to the neglect of the ideas of the people, their beliefs and avowed purposes, is a fieldwork recommendation that no one could ever follow and yet succeed in his task. The relationship between beliefs and actions is pragmatic and not contingent. Statistical regularities, or any deviations from them, are social facts ('things'), but they become meaningful to actors only in terms of their value system. On the other hand, the validity of certain value-imperatives in a society could be said to be independent of the frequency with which they might be shown to inform different spheres of social life. Filial piety is a value in Kashmiri Pandit society, not because most of the sons can be shown to observe its implications most of the time, and despite the fact that some sons maltreat their parents. We must distinguish between essential and general truths and try to apprehend the relationship between them.

The opposition between 'beliefs' and 'rituals' is, I suggest, false: their true relationship is one of complementarity. If the evasion of people's ideas is to be justified in terms of the notion of 'false consciousness', one is obliged to follow this theoretical stance to its logical conclusion: examine such consciousness to expose what it covers. In short, one simply cannot just brush aside the ideas of the people: the alternatives are either to consciously confront them or to let them enter surreptitiously into one's work. In my own fieldwork, the ideas of people assumed an increasingly compelling character as my research developed beyond the quantitative aspects of the household census. It is in this sense, I think, that the anthropologist's view 'from without' is not equivalent to the external vantage point of the natural scientist: it is incomplete (Dumont and Pocock 1960: 84; Madan 1966b: 12; Dumont 1966a; see also Chapter 4). This is, in fact, the bane of sociological functionalism: it teaches us to rest content with incomplete descriptions.

The foregoing considerations do not enter in quite the same way into the making of the perspectives of a researcher who chooses to study his own society.[11] He is placed in a particularly difficult position:

[11] This is, of course, the minority, if not the heretical, tradition in anthropology as it has been practised in Europe, Britain and the USA. It is obvious, however, that in most of the world today the study of one's own society by social anthropologists is emerging as a primary concern no less than it is among sociologists. It is in this sense, among others, that the distinction between social anthropology and sociology is obsolete.

he is an insider who takes up the posture of an outsider, by virtue of his training as an anthropologist or a sociologist, and looks at his own culture, *hoping to be surprised.* If he is, only then may he achieve new understandings. The insider–outsider dichotomy can never be a stark opposition in his case, nor indeed must it be allowed to break down. The encounter between anthropology and a culture in the person of the 'native' researcher is a dialectical and, *therefore*, a productive one. I completely agree with Dumont (1966a: 23): 'Duality, or tension, is here the condition *sine qua non* of social anthropology or, if one likes, sociology of a deeper kind.' Lévi-Strauss (1963b: 58) evocatively calls the anthropologist 'an amputated man'. If one may persist with this metaphor, the attempt to study one's own culture and society is the act of simultaneous amputation and restoration. Indeed, one might say that a person becomes truly whole, or wholly human, only through the study of his own society.

In anthropological research great value (at times bordering on a kind of mystique) has come to be attached to the study of 'other cultures'; only such an undertaking has been deemed to be enough of an intellectual and physical challenge. The virtues of cultivated empathy are, therefore, extolled; so overwhelming is this point of view that even anthropologists who have studied their own society have come to subscribe to it, at least in some measure (Srinivas 1966: 155–7). The study of a society other than one's own is, undoubtedly, important in itself; it could also be heuristically useful in refining one's conceptual tools which might later be employed in the study of one's own society. To maintain that the study of foreign societies advances sociological understanding more than the study of one's own society (Dumont 1966a: 23), or to suggest that the former is a prerequisite for the latter (Srinivas 1966: 155), seem to me overstated positions. The starting point of one's studies may well be one's own society, and empathy is not the only or the *principal* methodological precept in the understanding of social life everywhere.

It is not so much empathy as detachment—Dumont would call it 'distantiation' (1966a: 23)—that is the ability to step outside and look back sharply and deeply at one's own culture which a scholar studying his own society has unremittingly to cultivate. And it is not easy. Malinowski wrote about the Trobriand Islanders, perhaps in a fit of depression: 'I see the life of the natives as utterly devoid of interest or importance, something as remote from me as the life of a dog' (1967: 167). Needless to say, my own attitude towards the Pandits, even on the most luckless of days, was very different: I felt *personally involved*, no matter how slightly, in their affairs and fortunes. This naturally worried me, watchful as I had been advised to be of the dangers of sub- jective bias. Matters were made more difficult by the fact that, as was plain to me from quite early in my fieldwork, the people among whom I lived expected me to abide by the basic rules of social, moral, and ritual conduct prevalent among them. Once it was accepted by most villagers that there must be good reasons for a person to spend a year among them, obviously at considerable expense, to study their way of life in order to be able to write about it, they also accepted the new role of informant for themselves. The degree of the acceptance of this situ- ation varied considerably from person to person. There were Pandits, fortunately a small minority, who never went beyond the exchange of politely restricted salutations with me. What is important is that even those who accepted the ethnographer–informant relationship willingly or enthusiastically, implied that Pandit culture and society had to be the overall setting for our relationship.

Such a definition of their relationship with me imposed two kinds of restraint on my inquiries. Early during the fieldwork, my inquiries about the basic norms of social intercourse caused puzzlement among my informants: 'Surely you must know?' would be the usual query. I had to plead that, given my upbringing in an urban area, and my prolonged studies outside Kashmir (my 'desocialization'), I did not always know what I ought to know. This produced a positive response, I think, mainly because they believed me but, probably, also because some of them saw in the situation their opportunity to reclaim ('reso- cialize') me. Consequently, I was expected to observe even more faith- fully the fundamental rules of social intercourse prevalent among them.

The situation became more difficult with the passage of time: improving *rapport* with the villagers only meant that more insistent, though not always deliberate, efforts were made to absorb me, and my wife, into village life. I will very briefly give just two examples of the kind of situations that developed.

(1) I was asked on a few occasions during the later part of my stay in the village to intervene in some family disputes about property. In the process I was given access to information about conflict among kinsfolk that I had found very difficult to obtain in the course of my inquiries. This raised for me the ethical problem of what use I might make of what I had come to know. It was obvious that at least some households had taken me into the domain of their privacy, and thus bound me to secrecy.

130 *Pathways*

(2) Significantly, on the day of my wife's departure from the village, a few days before my own, one of my best informants, Vasadev Pandit, took us to his home and solemnly announced in the presence of his household members that, from that day, he would regard my wife as his sister.[12] To seal this bond, he requested her to name his infant daughter after herself. It is clear that, by this act, he was seeking to establish a new and permanent bond between me and himself (and the Pandit community of the village), overriding the temporary and, in the eyes of a Kashmiri villager, the less valued relationship between ethnographer and informant. The tension between the two roles was thus being symbolically overcome, at least so far as Vasadev was concerned. In the process, the other oppositions mentioned by me in the course of this essay were also being placed in their proper perspective. I realized this only later, however, by hindsight.[13]

[12] I interrupted my fieldwork after it had been in progress for five months to get married to, as it happened, a non-Kashmiri Pandit. Those of the villagers who had by then come to know me fairly well did not conceal their pleasure when they learned that my wife was a Brahman. Their disapproval of her not being a Kashmiri was never voiced: restraint in such matters is a basic principle of social intercourse among the Pandits. She was treated with considerable courtesy though she aroused much curiousity on account of her inability to speak Kashmiri and (to quote the village school second master, a Pandit) her 'sixteen years of education as compared to my fourteen'! My wife and I were soon able to settle down to a pattern of domestic life which was largely indistinguishable from that of other Pandits in the village.

[13] I read Leach's essay 'Ourselves and the Others' (1973) only after this paper had been completed. I find his remarks about participant observation most interesting. He writes that Malinowski substituted the 'illusion' of 'complete subjective understanding' through 'participant observation' in place of 'the illusion of objectivity'. He however found 'to his chagrin' that 'the others remained obstinately other'. He discovered an 'incompatibility' between doing ethnography and participating in 'Trobriand daily life as a human being. It is an incompatibility which all of Malinowski's successors, when fully honest with themselves, have had to recognize' (ibid.: 772).

It is a pity that Leach's discussion of the relationship of anthropologists ('ourselves') to 'the others' they study had to fit into a symposium on British social anthropology. It is obvious that, within this tradition, the opposition implied in Leach's title must remain unresolved. He does mention non-British 'members of the profession' from Africa and Asia, but does not examine their significance for the sociology of their own societies, or for social anthropology. The methodological problems that a Trobriand Islander wanting to study his own people would face can hardly be lacking in interest to Malinowski's successors.

On the Mutual Interpretation of Cultures

7

Each race contributes something essential to the world's civilization in the course of its own self-expression and self-realization. The character built up in solving its own problems, in the experience of its own misfortunes, is itself a gift which each gives to the world. The essential contribution of India, then, is simply her Indianness; her great humiliation would be to substitute or to have substituted for this own character (svabhava) a cosmopolitan veneer, for then indeed she must come before the world empty-handed.

ANANDA COOMARASWAMY

Anthropology will survive in a changing world by allowing itself to perish in order to be born again under a new guise.

CLAUDE LÉVI-STRAUSS

Anthropology as the Mutual Interpretation of Cultures

Anthropology sat proudly though briefly on a wall—the wall erected by the Enlightenment and buttressed by colonialism—viewing the non-Western cultures of the world and their disintegration with the detachment that behoves scientific inquiry! Our generation has had to witness its fall, however, and also the efforts to put it together again. It seems to me that a tragic misunderstanding of the possible scope of anthropology underlies some of these efforts. Thus the project which is called by such names as *native, spontaneous, autonomous,* or *indigenous* anthropology seems to me to misconstrue the very nature of the discipline. I would therefore like to begin this essay by clarifying what I understand by the term anthropology.

Written in 1978, and presented at a conference on 'indigenous anthropology' held under the auspices of the Wenner-Gren Foundation that year, the essay is reproduced from *Indigenous Anthropology in Non-Western Countries,* edited by Hussein Fahim, Durham N. C.: Carolina Academic Press, 1982. I would like to place on record my indebtedness to Lita Osmundsen for many acts of support and kindness spread over several years.

There have always been affirmations by the brave among the tribe that anthropology is about 'that wondrous creature man', 'in whatever place or time we meet him' (Evans-Pritchard 1951b: 129). That is the myth by which they have lived. In practice, however, anthropology has been the effort of certain intellectuals to make sense of non-Western cultures of the world in the manner dictated by Western science. In other words, the basic presupposition of anthropology is that we are able not only to obtain verifiable information about cultures other than our own through observation, but also to acquire scientific understanding of them. Men and morals are thus treated as objects of scientific study just as nature and natural forces are.

We need do no more here than recall that, although the founding fathers of anthropology relied upon their own cultural understandings, glorified by the widespread evolutionist ethos of the second half of the nineteenth century, to place other cultures in their 'proper' places on the lower rungs of an evolutionary ladder, a later generation admitted of varieties of understanding as well as of culture. It, however, took away with one hand what it gave with the other by promulgating a functional or scientific theory of culture (see Malinowski 1944). Neither Malinowski's own well-intended and forthright admonitions about the dangers of ethnocentrism, nor the prodigalities of the culture relativists, could really shake the positivist foundations of anthropology. The focus was on verbal and non-verbal behaviour as observed from the outside by the trained investigator called the anthropologist. Though the so-called natives did whatever could be done in front of the anthropologist's eyes, and said whatever could be spoken within his hearing, the anthropologist took his selected pickings and constructed his own image of the culture and society under observation.

In the process, however, two vantage points came to be recognized—the external and the internal. Durkheim had, of course, already formulated (in the 1890s) this distinction when he proposed that social facts be studied as 'things' as well as 'collective representations' (see Durkheim 1953, 1964b), but his views suffered at the hands of one-eyed exegetes. The importance of the dual perspective was later to be rediscovered under the reign of linguistics and reformulated as the etic and the emic dimensions of social reality (see Pike 1954). The important thing, however, is not the recognition of the two vantage points, or of scientific and 'home-made' models, but of the nature and importance of their nexus.

It seems to me that we must adhere firmly to the notion that *anthropology* resides in this nexus, that it *is a kind of knowledge—a form of consciousness—which arises from the encounter of cultures in the mind of the anthropologist*. What an outsider learns about an alien society's observable modes of behaviour will not yield anthropological understanding unless he is able to grasp, in the first place, the subjective purposes and meanings that make these modes of behaviour significant to the people concerned. But the knowledge about one's own beliefs and rituals which an informant may impart to the investigator is not anthropological understanding either. All fieldworkers know that well-informed and intelligent insiders often fail to provide exegetic commentaries on what they are able to narrate. At the same time, the insider's puzzlement about his own situation is hardly ever resolved through reference to other people's ways of life that the anthropologist might acquaint him with. The point, then, is not that anthropology is superior or inferior to the traveller's tale, or to autology (howsoever attained), but that it is different from both. Difference should not, however, be interpreted as the mutual irrelevance of the view from within and the view from without; if it is, the nexus I mentioned above becomes redundant and the promise of anthropology remains unrealized.

The anthropologist has been, by convention, an outsider who has tried to understand what the insiders of the society he wants to study believe and do. He seeks to enter another society, as it were, to live intensely in it, enveloped by it, but only for a while. His intention is to leave it and return to his own society. In the words of Claude Lévi-Strauss (1963b: 17), every anthropological study seeks 'to enlarge a specific experience to the dimensions of a more general one, which thereby becomes accessible *as experience* to men of another country or epoch'.

A risk which the outsider as anthropologist runs is that of going native and losing his perspective (often erroneously referred to as objectivity). Judging by the available evidence, however, anthropologists have been remarkably successful in overcoming this professional hazard. In view of this, I have elsewhere described anthropological fieldwork as the *art* of 'living intimately with strangers' (see Chapter 6).

In this sort of work it is understandable that what is relatively easily accessible through observation from the outside gets more emphasis than what is given in the people's own experience—that what people do gets more attention than what they think or believe in—that what they have is stressed more than what they are. Under the circumstances positivism comes to be regarded as a virtue and scientific knowledge (so-called) gets elevated to being considered the only valid understanding. Karl Popper's judgement may appear harsh but it seems just to me: 'The triumph of social anthropology is the triumph of a pseudo-observational, pseudo-descriptive, and pseudo-inductive generalizing methodology and above all marks the triumph of a pretended objectivity and hence an imitation of the methods of natural science' (quoted by Banton 1964: 99).

It is, therefore, all to the good that anthropologists have turned in a big way in recent years to the examination of cultural signs, symbols, and meanings—to structures of inference, implication, and signification. Structuralism and phenomenology (with their respective concerns with form and consciousness) are the intellectual streams which have significantly contributed to this development. It is obvious that unless we put people back into anthropology we will only deal with behaviour and institutions, and we will deal with them imperfectly, for what people do is never fully comprehensible unless we try to find out what they believe in and what their purposes, values, and norms are. This takes us into the realm of subjective experience which, needless to emphasize, is hard to penetrate.

What people believe in and do, and the relationship between belief and action, have first to be understood in the people's own terms— this is the first-order interpretation of facts—before one may translate these understandings into the language of anthropology. The anthropologist's task, then, is to establish a synthesis between the introversion of self-understanding and the extroversion of scientific method. This is a very difficult undertaking. A simple-minded aggregative approach does not lead to such a synthesis because, among other reasons, the two perspectives do not readily merge into a harmonious whole: they cannot, in view of their different presuppositions. This is, perhaps, why Louis Dumont says that 'duality or tension is here the condition *sine qua non* of social anthropology': 'Unless we maintain and combine both views we shall get adrift' (1970b: 156f.). Anthropology, then, may be defined as the mutual interpretation of cultures, one by another.

Stated differently, anthropology has to choose between intercultural communication, on the one hand, and cultural exclusivism, whether in the form of ethnocentrism or solipsism, on the other. In fact there is no choice, for the latter option would drastically diminish the scope of anthropology and eventually lead to its abolition. It is, however, important to recognize that anthropology defined as intercultural communication is beset with overwhelming conceptual and methodological problems. Thus the uncritical use of one particular language to establish such communication will result in 'understanding' which is based on misunderstanding. These problems have to be faced and overcome, for—to extend to culture what Goethe said about language—so long as we know no foreign culture we are in a sense ignorant of our own.

Anthropology as Heightened Self-Awareness

Anthropology, then, is a worthwhile endeavour inasmuch as it enables us to understand ourselves in relation to others: the old definition of it as the study of 'other cultures'—whether an honest confession or an expression of cultural arrogance—is no longer adequate. A question that must be faced here is whether the insider is prevented by the very fact of his cultural location from acquiring the kind of knowledge of his society that I have called anthropological. This seems to be an unwarranted misgiving; in fact, one could hardly hope to contribute to anthropology in any case without examining one's tacit assumptions.

One of the virtues of classical anthropology was the conviction of the scholars concerned that mankind had to be treated as one, that it *was* one. They did this using some arguments which we would readily reject today. What is important to note in their work and to preserve, however, is that they saw cultures in terms of their mutual relatedness (in evolutionary or, later, diffusionist schemes) rather than merely as isolated entities. Anthropology by implication, if not by formal definition, was the study of these *relations*. They even turned the anthropological gaze occasionally on themselves, through their concern with the classical roots of contemporary European civilization, as seen, for instance, in the work of James Frazer. Later, Franz Boas (1928) wrote about anthropology and modern life and Bronislaw Malinowski (1947) expressed his anguish at the grave threat that freedom and, therefore, civilization itself were faced with in Europe. Boas's distinguished pupil Margaret Mead, who began her anthropological research in Samoa, later on devoted considerable attention to the study of aspects of American society. In all such writings, however, the anthropologist's concern with his own society is either implicit or indirectly derived from his study of other cultures. The task that is before us now, it seems to me, is to formulate explicitly the legitimacy and importance of this concern with one's own culture in relation to other cultures.

While many anthropologists today write about their own societies with remarkable success (see, for example, Nakane 1970), and even discuss the methodological problems involved in this endeavour (see, for example, Srinivas 1966; see also Chapter 6), it is, perhaps, Louis Dumont who has sought to establish most explicitly the importance of the comparative study of cultures at the level of underlying principles. He defends his work on India generally and on the caste system in particular by stating his 'conviction that caste has something to teach us [Europeans] about ourselves' (1970a: 1). Elsewhere he writes: 'The sociologist can *name* without arbitrariness, in a given society, features which it neglects, because he has learnt their names from another society. For instance, the India of caste and *varna* teaches us hierarchy, and this is no little lesson' (1970b: 164). Dumont's present interest in aspects of European intellectual history—specifically, his concern with the genesis and triumph of economic ideology (see Dumont 1977a)—has taken the particular form and direction it has because of his earlier work on India. It is his effort to understand the ideology of caste—that is, hierarchy—which has created in him a particular kind of puzzlement about his own society and about the importance of individualism in it. It is this which has, in turn, enabled him to bring out explicitly the inversion of values which one encounters in the comparative study of *homo aequalis* and *homo hierarchicus*.

In this endeavour 'comparison is the fulcrum' (Dumont 1977b: 11). One has to learn not only to *live intimately with strangers* but also to *live (behave) strangely with intimates*. One has to cultivate empathy for other cultures; contrariwise one has to create distance between oneself and one's culture and society in order to be able to see oneself in the round, as it were. And that is how a heightened self-awareness may be expected to emerge. There is a remarkable passage in Lévi-Strauss's inaugural address at the College de France which is apposite in this context: 'this "anthropological doubt" does not only consist of knowing that one knows nothing, but of resolutely exposing what one thought one knew, and indeed one's very own ignorance, to the buffetings and denials which are directed at one's most cherished ideas and habits by other ideas and habits which must needs contradict them to the highest degree' (1967: 43). This, indeed, is the spirit which should animate the work of anthropologists, whether they are 'aliens' or 'natives' in the society which they choose to try to understand—particularly the work of the latter.

The 'connection' of societies—their theoretical comparison—is the first principle of anthropological knowledge. A problem that arises here is whether one needs to study personally an alien culture, as part of one's training and education, before turning to the exploration of one's own. M. N. Srinivas thinks that this is so: 'Fieldwork in an alien society constitutes an excellent preparation for the observation of one's own society' (1966: 155). Dumont goes further to assert that 'sociological understanding is advanced more by the social anthropologist looking at a foreign society than by the sociologist who looks at his own' (1970b: 157).

There seems to be a double misunderstanding here which in effect denies the collective nature of the scholarly enterprise that anthropology is. First, one certainly does not have to study personally alien cultures in order to acquire a critical perspective on one's own: one may read about them, as indeed all anthropologists do. In other words, fieldwork in an alien society is not a necessary precondition for the study of one's own society, but a comparative perspective is. If one were to begin with a description of one's own society without any exposure to comparative ethnography, one would produce the kind of narratives which Pocock (1973) calls personal anthropology. I would, in fact, hesitate to use the word anthropology in reference to such accounts. Second, apropos Dumont's observation, the study of a foreign society by itself will not do: this also has to be based on prior knowledge of societies other than it. Whether one begins one's anthropological quest at home or abroad, the comparative perspective is indispensable.

Another problem that arises in the context of mutual interpretation of cultures is whether this is guaranteed by the appearance of native or indigenous anthropologists on the anthropological stage. Some scholars seem to think so, but I do not feel assured about it. One would not like to minimize the importance of such a development in the non-Western countries of the world, in view of the shocking fact that about 90 per cent of all social scientists today belong to the so-called developed countries (see Madan 1977a). Nevertheless, I would like to argue against such a narrow interpretation, for this change of stage (from, say, the London School of Economics to the Delhi School of Economics) and of actors (South Asian anthropologists in place of Westerners) may be only a change in form and not in substance. The purpose of the play may remain the same, namely the ending of the puzzlement which the Occidental consciousness experiences in the mysterious Orient, and the direction of the play may remain the same as well. This is the well-known phenomenon of the imported 'intellectual baggage' of the Indian scholar (see Madan 1966b)—of 'the captive mind' in the non-Western societies (see Alatas 1972)—which is a product of academic colonialism.

The 'centres' of intellectual activity have been located in the West, Edward Shils pointed out many years ago (Shils 1961), and what exist out there in South Asia ('in here' for South Asians) are the 'peripheries', the outposts. It is a kind of hierarchical relationship between substance and shadow, between creation and imitation. In India, we talk of the 'brown sahibs' having taken over government from the 'white sahibs': in the domain of social sciences there has been a similar transfer from Western scholars to the native practitioners of the craft. The crucial question, therefore, is not Who is doing anthropology? but What kind of anthropology is being done?

Here I would like to draw attention to a seminal essay by Jit Singh Uberoi entitled 'Science and Swaraj'. He wrote: 'The aim and method of science are no doubt uniform throughout the world but the problem of science in relation to society is not' (1968: 119). This obviously applies much more forcefully in the field of social sciences than elsewhere. By the very nature of the academe as now constituted, Uberoi says, there is a congruence of national and international interests in the work of Western scientists but not in that of their non-Western contemporaries. Hence his plea that we 'concentrate on decolonialization, learn to nationalize our problems and take our poverty seriously'. 'A national school, avowed and conscious, can perhaps add relevance, meaning and potency to our science; continued assent to the international system cannot' (1968: 123).

The foregoing does not mean, however, that non-Western social scientists should retreat behind some kind of a curtain. The importance of 'self-rule' (*swaraj*) in determining what research to do and how to do it is not, Uberoi clarified later, a plea for native imitations of Western products of the mind: 'It is not a question of relying solely on home-grown or *swadeshi* ideas or of making ritual rules of purity and pollution in international intellectual relations' (1974: 136).

What Uberoi said in India has been echoed by many anthropologists hailing from other non-Western societies. To give just one example, Talal Asad has pointed out that anthropology, rooted as it was 'in an unequal power encounter between the West and the Third World', has contributed to the process that gave 'the West access of cultural and historical information about the societies it has progressively dominated', and has helped in 'maintaining the structure of power represented by the colonial system' (1973: 16f.). Similarly, a group of social scientists drawn from Africa, Asia, Latin America, and Europe meeting under the auspices of UNESCO in 1976 drew pointed attention to the need to end the 'cultural, intellectual and financial dependence' of social sciences in 'the developing countries'. It was further stated that:

> There has long existed an imbalance between intellectual 'imports' and 'exports' between Third World countries and the advanced nations of the West. There has been an abundant flow into the developing countries of ready-made conceptual models, theoretical frameworks, research techniques, etc., whereas the flow in the reverse direction has been the raw data, whether collected by foreigners or "native" scholars (Madan 1977a: 9).

The point, then, is that—to return to the metaphor used earlier in this essay—a mere change of the stage and the actors will not enable anthropology to be reborn. In order to replace the prevailing borrowed consciousness by a heightened self-awareness among the non-Western anthropologists—thus paving the way for a mutual interpretation of cultures—we need to produce a different kind of play under the direction of comprehensive theoretical frameworks, which admit meaning and purpose into our discourse, and, which integrate the views from the inside with those from the outside. In this endeavour, the perceptive insights of savants like Ananda Coomaraswamy and Claude Lévi-Strauss (see the epigraphs on page 131) on the nature of self-awareness, self-expression, and self-realization, and the significance of these processes for the emergence of anthropology as the mutual interpretation of cultures, should be our signposts.

Anthropology in India as a Fragmentary Discourse

At this point it might be useful to illustrate the preceding discussion by sketching the rise and growth of anthropology in India. It may be added parenthetically that what is true of India is generally the case throughout South Asia.

Anthropology as ethnography was brought to India late in the eighteenth century by Western, notably British and French, visitors who came here as Christian missionaries, civil servants, or simply travellers. They observed the natives as much as seemed necessary for the intended purpose of efficient administration or religious conversion. What they recorded is truly impressive in its comprehensiveness of coverage though not always in its depth of understanding. Alongside of fieldwork-based accounts of customs and manners and of tribes and castes, which required patience and interest in detail, but not much scholarship or respect for the people, there emerged a small group of dedicated scholars who devoted themselves to the study of written texts, particularly those in Sanskrit. Again, some of these texts were of interest to the administrators (for example, the commentaries dealing with inheritance of property), but many others were studied for their literary quality or metaphysical content. It was thus that Indology was born.

The work of Indologists, however, had little or no influence on the ethnographers. The unity of experience in the life of the people, and the vital connection between the past and the present, were destroyed by this artificial fragmentation of knowledge. It is instructive to recall that whereas the Indologists were deeply impressed by the literary and cultural achievements of ancient India, the ethnographers were repelled by the 'rituals', 'superstitions', and general 'degradation' of contemporary India. This fragmentation was seemingly neat but, of course, misleading or false. Equally pernicious was the uncritical distinction between tribes and castes, ignoring the fact that the so-called tribes were often not only involved in economic transactions with non-tribal people but were also in many situations culturally closer to their neighbouring castes than to tribes elsewhere in the country.

By the beginning of the twentieth century Indology and ethnography had made great progress and the former discipline had gained entry into academic circles not only in India but also in Britain and Europe. The great German philologist and Sanskritist, Max Müller, who taught at Oxford University in England, and others like him made this possible. Anthropology had to wait till the 1920s before it came to be taught at a university in India. W. H. R. Rivers of Cambridge was to have been the first professor of anthropology at Calcutta University, but he did not take up the assignment, and eventually his pupil K. P. Chattopadhyay played a leading role in the development of the subject as an academic discipline in India. At Bombay University, Patrick Geddes had already established the sociology department (in the previous decade) and, after he left, another Indian student of Rivers, G. S. Ghurye, took over the responsibility of nurturing the subject there.

Though Ghurye's interests and skills enabled him to span the three disciplines of Indology, sociology, and anthropology in his own work, a tripartite division of the study of society and culture in India had become almost formalized by the time India gained independence in 1947: Indology had become rigidified as the study of old Sanskrit and Pali texts; sociology had come to be defined as the study of Hindu society; and anthropology had emerged as the study of Indian tribes. This was a step backwards from the comprehensiveness of official ethnography. Academic anthropology thus turned its back on the millions who were considered non-tribal people and sociology largely ignored non-Hindus. The process of fragmentation mentioned above thus remained uncorrected.

This, then, was the situation at the time of independence. Though anthropology and sociology courses were taught at a few universities (notably at Lucknow University by the famous trio of Radhakamal Mukerjee, D. P. Mukerji and D. N. Majumdar) (see Chapters 1 and 2) within economics, political science, or philosophy departments, no new departments devoted to either of these two subjects had been established anywhere. Anthropology particularly seemed to have fallen foul of both the administrators and the nationalists. Things have changed very rapidly since then. Sociology departments now exist in over eighty universities and affiliated colleges and anthropology departments in over twenty. It should be added here that some of the courses taught in many sociology departments, and also some of the research carried out by students and teachers there, will be recognized as social anthropology in Britain and North America. Apart from the expansion of size, significant changes in the scope of anthropological and sociological studies have also occurred. At least three major developments need to be taken notice of.

First, social anthropology and sociology have, as stated above, drawn closer together. The distinction between them, as it was developed in the West and in the form it is maintained there, is generally seen as irrelevant in India today. Anthropologists have turned to non-tribal rural communities and urban groups and centres; similarly, sociologists engage in intensive fieldwork in rural and urban settings. The distinction has not, however, disappeared completely.

Second, there has been a diversification of theoretical frameworks. This can only be briefly mentioned here. The first generation of academic anthropologists in India were by and large functionalists who modelled their work on Malinowski and his followers. After the independence of India there was a convergence of interests in the work of M. N. Srinivas and some American anthropologists. Srinivas, who studied with G. S. Ghurye in India and A. R. Radcliffe-Brown

in England, opened a new approach to the study of local communities
and regional caste systems by showing how they relate to what he
called all-India Hinduism. In this context, he pointed out the central
importance of a long established cultural process of imitation of upper
caste lifestyles from below (and the propagation of cultural values from
above) which he called 'Sanskritisation' (see Srinivas 1952b; see also
Chapter 3).

Srinivas's work influenced and was itself influenced by the emerging
interest in India among American cultural anthropologists. The
work of Robert Redfield and Milton Singer (see Redfield 1956 and
Singer 1972) became a major driving force among both American and
Indian scholars who contributed to the making of this highly influential
new trend. Its most significant achievement was the effort to place
the local communities which anthropologists studied within the
overall framework of Indian civilization. The Indian village was thus
seen not as a self-contained social system but as a microcosm of Indian
civilization—in theory if not always in practice. Redfield's earlier
studies in Mexico had provided the foundation for the postulation of
the dialectic of great and little traditions in the history of civilizations. This development, however, created its own variety of fragmentation in Indianist studies in the hands of unimaginative scholars
who often produced inventories of the elements of the two traditions
and thus, in the process, opposed them to each other. This happened, for example, in the study of religious belief and practice.

Almost simultaneously (in the early 1950s), the French anthropologist Louis Dumont's work on India began to appear in print.
Within a few years it covered a wide range of subjects—kinship, caste,
politics, religion—and produced a sensitivity to the ideas of the people
which had generally been ignored under the regime of functionalism
(see Chapter 4). He proclaimed that 'we must learn from the people
themselves which modes of thinking we have the right to apply and
which we should reject' (Dumont 1970b: 7). He cautioned, however,
that 'ideology does not tell us everything about society'; the anthropologist must, therefore, attend to the 'facts of behaviour' as well and,
besides, 'add the necessary but implicit links to the principles that the
people themselves give' (ibid.). Dumont thus insisted that the sociology of India must lie at the confluence of Indology and ethnography—
that it must synthesize the views from within and without.

More recently, efforts have been made by some American and Indian anthropologists, who affirm the importance of native categories of thought but do not accept Dumont's methodology, to construct models of Hindu society which have been characterized as ethnosociological (see, for example, Marriott 1976a, Inden and Nicholas 1977, Das 1977; see also Chapter 5). This appeal to the ideas of the people and to texts is welcome so long as care is taken that it does not result in a retreat from one kind of ethnocentrism into another. Personally, I would insist that the mutual interpretation of cultures must remain at the centre of all our efforts.

What is important to note about these developments in the context of this essay is that although the contributions of Indian scholars have become increasingly significant, the primary impetus that has shaped them has lain in the work of Western anthropologists.[1]

The third major development in anthropological/sociological studies in India since independence has been a growing demand that the work of all social scientists must directly contribute to the most urgent tasks at hand. These were first defined as economic growth, development, or modernization; more recently they were restated as the removal of gross socio-economic inequalities and the provision of the basic needs of all citizens. There has been a continuing debate about the social responsibilities of intellectuals in general and about the criterion of *relevance* (sometimes curiously opposed to *quality*) in social science research in particular. Such compartmentalization of the work of anthropologists (and other social scientists) into relevant or irrelevant, applied or pure, introduces yet another injurious fragmentation into the field which cannot but diminish our understanding of the social reality under examination; for this reality is acknowledged on all sides to be a unified whole, though the nature of the unity may not be conceived in identical terms by, say, the Marxists and the non-Marxists. It would indeed be a rash person who would start with the assumption that some aspects of social life are irrelevant to our efforts to change others. This itself is a problem for investigation.

What the supporters of the movement for relevance seem to be saying is that, unlike the foreigner, the native or indigenous anthropologist has a stake in the future of his society and that he must, therefore, become an agent of social change—he must give a push to history in a particular desired direction. The outsider may perhaps be able to

---

[1] I have not made any mention of the influence of Marxism among Indian anthropologists and sociologists because this has remained the alternative rather than the dominant intellectual tradition (see Mukherjee 1977).

afford the luxury of a value-free social science, even elevate culture relativism to a dogma, but the insider can not. To quote Ramkrishna Mukherjee, one of the senior Indian sociologists:

> The role of social anthropology today is not merely to *describe* or to *explain* a phenomenon... [but also] to answer the... fundamental question... "what will it be?" To adopt this *diagnostic* role... social anthropologists must have a particular orientation towards their education and a distinctive ideology: otherwise the outcome of their efforts will be fragmentary, inconsequential, or even distorted. The ideology should be "value-accommodating" instead of "value-accepting" or "value-neutral" (1976: 83).

To put it somewhat differently, if it is still believed that social sciences do not issue ethically commanding directives, then the immediate task at hand is to make them do so by locating them in the domain of ethics. The anthropologist as anthropologist must participate in defining the goals of social effort, try to reckon the costs of certain choices as compared to others, point out better, more desirable, alternatives, and suggest appropriate strategies for their achievement. The fault of the economist has, perhaps, been his disregard of the human and cultural costs of development—his failure to realize that every act of development is also an act of destruction. The anthropologist must pay attention to these problems of choice and cost. He must not remain content with the description of other people's life styles but turn to the moral question of improving the lifestyle of his own people.

The question is, how to do this and yet prevent anthropology from being incorporated into the state? The role of the outsider-critic may easily degenerate into irresponsibility; the insider-participant often finds himself a prisoner of the establishment. This moral dilemma is the most trying part of the situation of the native anthropologist in the non-Western societies today and it calls for careful attention and reflection. Is the legitimate purpose of an anthropologist's work given by personal inclination, interest, and training or by social need? To pose the question thus is to set up an artificial opposition. I agree with Dell Hymes when he says: 'By virtue of its subject matter, anthropology is unavoidably a political and ethical discipline, not merely an empirical speciality' (1974: 48). The task that we face is that of working out the implications of this realization for our work.

Concluding Remarks

The brief examination of the nature of anthropological studies in India undertaken in the previous section of this essay highlights the problems which arise from a narrow conception of the nature and office of anthropology. This narrowness has its roots in the ethnocentrism which characterized, perhaps inevitably, the rise of anthropology in the West and which was later diffused from the Western centres of learning to academic centres in Asia, Africa, and elsewhere. Under the circumstances the emergence of a movement for the articulation of indigenous viewpoints may be welcomed as a step forward, but it will lose its usefulness and turn out to be sterile if it is treated as the final step.

It seems to me that intellectuals everywhere must cultivate the sceptical attitude that distrusts all simple-minded dichotomies or oppositions and must seek theoretical frameworks within which these may be resolved. This distrust must also apply to a contrast between indigenous and non-indigenous anthropologies. A substitution of anthropologists for anthropologies, of the actors for the act, does not really alter the formulation and must, therefore, be looked upon with suspicion as logomachy. What is needed is a better, a fuller, a richer anthropology, and not many partial anthropologies—a complete discourse rather than fragments of it. We need concepts and methods applicable to all societies and such as may be practised anywhere by anybody who calls himself an anthropologist. These concepts and methods must, however, enable us to preserve the historical specificity of cultures, and not dissolve them in generalizations masquerading as cultural universals. The task, it seems to me is also to 'typify' cultures and not merely 'classify' them. This is why I have pleaded in this essay that we ground ourselves firmly in a dialectical conception of anthropology.

When we adhere to such a conception, a question that haunts our discussions these days—namely, whether *insiders* lacking objectivity or *outsiders* incapable of empathy can become anthropologists—will have been laid to rest. Also, the superficiality of the belief that the cure for the excesses of colonial anthropology lies in its replacement by indigenous anthropology (or anthropologies) will have been revealed. I am convinced that anthropology will be saved by those who have been its objects in the past, but only if they learn to look beyond the confines of their own cultures without losing the capacity to be themselves. Anthropology will then become knowledge about man, a heightened self-awareness acquired through the mutual interpretation of cultures. In this respect, I find myself in agreement with Lévi-Strauss when he says that, in the ultimate analysis, no cultures are alien to any human being: 'myself is no more opposed to others than man is opposed to the world: the truths learnt through man are "of the world", and they are important for this reason. This explains why I regard anthropology as the principle of all research' (1966b: 248).

ON CRITICAL SELF-AWARENESS

8

> *The things that men inherit come alone to true possession by the spirit's toil.*
>
> GOETHE

> *A new figure has entered the scene, "the indigenous ethnographer". Insiders studying their own cultures offer new angles of vision and depths of understanding. Their accounts are empowered and restricted in unique ways.*
>
> JAMES CLIFFORD

The Study of Other Cultures

Anthropology—not the philosophical inquiry which the German idealists promoted, but anthropology the subject that is today taught in colleges and universities all over the world—was, as is well known, a late child of the union of the Enlightenment and colonialism. The Enlightenment restored human society to the domain of nature and proclaimed the freedom of its study from the stranglehold of theology and metaphysics, elevating it to the status of positive science. In Michel Foucault's formulation, this historical development in the closing years of the eighteenth century marked the replacement of 'the order of things' as the central theme of knowledge, or epistemology, in the West by the theme of history, manifested in such concerns as social evolution and progress. Sociology and social-cultural anthropology were, I would like to suggest, a motivated

Earlier versions of this essay were offered, first, as the William Allan Neilson Lecture at Smith College, Northampton, Mass. (9 Oct 1990) and, then, as the Platinum Jubilee Lecture to the Anthropology and Archaeology Section of the Indian Science Congress at Indore (6 Jan 1991). I am grateful to President Mary Maples Dunn and Professors Elizabeth Hopkins and Frederique Apfell Marglin of Smith College and to Dr D. P. Sinha, Sectional President, Indian Science Congress, for their kind invitations and for their criticism and encouragement. The essay is being published simultaneously by the Oxford University Press, Delhi, in a Festschrift in honour of Rajni Kothari, entitled *The Multiverse of Democracy*, and edited by Ashis Nandy and D. L. Sheth. I thank the editors and the publisher for permission to include the essay in the present volume.

internal (European) commentary on the historical process of ration-
alization in the West. The purpose of sociology, Auguste Comte
said, was to know in order to predict and to predict in order to control.

Turning to the other parent of anthropology, namely colonialism,
this emerged as the concern with the redesigning or remaking of
non-European lands and peoples. It may be recalled here that the
Latin root of the word colonialism is *colere*, meaning 'to design'.
This etymology hardly succeeds in indicating the violence that accompanied the redesigning. Moreover, colonialism treated anthropology
as one of the resources of easy governance, enhancing the power of
the governors. Christian missionaries and rapacious merchants, too,
found ethnography useful in their own pursuits, and they embarked
upon first-hand observations sooner than anthropologists. The latter,
in fact, derived their early data from the accounts of missionaries and
administrators as well as from travellers' tales. It was only towards
the end of the nineteenth century that academic anthropologists left
their homes to reach out to the furthest, and in their eyes often the
darkest, corners of the world. Historians of the subject have, however,
pointed out that, in the West, the concern with non-Western ways of
life goes back to Greek historians—Herodotus, Thucydides—and
with utopias to Greek philosophers, notably to Plato's *Republic*.

Given such historical beginnings, and given such an intellectual
background, as mentioned above, it is not surprising that social-cultural
anthropology should have come to acquire a well-recognized place
among the humanities as well as the social sciences. It owes this place,
it seems to me, to the belief that our knowledge of cultures other than
our own broadens the mind. The idea may, perhaps, be best expressed
by saying that, one who knows only his or her own culture in fact
knows none.

From its beginnings as a scholarly discipline to this day, anthropology has affirmed two truths which it has considered fundamental.
Namely, first, that humankind is one in its psychological make-up
and potential and, secondly, that humankind is divided by its ways
of life, its cultures. The dogma (for that is what it was to the founding fathers) of 'the psychic unity of mankind' was coupled with the
fact of cultural diversity. In our own time Claude Lévi-Strauss has
summed this up in his own succinct manner by proclaiming that the
savages do not *think* differently than the civilized, but they *symbolize*
differently. Through the recognition of a common capacity for culture
rooted in the structure of the human mind—which sets the limits of

creativity—and also of diverse creativity, human 'alterity' is both denied and acknowledged. Lévi-Strauss emphasizes in Le Pensée Sauvage that ultimately no culture-bearing human being can ever be the other to another human being. That is how, in his judgement, anthropology provides the principle of all humanistic studies, in fact of all research (see Lévi-Strauss 1966b: 248). He also emphasizes that the anthropological method for the comprehension of the universality of human thought and morality lies in the study of remote peoples, remote from one's own culture. It lies in the pursuit of what he calls 'pure anthropology' (see Lévi-Strauss 1977: 26). What does this mean in practice?

Studying anthropology in India, what impressed me early in my career (in the 1950s)—and the impression has stayed with me ever since—was that, notwithstanding the bow to the oneness of human-kind, united psychically by instincts, mental propensities, the com-mon structure of the mind, or whatever, anthropology had contri-buted not only to the recording of cultural differences, but also, and more significantly, to the gradation of cultures, with Western civili-zation providing the criteria of excellence. The manner in which anthro-pologists had written about cultural others vis-à-vis themselves, the bearers of Western culture, had, it seems to me, divided humankind more than united it. Christianity, the Enlightenment and Social Dar-winism had converged to make this inevitable.

It may be noted here that, although the recognition of cultural dif-ference is a very special concern of anthropology, it is not its original discovery. Cultural difference has been recognized throughout human history. It has been known in India for two millennia. Cultural dif-ference has been, in fact, used to define one's own cultural identity and also to assert its superiority. Foreigners of Greek or Persian origin as well as non-Aryan indigenous tribal peoples have since the Vedic times been differentiated as yāvanas or mlecchas and as dāsas or dāsyus respectively. Subsequently, Arabs, Mongols, Turks, and Pathans, too, were included among the mlecchas. Needless to add, all these terms are derogatory, pointing to the inferiority of language and manners. The term 'Hindu', too, pointed to difference and moral and political inferiority in medieval India: it was used by Muslim conquerors to refer to those Indians who had not yet converted to Islam. It may be added here that the famous religious reformer of the late nineteenth century, Swami Vivekananda, used to say that the decline of Indian thought began the day the notion of mleccha was conceived, for it entailed the closing of the mind.

For pre-Enlightenment Europe, the principal marker of cultural difference was religion: the saved Christians against and above the damned heathens. The Enlightenment focused on reason and knowledge and contrasted the same with superstition and ignorance. The latter included revealed religion. In the post-Enlightenment period, with anthropologists taking the lead as the West's very own specialists on cultural otherness, difference came to mean first, in the late nineteenth and early twentieth centuries, cultural gradation, which spawned 'primitives', 'Orientals', etc., and, then, cultural relativism, which valorized difference, but in the process (and rather paradoxically) devalued the content of cultural forms. Anthropologists *qua* anthropologists committed themselves to relativism—this meant in the American anthropologist Melville Herskovits's celebrated formulation that, truth, goodness and beauty had as many manifestations as there were cultures (see Herskovits 1948).

As the bearers of Western culture, however, anthropologists were committed to the superiority of their own culture. Anthropology which taught people to have respect for cultures other than their own, Lévi-Strauss, Kenelm Burridge and others have pointed out, bears the signature of the West. The superiority of the anthropologist's own culture over that of the people he studied was an implicit assumption, an obvious truth, that did not have to be stated. To quote Lévi-Strauss, 'if we [Western anthropologists] claimed to be able to estimate one form of society in its relation to another we were merely claiming, in a shamefaced and roundabout way, that our society was superior to all the others' (1963b: 383). More recently, Johannes Fabian (1983) has pointed out that the cultural 'others' that the anthropologist studied, and in fact constituted, not only lived outside the centres of Western civilization, they were also denied coevalness in time—they were pushed back chronologically, as it were, to become the contemporaries of the anthropologist's ancient and not so distinguished forebears. The 'other' was thus rendered absolutely the 'other', located in another place (the Orient, the Dark Continent, the South Seas, or the Amazonian jungles) and in another time, both remote.

Cultural relativism may well have defined the relationship of the non-Western peoples to one another in anthropological literature— 'all non-Western cultures are the same', unified and downgraded by their otherness—but, declarations to the contrary notwithstanding, it did not seem to be quite relevant in defining the relationship of the anthropologists' own culture to the cultures of the peoples they studied, for this was considered intrinsically an unequal relationship. After explicitly denying that 'primitive' means 'backward', Lévi-Strauss writes that primitives are non-literate peoples under the impact of an expanding industrial, that is Western, civilization. The French master would have been perhaps happier if he could have found really 'cold', 'archaic', societies, unaffected by 'time elapsed', which could in some sense be seen as equal because they would be radically different, but it is too late for that now. As he puts it rather nostalgically, 'A cracked bell, alone surviving the work of time, will never give forth the ring of bygone harmonies' (1963a: 117).

The fault lies not in recognizing cultural differences, nor even in the notion of the gradation of cultures, perhaps, and cultural relativism only evades the issue. It lies, it seems to me, in implying that, ultimately, the *alleged* benefits of Western industrial civilization will, and should, become available to all humankind. Karl Marx assured the unfortunate non-Western peoples of the world that they could see in European societies the face of their own future, and he was not alone in thinking thus. In our own times, while bourgeois liberals have proclaimed that the 'prognosis' for the new states has been standardized—'they will become industrialized, modernized, and Westernized' (Bell 1974: 50)—socialist intellectuals assure them that, though they may be 'retarded in their development', a world socialist system opens for them the possibility of a direct transition to socialism, without their having to tread 'the long and tormented route by which mankind as a whole has passed' (Semenov 1980: 52). In the words of W. E. H. Stanner, one of the most humane anthropologists of our time, 'I am much puzzled by one thing: that is the bland assumption that there *must* be some way of "modernizing" the [non-Western peoples]. Why "must"?' (letter to this author, quoted in Barwick *et al.* 1985: 42).

The message, if not always an explicitly acknowledged mission, was, in yesterday's language, to civilize (*read* Westernize) the non-Western peoples of the world (the white man's burden) and, in today's, to modernize them (the First World's obligation). It means the same thing, of course, namely political and cultural domination. These non-Western peoples themselves are, of course, considered empty-handed or, at best, bearing some exotic gifts such as yoga, acupuncture, herbal medicine, florid folklore, and Oriental arts and crafts.

After India became free in 1947, and the government launched various programmes of rural development, anthropologists (Indian as well as non-Indian) moved in as individual fieldworkers, or as consultants to the government and to foreign, mostly American, agencies to help in the effort—to help in identifying what were called the 'felt' needs of the people. These invariably turned out to be *imputed* needs, that is what people should want, judging by the Western conceptions of the good life. The experts are still at it, most of them, though some think differently now.

Development and modernization were intended to transfer Western technologies, institutions, and values to the non-Western world, but this did not mean that anybody believed that the latter would become the equal of the West. A westernized Indian, it was assumed by the good Samaritans, would be a better Indian than the one who was immured in his own tradition, but he would never be the same as a European. The universal modern cultural empire has produced dependent subjects all over the so-called Third World, through the processes subsumed under development, but not a common world citizenry. This fact alone is enough to generate fears that modernity can become the new colonialism. When the intellectual centres of the West look beyond their own campuses, they only create the peripheries (see Shils 1975a).

I am not trying to suggest that westernization should have been total. I only want to emphasize that inequalities were inherent in this homogenizing process. Further, I want to point out that the self-image of Western anthropologists as 'ourselves'—a community of scholars united by common professional goals, common cultural values, and common though unstated politico-economic interests—studying the 'others' is made up of many strands not all of which are explicitly acknowledged. Doing fieldwork abroad has been for most of them an intellectual pursuit and a physical tracking of the cultural trails of 'other', non-Western, peoples, but rarely a following in the latter's footsteps. In fact, doing so has had to be guarded against carefully.

Although Lévi-Strauss introduced himself at the prestigious Collège de France as a 'pupil' and 'witness' of 'the Indians of the tropics and others like them throughout the world' (1977: 32), this was a personal grand gesture. More generally, the anthropologist has been wont to keep his or her distance. One of the disasters that may overtake an anthropological career is for him or her to go native, i.e. succumb to the 'risk', as Lévi-Strauss put it, of 'the complete absorption of the observer by the object of his observation' (1977: 15). Should it be thought that, although this may have been the case when, say,

Frank Cushing went to work among the Zuni, but is no longer a live topic, one has only to recall the enormous discomfort that Carlos Castaneda's books caused in professional anthropological circles in the 1970s.

The explicit advice to the apprentice has been to cultivate 'skills, precision, a sympathetic approach, and objectivity'. Fair enough, but in practice the assumption has been that the threat to objectivity stems from the people being studied rather than from the anthropologist's own culture. The current appeals for cultivating reflexivity, although a step in the right direction, have still to be thoughtfully worked out: reflexivity should not become yet another empty posture. And so, while the anthropologist goes through the mystical experience of participant observation (usually this is no more than sustained observation), he or she is exhorted in effect to remain culturally, emotionally, and spiritually aloof. This is still the orthodoxy. It is sobering to ponder the fact that not many anthropologists have acknowledged learning anything specific from non-Western sciences or philosophies of life, although they have written evocatively about 'primitive' religions and with technical competence on marriage and kinship.

As for non-Western science, that is supposed not to exist beyond some techniques and craftsmanship. The typical anthropological attitude is loudly echoed by the Cornell astronomer Carl Sagan's refusal to accept that the accurate cosmological knowledge that the Dogon of Africa possess could be their own, and not borrowed 'from a Gallic visitor . . . a diplomat, an explorer, an adventurer or an early anthropologist'. Y. V. Mudimbe, a well-known African intellectual, calls this 'epistemological ethnocentrism', and points out how amazing it is that Sagan puts greater trust in his own just-so story of a Gallic visitor as the fountainhead of astronomical knowledge than pay heed to internal cultural evidence which would certify the knowledge that the Dogon did, in fact, possess (see Mudimbe 1988: 13f). But, coming to think of it, it is not at all amazing.

Besides the apparent cognitive distance between the anthropologist and the people he or she studies, there is also a deep emotional chasm that usually divides them. There are, of course, many known instances of warm feelings between anthropologists and particular informants (see, for example, Casagrande 1960), but these have rarely become generalized. An American anthropologist, who has written authoritatively on a New Guinea people, asked me (in 1990) if I expected every anthropologist to like the people he or she studies. The point, I guess, is not one of like or dislike, but of mutual respect, or at least of taking the other seriously as a human being.

In the absence of such an attitude, one wonders how many anthropologists, studying remote cultures—the more distant the better for the challenge that they pose—are able to capture their visions of the good life, their innermost spirit, though many gifted with a literary imagination and favoured by circumstances—Malinowski had both advantages—have succeeded in bringing them to life. But this does not perhaps matter. Writing about the speculative concerns of the late nineteenth-century anthropologists, the American anthropologist Paul Radin observes somewhere that 'primitive peoples were only pawns in a much larger game'. Raymond Firth, the doyen of British anthropologists, has gone on record as saying that students are taught that 'it does not matter so much if they get the facts wrong so long as they argue the theories logically' (1965: vii). British scholars perhaps more than the Americans have been disdainful of 'fact-worshipping, theory-dreading' (Malinowski's phrase) anthropologists. Lévi-Strauss, too, has pointed out how anthropologists only too often succumb to the temptation of wanting 'to reinterpret indigenous customs and institutions with the unacknowledged aim of making them square more adequately with the latest body of theory' (1977: 27).

In short, although anthropology has contributed richly to the recording of cultural diversity, it has not quite succeeded in working out a convincing philosophical attitude towards it, not to speak of cultivating a well-argued and therefore genuine respect for it. Not that this is easy, for it can shake the foundations of one's cultural confidence. In Lévi-Strauss's telling phrase, anthropology is, if properly pursued, the *'technique du dépaysement'* (1963a: 117) and the anthropologist, if he is true to his vocation, a 'mutilated', an 'amputated person' (1963b: 58, 384). But, then, that is perhaps the risky journey that opens a new path. The critical test of genuine respect for cultural diversity would be to go beyond mere acknowledgement of other cultures as possible critiques of the anthropoligist's own culture, whether this be Western culture or Indian culture, and to translate it into some rethinking of one's world-view and some redesigning of one's life-style (see Marcus and Fischer 1986). Researches like Margaret Mead's among the Samoans expressed fascination rather than respect for what she believed, it now turns out wrongly (see Freeman 1983), to be the values of Samoan culture.

Respect for other cultures does not consist in saying that they are all right, but could be better if they came closer to being modern. Such an attitude, in fact, only underscores the hubris of modern man. It does not consist in the philosophically absurd and self-contradictory doctrine of cultural relativism which relativizes all values except relativism itself, so that (to turn around a well-known Nietzschean aphorism)when everything is permitted, everything is false. Respect for cultures other than one's own consists rather in affirming that every culture needs others as critiques, so that the best in it may be highlighted, and held out as being cross-culturally desirable, *and* the worst abandoned. The cultivation of exceptional cultural self-awareness of this kind—not mere reiteration of tradition nor its uncritical rejection—is what I would like the goal of anthropology to be. The awareness itself is important and equally so is the process whereby it is arrived at, namely, *the mutual interpretation of cultures* (see Chapter 7). Anthropology should not merely tell us how others live their lives; it should tell us how we may live our own lives better. For any anthropologist who wants to study his or her own culture, as I have tried to do, this seems to be an inescapable responsibility.

Now, it may well be said that Western scholars have always engaged in such critiques. They have, however, done so with their backs turned on either other cultural traditions (in the case of, say, theologians and philosophers), or their own tradition (in the case of anthropologists). The anthropologist should actually be better able than anyone else to be Janus-faced and build hermeneutic bridges. But one can do this only if critical awareness is extended to one's own culture also and not reserved for other cultures. Moreover this critical awareness should be one seamless whole, not compartmentalized, along the lines of the 'ourselves-and-the-others' dichotomy.

To illustrate, when he first recorded his reflections on the sociology of India in the 1950s, Louis Dumont contended that anthropological knowledge resides in the tension between the internal view of a culture and the external, the latter being grounded in both anthropology and the anthropologist's own culture. An external viewpoint alone, he implied, would be presumptuous (see Dumont 1957a; see also Chapter 4). Later he used his understanding of Indian hierarchy, and of the ideology of holism, to obtain a critical understanding of the Western ideologies of equality and individualism. Without *Homo Hierarchicus* (1966, 1970b), *Homo Æqualis* (1977a) would never have been written quite the way it is. Dumont's studies are, of course, not

wholly free of problems. But the point is that he makes an attempt to
interpret through comparison at the level of civilizational principles,
and that is why his work is so important. His on-going work on
internal comparisons within Western culture is a good example of what
I mean by anthropology as critical self-awareness (see Dumont 1986b).

The Study of One's Own Society

The foregoing observations are based on the assumption that all anthropologists belong to the West. On the face of it, this would be a false
assumption. But we need to examine this equation more closely. The
arrival of non-Western anthropologists, in the sense of their travelling
from home to a modern university in their own country or to a university in the West to be trained as anthropologists, is a twentieth–
century phenomenon. It happened in the years between the two World
Wars. When one of Malinowski's African students, a chief's son from
Kenya, prepared his doctoral dissertation for publication, the master
readily wrote the foreword. Jomo Kenyatta had obviously done an
unusual thing for an African by writing an anthropological account of
his own culture, and it needed defending. Malinowski characteristically
chose to write the defence by attacking the need for it (Malinowski
1938). Why, he asked, should it be necessary to justify the claims of
an African to write about his own tribal culture when a European's
competence to study his own society is not questioned? Malinowski
must have known that this was rhetoric, that Europeans and not
Africans had given birth to the social sciences. In the following year,
another foreword by Malinowski, this time to Fei Hsiao–Tung's book
on peasant life in China appeared. Again on the defensive, arguing
conditionally, he wrote: 'If it is true that self-knowledge is the most
difficult to gain, then undoubtedly an anthropology of one's own
people is the most arduous, but also the most valuable achievement
of a fieldworker' (Malinowski 1939: xiii).

A generation had to pass, Africa and Asia had to win their freedom
from the chains of colonialism, before the truth could be spoken. For
instance, Kenelm Burridge, who has written insightfully on both
primitive and modern cultures, on cargo cults as well as individualism,
says with admirable candour: 'If today there are many anthropologists
who are not Europeans, it is because anthropology is but one of many
European ways of doing things which their cultures have been adopting, or in which, as individuals, they have become so involved as
to be, culturally, Europeans or as though Europeans' (1973: 7).

Now, I am not sure if all non-European anthropologists think of themselves as Europeans, or 'as though' Europeans—I certainly do not do so—but it is noteworthy that a sober scholar such as Burridge should write thus. Similarly, when I once asked the Austrian-born British anthropologist Christoph von Fürer-Haimendorf why he was distressed only by the Hinduization of Indian tribal peoples and not also by the westernization of Hindus like myself, his response to my question was one of puzzlement. The attitude is a familiar one in India. The great English historian Macaulay wrote in the middle of the nineteenth century that the goal of modern education in India should be to produce a class of Indians who would be brown in colour, but British in their attitudes and tastes and habits of thought. They would be, in Burridge's phrase, 'as though' British.

At this point a brief digression on my own education as an anthropologist seems to be in order. When I took my first course in cultural anthropology at Lucknow University in India in 1949, we were taught that the scope of the subject was the study of pre-civilized peoples. The first textbook we were asked to read was Robert Lowie's *Primitive Society*. India, we were taught, had its own 'primitives', though they were called by other names such as tribals, aborigines, and sometimes animists. Our teacher, Professor D. N. Majumdar, had studied several such societies and earned his doctorate at Cambridge in the mid-1930s, and became one of the renowned anthropologists of his generation (see Chapter 2).

When I began my doctoral studies, Majumdar said that I would have to do fieldwork among a tribal people. I tried this very briefly, but immediately realized that I was too shy and physically and emotionally incapable of immersion in the lives of strangers. What others called immersion seemed intrusion to me. If I was incapable of fieldwork, I would have, Majumdar told me, to write about tribal peoples on the basis of published work. But could I not study my own cultural group among whom I would not be an outsider? He was non-committal about this as a permissible option: ideally that was not what one should do, he seemed to imply. Anthropology was still for him, at that time, the study of other cultures. He did change his position, but that came a few years later (perhaps sooner than he himself would have then imagined it possible).

The person who encouraged me to go ahead with the study of my own society was the psychologist-anthropologist S. F. Nadel (who had done his fieldwork in north Africa). He came to Lucknow University in 1954 to give a lecture, and I spoke with him about my problem. As stated above (pp. 114–15), he told me that my studies as an undergraduate should have sensitized me to the importance of objectivity. Obviously, he thought that my birth and upbringing in an urban milieu, and my subsequent university education, would have created sufficient cultural distance between me and the peasants I wanted to study. He accepted me as a doctoral student at the Australian National University.

By the time I got there in 1956 he had just died and the role of advisers was taken up by others. One of them, Derek Freeman, cautioned me repeatedly to steer clear of Indological texts and not to get carried away by people's ideas. He called giving too much attention to such texts and ideas the 'besetting fault' of the work of Indian anthropologists on Hindu society. The anthropologist should, they all said or implied, draw his conclusions directly from observed behaviour guided by well-established fieldwork techniques.

The import of such exhortations is understood much better today than I was capable of doing then. My advisers emphasized, in today's language, that Indians were incapable of objective self-awareness and of reliable self-representation. They could be the objects of anthropological research but not its subjects, informants but not authors, unless of course they had been touched by Western consciousness and transformed into 'modern scholars'. Besides, my teachers were, I can now see, plainly uncomfortable with the idea of studying people who had a literary tradition enshrining their self-awareness. They were happier with oral traditions. Actually, in India too, around the same time, M. N. Srinivas was emphasizing the primacy of the 'field-view' over the 'book-view' rather than, as he might have, their complementarity (see Chapter 3). Such complementarity was in a limited way a characteristic of the work of his first teacher, G. S. Ghurye.

I have written about some of this in an essay on my fieldwork experience, published fifteen years ago (1975a) (see Chapter 6). It was Louis Dumont who gave me back through his writings a wholesome respect for peoples' own categories of thought, himself deriving the same from the teaching of Marcel Mauss. The message was clear: the ideas of the people must be the starting point of any anthropological inquiry, but ideology never tells us everything. To fill the gaps one must confront it with what people do and with other ideas derived from anthropological literature, theory as well as ethnography. But without the ideas of the people, nothing worthwhile was possible (see Dumont 1957a). To do anthropology at home I did not have to be a pseudo-European: I could be myself but not just myself. I could not rest content with being one, I had to be many. This too would be called 'reflexivity' today, or critical self-awareness.

My title, 'On Living Intimately with Strangers', had been a sincere bow to anthropological orthodoxy, but, unfortunately, not a clear clue to the content of the essay or its central argument, which was that genuine anthropological knowledge of one's own culture can arise only out of a sense of surprise, a looking at it with the eyes of others—seeing the hidden face of the moon, as it were. As I have already indicated (see page 136), the title of my paper might have been 'On Living Strangely with Intimates', emphasizing that anthropological knowledge arises more from the method of inquiry rather than from whom you study: that an excessive emphasis on the otherness of those studied only results in their being made the objects of study rather than its subjects.

This sense of surprise is perhaps better called anthropological doubt, a term that we owe to Lévi-Strauss: 'Indeed research in the field, by which every anthropological career begins, is mother and nurse of doubt, the philosophical attitude par excellence. This 'anthropological doubt' does not only consist of knowing that one knows nothing, but of resolutely exposing what one thought one knew and one's very ignorance, to buffetings and denials directed at one's most cherished ideas and habits by other ideas and habits best able to rebut them' (1977: 26). But Lévi-Strauss thinks that the exercise of such doubt is possible, or truly possible, only when one studies one's own culture after studying other cultures, the remoter they are the better for the enterprise. Louis Dumont (1966a) too holds a similar position, and so does M. N. Srinivas (1966) (see Chapters 3 and 4). My only reservation about this position is that these authors seem to suggest that the only way one can learn about other (remote) cultures is through personal fieldwork. This is the well-known mystique of 'participant observation' and plays down both the volume of extant, good ethnographical literature and what one can learn by studying it.

The point, then, is not to divide humankind into 'ourselves' and 'others', but to see ourselves in others and others in ourselves—to bring about what Lévi-Strauss himself describes as 'a conversation of man to man', or what Hans-Georg Gadamer calls 'the merger of horizons', or what I have called 'the mutual interpretation of cultures'. It is only through such mutual interpretation, the effort to see in the round what otherwise is flat, that one may develop that critical self-awareness which

I have suggested here as the goal towards which all anthropologists—
and not only those engaged in the study of their own cultures—
should aspire.

Facets of India's 'Otherness'

A dialogic anthropology in which the questioner and the respondent
speak to one another, and the latter is not merely an informant answering
questions, but also one who questions the questions, is at best in its
infancy. And the past is still too much with us. A few years ago, when
the Pakistani anthropologist, Akbar Ahmed, published a serious and
well-grounded critique of Fredrik Barth's well-known analysis of
Swat society and politics, complaining of, *inter alia*, Barth's 'methodological individualism' and other alleged preconceptions of Western
origin (see Ahmed 1976), some of his teachers in London (though not
Barth himself) felt deeply offended by his critical attitude (see Tapper
1985). It is in this context that James Clifford's insightful observation
about the great lies that make up the truth of anthropology is, I think,
best understood (see Clifford 1986a: 7).

What is worse, the 'received' image seems to possess seductive
power. Thus, what passes for Maori tradition today is arguably the
invention of anthropologists. I choose this particular example because
of the stunning fact that some very crucial elements of the so-called
Maori tradition—such as the arrival of the Maoris in New Zealand in
the middle of the fourteenth century in seven magnificent canoes
from Polynesia—was the brain-wave of a single Englishman of the
late nineteenth century, S. Percy Smith. He had a theoretical axe to
grind, and this was the diffusionist theory of culture. He fabricated a
past which the Maoris today are unwilling to let go (see Simmons
1976 and Hanson 1989). The psychologist Ashis Nandy would call this
'the loss of self'. The invented image takes root in the mind and becomes
'the intimate enemy' by attempting to invalidate other similar images
(see Nandy 1983). Nandy has nineteenth–century Indian intellectuals
rather than anthropologists in mind.

Let me, then, turn to India, to the images of India. In anthropological
literature India is the land of karma, caste, and renunciation. Karma
is the iron-fisted doctrine of retribution; caste *is* the typifying social
institution; and renunciation *is* the highest cultural ideal. This is what
I began to learn when at high school. As I moved from there to college
and university, and became a student of anthropology, I learnt more
and more about these ideas from acknowledged authorities and along

the same lines. The non-Indian anthropologist for whose work on India I have the highest respect, Louis Dumont, has written a *magnum opus* on caste (1980) and a masterly essay on renunciation (1960). Similarly, M. N. Srinivas, the doyen of Indian anthropologists, has devoted a lifetime to writing about caste and its impact on modern life.

But I have had a problem. My own upbringing and experience as a Hindu Indian speaks to me in another idiom—the idiom of moral responsibility rather than karmic choicelessness, of the family rather than caste, and of plenitude rather than renunciation. At first I thought that my experience was less important than the general picture, the former being a result of the peculiarities of a regional subculture rather than of an overall Hindu perspective. But the more I have read and thought about the matter, the more doubts about the emphases incorporated in the 'established' picture have bothered me.

It was, therefore, with great interest that I heard, in the mid-1970s, first from R. S. Khare, how his researches on the culture of food, cooking and eating in north India revealed an overwhelming concern with auspiciousness as a value in domestic life (see Khare 1976), and then from Frédérique Marglin, how her fieldwork on the *devadāsīs* and temple rituals in Orissa had yielded rich data on auspiciousness and related themes in relation to royal power and female sexuality (see Marglin 1977). Such work constituted, it seemed to me, a significant step forward from the preoccupation with caste, and the related ideology of ritual pollution, emphasized by Srinivas, Dumont and many other scholars. Recent ethnography on the subjugated traditions of Hindu society similarly points to gaps in the anthropological know-ledge of India (see e. g. Kolff 1990 on the ethnohistory of the military labour market). Most notably, traditional concepts of power, which are broader in scope than what the social sciences mean by the term, and the dialectic of 'purity' and 'power' in Hindu society, are now beginning to receive due attention in anthropological studies.

Let me not be misunderstood. Karma, caste and renunciation are not pure fabrication. They are real and they are very important in Hindu society, particularly among upper castes. What is misleading is their having been made the general and exclusive or premier categories of the kind that they, I think, are not. At the University of Lucknow, during my student days in the early 1950s, two of my teachers used to complain that social structure in India has been reduced to caste. While D. N. Majumdar was concerned about the place of the so-called tribes in what he used to call 'the mosaic of Indian cultures', D. P. Mukerji used to regret the lack of attention to class (see Chapters 1 and 2). The problem obviously is not with the categories but with what anthropologists have done with them, the kinds of significance they have attached to them, the kinds of relations they have mapped for them.

Thus, some scholars have questioned the emphasis on caste from various perspectives. The Marxists have for long seen in caste a cover for class exploitation, and they have a point though certainly not the ultimate explanation they claim. More recently, some historians have constructed a persuasive argument, duly backed by evidence, to the effect that caste came to acquire the importance that it has had in contemporary times, not as a result of its having deep historical roots, which it of course has, but because of the transformation of its social role following the establishment of British rule in India. Having emptied the Indian kingdoms of their political power by taking it into their own hands, it made good imperial sense for the British to say that Indian society was based on caste and caste had its roots in religious values. The Hindu tradition which is said to incorporate the institution of caste and the underlying values, viewing caste as a specifically Indian form of society, rigid and immobile, is largely a product of colonial times.

I do not, however, agree that caste was, as Nicholas Dirks, carried away by his own rhetoric, seems to suggest, an invention of the British. By their preoccupation with caste, and indeed by suggesting that the essence of the caste system is the disjunction of social status and political power, which is what Dumont does forcefully, anthropologists and historians have, in Dirks' judgement, only furthered the colonial project (see Dirks 1987, 1989). Earlier Ron Inden (1976) had similarly maintained that the increasing salience of caste in medieval Bengal was a result of the decline of Hindu kingdoms.

Other scholars too have in recent years persuasively argued that social formations such as caste and religious or linguistic community, which anthropologists like Clifford Geertz (1963) and sociologists like Edward Shils (1975a) have considered decisive impediments to the formation of civic bonds and the nation-state, are as much imagined communities as the nation-state is. At the microlevel there has been much confusion about the character of the family in Hindu society, seen by Western observers to be 'joint', 'extended' or 'undivided', in contrast to the nuclear family of the West, and also about the status of women, which has tended to be judged in terms of the value of individualism (see Madan 1962b, 1976). These alien judgements, enshrined in authoritative social science literature guide our students in their study of their *own* society.

The question I am trying to pose here is this: Have non-Western peoples, by having cultural 'otherness' of particular kinds held out as their most characteristic features, had their societies and histories misrepresented? Tradition is, of course, continuously reinvented in all societies, but has the anthropological enterprise been hegemonic, holding up a single version of the 'truth'? Have non-Western societies been studied but not listened to? Echoing Ashis Nandy's notion of 'the loss of self', this phenomenon of the distortion of tradition may be called 'the theft of culture'. There are many eye-witness accounts of such cultural thievery, just as there are economists' discussions of the drain of wealth from India. The process of impoverishment obviously was of wide scope.

Bhudev Mukhopadhyay, a late nineteenth–century Bengali intel-lectual and gentleman, having declined a European friend's invita-tion to eat at his home, explained: 'Dining with you would have been an act of violation of our social code. Could there be a stronger reason? Besides, consider, what else are we left with? We have lost our political freedom, our religion is under your attack, our vernacular literature has not yet reached a level one can be proud of. What else have we got to give us a sense of pride or help maintain our (cultural) individuality? You may call it superstition or a social code, the system of caste and the codes of ritual conduct are all that we know now. These I cannot abandon' (see Raychaudhuri 1988: 49). The only false note in this statement of cultural self-awareness, the only crack in the armour, was the point about Bengali literature which reproduced a European judgement about it rather than stated its true worth.

If anthropologists take seriously statements such as the above, and attempt to understand them contextually, rather than dismiss them as mere rationalizations, they may be able to enter into dialogue with the peoples they try to represent, perhaps understand what moves them, and themselves move beyond mere description of cultural otherness. So far as the so-called native anthropologists are concerned, I do not see how we can abandon our responsibility to the past, which is discharged by evaluating it critically, and not by a paleocentric lauding of it as the golden age, or its uncritical excoriation as the dark age. Besides, this is one of the ways we can protect our future. If we do not act responsibly it is not our cultural tradition that will speak to us but strange voices, our own and others', ours being the stranger for being borrowed. These voices have propagated varieties of India's cultural otherness, which have misled many students, not to speak of the anthropologists who have been mostly accomplices in this game. In Salman Rushdie's apt words (written about hosts and migrants), 'They describe us. That is all. They have the power of description, and we succumb to the pictures they construct' (1988: 168).

As non-Western peoples reach out today to recover their lost selves through the reaffirmation of their cultures, a new wind is blowing among the anthropologists too. Although they do not speak with one voice, there are quite a few among them today who are ethnomethodologically oriented. Those among them who specialize on India have contributed to the project, initiated by Louis Dumont, of studying people's own categories of thought, the so-called emic categories. They have produced rich ethnography, but their theoretical preoccupations sometimes give rise to serious problems of interpretation.

In an emphatic rejection of Western dualistic categories of thought McKim Marriott has constructed complex images of Indian thinking, emphasizing the sharp contrasts between Western and Hindu cognitive categories (see Chapter 5). These seem all right at first blush, but when he moves on to write of such themes as 'three dimensional' Hindu thought, and invokes the imagery of cubes, one begins to wonder. The images are understandable—after all Marriott is only saying that Hindu cognitive categories generally employ three variables and are not based on binary opposites, but they do not seem either exhaustive or of primary importance to Indian anthropologists. In fact, it is remarkable how little Marriott draws from the work of Indian anthropologists and they from his. Marriott has suggested that the reason for this lack of communication could be that Indian intellectuals have been brainwashed by Western scholars (see Marriott 1976, 1989). It is a peculiar predicament: both the captivators and the would-be liberators of Indian minds are Western gurus. The chorus of strange voices that I wrote of above seems to get curiouser and curiouser! Obviously, Indian anthropologists should be playing a more significant role in the making of the anthropology and sociology of India than they have done in the past.

The Cultivation of Critical Self-awareness

Let me conclude. I have tried to point out in this essay that the anthropologists' preoccupation with the exploration of cultural difference, even when placed within a framework of the oneness of humankind and cultural relativism, has not saved them from the very pitfalls (such as ethnocentrism) that, they have maintained, they wish to avoid. Not only have different cultures invariably surfaced as unequal ways of living in the anthropological mirror, but the promise of a future equality *via* modernization has turned out to be both distant and destructive of cultural variety. Moreover, the open invitation to join the club of anthropologists has often turned out to entail heavy membership fees for the bearers of the so-called other cultures, for they have often been invited to subscribe to images of their cultures which their native sensibility does not approve of. Anthropology thus turns out to be, in terms of Michael Foucault's analysis of knowledge, a discourse of power, a discourse that must needs be divisive.

The contemporary predicament of non-Western societies arises partly from the fact that they are thrice deceived. First, they have had their traditions tampered with, eroded and invented, often with the help of anthropologists and historians. Ironically, they are called traditional societies, that is societies immune to change.

Secondly, they are deceived societies as they have had their present transformed into a permanent transition: the developing societies will forever remain that way if they are to catch up with the so-called developed but, in fact, runaway societies. Finally, these societies are deceived the third time over because their future has been pre-empted. In a faceless French journalist's phrase they are the 'Third World', economically, politically, and even culturally dependent on the first two worlds.

The world-view that these societies are invited to embrace is modern, secular, technological, and statist: it is at once hegemonic and hom-ogenizing. Dazzled by what technology and the 'market,' and the power of the state, have to offer, unmindful of the stupendous costs (such as destruction of the environment and loss of cultural autonomy), non-Western societies make choices that constitute their self-deception. One would have thought anthropologists, the devotees of cultural difference, would be aware of this, but they relish doing development work as much as anybody else. Alongside of many improvements in the human condition, the modern world-view has produced a heavier load of the debris of destruction than history has ever known. Gandhi saw that this would happen as a result of a mindless surrender to the industrial culture, and he said so too, although not always in terms that I personally find acceptable. About the time that Gandhi made his major pronouncement on the subject in his *Hind Swaraj* (1909), Max Weber, too, was writing about modern man being trapped in 'an iron 'cage', faced with 'nullity', and engaged in the destructive 'sport' of 'machine production' that would be played out only when 'the last ton of fossil fuel' was burnt out (see Weber 1930: 181–2). Barely a decade later, in 1916, he spoke of the future, though in the context of politics rather than economics, as 'not summer's bloom . . . but the polar night of icy darkness and hardness' (1948: 128). What prophetic phrases!

So, it seems that, ultimately, everybody is deceived. But must that be so? Can people who live and experience their culture, not in an unquestioning attitude, but self-consciously, in critical self-awareness, and in similar awareness of others, be ever deceived? This may sound like a pious hope in these days of the mindlessness of modernization and the madness and terror of various kinds of fundamentalism. But the tougher the challenge, the greater the need for perseverance. In such a situation, surely, anthropologists, who despite many limitations and distortions, have produced much good and even great ethnography, could do something to bring out the wealth and value of cultural diversity and the poverty of cultural insularity and sameness. But for that they would have to enlarge their own vision and learn new ways of doing anthropology—doing it in such a manner as will help it overcome the division of humankind into 'ourselves' and 'others' and enable it to heal the schism in its soul. Then, and then alone, may one say, with Terence, *Homo sum, humani nihil a me alienum puto* (being a man, nothing human is alien to me).

The Social Construction of Cultural Identities in Rural Kashmir

9

> I borrow myself from others; I create others from my own thought. This is no failure to see others; it is the perception of others.
>
> MAURICE MERLEAU-PONTY

> How will you know who the 'person' out there is? Watch him do the things he does, listen to him speak about them. And hear others, too, talk about him. If the second story is the same as the first, it is no good!
>
> W. E. H. STANNER

In this chapter I am concerned with defining the socio-cultural identities of the Muslims and Hindus of rural Kashmir. Such an exercise will have first to take note of those attributes that the two categories of people themselves judge to be of critical importance. I shall thus examine the images that Muslims and Hindus have of themselves and of each other. Once the attributes have been defined, discussion will be focused on real life interaction observed in the course of field-work. To give historical depth to the materials obtained through interviews and observation, limited use will be made of selected published works. I will not burden the discussion with ethnographical and historical details, but concentrate on exploring the general principles that may be shown to underlie what people believe in and what they do. In other words, an effort will be made to combine the views from *within* and *without*. Needless to emphasize, doing so is not an exercise in simple accumulation of points of view—the

Written in 1972, this essay benefited immensely from the criticisms of Edmund Leach, Kris Lehman, Kim Marriott, Jit Singh Uberoi, and Nur Yalman. It was first published in *Contributions to Indian Sociology* (NS) 6, 1972, and reprinted in *Ritual and Religion among the Muslims of India*, edited by Imtiaz Ahmad, New Delhi: Manohar, 1981.

effort is to examine not the two views *per se* but the relation between them (see Chapter 4).

Situated in the Himalayas at an average altitude of 6,000 feet above sea level, Kashmir proper—not to be confused with the state of Jammu and Kashmir of which it is a part—is a basin, 85 miles long and 25 miles broad. It is located approximately between 33–35°N and 74–76°E, and has an area of 6,131 square miles. The people of Kashmir partake of the common cultural heritage of the subcontinent of India, Bangladesh and Pakistan. At the same time, they have their own distinctive cultural traits, social structure, and historical experience. In this respect, the Kashmiris are like any other regional community such as the Bengalis, Maharashtrians or Tamils; but the insights which our study of them is likely to offer would seem to be rare if not unique.

As a culture area, the Kashmir Valley is of crucial importance for our understanding of, for example, the synthesis of Muslim and Hindu world-views and such fundamental principles of social organization as caste. It has not, however, received from anthropologists and sociologists the kind of close attention that it richly deserves.[1]

Kashmir has a population of 2,435,701 of whom 832,280 live in the southern district of Anantnag. It is primarily from a village of this district that the ethnographical content of this paper is drawn. I have also visited a few other villages in this district and in the central district of Srinagar (population: 827,697). The rural areas of these two districts are generally believed by Kashmiris to be culturally similar. The northern district of Baramulla (population: 775,724) is, however, said to be culturally somewhat distinct in several respects. The present essay may be, therefore, said to be generally descriptive of the rural areas of the two districts of Anantnag and Srinagar. The rural population of Anantnag is 758,046, or 91 per cent of the total. The corresponding figure for Srinagar is 404,444, or 48 per cent (India 1972a, 1972b).

Muslims occupy a position of overwhelming importance in the

[1] Literature of general interest on Kashmir, including travellers' accounts, is considerable; sociological studies of Kashmiris are few. Lawrence's book (1895; reprinted 1967) and gazetteer (1909) are invaluable sources of information. He toured the valley during the 1890s in his capacity as settlement commissioner. The only published, major social anthropological study is Madan 1965. For a general introductory account and bibliographies, see Crane 1956. Suggestions regarding future research are given in Madan 1969.

population of Kashmir. They call themselves Musalman which is the Persian form of the word Muslim (see Hughes 1935). They form 94 per cent of the total population in the three districts taken together— 95 per cent in Anantnag and 91 per cent in Srinagar. If we consider only the rural population of Anantnag, Muslims again account for over 95 per cent of it. The rest of the population consists almost exclusively of Hindus, though Sikhs also are present in a few villages. It must be noted here that there are no Hindus at all in about 56 per cent of the villages of the Anantnag and Srinagar districts (India 1943). Village boundaries are not, however, impassable barriers, and exclusively Muslim settlements would often seem to have various kinds of relationships with Hindus in adjoining villages.

The native Hindus of Kashmir all belong to the Brahman *varna*, and are divided into two endogamous subcastes. The Kashmiri Brahmans call themselves Bhatta and are generally known in India as Kashmiri Pandits. 'Bhatta' is the Prakrit form of the Sanskrit *bhartri* which means 'scholar', 'doctor', or the same as the Sanskrit *Pandit*. Since I have elsewhere used the term Kashmiri Pandit (see, for example, Madan 1965), I will continue to do so here. How Kashmir came to have a single Hindu caste will be described later. I will first take up the problem of Muslim identity.

Muslim Identity: Muslim Representation

The problem of mutual identification among the Muslims of rural Kashmir does not arise very often. Within a village all adults know each other. The average population of a village in the district of Anantnag is 511 (India 1966: 5). When a person goes to another village, he stays with his relatives; the purpose of the visit most often is to renew contact with them. A Muslim tenant on a visit to his landowner in another village will stay with him and, if the latter also is a Muslim, eat with him. A Pandit landowner will supply uncooked victuals to the tenant, who will cook his own meal in the compound. Utensils for the purpose will be borrowed for him by the landowner's household from one of their Muslim neighbours. Mutual recognition in such situations is not problematic, but it is important, for Hindus and Muslims observe different degrees of mutual avoidance.

Even when one encounters total strangers, there are several visible signs which identify them as one's co-religionists or otherwise. Thus, Muslims and Pandits do not dress identically: the differences may not appear striking to an outsider but a Kashmiri would never make a mistake in this regard. Besides differences of male and female dress (of hedgear, gown, trousers, and sometimes even footwear), many Pandits wear *tyok* on their foreheads: it is a mark of saffron or some other coloured paste, elongated among men and round among women. Muslims grow beards more often than Pandits, and of a distinctive cut. There are differences of speech, mainly lexical (see Kachru 1969: 21–7). Though native Kashmiris look very much alike (see Raychaudhuri 1961 and also Bhattacharjee 1966), two recent Muslim immigrant groups have distinctive features and speak a non-Kashmiri dialect called *Paryum* (literally, 'foreign', 'alien').

Identification of people in terms of the Muslim-Pandit dichotomy is thus not difficult in the rural areas, except perhaps when the stranger is from a town or is an urbanized villager, and thus likely to be without any of the above visible signs. Purposive interaction with a stranger is dependent upon the initiation of a specific process of identity establishment. This process usually follows a predictable pattern.

The most crucial cue lies in the family name. Muslim personal names in rural Kashmir are identical with similar names anywhere in the world. Family names often refer to the fact of descent: the Baig, Mausodi, and Sayyid are descended from early immigrant families, and the Shaikh, who constitute the overwhelming majority of the Muslims, from converts.[2] The immigrant families fall into three categories: Arabs, Mughals, and Pathans. There is a fourth category of immigrant Muslims who entered the Valley late in the nineteenth century. They are called Gujar ('cowherd') or Bakarwal ('goatherd'), and constitute two somewhat distinctive groups. They are the Muslims who, as mentioned above, speak a non-Kashmiri dialect among themselves.

Not many Shaikhs use that appellation along with their names. It is more common to use other types of family name. One of the most widely prevalent of such names among Kashmiri Muslims is Bhat, which is, of course, the same as Bhatta, and obviously bears testimony

---

[2] Shaikh, an Arabic word (pl. *shuyukh*), literally means an old man or man of authority. The term seems to be widely used in South Asia to designate Muslims descended from Hindu converts (see Gait 1911; see also *Chambers's Twentieth Century Dictionary*). In Kashmir: 'The census of 1891 does not show the divisions into which the Musalmans of the valley fall, but it may be stated that the great mass of the village people come under the head Shaikh, and are descendants of the original Hindus . . .' (Lawrence 1967: 306). It is likely that some Shaikhs, particularly in urban areas, may be descended from immigrants.

to the fact of conversion. There are other examples of this kind of surname such as Pandit, Koul (Sanskrit *kaula*, originally the name of a Brahman sect), Naik and Ryosh (Sanskrit *rishi* or saintly, learned man). There is still another category of common family names which either directly refer to one's hereditary family occupation or indirectly through association. Thus, an Ali Khar is a blacksmith (*khār*) and a Rasul Navid is a barber (*nāvid*). A Samad Vagay will readily be recognized as a milkman, and even referred to as Samad Gur, for the Vagays are milkmen (*gūr*).

All types of surname are called *zāt*, and enquiries about them are made in the effort to obtain identity specification. The important question is what does *zāt* denote? Apparently it points to birth, as does the well-known word *jāti* used elsewhere among Hindus. The Kashmiris, however, use the word *zāt* in a broader sense to connote essence or inherent nature. *Bad-zāt* is a term of abuse and is used to condemn an evil–natured or mean person rather than to refer to lowly birth, which would seem to be the primary meaning of the term in the original Arabic–Persian (see Steingass 1957). Similarly, Kashmiri Muslims refer to God as *Zāt-i-pak*, the one whose nature is pure. *Zāt* is also used in classifying breeds of cattle or varieties of inanimate objects such as paddy or timber.[3]

When used as part of a person's name, *zāt* has the narrower meaning of either birth (e.g. Sayyid, Shaikh) or hereditary occupation (e.g. Khar, Navid, Gur). It does not, however, necessarily indicate a person's actual source of livelihood: a family of any occupational category may have enough land not to want to exercise their traditional calling; or, a particular individual may choose to enter a new occupation. These facts are ascertained by inquiring about *kār*, a

---

[3] Gould mentions a similar use of the term *jāti* among villagers in eastern Uttar Pradesh: 'One also speaks of *jatis* of . . . animals . . . of botanical objects . . . (and even of) woven fabrics . . . . What we see operating here is *ethno-conceptualization*. In this instance Indians are manifesting a long established, culturally patterned tendency to regard endogamous, ritually and functionally differentiated social units as *if* they were natural species' (1969: 23). Marriott and Inden have been engaged in working out a general thesis regarding *jatis* as natural genera (see Marriott and Inden 1974).

Eglar reports from the Punjab in Pakistan: 'When a mature person is asked about his *zat*, which means caste and also identity, he is most likely to answer: "What identity can a human being have? The only one who has an identity is the Almighty. I am a carpenter (or *zamindar*, or barber or this, that) by occupation"' (1960: 29).

An interesting use of the world *zāt* appears to have been made in Mughal administration. A *mansabdār*, or noble, was accorded a double rank. His so-called *zāt* rank apparently gave recognition to his social status, and his salary was determined in terms of it; his *sawār* rank stipulated the number of troopers he was expected to maintain (see Gascoigne 1971: 105).

general term for work or occupation, or about *kasb*, skills.[4] It may be noted, however, that people rarely move from one skilled or specialist occupation to another, though agriculture is deemed to be open to all. Agriculturists are called *zamīndār* and non-agricultural artisan groups are designated *nāngār*, literally 'those in search of bread'.

At this stage it will be helpful to introduce some ethnographical details from a village.[5] Utrassu–Umanagri is situated 12 miles east of the town of Anantnag. It is a rather large bi-nucleated—hence the hyphenated name—village of about 1,542 acres, inhabited by 2,644 persons (see Madan 1965). Of these, 2,122 persons (80 per cent of the total population) are Muslims and the remaining 522 are Pandits. The Muslims are divided into two cultural subgroups; 1,352, or 64 per cent are natives and 770, relatively recent immigrants.

   The natives engage in a variety of economic pursuits. Over half of them, totalling 121 households (728 persons), are agriculturists—peasant proprietors or proprietors-cum-tenants. Another 111 households (624 persons) fall in the traditional category of Nangar, though after the abolition of big landed estates in the State in 1950 (see Bamzai 1962: 716–18), there are no completely landless Muslim households in the village. Enquiries made by me in other villages indicate that the Nangar generally account for about one-third to one-half of all Muslim households. They never seem to outnumber the Zamindar. As will be pointed out below, several of the households of Utrassu–Umanagri that I have classified as Nangar in arriving at the above proportions are doubtful cases. But I will first give the distribution of the Muslim households in terms of occupation (see Table 1).

   Besides the occupational categories listed in Table 1, I came across the following in other villages or in the town of Anantnag: (i) Aram (vegetable gardener); (ii) Band (minstrel); (iii) Barbuz (grain parcher); (iv) Gada Hainz (fisherman); (v) Hainz (boatman); (vi) Kawuj (attendant at Hindu cremation sites); (vii) Sangtarash (stone-cutter); (vii) Tor-kachhan (wood carver); (ix) Vonya (grocer).[6]

---

[4] Barth (1960: 118) has recorded an identical use of these two terms among the Swat Pathans who, however, use *quom* for caste status.

[5] My first period of fieldwork in Kashmir, the longest so far, was in 1957–8 when I was a scholar at the Australian National University. Since then I have returned to the area of original fieldwork for several short spells. I was there last in 1986. The tense employed in this essay is of the ethnographic present.

[6] Various census reports on Kashmir seem to have failed to distinguish between traditional role and hereditary occupational groups. Thus, the 1931 report lists groups like Derwish (Muslim mendicant) and Jogi (ascetic) which are not such groups. Many

TABLE 1
NATIVE MUSLIM HOUSEHOLDS BY TRADITIONAL OCCUPATION

Occupational Category	Number of Households
1. Zamindar (landowner–cultivator, tenant)	121
2. Nangar	
(i) Dob (washerman)	2
(ii) Dosil-Chhan (builder–carpenter)	8
(iii) Domb (messengers of revenue officials)	2
(iv) Dun (cotton carder)	6
(v) Gur (milkman, cowherd)	5
(vi) Hakim (physician)	2
(vii) Jalakhdoz (rug-maker)	1
(viii) Kandur (baker)	2
(ix) Kanyul-Shakhsaar (basket-maker)	10
(x) Khar (blacksmith)	6
(xi) Kral (potter)	4
(xii) Navid (barber)	6
(xiii) Puj (butcher)	3
(xiv) Sech (tailor)	6
(xv) Sonur (silversmith)	1
(xvi) Tabardar, Arikash (wood-cutter, sawer)	10
(xvii) Tilawoni (oilseed-presser)	3
(xviii) Thonthur (copper-smith)	2
(xix) Vatul (cobbler)	3
(xx) Wovur (weaver)	19
(xxi) Mallah (religious functionary)	10
Total	232

The Muslim Zamindar households of Utrassu-Umanagri may be deemed to be those who have no source of income other than cultivation of land, whether self-owned or leased in, or of both types.[7] There are no landless labourers in the village though many agriculturists work on daily wages for other landowners during busy seasons. Muslim Zamindars are small landowners. The average size of the holding is just under an acre and three quarters, but this figure is

other functional roles could be mentioned: e.g., *dāndur* (vegetable dealer) *galadār* (grain dealer), *ghāsi* (grasscutter), *hamāmi* (attendant at public baths), *vārinya* (midwife) and *vāza* (cook). A hereditary group which I heard mentioned was that of the Galawan who reared and stole horses (see Lawrence 1967: 311). The 1941 census report lists Potters, Blacksmiths, Carpenters and Oilpressers, and groups all the rest together as Shaikh unless they happen to be Sayyid, Mughal, Pathan or Rajput. (See India 1943).

[7] There were only a handful of literate Muslims in Utrassu-Umanagri in 1958; the oldest of them was about 18. This fact ruled out government service as a major source of livelihood for them. The two *lambardār* (revenue collectors) of the village were, however, Muslims. A few more were employed as forest guards.

somewhat misleading in respect of the Muslims since it is based on all holdings, including those of Pandits. There are 636 landowner-ship registrations among the native Muslims of the village, the basis of registration being the individual and not the household. Recalling that there are 1,352 native Muslims, it will be noticed that the regis-trations are indicative of the already mentioned fact of widespread ownership of land. Of these registrations, 139 are in respect of holdings of 1 to 3 acres, 27 in respect of holdings above 3 but below 6 acres, and only 2 in respect of holdings above 6 acres. All the rest are below one acre. The ceiling on agricultural land was fixed at 20 acres through legislation in 1950. No Muslim household lost any land at that time. Only one Muslim landowner had more than 12 acres and was thus affected by the tenancy reforms which fixed the share of the tenant at three-quarters of the produce in respect of such holdings. A large number of tenants, mostly Muslims, received small shares from about 170 acres of land that were compulsorily acquired from Pandit landowners and redistributed among the tillers by the Government.

Turning our attention to the Nangar, it may be noted that:

(i) The names of all such groups, except the Domb, are directly descriptive of skilled work of some kind, or of non-skilled but special-ized services. The Domb have a traditional calling but their name does not originate in it. They seem to be descendants of a low caste (see Lawrence 1967: 311), maybe of the Domba mentioned in early historical accounts of Kashmir (see Pandit 1968).[8]

(ii) Whereas most of the Nangar in the village are stable groups following their respective hereditary occupations, some of them represent the arrival of relatively recent skills in the village, or seem to be more open to recruitment than others. The Bakers, Rugmakers and Tailors of the village, though natives, have had no predecessors there. Butchers and Weavers seem to be relatively open categories. Only one of the four Butcher households have a tradition of being meat sellers. Similarly, the Weavers seem to be an assorted category, only some of whom are Weavers by birth. Incidentally, most of the Weaver households have a secondary occupation—the breeding of silkworms. Sericulture and silk-weaving have been carried on in Kashmir for several hundred years (see Bamzai, 1962: 451).[9]

[8] 'Dom: A widespread caste of scavengers, musicians, and sometimes weavers, traders or even money-lenders; possibly representing an aboriginal tribe of some influence and power (-Domra, Dombu)' (Hutton 1951: 279).

[9] See footnote 6.

(*iii*) Some of the households following the above occupations own shops. The Butchers are a good example and so are the Tailors; but the former also sell meat at their homes and the latter divide work between home and shop. Shopkeeping is not treated as an occupation by any group in the village, but grocers in the nearby town of Anantnag have a long tradition of it. Generally speaking, shopkeeping in the rural areas is merely indicative of a group's or a household's mode of augmenting income.

Finally, a few words about the Gujar and Bakarwal. As already stated, they number 770, and constitute 98 households. They live on the upper boundaries of Utrassu-Umanagri, along and deep inside the forests. Some of the Gujar—the group which came earlier than the Bakarwal—have taken to agriculture and sedentary life, and a few have even intermarried with native Muslims. There are 71 registrations of landownership in the names of the Gujar. However, most of them continue their traditional occupation, as do the Bakarwal: they graze sheep and cattle, their own and those of other people in exchange for grain, and sell dairy products. Most of them leave the village during the winter months in search of warmth and pastures for their flocks. The Gujar and Bakarwal are an important element in the life of the village but they are not of it. They look different from native Muslims, speak their own dialect, live in distinctive huts, follow their own traditional pursuits and customs, and have a system of social control centred round the *jirga* or tribal council.

Occupations such as the above are widespread and stable categories in rural Kashmir and are, therefore, employed by the people themselves as indicators of socio-cultural identity. In any particular village one encounters them as groups of households, usually but not necessarily related by ties of kinship and/or marriage. The Zamindar category is the melting pot, as it were, inasmuch as anybody might become a cultivator, even if he has no land of his own. The various Nangar groups are, however, characterized by a low degree of occupational mobility and a high incidence of endogamous marriages. Only 9 per cent of the adult Muslims of the village are in skilled or specialist occupations other than those indicated by their *zāt*. A count of marriages among the Nangar, spread over two generations, revealed a little under two-thirds of them to be endogamous. (Here it may be noted that marriage between both parallel and cross cousins takes place among Kashmiri Muslims, but is not prescriptive.)

When asked to explain these cultural regularities, my Muslim informants generally stressed three considerations. (*i*) The most specific of these is what may be called practical considerations. Since every Nangar is assured of a clientele for his goods or services, it is only reasonable that he should pursue his traditional occupation. His relations with his clients are generally on a hereditary and family-to-family basis; landowning households pay for goods and services in kind according to pre-determined scales, while the others pay in cash. Barter is rarely practised nowadays. The most practical as well as efficient way of learning a craft is to start when quite young, by helping the older members of one's household in their chores. One's son is one's natural apprentice as well as one's successor. (*ii*) Endogamous marriages are desirable for reasons of compatibility. There are often differences in the lifestyles of different groups. Boatmen and Mallah are good examples. Moreover, women often help men in their chores; a Carpenter's daughter would obviously be of no help to a Potter, or a Barber's daughter to a Boatman. (*iii*) Both pursuit of hereditary occupation and endogamy are commendable as being *inherently* right. The word *zāt* (in its adjectival form of *zāti*) is employed in this context also.

It follows from the foregoing that we ask, how does one acquire one's essential nature, one's true identity, or *zāt*, in terms of which certain actions become inherently right or natural? This was not a question which my informants generally welcomed as they felt that they were being pushed against the wall. Several of them, however, interpreted the world *zāti* as meaning 'at the root or base', which was further paraphrased as 'at or by birth'. One might translate this statement to mean that one's essential nature is endowed upon one by the circumstances of birth. The notion of *zāt* is genealogical, but stands for more than the fact of birth.

If the foregoing is a culturally valid position to adopt in respect of the self-ascription of Kashmiri Muslims, the most crucial question that arises is, who is a Muslim?

There seems to be general agreement among the Muslims of rural Kashmir that anyone who avows to be a Muslim is to be regarded as such. They maintain that this is what the Koran teaches. They further assert that a pious Muslim (*i*) believes in the oneness of God and in Muhammad as His prophet; (*ii*) offers prayers (*namāz*) at the appointed times; (*iii*) gives alms (*zakāt*); (*iv*) keeps the prescribed hours of fasting and eating (*roza*) during Ramazan; and (*v*) performs the pilgrimage to Mecca (*hajj*) when he has enough savings for the purpose. My informants pointed out that lack of means, poor health, and preoccupation with household responsibilities often prevent a person from offering prayers, giving alms, observing *roza* or performing *hajj*. Such unwilling transgressions of the desired conduct are to be forgiven a person if he reaffirms the most important tenet of Islam by solemnly reciting the *Kalimah* on being challenged: *Lāillāh illallah Muhammadur Rasūl Allah*, there is but one God and Muhammad is His prophet.[10]

To deny such a person the status of Muslim is to turn against the will and voice of God and the Prophet. The *accident* of birth is irrelevant in this regard. One of my educated urban informants, a Shaikh, stressed this point by asserting that he who embraces Islam out of conviction is a better Muslim than he who follows it as the religion of his parents. 'Such a man is deservedly called *shaikh*, the leader who points the path to others'.

In the course of my fieldwork I heard of about a dozen cases of recent conversion of Pandits to Islam. I was able to interview one of these converts and to discuss his case with a number of my informants, Pandits as well as Muslims. Since this case throws considerable light on the notion of *zāt* in relation to religious identity, I will briefly discuss it here.

He told me that his name was Ghulam but that, before conversion to Islam, which took place about twenty years ago, he was known as Darshan Krad, and belonged to a Pandit family of Utrassu-Umanagri. His *gotra* name was Shandalya. He had been much persecuted by his cousins, particularly because he was a bachelor.[11] He had several Muslim friends in the village and they showed him greater sympathy and understanding than his own kin, who robbed him of his property and would have willingly starved him to death. His Muslim friends fed him and gave him shelter in their homes. Ultimately, he became a Muslim. He was, however, very badly treated by Muslims once he

[10] Whenever Kashmiri Muslim villagers have to cite the authority of religion, they invariably invoke the Koran. Being generally illiterate, they are unable to cite a specific chapter or verse. Far from being a disadvantage, their illiteracy and ignorance have emerged as a source of strength inasmuch as doubt has been banished from their lives. Whatever the source of their beliefs, they attribute them to the unimpeachable authority of the holy book. Distinctions between the *sunnah*, *hadīth*, and *īmān* (see Hughes 1935) are not generally made by common people; only the literate are aware of them.

[11] On the sad lot of a bachelor among Kashmiri Pandits, see Madan 1965: 101–2.

changed his religion, he said. Though he is living with a Muslim household of the village, he is doubtful whether they will give him a decent burial. It is for this reason that he begs and not merely to keep himself alive. He is obviously saving for the rainy day and hopes to have enough money for a shroud for his dead body and for its burial. He lamented over his moral and physical condition and called his act of conversion 'a stupid act' (*budhi-vināsh*) by which he became a 'breaker of *karma*' (*karma-khandit*). As he sees himself, he is a totally lost man.

The Pandits, to whose homes he comes to beg, generally pity him, but treat him as a fallen man who is of course no longer a Brahman, even though he had been born one. Small urchins ask him to sing Brahman devotional songs (*līlā*) and promise him handfuls of rice. He often obliges them. My Pandit informants said that he had given me a fairly accurate account of what had happened, but that he had omitted to tell me that he had been promised a Muslim girl in marriage to make him give up his religion. This might in fact be true as Ghulam told me that Muslims often tempt Hindus by 'showing them birds' and by making false promises. He did not say, however, that this had been his own undoing too. The Pandits look at such cases as a kind of wicked game which some Muslims play at the former's cost. It was alleged that such Muslims derive mean satisfaction from a Pandit's fall.

When I discussed this pitiable man's case with some Muslim informants, they made two points. First, they maintained, it was imperative that one should distinguish between a person who becomes a Muslim out of conviction and one who embraces Islam in the hope of material gain. To them Darshan's conversion was not a true conversion: he had not been impelled by the best of motives. Nevertheless, a Muslim household has given him shelter, though nobody gave him a wife. What more could he expect?

Secondly, my informants said, Ghulam is a bad Muslim. He does not observe the essential rules of behaviour. For example, he begs and eats at Pandit homes. No good Muslim eats food cooked by Pandits. 'The plain truth', as one informant put it, was that Darshan was born a Pandit and could not possibly be as good a Muslim as he himself, i.e., the informant, who was a *zātī* Muslim.

The conclusion that seems permissible on the basis of the foregoing discussion is that, the alleged teachings of the Koran notwithstanding, in actual practice the Muslims of rural Kashmir attach crucial importance to the fact of birth in the determination of a person's nature and his legitimate socio-cultural identity. Whether this is an Islamic notion or not, it certainly accords well with Hindu belief.[12]

Hindu Identity: Hindu Representation

One of the most striking characteristics of the social organization of the native Hindus of Kashmir is that they consist mainly of two Saraswat Brahman subcastes. There is also one Vaishya caste, but it is very small in number and is found only in some towns. To the best of my knowledge, this is a social situation unparalleled in any other cultural region of the subcontinent. It is almost like a deliberately set up laboratory situation, and its study should yield insights into the Hindu caste system unobtainable elsewhere. The first question that must be answered is, how has this peculiar situation arisen?

Fortunately we have a precious historical document to fall back upon: the twelfth–century Sanskrit chronicle *Rājataranginī* by Kalhana.[13] A perusal of this work yields two relevant conclusions regarding the social structure of Kashmir before the arrival of Islam early in the fourteenth century. First, it is obvious that there were many castes among the Hindus. All the four *varṇa*—Brahman, Kshatriya, Vaishya, Shudra—are mentioned and, besides, we read of castes, sects and classes such as the Chandala, Damara, Domba, Kayastha, Kirata, Nishada and Tantrin. It is not always clear, however, which is which. Thus, the Damara and Kayastha, it seems were classes of landowners and civil servants respectively, rather than castes. Tribal groups of various kinds are also mentioned. Of these, the Ekanga and Lavanya seem to have been professional soldiers.

The second relevant conclusion is that the caste system in Kashmir between the seventh and fourteenth centuries does not seem to have been characterized by stringent exclusiveness in the relations between social groups. We read in the *Rājataranginī* of low caste Domba

[12] Though all believers are called brothers in the Koran (49, 10) and a *hadīth* (saying attributed to the Prophet Muhammad) contends that genealogies count for nothing among Muslims (see Levy 1962: 56–7), it is well known that Islam was never able to eradicate earlier social inequalities among Arabs (see Smith 1903: 42–55 and Levy ibid.: 53–90). Besides, 'Birth as a principle of status honour was considerably important in the early Muslim society in India' (Imtiaz Ahmad 1966: 270; see also Ashraf 1959: 61–3).

[13] Kalhana composed the *Rajatarangini*, 'River of Kings', in eight cantos of Sanskrit verse in the middle of the twelfth century. Though he draws upon both legendary and historical materials, his work has been acclaimed as a historical text in the true sense of the term (see Pandit 1968: xiii ff.).

queens of Kshatriya kings and Kalhana particularly mentions a low caste *āramika* (vegetable grower) who had successfuly entered the ranks of the Kayastha. A probable reason for the relatively flexible social organization may well have been the influence of Buddhism, which was introduced in Kashmir during Ashoka's reign in the first quarter of the third century BC and dominated the cultural life of the Kashmiris for almost a millennium.

By the beginning of the eighth century, Hinduism had reasserted itself in Kashmir—the Brahmans, who led the resistance to Buddhism, seem also to have spearheaded this revival. They continued to play a prominent role in the political and cultural life of the Kashmiris until the arrival of Islam in Kashmir. The presence of Muslim (Turkish) mercenaries during the eleventh century is noted by Kalhana. It was only a couple of hundred years later, however, that the Islamization of the Valley began, first through the persuasion of missionaries and then through the persecution by some of the early Muslim kings. The most prominent of the early missionaries was Sayyid Bilal Shah of Turkistan, who was associated with the Suhrawardi school of Sufis (ses Hughes 1935).[14]

The Hindu dynasties had an inglorious end. External invasion, court intrigues and internal disorder resulted in the emergence of the first Muslim king of Kashmir, Rinchana (1320–3). He was a Buddhist prince, a refugee from Tibet at the court of the Hindu king. This combination of circumstances and Rinchana's personal valour led to his seizure of the kingdom. He beseeched the Brahmans to allow him to become a Hindu but they refused. He then turned to Bilal Shah who readily accepted him within the Muslim fold. Thereafter, the Sayyid's mission as a proselytizer seems to have met with success after success. Of later missionaries who carried Islam into the length and breadth of Kashmir mention may be made of the saintly Sufi scholar, Sayyid Ali of Hamadan, who paid several visits to the Valley beginning in 1327. Many Sayyids came to settle down in these parts around that time.

The scholarship, saintliness and peaceful intentions of some of the Sayyids found their counterpoint in the bigotry and fanaticism of some of the early Muslim kings. The most notorious of these was Sultan Sikandar (1389–1413), whom historians have given the name of *butshikan* (iconoclast). Not only did he destroy practically all the

[14] The following account of the political history of Kashmir is based on Kak 1936.

Hindu temples of Kashmir (see Kak 1936, text and plates), he also compelled his Hindu subjects to choose between Islam, exile or death. Whereas some chose one of the latter two alternatives, the majority of those who had resisted the missionaries now accepted defeat. It was thus that the Hindus of Kashmir, along with whatever Buddhists had remained, were converted *en masse* and Islam established in Kashmir during the fourteenth century.[15] It seems that only a handful of Brahmans survived in Kashmir at the time of Sikandar's death in 1414; tradition puts the number at eleven. It is from them that the Pandits of today are said to be descended.

The most celebrated of the Muslim kings of Kashmir is Zain-ul-Abidin, remembered to this day as the *bud shah* ('great king'). His reign, spanning half a century (1420–70), reversed the policies of the preceding hundred years of Muslim rule by making it possible for Hindus and Buddhists to live in safety and with honour in their homeland. He abolished the *jizya*, a tax imposed on non-Muslims by his predecessors, called a halt to the destruction of non-Muslim places of worship, showed keen interest in Buddhist and Hindu philosophy and scholarship, and appointed the followers of these religions to high positions in his administration. In his magnanimous treatment of his non-Muslim subjects, he was the true precursor of Akbar, the Great Mughal, who followed a hundred years later.

Encouraged by the king, many Brahmans returned to Kashmir. The descendants of those who stayed behind during the darkest days, and of those who went into exile to return later, maintain a distinction amongst themselves to this day: the former are called *malamāsi* and the latter *bhānamāsi*.[16] More significantly, the Brahman families, presumably acting together,[17] seem to have taken the major decision to study Persian and thus laid the foundation of a changed social organization.

[15] The similarity between the Kashmir and Bangladesh situations is striking. 'Here [in Bengal], in the course of the thirteenth and fourteenth centuries, a whole countryside turned to Islam. It is thought that the decaying Buddhism of the Pala dynasty in Bengal had been superimposed upon their rustic animism, that the substitution of the Brahminical Sena Kings for Palas had meant a lowering of status and caste restriction, and that the Muslim conquests of Bengal with its casteless religion offered a welcome avenue of social escape' (Spear 1967: 34). See Chapter 10.

[16] I have been unable to establish the exact meanings of the two terms. The common suffix *māsi* (probably derived from *mās*, month) suggests a calendrical connotation; the two groups do, in fact, observe the same important ritual occasions on different dates during the Hindu leap year.

[17] There is evidence in the *Rājatarangiṇī* that Brahmans often acted as a corporate group, for instance, to effectively intervene in the affairs of the state.

It is clear from Kalhana's account that the Kayastha category had traditionally been recruited mainly from among the Brahmans. They had for long been accustomed to playing an important role in religious, civic and administrative affairs. Zain-ul-Abidin, who had inherited an administration which was in a shambles, held forth to them the renewed possibility of a similar role. The language of the court and administration had meanwhile been changed from Sanskrit to Persian. The Brahmans' decision to acquire proficiency in the latter language indicated their earnestness to seize the newly offered opportunities and become *kārkun* (the Persian word for civil servants, revenue collectors, etc.).

The Brahmans' decision raised a problem: what was to become of their traditional scholarship and philosophical heritage, and who was to ensure the proper performance of rituals so crucial to a Brahman's life? During the days of Hindu rule they had not faced such a problem, obviously because the Brahman and the king belonged to one and the same socio-religious system and used the same language—Sanskrit— in the performance of their respective roles. The problem that resulted from the separation of the socio-religious and politico-administrative spheres was resolved through a curious strategem: a daughter's son would study *bhāshā* ('the language'), i.e., Sanskrit, and administer to the spiritual and ritual needs of his mother's natal family (see Kilam 1955: 53).[18] Designated Bhasha Bhatta, they were regarded as the privileged category compared to the Karkun; they were the Brahmans *par excellence*, in deed as well as in name. What began as an arrangement of convenience has since frozen into a rigid division into two endogamous subcastes. What is more, the Karkun have arrogated to themselves the higher status. The Bhasha Bhatta are now called Gor (derived from the Sanskrit *guru*, 'preceptor', 'teacher'), which term today is unmistakably one of social contempt.

Both the Karkun and the Gor are divided into exogamous *gotra* categories. According to Lawrence (1967: 304) there are 103 Karkun and 18 'Levite' *gotras* among the Pandits. Koul (1924) mentions 199 *gotras* and names 189.[19] Within each *gotra* there are families which are

[18] The choice of a daughter's or sister's son would seem to have been made in view of the fact that, since agnates suffer pollution together, such a kinsmen would be unable to help in the performance of purificatory rituals of his *yajamān*; non-agnatic kinsmen would not be similarly handicapped except by rare coincidence. The practice seems to have been prevalent in the Punjab also and Hutton curiously considers it as evidence for the fusion of matrilineal and patrilineal cultures (see Hutton 1951: 156–7).

[19] For a discussion of the nature of *gotra* among the Pandits, see Madan 1962a.

identified by surnames called *zāt* or, relatively rarely, *kram*, meaning 'hereditary descent', and possibly indicative of social ranking. The *zāt* among Pandits are sectarian or family nicknames, the latter oftener than the former. These nicknames have their exact parallels among the Browns, Blacks, Longmans, Pidgeons, Swindlers and such other Anglo-Saxon surnames.[20] The Gor also have *zāt* but they rarely use the surname. It is instead customary to use the suffix *boi* (brother) with the personal name of each male priest. I have already pointed out that *zāt* has to do with the establishment of identity by birth among Kashmiri Muslims; the same applies to Pandits.

In none of the villages in the district of Anantnag which I visited did I encounter any other kind of Bhatta except the Gor and Karkun. All the 87 Pandit households of Utrassu-Umanagri are Karkun. The adjacent village of Kreri has seven Karkun and five Gor households. Pandit informants drew my attention to the presence of a doubtful and small category of Bhatta, the Buher, who are to be found only in urban areas. (There is a ward in the city of Srinagar named after them.) The Buher (also called Bohra) are Khattris, probably of Punjabi origin (see Lawrence 1967: 302; 1909: 40). Hutton (1951; 282) describes the Khattri as a trading caste of the Punjab and north-west India. The Buher are an endogamous caste of grocers and *halwai* (makers of confectionery, cheese, yoghourt and savouries of various kinds). In fact, the word *buhur* (singular of *buher*) is used in Kashmir in the sense of a grocer. The Pandits do not interdine with the Buher, nor allow them entry into their temples. The Gor do, however, perform priestly functions for them. The Buher have built a Vishnu temple of their own in Srinagar. On their part, they have adopted the lifestyle of the Pandits and would obviously like to be called Buher Bhatta. Already there are signs that, barring intermarriage, the Karkun and the Buher are coming closer to each other in urban areas. The problem does not exist in rural Kashmir.[21]

In Utrassu-Umanagri and surrounding villages the Karkun are served by a large number of occupational groups. The first of these are, of course, the Gor. Each Gor household has a clientele fixed on a hereditary basis, of both Karkun and Gor households. The latter are referred to as *yazaman* (derived from the Sanskrit *yajamāna*). When a Gor household dies out, its clientele is usually inherited by the nearest

---

[20] For an account (partly fanciful perhaps) of Pandit family names, see Fauq (n.d.).

[21] There are a few Kashmiri speaking Hindu families in Srinagar called the Purib or Purbi. They are probably descended from an immigrant Brahman group. Some informants told me that the Purbi came to Kashmir from the Chambha valley.

agnatic kin. A Karkun household may employ the services of the most readily available priest for minor purposes—such as consecrating routine food offerings, or determining auspicious dates for doing or buying some thing—but on all important occasions only the *kola-gor* (family priest) will do. If he is ill, in a state of pollution, or otherwise unavailable, it is his duty to provide a substitute.

Formerly the Gor were also teachers, not only of priestly lore but also of astrology, Sanskrit and *shāstra* (religious literature) in general. Nowadays, the only pupils they have are their own sons, though not even all of them are willing to follow their traditional calling. The performance of all but the most essential rituals is coming to be viewed as dispensable. The Karkun feel that they do not have the time or the resources for them. The Gor lament the decline of faith and they complain that even the essential rituals are sought to be abridged. Whatever the reasons, the Gor are beginning to turn away from priestcraft. One of the young Gor of Kreri is a school teacher; another has joined the state militia. I was informed that the process of occupational change among the Gor is more visible in urban areas than in the villages.

The Karkun are, of course, dependent on the Gor for the performance of rituals. There can be no Pandits without the Gor. The latter's dependence on the Karkun is merely economic. It is not inconceivable that a small community of Gor could exist without the Karkun and draw their sustenance from land or service. The Karkun on their part look down upon the Gor and even consider them inauspicious. Several times during my fieldwork I noticed how a Karkun would return home if he met a priest just after he had started on an errand. There is general denigration of the Gor on account of their style of life and their alleged greed and lack of learning. Their worst fault would seem to be that they accept food and other gifts offered to the dead.[22]

The Karkun-Gor relationship has always been hierarchical, being ordered in terms of religious values and moral judgements. The two groups seem to have changed places, however, since the emergence of the division between them about 500 years ago. Even so, as a category, the Gor are essentially pure, irrespective of how particular Gor may be regarded by their Karkun patrons. In principle the Karkun and the Gor are one: they are Brahmans—they are the Pandits.

[22] I was told that in Srinagar there is a special category of Gor called *Achor*, who alone accept such offerings. They collect the goods under cover of darkness, either from the home of the gift-givers or from the nearest bathing ghat. See Dumont 1970a: 58 on the 'Mahabrahman'.

For all other services the Pandits are dependent upon Muslims. An examination of these services is of great importance from the point of view of this discussion as it will enable us to grasp the definition of Muslim identity by the Pandits.

Muslim Identity: Hindu Representation

As stated earlier, Utrassu-Umanagri is a bi-nucleated village. The settlement of Utrassu is older than anybody can remember. Umanagri is, however, quite recent: it was founded about 200 years ago. I have given the details elsewhere (see Madan 1965: 38–40), and will here confine myself to pointing out that originally there were no Muslims in Umanagri. The Pandits found it impossible to carry on without the services of Muslim cultivators, artisans, village servants, and other specialist groups, and therefore invited them to come from other villages and settle down in Umanagri. This historical fact only serves to underline what my fieldwork has revealed.

Being Brahmans, the Pandits are traditionally debarred from a large number of occupational activities. Thus, they cannot engage in polluting activities such as barbering, washing clothes, obtaining oil from oilseeds, removing and skinning dead animals, making shoes, winnowing pans and drums, slaughtering goats and sheep,[23] and so on. There are so many other types of activities which are not polluting, but which no Pandit would engage in because they involve manual labour, no matter how light. Some of the poorer Pandits in Utrassu-Umanagri do engage in cultivation or cooking—the former only in their own village and the latter only outside it—but at the cost of being treated as socially inferior by the others.[24] Ownership of land, service (public or private) and shopkeeping are the only sources of household income among the Pandits of Utrassu-Umanagri (see Madan 1965: 149–50).[25] In such a situation it is not at all surprising that the Pandits should regard Muslims as an essential component of their social system. In this connection it is worth mentioning that the 1941 census shows only two villages in the Srinagar-Anantnag districts inhabited by Pandits alone though, as stated earlier, 56 per cent of the villages are exclusively Muslim.

[23] Kashmiri Pandits eat mutton, wild fowl and fish, but not domestic fowl or their eggs (see Madan 1975b).
[24] Things have begun to change since 1947 following the many drastic political and economic changes that have taken place in the state. During 1957–8, nine Pandits of Utrassu-Umanagri were working as labourers in an Indian Army ammunition depot four miles from the village (see Madan 1965: 146–8).
[25] The 1931 census report lists government service as the traditional occupation of the Pandits (see India 1933).

In the Pandits' conception of them, Kashmiri villages are characterized by the simple but sharp distinction between themselves and
the Muslims. The latter are regarded in principle as being ritually
impure. They are referred to as *mleccha* (of lowly birth, outsiders);
theirs is the world of *tamas* (darkness, ignorance). Muslims are outside
the pale of values by which a Pandit is expected, as a Brahman, to order
his life. In practice, however, the Pandits consider some Muslims less
polluting than others.

In Utrassu-Umanagri no Pandit eats food cooked or even touched
by a Muslim. There are no exceptions to this rule except the acceptance of clarified butter from Milkmen, Gujars and Bakarwals. (Some
Pandits also accept yoghurt and fresh cheese from these three groups
but others disapprove of the practice, which seems to be recent.) If
transgressions occur they are so secretive that no Pandit claimed having
actually seen another Pandit eating with a Muslim. There seems to have
been some kind of a sumptuary ban on the consumption of such forbidden food until about 1925, when Maharaja Pratap Singh, a very
orthodox Hindu ruler, died.

Pandits accept uncooked food from all but the lowliest of Muslims
(namely, Domb and Vatal). Grains, vegetables and fruits are included
in this category. Uncooked meat also is generally accepted but may
be refused for fear of its being beef. (Killing beef cattle is a penal offence
in the state, but it would seem that Muslims do sometimes slaughter
such animals.) Unboiled milk is freely accepted from Milkmen,
Gujars, Bakarwals, and Zamindars but usually not from any other
group. The Pandits are much more hesitant to accept water from
Muslims. Some well-to-do households employ water carriers but
invariably choose a Milkman or a Zamindar for the chore and provide
him with a pitcher. A Pandit is not expected to drink even milk from
a container belonging to a Muslim.

There is no sharing of the *hookah* between Pandits and Muslims. A
Pandit does not touch any part of a Muslim's *hookah*—its vase of
water, pipe or the *chillum* (tobacco-cum-fire bowl). A Muslim is
allowed to smoke the *chillum* of a Pandit's *hookah* by holding it between
his palms but is never allowed to use the pipe.

The Utrassu-Umanagri Pandits avoid any physical contact with
the cobblers and winnowing-pan makers (Vatal), who skin dead
animals and have traditionally been suspected by everybody of being
carrion eaters. (I was informed that in urban areas, where there are
two types of Vatal, namely, leather-workers and scavengers, the latter

are treated with less repugnance than the former.) The Pandits do, however, buy the articles these craftsmen make. The Domb are also regarded as being very polluting and physical contact with them is strenuously avoided. In relation to other Muslims in the village, the Pandits are less anxious to avoid total physical contact. The more fastidious among them will wash their hands after touching a Muslim. I once saw a Muslim servant (a Zamindar) press the feet and legs of his Pandit master but the latter did not wash afterwards. (Only half a dozen or so Pandit households in Utrassu-Umanagri employ Muslim servants, all of whom are Zamindars.) Muslim-Pandit marriages are, of course, ruled out. Illicit sexual intercourse does seem to occur once in a while. This is a subject on which one has no evidence more reliable than village gossip. Among all Muslims, it is the Barber (Navid) and the midwife with whom Pandit men and women, respectively, come in most intimate physical contact. The Barber's services are particularly noteworthy and may be elaborated upon.

The Navid renders routine and occasional services to his Pandit patrons. The routine services consist of shaving the face and the head or cutting the hair. Shaving is regarded as *varzit* (derived from the Sanskrit *varjit*, forbidden) on certain days of the week and on most occasions when one has to perform a ritual. The act of having one's beard or hair shaved on such days is inauspicious in itself, and does not seem to have anything to do with the desire to avoid contact with a Muslim. That this is so is indicated by the fact that the Barber is called in to render his services on four highly important occasions of ritual performance. Sanskritic rites are interrupted to have a boy's *zarakāsai* (*zara* = baby hair, *kāsai* = shaving, cutting) done; to have a neophyte's head shaved during *mekhlā* (the investiture ceremony also called *yagnopavit* or *upanayana*); and to shave the beard and hair of a mourner at the end of the period of pollution. These rituals would remain incomplete without the Barber's services. The Barber's touch is polluting, however, and the person who has been served by him on the special ritual occasions mentioned above must have a bath. On other occasions too having a bath is desirable, but washing of the face and head is all that may be done. The Barber also shaves and gives a haircut to a bridegroom before the latter leaves for the bride's home for the marriage ceremony. During the *lagan* (marriage ritual), one of the rites involves letting the bride and the bridegroom see each other's faces in a mirror. This mirror is customarily provided by the Barber of the bride's natal household.

For his routine services the Barber receives a number of measures of paddy from his patrons at harvest time. Several Pandit households of Utrassu-Umanagri buy grain so as to meet the requirements of such payments to the Barber and other specialists. Many families pay for them in cash. On all special occasions the Barber receives the clothes, at least some of them, which the individual recipient of the services has on him at that time. The Barber also receives other gifts. He is treated as a well-wisher by his patrons, with whom he has hereditary relations.

I have described the Barber's services at some length because of their value as a paradigm of the relations between the Pandit and Muslim occupational groups. The essential elements of the paradigm may be recapitulated:

1. The services are of routine and special kinds;
2. they have a ritual significance for the Pandit and this is known to the Muslim specialist;
3. the specialist himself views them in economic terms, but recognizes their traditional character;
4. the threat to his state of ritual purity arising from contact with a Muslim is tolerated by the Pandit because he is otherwise even more seriously in danger of being unable to enter or re-enter such a state; and
5. the relations between the patrons and the specialists are on a hereditary basis and are paid for in kind, if possible.

I will take another crucial example: that of the relations between the Muslim Potter (Kral) and his Pandit patrons. The Potter supplies pots and pans of various kinds which he makes both for everyday use and for special occasions. Storage jars for grains, pickles and water; utensils for cooking, storing and serving food; smoking bowls; toys; and many other types of pottery are supplied by him. He provides a wide range of utensils in large quantities at weddings. It is on the occasion of Herath (a feast in honour of Shiva), however, that he makes for his Pandit customers the most unusual of all pieces of pottery.

As I have described elsewhere (see Madan 1961b: 129–39), Herath is celebrated over fifteen days during the dark fortnight of the month of Phagun (February–March). Each day has its appointed task; on the eleventh day the Potter carries a basket load of pottery to each patron household for use in the kitchen and in the climactic rites during the last four days. The number of each type of the various pieces of pottery has to be just right. Shortages are regarded as bad omens and the Potter is rebuked for such lapses. Among the many objects he makes is the rather inconspicuous looking *sanipotul* (*sani* = worship, *potul* = idol), which is the *lingam*, to be installed as Shiva during the rites. It is obviously phallic in shape.

Though the Potters whom I questioned at Utrassu-Umanagri do not exactly know what kind of an idol the *sanipotul* is, they are all aware that it is an object of worship for the Pandits. As Muslims they have no use for such idols, and abhor idol worship, but as Potters they readily make the objects for their patrons. They look upon the work they do in economic terms; but not so the Pandits, who view the Potter's services in relation to such basic activities as the preparation of food and the performance of one of the most important domestic rituals of the year.

More examples of such relationships between Muslims and Pandits could be given, including that of the familiar Washerman and the unfamiliar (among Brahman communities) Butcher. The latter supplies the meat which the Pandit offers to some of his gods and goddesses. In fact, it is the Muslim Butcher who slaughters the sacrificial ram after the Brahman Gor has ritually rendered it sacred. Further, it is worth mentioning that, since the Pandits are major consumers of meat in Utrassu-Umanagri, the Muslim Butchers keep track of the capricious Hindu lunar calendar and avoid slaughtering too many animals on days on which Pandits abstain from eating meat.

Limitations of space prevent me from going into the details of more cases.[26] Suffice it to add that most of the services that Muslim specialist groups render to their Pandit clientele are ritual liturgies when viewed from the receiver's end; but they appear as economic transactions, sanctioned by village tradition, when judged from the perspective of the giver. What are legitimately seen as occupational groups from the Muslim angle are castes, 'caste analogues', or 'caste substitutes' when viewed in terms of the Hindu caste system which they, in fact, help to constitute in Kashmir.

We will be justified in speaking of the social organization of mixed Kashmiri villages as a regional variant of the caste system if the cardinal principle of hierarchy is found applicable. It is obvious from the foregoing discussion that this certainly is so in the Pandits' ideological reconstruction of empirical reality. Moreover, the Pandits do not

[26] The case of the Muslim Kawuj—attendants at Pandit cremation sites in Srinagar, and probably in other towns—requires close study; particularly their relations with other Muslims should be of interest. Kashmiri Muslims regard everything dead (except fish) as polluting.

normally render any services to the Muslims, nor do they provide them
with any goods. The only exceptions to this rule in Utrassu-Umanagri
are a Pandit *hakim* (practitioner of Graeco-Arab medicine), and some
money-lenders, and (if we may include them) shopkeepers. I encountered several instances of a Pandit astrologer being consulted by
Muslims. It is clear that all these roles are prestigious. The Pandits'
representation of village society is shown in Figure. 1.

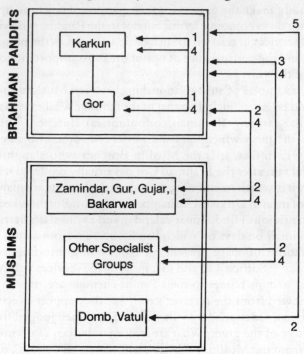

FIGURE 1

1 Acceptance of cooked and uncooked food.
2 Acceptance of uncooked food, milk, water.
3 Acceptance of uncooked food only.
4 Flow of goods and/or services without avoidance of physical contact.
5 Flow of goods and/or services with strict avoidance of physical contact.

It will be agreed that (*i*) the inferior status of Gor *vis-à-vis* Karkun,
(*ii*) the inferior position of the Muslims *vis-à-vis* the Brahmans, and
(*iii*) the division of Muslims into three ranked categories are all ultimately based on the same governing principle of superior dignity
arising out of moral, i.e. religious considerations. As we move

downwards from the Gor through the three rungs of Muslim occupational groups, the element of ritual impurity becomes increasingly salient.

The admission of Muslims into a common social fold is surreptitious, by the backdoor as it were: it cannot occur in terms of ideology but, paradoxically, is defended on the ground that without them the Pandit would lose caste or ritual purity. In other words, the empirical situation in which the Pandit finds himself compels him to establish relations of various kinds with Muslim occupational groups; he orders them in terms of hierarchy. Ideally he should have no relations with the Muslims: they are *mleccha*, and this word means both 'an outsider' and 'a person of lowly birth'. Common stereotypes about Muslims which I found prevalent among Pandits included, besides *mleccha*, 'dirty', 'polluted', 'unprincipled', 'omnivorous', and 'lustful'. Individual Muslims are respected for personal qualities; the two Lambardars (minor revenue officials) of Utrassu-Umanagri are Muslims, and I saw Pandits treat them with the courtesy due to their official position. Muslim households with wealth may even be accepted as patrons: one Pandit household of the village cultivates a portion of the biggest Muslim Zamindar's land, though I was told that such a relationship is rare and amounts to a reversal of familiar roles.

As a category, however, Muslims are polluting and contact with them should be restricted as far as possible if it cannot be avoided. It is obvious that Pandits have accepted compromise to avoid being defeated. They are faced with a moral dilemma: to preserve their status as Brahmans they need goods and services which only the Muslims provide, but the latter are themselves a source of pollution. Since the danger emanating from Muslims can be controlled and rectified, the Pandits' choice has its merits. A Pandit saying is apposite in this context: *Yath na pūsh tath na dūsh* (whereof one is helpless, thereof one attracts no blame). This may be regarded as evidence of Pandit pragmatism; in Dumont's phrase, a concession to coexistence (see Dumont 1970a: 206).

That this has not been an easy choice is illustrated by the manner in which Pandits switch codes when talking to Muslims. Though they all speak the same language, Koshur or Kashmiri, there are striking differences of lexical elements so that linguists have classified it into Sanskritized Kashmiri (SK) and Persianized Kashmiri (PK) (see Kachru 1969: 21–7). The speakers of PK are Muslims. I found in Utrassu-Umanagri that their use of PK words is consistent: they employ

them with whomsoever they are speaking. The Pandits switch from
SK to PK when certain crucial words have to be used in conversation
with Muslims. A Pandit will generally stick to such SK words as
ponya (water; PK equivalent, *āb*), *khovur* (left; PK, *khofur*), *shokrawār*
(Friday; PK, *jummah*). He wavers when it comes to such words as
God (SK, *Bhagvān*; PK, *Khodā*) and religion (SK, *dharma*; PK,
mazhab), but generally uses the PK words when talking with a Muslim.
I never found a Pandit use the SK greeting of *namaskār* when addres-
sing a Muslim: there is no ambiguity at all on this point. A Muslim
greets all, whether Muslim or Hindu, with *salām*; but a Pandit always
says *salām* to a Muslim and *namaskār* to another Pandit. *Namaskār* is
thus a marked term: when one hears it said, the only conclusion that
may be drawn is that one Pandit has greeted another.

On being questioned, even the most intelligent of my Pandit
informants would tell me no more by way of explanation than that it
would be improper to say *namaskār* to a Muslim. 'Is that not obvious?',
they asked me. It is apparent that saying *namaskār*, 'I bow to thee', to
a Muslim is improper, for he is *mleccha*, an outsider. He cannot be
fully admitted into the Pandits' company. There must be no blurring
of *zāti* or natural distinctions, that is, of socio-cultural identities.
Words like *Bhagvān, dharma* and, above all, *namaskār*, are signposts
which the Pandits have set up as a boundary maintenance device.
Those within are Brahmans; those outside, *mleccha*. It is a kind of last
ditch defence.

Hindu Identity: Muslim Representation

A question that arises from the foregoing discussion is, do Kashmiri
Muslims also feel threatened by the Pandits? The answer, it seems to
me, has to be in the negative, although Muslims regard Pandits as
being outsiders, non-Muslims. To understand this situation we shall
now examine the Muslim representation of Pandit identity in relation to their own.

The Muslim's view of Pandits as non-Muslims has to be disen-
tangled from his image of them as clients or patrons. Just as Pandits
qua Hindus see themselves in opposition to the *mleccha*, Kashmiri
Muslims *qua* Muslims identify themselves with the *umma*, the universal
Muslim brotherhood, and regard Pandits as *kāfir* ('misbelievers'),
destined to go to hell. Internal divisions among the Pandits do not
interest the Muslims in the least.

The relationship is hierarchical, based on Islamic values. The exclusion of Pandits stems from moral abhorrence but has nothing to do

with ritual pollution. Earlier I mentioned Pandit stereotypes of Muslims; these may now be matched by Muslim stereotypes of Pandits, equally derogatory and expressive of the wish to exclude the other. 'Faithless', 'unfaithful', 'double-dealer', 'mean', 'cowardly', 'corrupt' and 'dirty' are some of the epithets I heard Muslim informants use for Pandits.[27]

Kashmiri Muslims countenance marriage with Pandits no more than the latter do so. They have no objection, however, to physical contact with the Pandits. The latter have free access to all parts of a Muslim house though they themselves do not allow Muslims into their kitchens and into any room where a ritual is in progress or where rituals usually take place (see Madan 1965: 46–50). The Barber and the Butcher, whose role in Pandit religious ceremonies was discussed earlier, perform their assigned tasks just outside the ritually demarcated area. Similarly, the water carrier pours water into a vessel in the kitchen without stepping inside. Pandits are, however, debarred from entering mosques. Moreover, the Muslims of Utrassu-Umanagri do observe strict avoidance in respect of food cooked by the Pandits. 'It is *harām* (forbidden)'—the Koran prohibits it—is the most general explanation given. When pressed to elaborate this cryptic remark, some informants used the word *nāpāk* (impure) to describe Pandit food. (Several other less significant explanations were given, including the belief that Pandit food is injurious to health because their curries contain asafoetida, and is tasteless as it lacks onions and garlic.) A few Zamindars who have intimate relations with Pandit land-owners were reported as given to eating food from their patrons' kitchens, but the number of such cases is negligible. Those who transgress this restriction are believed to be guilty of a moral lapse and therefore liable to suffer supernatural punishment. One of the villagers drew attention to his own brother, a sickly and poor Milkman, saying that the latter was an eater of Pandit food.[28]

[27] Probably the stereotype of Pandits most widely used by Kashmiri Muslims is *dāli-Bhatta*, 'the *dāl* or lentil curry Pandit'. *Dāl* is considered the very opposite of mutton curries; *dāl* eaters are represented as cowardly and meat eaters as brave and courageous. Vegetarianism is actually no more than an occasional dietary restriction among the Pandits. Exceptions apart, I have encountered no vegetarian Pandit households in many years of contact with rural Kashmir, though there are vegetarian individuals. The Muslims also eat *dāl* but never on festive occasions (see Madan 1975b). A well known Kashmiri saying is: *Bhattas phaka, Musalmanas shraka, Shias baka*, the Pandits fast on important occasions, the Muslims wield the sword (to slaughter sheep and goats), and the Shiahs weep.

[28] I discussed the Muslim attitude to Pandit food with a *mufti* (a person 'learned in the Koran and Hadith and in the Muslim works of law' (Hughes 1935)) who is

There is one more category of people whose cooking the Muslims of the village do not accept because it is considered impure. The people concerned are the Domb and the Vatal. Whenever these families arrange a feast, they engage professional Muslim cooks who bring their own cooking and serving utensils. Other Muslims then readily join such feasts in the houses of these lowly groups, but do not otherwise eat with them. In turn they get invited to the homes of other Muslims but they are excluded in a subtle manner. On such occasions four persons eat from a single plate. Domb and Vatal guests will not be asked to share a plate with one another, or with any other Muslim, even if there are less than four of each of these groups present. Needless to add, the Domb and the Vatal are the two most strictly endogamous Muslim groups in the village.

Kashmiri Muslims clearly distinguish between dirty (*mokur*) and impure (*nāpāk*). The two conditions may exist together as in the case of the legendary pig—the animal is non-existent in Kashmir—whose very sight is forbidden to the Muslim. The best example of the distinction between dirt and impurity was given to me by one of my informants when he explained why Muslims are expected to dry the penis with clay after urination. 'I may have put on new or washed trousers, but if even a drop of urine falls on them, I cannot enter the mosque for prayers.' Muslim ablutions prior to the saying of prayers (*namāz*) are quite an elaborate affair. However, their notion of pollution is in principle different from the Hindu notion inasmuch as they do not consider it permanent in any circumstances whatsoever. I was told that if the Domb or the Vatal should give up their present occupations, they too would be accepted as equals by other Muslims. This is of course difficult to confirm, and though there has long been evidence of upward mobility among Muslim occupational groups, I doubt if these two groups could easily live down the stigma of their

---

also a college professor. He disapproved of the villagers' attitude and maintained that they were acting out of ignorance and under the influence of long established habits. In this connection it is worth noting here that a Muslim Washerman of Utrassu-Umanagri once told me of how he had fallen ill after he had eaten 'unusual meat' with some acquaintances in a neighbouring village. On my asking for clarification, he said he suspected that he had been served beef. I doubt if many Kashmiri Muslims would feel likewise about eating beef; what is remarkable is that even a few of them should. The influence of Pandit neighbours is an obvious but unsatisfactory explanation. I guess one has to fall back upon Dumont's other suggestion, 'psychological dispositions' (see Dumont 1970a: 211), preferably qualified as *residual*.

names, which proclaim their *zāt*.[29] The Muslims point out that even a Pandit—any non–Muslim for that matter—can acquire true faith and become a believer (*mūmin*). This is of course the ideological position, but we have already noted the case of the convert Ghulam alias Darshan and have discussed the significance of the circumstances of birth in the determination of *zāt*.

Before we complete this discussion of the Muslim representation of Pandit identity, I would like to make a final comment on the notion of *zāt* among Muslims. The status of Sayyids is the key to this problem. I have already pointed out that Kashmiri Muslims are not an undifferentiated category, and that they themselves acknowledge this fact. My informants in Utrassu–Umanagri spoke to me of the division between the Sunni and Shiah (see Levy 1962: *passim*), though there are no Shiah in the village.[30] They also mentioned Sayyids, Mughals and Pathans with a certain degree of deference. Muslims falling into these categories are to be found in the town of Anantnag.[31] The position of the Gujar and the Bakarwal has already been mentioned. I have also described how the native Muslims are composed of many occupational groups including the Domb and the Vatal.

The Sayyids are the descendants of Ali and his wife Fatimah, daughter of the Prophet Muhammad. They are, therefore, entitled to respect. The Mughal and Pathan families are also entitled to respect, but why? The Muslims of the village are dimly aware that these people were once the rulers of Kashmir. An equally important reason would seem to be that these groups have been Muslims longer than the others. The principle of proximity to the founder of Islam,

[29] Lawrence calls the 'social system in Kashmir . . . delightfully plastic': '. . . there is nothing to prevent Abdulla, the Dum [Domb], calling himself Abdulla Pandit if he chooses. At first the people would laugh, but after a time, if Abdulla Pandit prospered, his descendants would exhibit a lengthy pedigree table tracing their family back to one of the petty Rajas, lord of three villages and possessor of a fort, the ruins of which still stand in Abdulla Pandit's village . . .' (1967: 307). Unless things have changed beyond recognition over the last 75 years, which I doubt, Lawrence's account seems rather exaggerated. I found no forts in ruins in the Kashmir countryside and the people, Muslims and Pandits alike, take little interest in genealogies beyond half a dozen generations at best.

[30] 'At the census of 1890 no distinction was made between the Musalmans of the Sunni and Shiah persuasions, but it may be roughly said that the Shiahs form only about 5 per cent of the total Musalman. The Shiahs chiefly reside in Zadi Bal ward of Srinagar and in the Kamraj (Baramulla) district, though they are found in other parts of the valley' (Lawrence 1967: 284).

[31] According to the 1941 census Sayyids formed 7 per cent of the Muslim population of Anantnag district, Pathans 3 per cent, Rajputs 2 per cent and Mughals 1 per cent.

which is apparent in view of the genealogical connection in the case of the Sayyids, and acknowledged by the Muslims, is also applicable to the Mughals and the Pathans. In terms of this logic Gujars and Bakarwals should also be accorded deference but they are not, though they themselves look down upon the natives. The empirical situation is, therefore, somewhat ambiguous, but the cardinal principle of genealogical relationship emerges clearly in the exalted position of the Sayyids. It is misleading to regard them as the Muslim equivalent of Brahmans, as some writers have done, because the criterion of ritual purity—or perhaps even of moral superiority—is not applicable.

All the above internal divisions among Muslims are ignored when Muslims are juxtaposed with Pandits. The situation then is dramatized by being reduced to stark opposition between the believer and the 'misbeliever', the Muslim and the non-Muslim. The Pandit lies completely outside the fold of Islam. His present status is inconsequential to the Muslim; his potential status as a convert, though significant in ideological terms, does not really excite the Muslim, given the latter's notion of *zāt*. In any case, the convert is not a threat to the community of believers, which is open and to which he is in principle welcome. The contrast with the completely closed community of Pandits is too obvious to need further comment.

The answer to the question posed at the beginning of this section—namely why Muslims do not feel their identity threatened by interaction with Pandits—may now be given. As already explained, Kashmiri Muslims enter into relations with Pandits which they view as traditional economic transactions. The relationship is between a supplier of goods and services and his patron; religious differences are held in abeyance. It is a relationship of mutual dependence, but is asymmetrical. Whereas the Pandit cannot find substitutes or surrogates for Muslim occupational groups in his own community, Muslim specialists are free, at least in principle, to make their living by attending to the needs of their co-religionists alone. This is what happens in fact in many villages where there are no Pandits within the settlement or nearby. It is true that in mixed villages Pandit households have generally enjoyed enough economic power to make it worthwhile for the Muslims to serve them. The Pandits were favoured by and identified with the ruling class during the hundred years of Hindu rule between 1846 and 1947 (see Bamzai 1962: 553 ff.).[32] Economic need or advantage

---

[32] Lawrence notes that the Dogra rulers had vested revenue administration in the hands of the Pandits, who manned it from the lowest to the highest levels (see Lawrence 1967: 400–1).

and political subordination of the Muslims do not, however, create among them a dependence on the Pandits in principle, which alone would be immutable; the existing dependence is purely circumstantial.

Dependence in deference to a principle characterizes the relationship of the Pandits with the Muslims. A Pandit cannot retain his ritual status without the crucial services of at least some of the Muslim occupational groups. The dependence is absolute, in principle as well as in practice. To put it differently: the Pandit keeps Muslims out of the *sanctum sanctorum* of his cultural universe, but has to let them into his social world; hence the strain and anxiety that he experiences. A Muslim, on the other hand, considers Pandits as outsiders, both ideologically and empirically. He does not feel threatened on either plane. This sense of security has been considerably heightened since 1947 by the policies followed by a succession of democratically chosen governments of the state which have been dominated by Muslims. The most noteworthy of the decisions taken have been in respect of land and tenancy reforms (the most radical in India), abolition or reduction of the debt burden of the peasantry, and provision of extensive education, health and transportation facilities in rural areas. Educationally, and perhaps economically, the Muslims of Utrassu-Umanagri are not yet the equals of their Pandit co-villagers, but politically they are on the right side of the fence. This would seem to be generally true of rural Kashmir (see Madan 1966c).

The Muslim representation of village society is shown in Figure 2.

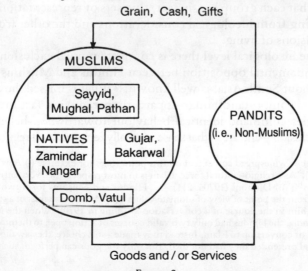

Grain, Cash, Gifts

MUSLIMS

Sayyid, Mughal, Pathan

NATIVES
Zamindar
Nangar

Gujar, Bakarwal

Domb, Vatul

PANDITS
(i.e., Non-Muslims)

Goods and / or Services

FIGURE 2

If we compare it with the Hindu representation of the same society presented in Figure 1, it becomes clear that we are faced with a situation of dual identities and of dual social orders. The only respect in which the two social orders appear identical is the position accorded to the Domb and the Vatal. In this parallelism between the two representations may be seen the exemplification of the Hindu ethic of ritual purity. What explains it? This is a difficult question to answer. With Dumont, we might attribute it to the permanence of 'psychological dispositions' (see Dumont 1970a: 211). What I would like to stress, however, is the marginal nature of these two groups in both the versions of Kashmiri rural society.

Conclusion

It will be recalled that this examination of data, drawn primarily from a Kashmiri village, was undertaken with a twofold purpose. It was hoped that it would, first, enable us to define the respective places of Muslims and Hindus in Kashmiri rural society and, secondly, provide some fresh insights into more general problems, such as the nature of Hindu-Muslim cultural 'synthesis' and of caste society.

We have seen that the Muslims and the Hindus differ in the images that they have of themselves, of each other, and of Kashmiri rural society. This is a familiar situation in societies characterized by cultural pluralism, with each ethnic category being 'self-ascribed' as well as 'other-ascribed' (see Barth 1970). The data from Utrassu-Umanagri reveal that each group has, in fact, two sets of representations, one stemming from ideological considerations and the other from the compulsions of living.

At the ideological level there is complete mutual exclusion. That this fundamental opposition between Hindus and Muslims exists throughout South Asia, is well known.[33] What is missed, however, is the very important though apparently paradoxical fact that both ideologies command identical behaviour towards non-believers—total exclusion—and are in that sense mutually reciprocal and reinforcing.

[33] There is widespread agreement on this point. See, for example (*i*) Aziz Ahmad (1964: 73): 'As a religio-cultural force, Islam is in most respects the "very antithesis of Hinduism"'; (*ii*) Dumont (1970a: 211): '. . . Hindus and Muslims form two distinct societies from the point of view of ultimate values'; (*iii*) A. K. Saran (gist of a statement made by him in the course of a conversation with me in 1970): 'When the Muslims came to India, the Hindus had only two valid courses of action open to them: a fight to the finish or conversion to Islam. Instead they made a soft choice: they swallowed the poison and pretended they had not died. But only the gods can perform such feats'.

In other words, Kashmiri rural society, when subjectively defined, comprises two social orders, not one.

At the empirical level we encounter another set of relations, those between the Muslim occupational groups and their Pandit clients or patrons. As we have already seen, the Muslims view these relations in economic terms, while the Pandits regard them as ritual liturgies with an economic content. This content is not to be equated with the value of goods or services transacted, for the Pandits' stakes are higher than can be measured by the economic yardstick. Thus, though the Muslims and the Pandits are mutually dependent, there is no reciprocity of perspective, if we take the surface level view of the situation. At the deeper level, however, there is agreement. The duality of the social orders is thus overcome. In the words of Lévi-Strauss (used, of course, in another context), 'it is not the resemblances, but the differences, which resemble each other' (1962: 77).

The relationship of the ideological and empirical situations may thus be seen as one of complementary opposition. The emic definition of the relationship would, however, seem to be as that of independence. Viewed in its own terms the empirical situation is a harmonious whole; in ideological terms it is a compromise, a concession to the exigencies of co-existence (see Dumont 1970a: 206). Compromise and concession spell ideological defeat; and it is as much in terms of it as of economic interdependence that, viewed from the outside, a synthesis may be seen to have been worked out by the peoples of Kashmir.

Turning to the problem of caste, we have seen that both Muslims and Pandits recognize the notion of *zāt* as the crucial factor in identity specification and in determining an individual's natural or moral conduct. Further, Muslim specialist-Pandit patron relations were seen to be a close approximation to the familiar *jajmānī* pattern. It was, in fact, argued that from the Pandit's point of view a caste system does exist in Kashmir. The significance of this situation lies in that it demonstrates more clearly than any other regional social framework that the castes of a 'Hindu' society, other than Brahmans, are not necessarily 'Hindu' by religion. The Kashmir data reveal how the Brahman will conjure up a system of caste substitutes even out of a non-Hindu environment. His capacity to do so is, of course, dependent upon both ideological compromise and politico-economic power. In the recent past—between 1846 and 1947—the Pandits had the monopoly of both political and economic power in rural Kashmir. In 1947 they lost the former. Though economically they are yet no

worse off than they were earlier, their economic monopoly has certainly been broken and their association with landownership has been
abolished. The future may yet hold an unprecedented challenge to
the Pandits in the form of the withdrawal of co-operation by Muslim
specialists. There have been a few straws in the wind to indicate that
such an eventuality cannot be ruled out.[34] It remains to be seen what
solution the proverbial Pandit ingenuity will find for such social and
ritual lacunae.

The above considerations should not mislead us to conclude that
the Kashmiri Muslim social order itself is a modified system of castes
as might be suggested by the manner in which some scholars have
dealt with so-called Muslim castes (see, for example, Dumont 1970a:
210, Ansari 1960; and Hutton 1951: 2). The temptation to do so is
particularly strong in Kashmir where the bulk of the Muslim population is of Hindu ancestry (see Lawrence 1967: 286 but also 306). It is
an easy way out but fails to attach sufficient importance to the Muslims'
self-ascription today. I do not mean to suggest that the anthropologist
should not venture beyond native models of social reality; he must
not, however, ignore them.

Another pitfall would be the temptation to discuss Kashmiri rural
society solely in terms of a system of economic classes based on
occupation, on the ground that the caste model is totally inapplicable
to Muslims in view of their ideology (see, for example, Saghir Ahmad
1970). I trust this discussion has convincingly shown that our understanding of the peculiarities of rural social organization in Kashmir is
dependent upon a prior knowledge of the Hindu caste system, which
is not the same thing as saying that Muslim groups are modified
castes.[35] The class model is an idependent construct.

The inescapable conclusion—it seems so to me at least—is that,
instead of trying to completely assimilate the Muslim and Pandit
representations of Kashmiri rural society, we should acknowledge
the existence of dual social orders, which are, however, accommodated within one overarching framework. The latter is defined partly

[34] Since 1947 some Muslim specialists of Utrassu-Umanagri have on two occasions
threatened to deny their services to the Pandits: the Potters in around 1948 and the
Barbers in 1967. See also Madan 1966c.

[35] Imtiaz Ahmad has, for several years now, been pleading for the study of the
nature of interaction between Hindus and Muslims (see, for example, Imtiaz Ahmad
1965, 1966), He believes that the Muslim occupational groups of Uttar Pradesh whom
he has studied are appropriately described as 'caste analogues' but does not clarify
from whose point of view—the anthropologists', the Hindus', or the Muslims'.

in cultural terms (language, customs, etc.) and partly in terms of the politico-administrative set-up. Its members are not, as such, the Muslims and the Pandits, but rather people, *Kashir* (that is, Kashmiris), who either have the Muslim identity or the Pandit identity. Within this overall framework, the Pandits need the alternate Kashmiri identity to function, whilst the Muslims do not, but only use it conveniently because that is the framework within which they can, given the Pandit requirement, deal with their Hindu co-villagers. This is precisely what I mean when I claim that, while Pandit identity is intrinsically a caste structured one, Muslim identity is not so, and, again, the Kashmiri one is. Moreover, such a view of the relation between religious ideology and ethnic identity may turn out to be of value beyond Kashmir in helping us comprehend the situation not only of Muslims but also of other non-Hindu groups in South Asia and, *mutatis mutandis*, even of Hindus in such places as Sind in Pakistan or in Afghanistan.

POSTSCRIPT

The social organization of rural Kashmir, evolved over more than six centuries, came under severe pressure in the mid-1980s with the emergence of Muslim fundamentalist and secessionist (pro-independence) forces. In early 1990 the Kashmir Valley was literally taken over by armed Muslim militants, who resorted to terror tactics, including abduction, arson and murder. Many groups called upon the Pandits to agree to live under Islamic laws (*Nizām-i-Mustafā*) or go away. One of the Pandits of Utrassu-Umanagri was killed, a couple of others barely escaped the same fate. This resulted in unprecedented panic, and well over 90 per cent of the 200,000 or so Pandits of the valley abandoned their hearths and homes and migrated to safer places or refugee camps outside Kashmir. The situation remains the same until today (June 1992). Recently some militant groups have called for the return of the Pandits; it remains to be seen what comes out of it.

These developments have delivered a death blow to the composite culture and harmonious social relations described in this chapter. A return to the traditional ways of life in rural Kashmir appears very remote.

Two Faces of Bengali Ethnicity: Bengali Muslim or Muslim Bengali

10

> *There will be time, there will be time*
> *To prepare a face to meet the faces that you meet;*
> *There will be time to murder and create . . .*
> *And time yet for a hundred indecisions,*
> *And for a hundred visions and revisions,*
> *Before the taking of a toast and tea.*

T. S. ELIOT

The Significance of Bangladesh

The birth of Bangladesh in 1971 was an event of historic importance if ever there was one. Its importance is not merely political, measured in terms of a new balance of power in South Asia. More than such a consideration, which may turn out to be transient, it is its importance to our understanding of the widespread phenomenon of cultural pluralism, or ethnic difference, and the consequent problem of 'national integration' in old states and new,[1] which needs to be stressed. Laboratory situations are practically non-existent in the experience of social research, so that when one does arise—we cannot set them up—the opportunity must be seized and its implications examined to improve our historical and theoretical understandings of the concerned social processes. In what follows, an attempt is made to

This essay (written early in 1973) is reproduced here from *Studies in Asian Social Development* (No. 2), edited by Suren Navlakha, New Delhi: Vikas, 1974. It is a revised and extended version of an earlier paper which appeared in *Developing Economies*, Tokyo, X, 4, 1972, pp. 74–85. I owe thanks to Shernawaz Billimoria for assistance in the location of materials in various libraries, and to Ed Bruner, Clark Cunningham, Hal Gould, Kris Lehman, and Dave Plath for their comments on the first draft of the essay, which was presented at a seminar at the Anthropology Department, the University of Illinois, Urbana, on 17 December 1971.

[1] It is sometimes suggested that cultural pluralism is a problem specific to the 'old societies' of the Third World which have only recently emerged as 'new states.' Whereas this may be broadly true, the phenomenon of ethnic difference is a prominent feature of many so-called advanced nations as well, including the United Kingdom and the United States.

briefly bring out some of the implications of the birth of Bangladesh
as an independent nation for research into the phenomenon of cultural difference within a state. A more detailed study would require
both a fundamental rethinking of conceptual categories current in
the field as well as a re-examination of historical records and ethnographic accounts from new perspectives.

The question that seems to me to be the crucial one is how we
might render sociologically intelligible the choice which the Muslims
of Bengal made in 1971, seemingly rejecting the choice which they
had made a generation ago when they enthusiastically supported the
demand for Pakistan, and helped in a big way to win it in 1947. In
other words, why did these Muslims choose yesterday to give first
place to the bond of religion, grouping themselves with Muslims in
other parts of the Indian sub-continent, and have opted today for their
exclusive cultural identity? Are we to assume that the earlier choice
had been a mistake and, therefore, had to be reversed, implying that
what has been decided now is final and valid? Are Islam and Bengali
culture being treated as 'values' or 'essences', important *per se*, or as
'signs', used for other purposes?

The Advent of Islam

Before an answer to the above question may be given, it appears
relevant to describe who the Muslims of Bengal are and how they are
historically related to Muslim communities in other parts of the sub-
continent.

The Muslim presence in India is generally dated back to the eight
century. The Arabs are said to have had trade relations with Malabar,
on the western coast of India, before the advent of Islam, and when
Arabia became Muslim, Arab settlements in india (and elsewhere)
became so too. A limited political foothold in Sind, further north,
followed soon after. It was only in the eleventh century, however,
that waves of Muslim conquests across India began. And these
had far-reaching political, social, cultural, and economic consequences (see Aziz Ahmad 1964, Qureshi 1962 and Tara Chand
1936).

The conquerors differed in their aims, aptitudes and habits. Thus,
though some of them, such as the first major invader of Indian kingdoms, Mahmud Ghazni, came to conquer and then return, others
stayed on. The presence of immigrants—Arabs, Mongols, Turks,
Iranians, Afghans—inevitably resulted in proselytism, voluntary as
well as forced. Percival Spear (1967: 30–50) points out that there

were conversions of individuals and of groups (for example, castes, clans) and even of large masses of people. Moreover, an interesting and significant geographical pattern of distribution of Muslim communities seems to have developed. The immigrants were prominent in and near the areas of original entry but were increasingly outnumbered by converts in remoter areas. (Some exceptions to the general pattern, such as the Kashmir Valley, may be mentioned, but the relative inaccessibility of this area may well be equated with spatial remoteness. See Chapter 9.)

Among areas of mass conversion East Bengal is particularly notable. By the time Muslim missionaries and kings arrived here, in the thirteenth and fourteenth centuries, the area had already seen the displacement of a Buddhist socio-political order by the Brahman Sena kings who brought the caste system with them. The local people must have found the new social order constrictive. Conversion to Islam must have, therefore, been welcomed by them. But a complete break with the past does not seem to have occurred. 'They also carried their customs with them, so that it could be said that the Islamization of India (so far as it went) also involved the Hinduization of Indian Islam' (Spear 1967: 34).

In retaining their customs, many Muslims also retained their former low social status. 'How many?' and 'How low?' are historical questions for which there are no straight, doubt-free answers. The manner in which they have been answered is, in fact, of great interest to our understanding of the problem of cultural difference in Bengal.

The state of general opinion on this issue about a hundred years ago was recorded by J. C. Lyall when he wrote that, while the offspring of conquerors 'count(ed) perhaps their hundreds', the majority of Muslims were descended from low caste converts, drawn particularly from rural areas. Upper caste Hindus of 'high culture' had obviously resisted conversion. 'The Hindu element of the population, there-fore . . . represents a higher social stratum, the Muhammadan element a lower one' (see Seal 1971: 301). Similarly, W. W. Hunter (1885), writing about the same time as Lyall, noted that wherever the Muslims formed the bulk of the population in Bengal, they were the cultivating classes, while the upper and mercantile classes were Hindus (see Seal 1971: 301).

There seem to have emerged at least three kinds of reaction to the above situation. The most significant of these was the effort to purify the Bengali version of the Muslim way of life by purging it of Hindu elements. This, as Hunter noted, widened the gulf between Hindus and Muslims. In the early nineteenth century, a sect knowns as the Faraizis, led by one Sharaitullah and his son Dudhu Miyan, spearheaded the movement for a return to Islam in its pristine purity, free from Hindu contamination. Among their followers, the peasantry were prominent. Conflicts with landlords and money-lenders, who were mainly Hindus, ensued. Thus 'the movement to resist the exactions of the latter took on a communal tone and brought Muslims into conflict with the government' (Seal 1971: 310 n2).

The second and third reactions represent the response of Muslim intellectuals and belong to two different periods. In the first place we find an effort being made to show that conversions had been peaceful and had drawn people almost equally from lower and higher castes. M. A. Rahim (1963: 68) estimates that 'the Bengali Muslim population was formed of about 30 per cent converts from the upper class non-Muslims (Buddhists and Hindus) and 35 per cent converts from the lower strata of the Hindu society'. He also cites Hindu authors and other sources to conclude that, between the thirteenth and sixteenth centuries, Bengali Muslims regulated their life in accordance with the tenets of Islam (ibid.: 271). More relevant than such efforts to estimate proportions and establish an earlier period of pure Islamic living, perhaps, is the fact that Hindu society in Bengal was itself less severely caste ridden and had evolved a simplified version of Hinduism called *Sahajiya* (see Mukherjee 1972: 143).

The third reaction, which is also more recent, stresses the distinctiveness of Bengali culture, of the Bengali synthesis of Hindu and Muslim ways of life supported by economic interdependence, at least in the earlier days. Thus, A. M. Khan (1960: 21–2) complains:

> The whole thesis about the Bengali Muslims centred round two alternatives: either they were low caste Hindus converted to Islam or they were immigrants.... The third and possibly the more correct assessment, *viz.*, that they were essentially neither but a distinct cultural entity, *could never occur to any one.* Bengali soil and Bengali blood are admittedly of innumerable origins but they are distinct identities in themselves. History of the growth and development also made the Bengali culture a distinct culture and the people a distinct people.... *So long as the traces of peculiar origin are preserved the immigrants will remain alien residents in Bengal rather than* become people of Bengal (quoted in Mukherjee 1972: 145, emphasis added).

The foregoing, written more than a decade before the birth of

Bangladesh, is a most important statement to which I will return below. Suffice it to point out here that it represents the turning away of the Muslim Bengali intellectual from the ideology on which Pakistan had been built.

Roots of Muslim Separatism

Wherever they lived in India, and whatever their ethnic status, Indian Muslims were equally under the protection of the Muslim state from 711 AD, when Sindh was incorporated in the Umayyad Caliphate, until the beginning of the nineteenth century. In 1803 a theologian, Shah Abdul Aziz, formally acknowledged that such protection had ceased. The rather rapid decline of the Mughal Empire, the rise of non-Muslim (Hindu and Sikh) kingdoms, and finally the emergence of the British as an imperial power in India, caused much distress among the new leaders of Muslim communities in north and east India. These leaders were theologians. They exhorted Muslims to purify their lives and at the same time sought to re-establish Muslim political authority. Sharaitullah and Dudhu Miyan in Bengal have already been mentioned. They not only tried to expunge the way of life of Muslims of Bengal of its Hindu excrescences, but also defied Hindu landlords and their protector, the East India Company, by rising in revolt. In north India Shah Waliullah led a similar but much more powerful movement. He helped in shaping the alliance between Ahmad Shah Abdali, the king of Afghanistan, and an Indian Muslim chief, Najibu-l-Daulah of the Rohillas, whom he invited to wage 'holy war' (*jihād*) against Hindus. It was his son, Abdul Aziz, who made the 1803 declaration about the end of the Muslim state mentioned above. Later, Sayyid Ahmad Barelvi, a follower of Abdul Aziz, strongly denounced borrowing from the Hindu way of life by Muslims and other kinds of deviation from the pure faith. He finally went to war against the Sikhs and temporarily occupied some territory in the north-west of the Sikh kingdom. The north and east Indian movements for the restoration of Islamic purity and Muslim power were originally independent of one another, but became linked later in the time of Barelvi and Dudhu Miyan. The ideology underlying them was that the purity of Islam could not be guaranteed except in an independent Muslim state (see Aziz Ahmad 1964: 201–17; Qureshi 1962: 193–211; Smith 1962: 39–51).

It would be historically misleading to maintain that Waliullah and Sharaitullah were the founders of Muslim separatism in India. The perception of a distinctive Muslim identity had existed from the very beginning because of essential differences between the Hindu and Muslim ways of life. The many varieties of syncretism in medieval and modern India have failed, or at best, remained incomplete.[2] It would be legitimate to claim, however, that these movements not only anticipated the emergence of Pakistan, with its two 'wings' in the north-west and the east of the sub-continent of India, but also provided its principal ideological basis.

It was economic deprivation that added a sharp edge to Muslim separatism in the nineteenth century. This happened in Bengal, where more than half of the Indian Muslims lived, earlier than in north India. Dudhu Miyan's uprising was a peasant revolt. The Permanent Settlement of Bengal had resulted in the expropriation of Muslim landlords and the impoverishment of Muslim peasantry. By the end of the century most of the land in Bengal had come under Hindu ownership. The replacement of Persian by English in 1835 resulted in the Muslims being edged out of the administrative and judicial services and also the professions. A National Mohammedan Association was formed in 1878 in Calcutta with the purpose of improving the condition of Muslims through the help of the government, and not by fighting it. It was thus that the demand for separate Muslim representation came to be made in the Bengal Legislative Council. The argument was simple: Hindu and Muslim interests were not identical because their socio-economic conditions were not (see Seal 1971: 31).

Muslim leaders in north India took up a similar stand on the exclusiveness of interests, but the conditions there were the opposite of those in Bengal. According to Seal, in the North-Western Provinces and Oudh 'the [Muslim] community was a minority of some 13 per cent, but as a whole it was more influential, more prosperous and better educated than its co-religionists in any other province of British India' (1971: 303). Moreover, it has been pointed out that, from the nineteenth century onwards, north Indian Muslim leadership consistently demanded such favours as would not only increase their political effectiveness, but also help them retain their existing privileged position in the larger society (see Brass 1970: 14).

[2] For a most illuminating discussion on this point see Louis Dumont (1964b: 30–70). In a later publication, the same author sums up the position succinctly: 'Hindus and Muslims form two distinct societies from the point of view of ultimate values' (Dumont 1970a: 211). On the complicated relationship of ideological difference with Hindu–Muslim contacts at the empirical level, see Chapter 9.

A major development in Bengal was its partition in 1905, which the government defended on grounds of administrative convenience. Its critics—the nationalists—complained that it was intended to divide Indians so that the British may continue to rule India. Muslims generally 'welcomed the measure as their chance to escape from Bengali bhadralok (Hindu gentry) domination' (Broomfield 1968: 31); their position did improve in some respects as a result of it. Muslim separatism in Bengal was thus much strengthened by the partition of the province; its reunification in 1912 reinforced rather than curbed this separatism (McLane 1966: 221–37; see also Broomfield ibid.: 40, 44).[3] It has been asserted by some observers that there was direct connection between the partition of Bengal and the founding of the Muslim League—the political organization which ultimately formulated the demand for Pakistan—in 1906 at Dacca under the leadership of, among others, Salimullah, the Nawab of Dacca (see Wasti 1964: 59–88).

Political and economic considerations received renewed and forceful ideological support from the philosopher-poet Muhammad Iqbal, who belonged to the north-western province of Punjab. After an early phase of intense nationalistic fervour, during which he wrote the famous patriotic song *sāre jahān se achhā Hindustān hamārā* (Our India, the best of all lands), he gradually came to stress that state and society are inseparable in the teaching of Islam, and that Indian Muslims were primarily the inheritors of a universal Islamic culture. He announced in his presidential address to the Muslim League in 1930 that 'the formation of a consolidated North-West Indian Muslim State appears to me to be the final destiny of the Muslims, at least of North-West India' (see Aziz Ahmad 1964: 273–4). Bengal, it will be noticed, found no place in Iqbal's vision of a Muslim state in the subcontinent. Nor did it in the name of Pakistan, suggested by a group of Muslim Indian students of Cambridge in 1933. 'This name . . . was mnemonically formed from the name of Muslim majority areas of the north-west: Punjab, Afghania (North-West Frontier), Kashmir, Sind, and Baluchistan' (ibid.: 275).[4]

From the point of view of the Muslims of Bengal everything was patently wrong with such a turn of events. They were the single

---

[3] As for the attitude of Bengali Hindus, a very perceptive observer recalls: 'It was from the end of 1906 that we became conscious of a new kind of hatred for the Muslims, which sprang out of the present and showed signs of poisoning our personal relations with our Muslim neighbours and school fellows' (Chaudhuri 1951: 229).

[4] Later these enthusiasts called for three Muslim states: Pakistan, Hyderabad and, in the east, Bang-e-Islam.

largest category of Indian Muslims, and accounted for over half of all Bengalis. It is they who had led the vanguard of modern Muslim separatism in the country (see Broomfield 1968: 238). The Muslim League had been born on their soil. Reorganization of administrative boundaries on the basis of what was in effect—official explanations to the contrary notwithstanding—the communal principle had been tried in their province with beneficial results for the Muslims. A Muslim middle class had grown up in Bengal since the early years of the present century, helped by special facilities in the fields of political representation, education and employment afforded by the government, and by emerging or fructifying economic forces. This middle class now found itself caught between the persistent threat of Hindu domination within their own province on the one hand and the indifference of the Muslims of north and north-western India on the other.[5] They once again made the bid to outdo other Muslims in their demand for the division of India. The Muslim League met for its annual session in 1940 at Lahore and adopted its historic resolution demanding independent Muslim *states* in north-western and eastern India. This resolution, it should be noted, was moved by A. K. Fazlul Huq, one of the outstanding leaders of the Muslims of Bengal. During the next half-a-dozen years, the political estrangement of the Muslims from the Hindus of Bengal was complete, and they came to look upon themselves primarily as Muslims, bound to other Muslims of India by a common destiny. In 1946 the Muslim League swept the Muslim polls in Bengal, winning 116 out of 119 seats reserved for the community. Later that year, it was another prominent Muslim leader of Bengal, H. S. Suhrawardy—the premier of the province—who moved the resolution demanding the

[5] Mukherjee (1972: 151, 153), writes: 'The Hindu middle class... was solidly entrenched in Bengal's economy. The corresponding Muslim interest could not compete with it, even though it held political power since 1937.... In the circumstances, the Bengali Muslim middle class envisaged a quicker and easier way for furthering its interest, by responding to the call of the All-India Muslim League which was steadily gaining strength with its demand for a Muslim homeland'. Similarly, Broomfield (1968: 326–7) observes: 'It is not difficult... to understand the Bengali Muslim politicians' distrust of the Congress. The domination of the nationalist organization in Bengal by Hindu bhadralok, their equivocation over liberal, secularist principles, and, from the time of partition [of 1905], their recurrent appeals to Hindu symbolism, all served to convince the Muslims that Congress rule would mean Hindu rule'. Richard D. Lambert adds: 'The term *Bhadralok* (gentry) ordinarily referred to Hindus only.... [At least] the top layer of [landowners] was Hindu—out of 2,237 large [landholders'] Constituency at the time of Partition [of 1947], only 358 were Muslims. Eighty out of 89 estates with an annual income of over Rs 100,000 and 122 out of 137 estates earning between Rs 50,000 and Rs 100,000 annually were owned by Hindus' (1959: 52).

formation of Pakistan at a convention of Muslim League legislators held in Delhi.[6] The demand was accepted by all concerned parties within the year, after much intervening violence in Bengal and elsewhere. India and Pakistan came into existence as independent states on 15 August 1947. The sub-continent of India had been divided on the basis of religious difference beween the two major communities, the Hindus and the Muslims.[7]

Bengali Muslims or Muslim Bengalis?

Each of the two successor states, Pakistan and India, was multi-ethnic in composition. The Muslim League had won Pakistan by simplifying this situation, maintaining that there were just two major 'nations' in India, the Muslims and the Hindus. The Indian National Congress, which unsuccessfully opposed partition of the country, altogether denied the relevance of ethnic difference to the question of national independence. The Muslims of Bengal had chosen to ignore their racial, linguistic, and cultural distinctiveness[8] and to identify themselves with the other Muslim communities of India, because it suited their economic and political interests to do so. It is clear that

[6] The resolution demanded, *inter alia*, 'that zones comprising Bengal and Assam in the north-east and Punjab, North-West Frontier Province, Sind and Baluchistan in the north-west of India, namely Pakistan zones, where the Muslims are in a dominant majority, to be constituted into a sovereign independent state and that an unequivocal undertaking to be given to implement the establishment of Pakistan without delay' (see Mankekar 1971: 48).

The figures regarding the 1946 elections have been taken from the same source. (ibid.: 47).

The 1946 resolution calling for the formation of a single state was a reversal of the 1940 demand for Muslim states. Aziz Ahmad (1964: 275) explains: 'Despite the reference . . . the possibility of the creation of a plurality of Muslim states, the unanimous comments of the Muslim League leaders made it clear that the resolution actually envisaged the creation of a single Muslim state, embracing both zones, north-western as well as eastern.'

The point that I wish to stress here is that Bengali Muslims played a prominent role in shaping the events which ultimately resulted in the formation of the state of Pakistan in 1947. Suffice it to add, as late as 1968, Sheikh Mujibur Rahman himself stated before the tribunal which was trying him on the charge of treason: 'Ever since my school days, I had ceaselessly worked for the achievement of Pakistan and was a very active member of the Muslim League organization in pre-Independence India and Bengal and worked for the realization of Pakistan even at the cost of my studies' (see Dasgupta 1971: 78).

[7] Several hundred princely states also became independent after what was described as the lapse of British paramountcy in India. It was expected, however, that these states would accede to one or the other of the two successor states of Pakistan and India.

[8] For a brief description of internal diversities in Pakistan before the break-up of 1971, see Madan 1968b: 82–3. See also Qureshi 1957: 1–16.

religion was being used by them as an integrative device to cover ethnic differences. In other words, religion was being employed as a 'sign', or a 'mask', as it were, to safeguard and promote political and economic interests. Herein lay a serious flaw in the edifice of Pakistan. This is, of course, a retrospective judgement. It would be misleading to suggest that the Muslims of Bengal were deliberately indulging in a kind of 'mask play': their involvement in the events of the day was too deep to permit of such a differentiation between 'essence' and 'sign'. It was the kind of situation in which the mask came to fit the face.[9] It is imperative, however, that we make this distinction in our analysis so as to reveal the underlying contradiction.

Though both were multi-ethnic states, there were two crucial differences between Pakistan and India. First, Pakistan lacked territorial integrity, about 1,900 kilometres of Indian territory separating its two wings. Second, whereas no single ethnic category was numerically or politically dominant in India, Bengalis accounted for more than half of Pakistan's population. The political and administrative centre of the latter country was located in its western wing, however. Economically also, West Pakistan was in a somewhat dominant position, though not decisively so (see Sengupta 1971). West Pakistan itself was more like India, being constituted of major ethnic categories, namely, Pukhtuns, Baluchis, Sindhis, and Punjabis. Each one of these ethnic categories has distinctive racial, linguistic, and cultural affinities. East Pakistan, however, was characterized by overwhelming cultural homogeneity, about 85 per cent of its people being Muslim Bengalis.[10]

Pakistan was thus a 'multi-national', or 'non-national', state, composed of several societies within one political system. This characterization is at variance with the proclaimed ideology of the Muslim League which secured a homeland for Indian Muslims (or at least for some of them, as 45 million Muslims, out of a total of 102 million, were left behind in India at the time of partition) on the ground that they constituted one nation. It is clear that if the fact of

[9] Cf.: 'Words and images are like shells, no less integral parts of nature than are the substances they cover, but better addressed to the eye and more open to observation. I would not say that substance exists for the sake of appearance, or faces for the sake of masks . . . nothing arises in nature for the sake of anything else; all these phases and products are involved equally in the round of existence' (Santayana 1922: 131–2).

[10] Hindus, Buddhists and Christians accounted for about 11 million out of East Pakistan's 75 million people in 1971. There were also about two million Biharis among the Muslims, who had migrated there at the time of partition in 1947. They were culturally distinct from the Bengalis and have remained so.

cultural pluralism in Pakistan had been adequately recognized after partition, the advisability of adopting a policy of 'equivalent integration' between the Bengalis and non-Bengalis, and among the four ethnic categories of West Pakistan, would have seemed imperative.[11] Far from recognizing the reality of cultural pluralism, efforts were made, in fact, to suppress it. Consequently, certain communities became politically and economically stronger, and also culturally arrogant at the cost of others. Cultural pluralism hardened into 'structural pluralism', and the treatment of Bengalis within the politico-economic framework became blatantly 'differential'[12] and disadvantageous to them. It did not take long for the Muslims of Bengal to realize that the costs of the choice they had made—the price of the mask they had chosen to wear—had been very heavy.

During the years immediately following the creation of Pakistan, Bengali Muslims resorted to the old practice (mentioned earlier in this chapter) of making themselves better Muslims. Arabicization of Bengali language and literature was much in evidence, as was a large increase in the numbers of those who could claim proficiency in Arabic and in Urdu (see Mukherjee 1972: 159–60). However, as soon as Urdu emerged as a tool of cultural domination by the western wing, accompanied by the spectre of politico-economic victimization, the Muslims of Bengal reacted sharply to the threat to their ethnic identity. Territorial integrity and total cultural identity (as against partial religious identity), the legitimacy of which had earlier been driven underground by them, soon began to be reasserted.

In March 1948, less than a year after the formation of Pakistan, the founder, M. A. Jinnah, himself announced, in the course of a convocation address to the Dacca University, that Urdu would have to be the sole *lingua franca* of the country. This caused much

[11] The terminology has been taken from Smith (1971: 433–40). See particularly on p. 435: '[there are] three alternative bases of societal organization and unity, namely, the modes of differential, equivalent, or uniform incorporation. By the first the society is constituted as an order of structurally unequal and exclusive corporate sections, that is, as an explicitly plural regime. By the second, it is constituted as a consociation of complementary or equivalent, but mutually exclusive, corporate divisions, membership in one of which is prerequisite for citizenship in the wider unit . . . . But, for "a more perfect union" than consociation, uniformity in the units and conditions of incorporation is essential . . .'. I do not entirely share Smith's scepticism with regard to equivalent incorporation; in fact, it seems to me to be ideally suited to the situation obtaining in South Asia.
[12] The terminology used continues to be borrowed from Smith: 'Structural pluralism consists . . . in the differential incorporation of specified collectivities within a given society and corresponds with this in its form, scope and particulars. It institutes or presupposes social and cultural pluralism together . . .' (ibid.: 440).

resentment (see Mankekar 1971: 35ff.). [13] Urdu written in the Persian script was the product of Muslim rule; it had become exclusively associated with Muslims, as separatist tendencies gained ascendance, only from the late nineteenth century onwards. [14] Bengali, written in a Nagri script, similar to that of Sanskrit, was, by contrast, an ancient language rooted in the soil of Bengal, and had a rich body of literature. The Muslims of Bengal had contributed to its shaping over the centuries and they felt a deep sense of identification with it. [15] Beginning in February 1952, and by 1954, Bengalis had successfully agitated and won recognition for their language as one of the two state languages of Pakistan. The resentment against alleged West Pakistani domination was proclaimed at the polls that year when a united front of Bengali political parties led by A. K. Fazlul Huq, the mover of the 1940 Lahore resolution, contested provincial assembly elections against candidates put up by the Muslim League, the political organization that had won Pakistan. The League's rout was decisive: it won only nine out of 310 seats and only 2·5 per cent of the votes cast (see Roy 1968: 96–7). Fazlul Huq became the premier of the province. He visited Calcutta in West Bengal (India) and spoke there of building bridges between the two Bengals. Back home, he continued to speak of provincial autonomy and was dismissed on 30 May on charges of treason. The verdict of the electrorate was thus nullified by the central government (see *ibid.*: 98–102). [16]

The relationship between the two wings of Pakistan never again was cordial. As a Muslim Bengali scholar put it in 1967: 'Since Independence, Pakistan had been dominated by the bureaucracy and the military, both of which have in turn been dominated by non-Bengalis' (Rashiduzzman 1967 quoted in Franda 1971: 264). Pakistan

[13] It may be of interest to add here that, according to the 1951 census (quoted by Dasgupta 1971: 21), 54·6 per cent of the people of Pakistan returned Bengali as their mother tongue, 28·4 per cent Punjabi, 7·2 per cent Urdu, 7·1 per cent Pushto, 5·8 per cent Sindhi, and 1·8 per cent English.

[14] For an account of the rivalry between Hindi and Urdu, and its political ramifications, see Das Gupta (1970).

[15] According to some Muslim writers, the Muslim contribution to the development of Bengali language and literature was more significant and substantial than that of the Hindus. Such claims obviously are an effort to belittle the role of Hindus in the formation of Bengali culture. We will see below how drastically the position has changed, eliminating the necessity of such exaggeration of Muslim contributions to Bengali literature. Also see Dasgupta (1971: 11–12): 'The finest example of the liberal religious imagination of the Bengali Muslims is the Baul poetry, a body of devotional songs which represent . . . a synthesis of vedantism and sufism'.

[16] Before and after the partition in 1947 several Bengali leaders continued to talk of united Bengal. H. S. Suhrawardy was said to be sympathetic to the idea at one time. See Bose 1968.

came under the rule of the military in 1958. During the next 15 years East Pakistan was treated as a domestic colony by the central government located in the western wing. It is unnecessary here to give the details of this exploitation as these have been widely discussed and are well known.[17]

The falling apart of Bengali Pakistanis from non-Bengalis found expression in mutual stereotypes which were freely bandied about and reported in the press. An excellent specimen of the cultural arrogance of the leaders from West Pakistan is the following characterization of the peoples of Pakistan by the former President, Mohammad Ayub Khan:

> The people of Pakistan consist of a variety of races each with its own historical background and culture. East Bengalis, who constitute the bulk of the population, probably belong to the very original Indian races. It would be no exaggeration to say that up to the creation of Pakistan, they had not known any real freedom or sovereignty. They have been in turn ruled either by the caste Hindus, Moghuls, Pathans, or the British. In addition, they have been and still are under considerable Hindu cultural and linguistic influence. As such they have all the inhibitions of down-trodden races and have not yet found it possible to adjust psychologically to the requirements of the new-born freedom. Their popular complexes, exclusiveness, suspicion and a sort of defensive aggressiveness probably emerge from this historical background . . . .
>
> The population in West Pakistan, on the other hand, is probably the greatest mixture of races found anywhere in the world. Lying on the gateways to the Indian sub-continent, it was inevitable that each successive conquering race should have left its traces here. Consequently, this forced mixture of races has brought about fusion of ideas, outlook and culture, despite the linguistic variety that obtained (1967: 187).

Elsewhere in the same book, the author mentions the Bengalis' grouse against the 'patronizing' attitude of 'exclusive' and 'aggressive' West Pakistani civil servants, only to brush it aside. 'It might well be that the mannerisms of the West Pakistani irritated the East Pakistani. . . . I told an East Pakistani friend once, "You have such sweet music. I wish to God you were half as sweet yourself"' (ibid.: 27). That Ayub Khan should have thought it wise to reproduce this comment in his autobiography, while still the President of Pakistan, is testimony to the cultural schism that afflicted the state of Pakistan. The Bengali attitude was summed up thus in 1971:

[17] See Mukherjee 1972: Table 7, 156–9, which sums up a considerable body of materials on the comparative socio-economic characteristics of the two wings of Pakistan.

The hatred towards the Bengali was total: his culture was belittled, his efficiency suspected and even his eating habits and his way of life were held in the greatest contempt. As a result of all these factors, there developed, over the painful years, seething hatred towards the West Pakistani.... The revolution in Bangladesh therefore is not merely against exploitation by West Pakistan—it is to preserve our race, our language, our culture that we are fighting. For once and for all, we wish to break the myth created by the British, and prolonged by West Pakistanis, that Bengalis, in some inexplicable way, are 'inferior', and prove to all, that the awakened Bengali is a viable force to contend with.[18]

When Pakistan held its first nation-wide elections, late in 1970, East Pakistani Muslims had come a long hard way: they had redefined their ethnic identity; they had decided to discard their earlier mask and wear a new one. They went to the polls as Muslim *Bengalis* rather than as Bengali *Muslims*. The political platform of the Awami League Party of Sheikh Mujibur Rahman, demanding a substantial degree of autonomy, was overwhelmingly endorsed.[19] This created an impasse between the two wings of the country which the central government, deeply identified with West Pakistan, tried to resolve by military force. The massiveness and brutality of this force ensured the independence of East Bengal, which finally became a fact in December 1971. Indian military intervention hastened the process, but it was the Bengalis themselves who had won their freedom.

Bangladesh is based on a political ideology very different from that of the old Pakistan. This ideology is nationalism and secularism. Iqbal, upholding the banner of pan-Islamism, had maintained that for a true Muslim nationalism was a heresy and 'native land' (*wattan*) a 'false god'.[20] Jinnah's successors had proclaimed Pakistan an Islamic

[18] Anonymous 'observer' in a bulletin issued by the Bangladesh mission in New Delhi, quoted in Mankekar (1971: 34). See also Michener (1972: 43): '... invariably, when a West Pakistani spoke of his Bengali fellow national, he did so with the deepest scorn. Indeed, a Punjabi rarely spoke of an Indian Hindu with the contempt he reserved for his fellow Bengali Muslim. "Filthy peasants" was a common description. "Impossible black monkeys" I heard once. If the Bengali had tried to better himself by study he was dismissed as a "book-wallah". If by some miracle he landed a job with the government he was known as an "ink-stained babu" (clerk).'

[19] The East Pakistan Awami League won 160 of the 162 national assembly seats and 288 of the 300 provincial assembly seats. The percentage of votes polled was 72·6 per cent and 75·5 per cent respectively in the national and provincial elections. See Franda 1971: 270. For the events that followed, see Ayoob and Subrahmanyam 1972.

[20] Iqbal, as stated earlier, began with a deep fervour for nationalism. A pan-Islamist phase followed, with the attendant denigration of nationalism. Finally, there emerged a compromise between these two positions, when he devoted himself to propagating the idea of a homeland for Indian Muslims. Still later, he turned to democratic socialism and revolution. See Malik 1971 and Ahmad 1967.

state. Bangladesh is a nation state characterized by territorial integrity and it has declared itself secular. Muslim Bengalis have learned, the hard way perhaps, to take a new look at their culture. The reference group no longer consists of Muslims somewhere in the west, and purification of the Bengali way of life is no more a meaningful slogan. Bengali culture is the over-arching framework within which all citizens of Bangladesh must find their place. Differences of religion, which were given heightened salience in the years before the establishment of Pakistan, have now been accorded a secondary place.[21]

When, after the military crackdown of March 1971, Bangladesh was proclaimed an independent state, the search for a national anthem dramatized the relationship between the different religious communities of the new country. The choice was an early but popular Tagore song, *Amar sonar Bangla, ami tomai bhalo bashi* (My golden Bengal, I love you). Rabindranath Tagore was the greatest figure in Bengali music and literature in the first half of the present century. He had been born in a Hindu (Brahmo) family and had died 33 years ago in 1941, but these latter were irrelevant facts.[22] The fact that India's national anthem, chosen in 1947, also was a famous Tagore song, seemed to signify no more than that Muslims and Hindus, Bangladesh and India, did not have to subsist on relations of mutual exclusion and cultural difference.

Some statements by Bangladesh intellectuals during the difficult days late in 1971, emphasizing the new cultural relationship between Hindu and Muslim Bengalis, verge almost on the extravagant. Two examples may be cited:

> We Bengali Muslims always had considerable respect for Hindus because of their talent, skill and scholarship. We are great fans of them in the field of literature, cinema, theatre, music, education, etc. . . . We are very fond of their composers, singers and performers. We Muslims appreciate the artistic talent and other excellent qualities of Hindu Bengalis and we do not need to feel ashamed of it. [The author then refers to the excellent craftsmanship of Bengali Hindu goldsmiths, potters, weavers, and the

[21] '. . . opinion surveys of students of Dacca University, taken in the sixties, revealed that there was no longer great regard for the Islamic bond of unity. A breaking away from Islam among educated youth is acknowledged by many observers of the Pakistan scene', wrote John Owen (1968), quoted in Mankekar 1971: 157.

[22] See Kripalani 1961. As is well known, Bengalis are a people with rich traditions of song and music. How important these are even in political life is borne out by, for instance, Nirad Chaudhuri's statement (1951: 221) that during the early years of this century, nationalistic fervour in Bengal seemed almost totally dependent upon patriotic songs. Incidentally, Chaudhuri grew up in what is now Bangladesh.

skill of sweetmeat makers.] In this connexion I would like to mention about a village some ten miles away from Dacca which is famous for its sweetmeat industry. It is a typical Hindu village where the people, keeping intact their traditional art of making sweets, were doing a flourishing business.... I am afraid this village is destroyed now and the people might have been killed [by West Pakistani soldiers (Shahab-ud-Din 1971)].

Pakistan is the "angry orphan" in Asia. It neither knows nor recognizes its parents. What is it actually? Indian? Persian? Arab? Central Asian? Who knows? The people of Bangladesh, on the other hand, know that they are first and foremost Bengalis and in a broader sense they are Indians too—and they are not ashamed to say so. *They do not need to deny their birth on the Indian subcontinent, conceal their genuine ethnic roots and mask their real identity with a pseudo-religious coating* . . . . (Shahab-ud-Din 1972, emphasis added).

What is most noteworthy about the above statements, and the one by Abdul Majeed Khan, quoted earlier (see p. 205), is that they bring out clearly the dynamic character of ethnic identity. Khan, it will be noted, complains that in earlier times it 'could never occur to any one' to define the Muslims of Bengal in terms of Bengali culture. Shahab-ud-Din does precisely this, because the situation has now changed and calls for identity-redefinition or, as we might say, for a new mask to wear.

The choice that was made by the Muslims of Bengal in 1947 was not wrong or invalid. It seemed the best choice at that time. The grievances of Bengali Muslims against economic exploitation by Hindu landlords and mill-owners found expression through identification with the demand for a Muslim homeland. In Pakistan, however, the Bengali found not only that his economic exploitation was becoming worse but also that he was being denied political rights, and even his cultural identity was bing threatened.[23] The bond of common religion turned out to be too narrow a base for nation building and state formation. In the light of the feedback from experience, it became imperative for the Muslims of Bengal to redefine their identity in broad cultural and territorial terms.

[23] Lambert (1959: 51–2) observes: 'The separation of East from West Bengal and its increasing absorption into the greater Pakistan society might have gone smoothly enough had it not been for several factors, some inherited from the past and some special features of the current situation. Most important was the fact that a set of attitudes held by East Bengal Muslims and previously directed at the Calcutta and East Bengali Hindus were now directed towards the *paschimas* (people from West Pakistan). It is clear that the demand for the creation of Pakistan drew much of its strength from the "underdog" feelings of the Muslims in pre-Independence India. . . .'

V. Conclusion

The purpose of this essay was stated at the very outset to be an attempt to bring out some of the implications of the birth of Bangladesh as an independent nation for research into the phenomenon of cultural difference within a multi-ethnic state. The materials examined have been historical, but the intention has not been to write a historical interpretation of the concerned events. I have rather attempted to highlight the fact that the Muslims of Bengal have shifted the emphasis from some elements in their ethnic identity to others in the course of a generation. The reasons for each of these two choices have been, it seems to me, the overriding need which they have felt to safeguard their interests, including the preservation of their identity *vis-à-vis* other groups, first in undivided Bengal and then in Pakistan. The strategy employed has been the same on both occasions: withdrawal from the larger institutional framework. In this respect they have acted, I suggest, as cultural categories always will at least attempt to act in a multi-ethnic state, if it operates, intentionally or by default, in terms of a policy of differential integration.

The key to the situation would seem to be the pursuit of economic advantage and political power. Here we must recall that, quite some time ago, Furnivall had summed up such a situation in his notion of plural society. He saw such a society as being constituted of peoples who 'mix but do not combine. Each group holds by its own religion, its own culture and language, its own ideas and ways. As individuals they meet, *but only in the market place*, in buying and selling' (1948: 304).[24] Furnivall was concerned with the colonial situation, but the insights his analysis affords still help to illumine the problems faced by the so-called 'new nations'. Thus, it is obvious that if the meeting in the market place consistently favours one group of people at the cost of another, and the state seems to connive over this, the deprived people, if concentrated in a particular area, are likely to activate nationalism—which sums up economic and political aspirations as well as cultural pride—within the state. This is what happened in Pakistan. And it could happen anywhere else, given a similar overall situation.

To generalize, one may say, that in multi-ethnic societies, each ethnic category will seek to pursue political power and economic

[24] Earlier, Furnivall had given his oft-quoted definition of the plural society as one 'in which two or more groups live side by side but separately, within the same political unit' (1945: 167).

advantage, by itself or in association with other chosen people. In the context of such dynamic interaction, what is of crucial importance is, as Barth (1970) so very rightly emphasizes, the effort at boundary maintenance, and not the content of ethnicity at any particular time. To be able to effectively manage the task of boundary maintenance, it is of prime importance that people retain the freedom to choose, reject, and choose anew the dimension of their total identity that they will most emphasize. There is no inalienable association between an ethnic category and any particular element in its identity, because such lack of flexibility might be fatal to its political aspirations and economic interests. A process of feedback enables people (or their leaders) to evaluate past choices and redefine identity if that is felt necessary. Culture is treated as a repertoire of masks, a pool of signs and symbols, as it were, from which to choose. The availability of alternatives and pragmatic choice-making are of critical importance.[25]

If the foregoing analysis is valid, it follows that any attempt to see the events of 1971 as a 'rectification' of an 'error' committed in 1947 is misleading. It is not as if the appeal of religion has been banished for ever, with the Bengali Muslim society moving along a straight path of secular development. It is not at all unlikely that in the years to come, the salience of religion will re-emerge among the Muslims of Bengal—though in a changed context—for Bangladesh exists independently of the *Indian state of West Bengal because it is predominantly Muslim*. It is also likely that conscious efforts will be made to widen the cultural and linguistic distance between Bangladesh and Indian Bengal. Further, it is not unlikely that Bangladesh will seek to move closer to Malaysia and Indonesia in some kind of a South-East Asian brotherhood of Muslim countries. This could happen without prejudice to the domestic policy of secularism; it would be more a response to Bangladesh's evolving relations with India, Pakistan and other countries of the region.

The foregoing discussion, we may conclude, points to the imperative of rethinking such well entrenched notions as 'ethnicity' and 'national integration'. In respect of the former concept, it is obvious that the self-ascription of ethnic groups must receive adequate *attention*

---

[25] 'It is of course perfectly feasible to distinguish between a people's model of their social system and their aggregate pattern of pragmatic behaviour, and indeed quite necessary not to confuse the two. But the fertile problems in social anthropology are concerned with how the two are interconnected, and it does not follow that this is best elucidated by dichotomizing and confronting them as total systems' (Barth 1970: 29).

in sociological studies of cultural difference. This is not, of course, a plea for unqualified *acceptance* of emic categories: the social scientist has to go beyond such formulations. What has to be stressed is that the magisterial dismissal of the ideas that a people have of themselves as 'false consciousness' obviously has proved sterile. Any hiatus that may be perceived here between the traditional aims of sociological and anthropological research and the ideas and doings of peoples must be bridged. The social scientists' categories are, in the first place, for the description of the specific and the concrete. Understanding is expected to result from complete description. The 'order' that he seeks to portray is, in fact, imposed by him upon the flow and flux of social events. One wants to write the definitive account of a people—be they the Trobriand Islanders, the Pathans or the Bengalis— in terms of objective attributes that are seen by social scientists as being relevant to the purpose at hand. This attitude arises out of the positivistic legacy (hubris?) of sociology and social anthropology. It may have served well in the past in the analysis of certain kinds of situations, but is unable to cope with cultural pluralism in the new states.

The Bengali example demonstrates that an exclusive preoccupation with 'objective' and 'fixed' attributes has to be abandoned. The student must focus on *processes* as well as on *attributes*—above all on the dialectical interplay between them. He must operate with a 'generative' concept of ethnicity. In other words, the most meaningful way of studying cultural difference in society seems to be to study it in history. For this we need appropriate concepts. The shift from ethnic *attributes* to ethnic *boundaries* seems to be a major step in the right direction. This concept enables us to lay down the limits of a cultural category much more precisely than the misleading notion of immutable attributes, for they are not unchanging. What is more, the concept of boundary has the virtue of focusing our attention on unfolding potentialities and opportunities—on the possibilities of becoming—than on the assumed fact of being. This approach clearly offers us a way out of the claustrophobia of traditional social anthropological analysis. As Barth has pointed out:

> . . . most of the cultural matter that at any time is associated with a human population is *not* constrained by this boundary; it can vary, be learnt, and change without any critical relation to the boundary maintenance of the ethnic group. So when one traces the history of an ethnic group through time, one is *not* simultaneously, in the same sense, tracing the history of "a culture": the elements of the present culture of that ethnic group have not

sprung from the particular set that constituted the group's culture at a previous time, whereas the group has a continual organizational existence with boundaries (criteria of membership) that despite modifications have marked off a continuing unit (1970: 38).

It is generally conceded that the reign of functionalism in the social sciences had resulted in an overweening accent on integrated social systems. Consequently, cultural difference had tended to be judged as pathological. The adoption of the 'conflict' model, and other developments in theory and methodology, have already made us aware of short-circuiting of research on pluralism in functionalist anthropology. The recent history of the Muslims of Bengal confirms the importance for anthropology and sociology of the study of situations characterized by various kinds of 'disintegration' and 'breakdown'.

The counterpart of the integrated social system in comparative politics has been the notion of nation-state. Here our thinking has been dominated by the unitarian model of national integration. The view of the political system from the top, which was a natural concomitant of colonial regimes, has survived the disintegration of empires and clouded the thinking of the elites in the successor states. Consequently, a kind of misplaced concreteness has come to be attached to the notion of nation-state, and certain other kinds of identity have come to be labelled as 'primordial' and regarded as being opposed to the growth of civil society and national integration (see e.g. Geertz 1963). Thus, in India, national unity has been considered to be under the persistent attack of fissiparous forces—notably 'casteism', 'linguism,' 'regionalism,' and 'communalism' (see e.g. Harrison 1960).[26] Here, too, rethinking of categories is called for and the notion of national *accommodation* of regional communities has to supplant the rigid concept of national integration: instead of viewing the situation from the top, it has to be looked at from the bottom, that is, from the perspectives of the peoples involved. The segmentary model of national unity should, it seems to me, replace the unitarian model. The 'centre' will then be seen as resting upon fully articulated regional identities rather than upon their suppression. Adherence to the 'centre' by the 'states' or 'provinces' has to be *won* for it cannot be *imposed* from above, particularly within a democratic

[26] For a rebuttal of Harrison's arguments regarding the divisive influence of 'linguism', see Das Gupta 1970.

political set-up.[27] This is the lesson the Muslims of Bangladesh seem
to have given to the 'new states' of South Asia and elsewhere.

POSTSCRIPT

In the two decades since this essay was written, Bangladesh has seen
many political upheavals and changes of policy. Bangladesh specialists,
including Bangladeshis themselves, have provided a running commentary on these events in the form of a large number of books and
articles. As far as I am able to make out, neither the political happenings
nor the scholarly publications have invalidated the analysis presented
in the above essay. In fact, my anticipation that religion would regain
salience in the political arena has been confirmed. The country has not,
however, moved closer to South-East Asia as I thought it would.
Bangladesh remains firmly rooted in South Asia, and I should have
known that this would be so, for my analysis itself had revealed Islam
and Bengali culture as the two crucial elements of Bangladeshi identity,
the latter no less important than the former.

As was noted in the essay, it was out of the dialectic of religious
and ethno-linguistic identities, which had reached their climax in the
years between 1940 and 1971, that the new nation-state of Bangladesh
was born and with it the Bangladeshi identity. Under the leadership
of Sheikh Mujibur Rahman, hailed in 1971 as the 'father' of the new
nation, the country adopted nationalism, democracy, secularism
and socialism as the fundamental principles of state policy. Islam was

[27] This is one of the central arguments of Rajni Kothari's thesis on the nature of
Indian politics: '. . . a country as vast and pluralistic as India can be effectively united
only through a participant and accommodative model of politics. (It is impossible to
rule India from New Delhi.) A concomitant of such a model is the autonomous and
creative role of politics, and its penetration all the way down to the social infrastructure'
(1970: 337).

There are several streams of anthropological literature which would seem to con-
verge on this point. Thus, there is the affirmation, emerging from a critical examination of ethological literature, that 'individual human beings are capable of identifying
with more than one set or type of phenomena (territory, social groups, ideas). For
man, at least, identification is more real and fundamental than territoriality, which is
only one possible outcome of the identification process' (Alland, Jr. 1972: 162). In
India, M. N. Srinivas has for several years now stressed the non-exclusiveness of
primordial and civic identifications. (see Srinivas 1962b: 12–14, 98–111). [I too have
developed a pluralist position in several papers (see particularly Madan 1979 and 1984)].

not included in this supremely important list of ideals. Speaking in the Constituent Assembly in 1972, Sheikh Mujib proclaimed: 'Secularism does not mean absence of religion. . . . Our only objective is that nobody will be allowed to use religion as a political weapon' (quoted in Maniruzzaman 1983: 192).

As Maniruzzaman notes, 'Sheikh Mujib was clearly advocating the negative, non-discriminatory, Indian type of secularism', and adopted 'the policy of equal opportunity of all religions' (ibid.: 192, 193). The fundamentalist Jama't-i-Islami was banned for its collaboration with the central government during the 1969–71 revolution.

Mujib was moving much faster than his people could appreciate, and his critics were quick to take advantage of the situation. His efforts to secularize education were confronted with the results of a survey showing that 75 per cent of the people would like to see religious instruction as part and parcel of general education (ibid.: 195). The country's close ties with India, which were a result of the role the latter played in support of the East Pakistanis in the 'civil war' of 1971, were frowned upon by the critics who portrayed India as a 'Hindu' country. Close ties with the socialist countries were not welcomed either as these were seen as 'godless' regimes. Within two years of the birth of the nation, its founding leadership was under attack for the neglect of Islam. A chasm had opened between Bangladesh society and the state (see Raonaq Jahan 1980).

Mujib tried to correct course. He began to cultivate ties with Middle Eastern (West Asian) countries. He introduced words and phrases in his public speeches which had a religious ring. He even substituted the Persian-Urdu 'Khuda Hafiz!' (God be with you), for the Bengali 'Joy Bangla!' (Hail Bengal or Bangladesh) of the days of the revolution, at the end of his public speeches. But before he could really turn the corner, he along with his family was assassinated on 15 August 1975.

The next regime, under a civilian president, did not last long enough, and General Zia-ur-Rahman took charge of the country a little over a year later, though he assumed the presidency only in 1977. Zia very shrewdly dropped secularism as a principle of state policy and substituted it by 'Absolute Trust and Faith in the Almighty Allah as the basis of all actions' (see Franda 1982: 299). He introduced Islamic teachings into general education and vigorously pursued the newly enacted constitutional directive 'to pursue friendly relations with Islamic countries' (ibid.: 300). He brought Bangladesh into the Islamic Conference. At home, he lifted the ban on Jama't-i-Islami in 1979.

In following this course, the young, politically inexperienced
General showed himself to be a more astute national leader than the
temperamental Sheikh Mujib. Although he talked of encouraging
Islam (the time for recitations from the Quran on the radio was raised to
fifteen minutes, while readings from the scriptures of other religions
were restricted to five minutes which was what Mujib had fixed for all
such programmes), he also tried to maintain a positive and protective attitude towards Hindus (the major religious minority) (see
Franda 1982: 236). More importantly, he laid great emphasis on the
Bangladeshi identity of his people; he did not revert to their Islamic
identity. To that extent he did not break away entirely from the secular
perspectives of Mujib. Zia, too, did not live long enough to see his
policy bear fruit. He was killed in a military coup in 1981.

After another short interlude of civilian rule, General H. M. Ershad
became the sixth President of Bangladesh. Under him the country
experienced a mixture of dictatorship and the semblance of democracy.
Political parties were allowed to function, and their principal goal
was the restoration of democracy. In this setting the fundamentalist
Jama't-i-Islami seemingly acquired new strength. To take the wind
out of the Jama't's sails, Ershad resorted to a number of measures
which had an Islamic appeal. The most important of these was, of
course, the declaration of Islam as the state religion of Bangladesh in
1988. This constituted an abandonment of the principles of nationalism, democracy and secularism that Mujib had espoused.

What is more significant than this development, perhaps, is that
the general elections of 1991, which saw the defeat of Ershad and his
political party, and the victory of Bangladesh Nationalist Party (BNP),
under Begum Khaleda (Zia-ur-Rahman's widow), gave the fundamentalist Jama't-i-Islami, its terror tactics notwithstanding, only
6 per cent of the votes cast. Moreover, an organization was formed
to pursue the issue of due punishment for those who had collaborated
with the Pakistan army in 1971. Under its auspices, a 'people's court'
asked, in March 1992, for the death penalty for Golam Azam, a Jama't
leader. It was clear that most Bangladeshis did not consider Islamic
governance as their first preference, but put greater trust in nationalism
and democracy, which were heavily emphasized in BNP's election
campaign. After assuming power, Begum Khaleda has reverted to
the parliamentary (prime ministerial) form of government as truly
democratic, and has projected the ideal of Bangladeshi nationalism
in the manner of her late husband.

It seems as if the old dichotomy of Bengali *Muslim* or Muslim *Bengali* may now have been transcended. Religion (Islam) has indeed become salient again in Bangladesh, but not at the cost of ethnolinguistic identity (see Raffiuddin Ahmed 1991). The Muslims of Bangladesh, who form 85 per cent of the population, are all Bengali speaking and are not riven by ethnic divisions. They thus present an excellent combination of attributes (one religion, one language, one ethnic stock) for the making of a stable nation–state. What they need, besides more education, better health, and faster economic growth, is the principle of equal opportunity for all citizens, irrespective of religious identity, which Mujib advocated. In Pakistan, Islamic identity has to carry the much heavier burden of half a dozen ethno-linguistic groups competing for economic advantage and political power. In this respect Pakistan is more like India than Bangladesh. Also, in the Pakistani situation, the prospects of a Muslim fundamentalist stronghold over politics are stronger than they have so far proved to be in Bangladesh.

ASIA AND THE MODERN WEST: INDIAN AND JAPANESE RESPONSES TO WESTERNIZATION

11

Magnificent! Magnificent!
No one knows the final word.

FUMON (1302–69)

The Impact of British Rule on India

During the 1950s and 1960s Professor M. N. Srinivas made many seminal contributions to the sociology of India (see Chapter 3). Among the thematic areas in which he stimulated research interest, the process of westernization as a form of social mobility was particularly noteworthy. He first published an essay on this subject in 1956 in *The Far Eastern Quarterly*, exploring the historical linkages between Sanskritization (or endogenous social mobility) and westernization (or exogenous social mobility) (see Srinivas 1962a: 42–62). He then returned to it for a more elaborate statement in his Tagore Lectures at the University of California at Berkeley in 1963 (see Srinivas 1966: 46–88 *et passim*).

Srinivas traced the roots of westernization to India's encounter with the West in the form of British rule, which he considered responsible for laying 'the foundation of a modern state' in the subcontinent and for other 'radical and lasting changes in Indian society':

This essay, written in 1983, is a revised version of a lecture I was privileged to give at the centennial symposium of the Kokugakuin University in Tokyo earlier that year (see Madan 1983a). I am grateful to the University for the invitation and to it as well as to the Japan Foundation for their hospitality. I also owe the warmest thanks to Professors Chie Nakane and Yoshiya Abe for their many acts of kindness.

I am obliged to Professor Savitri Vishwanathan for pointing out some factual errors in the first draft of this essay and to Professor David Plath for his unfailing encouragement and the insights of his own excellent work on Japan. The inadequacies that remain are, of course, my own fault.

The essay is reproduced here from a Festschrift in honour of Professor M. N. Srinivas which has been edited by A. M. Shah and B. S. Baviskar and is being published by Sage Publications India Private Ltd., New Delhi.

'profound, many-sided and fruitful', embracing 'technology, institutions, ideology, values' (ibid.: 47). He further maintained that 'implicit in Westernization are certain value preferences', among which he made particular mention of 'humanitarianism', including in its ambit equalitarianism and secularism (ibid.: 48). The fact that religious beliefs and social customs had now to meet the challenges of 'reason and humanity' emanating from the 'British Western' attack on the traditional culture led to a 'reinterpretation of Hinduism at both ideological and institutional levels' (ibid.: 49, 50). Apart from the good that ensued, however, certain 'pathologies of moderniza-tion' also became manifest, but these were held by Srinivas to be the result of 'partial or disturbed modernization itself' (ibid.: 52). He concluded: 'The Westernization of India produced in Indians an urge to change their traditional society, but in the course of time it came to occupy a secondary place beside the even more powerful, in fact almost elemental, urge to freedom' (ibid.: 87). This urge too was inspired by Western political ideals and quickened, perhaps ironically, by the very same British rule.

In sum, Srinivas's assessment of the processes of westernization in India was largely, and by implication in principle, favourable. In this respect his views reflect the mood of optimism about the future of the so-called modernizing societies that prevailed among India's political leaders and intellectuals during the early years after indepen-dence in 1947. This mood was born of faith in social intervention for the solution of socio-economic problems and encouraged a confi-dent view of the course and outcome of the process of modernization of traditional societies. It would seem that Srinivas did not quite share the ambivalent attitudes of some sections of the intelligentsia towards Westernization, which he wrote, had resulted from pro-longed contact with the West. This ambivalence, he pointed out, was characterized by a curious mixture of 'self-criticism'—even 'self-debasement'—and 'paleocentrism', of 'crude caricaturing of Western life' and 'Xenophilia' (ibid.: 79). It is obvious that Srinivas's own viewpoint not only recorded the existence of this ambivalence but was also itself incorporated in it.

Westernization and the Indian Middle Class

Now, as is well known, many Indian intellectuals have, over the last two hundred years or so, borne evidence in their life and work of this split in consciousness. Rammohan Roy (1772–1883) in Bengal was perhaps the first outstanding intellectual to articulate it: and he has

been generally acclaimed as the first modern Indian. While he thanked
Providence for the blessings which British presence in India seemed
to him to promise in many fields, including administration, education,
and the moral life of the people, he endeavoured at the same time to
evolve a synthesis between diverse cultural heritages—Vedantic,
Islamic, and Christian.

The concern with a Vedantic foundation for the new world-view
he endeavoured to shape remained prominent in the midst of efforts
to broaden and enliven the intellect, and reform and refine the social
order. In a famous letter addressed to Lord Amherst, the British
Governor-General, in 1823, he protested against the establishment
of yet another Sanskrit College, for he wanted Indians to learn the
rational sciences of the West and not be engrossed in Sanskrit grammar
and Indian metaphysics. He favoured westernization, using in his
writings and speeches emotive words such as 'enlightenment',
'amelioration', 'improvement', 'benefit', 'happiness', and so on to
describe its expected results. Above all, he laid great stress on the
superiority of the moral principles in the teachings of Jesus.

This ambivalence, or the desire for synthesis, whichever one pre-
fers to call it, has remained with us ever since. A couple of generations
after Rammohan Roy, Mahadev Govind Ranade (1842–1901) in
Maharashtra gave expression to almost identical sentiments concerning
the providential nature of the good that was part of the dispensation
under British rule. He, however, added: 'We could not break with
the past if we would. We must not break with it if we could' (quoted
in Ganguli 1975: 5).

In the twentieth century no one has given more poignant expression to the ambivalence and the desire for the synthesis we are talking
about than Jawaharlal Nehru (1889–1964). He wrote in his autobiography: 'I have become a queer mixture of the East and the West, out
of place everywhere, at home nowhere. Perhaps my thoughts and
approach to life are more akin to what is called Western than Eastern,
but India clings to me . . . in innumerable ways' (1941: 341). Apropos
of British rule, while he held it responsible for the political subjugation
and the economic exploitation of India, and castigated the British
for obstructing social change except when it suited their imperial
interests, he yet paid a tribute to the 'inspiration' of Western socio-
political thought and institutions.

Nehru's assessment of the Indian middle classes, who were sup-
posedly moved by this inspiration more than others, is, however,

very negative. Writing about the time when Mahatma Gandhi (1869–1948) assumed the leadership of the national movement (c. 1915), he observed: 'Incompletely developed and frustrated, they [the middle classes] did not know where to look, for neither the old nor the new offered them any hope. There was no adjustment to social purpose, no satisfaction of doing something worthwhile, even though suffering came in its train. Custom-ridden, they were born old, yet they were without the old culture. Modern thought attracted them, but they lacked its inner content, the modern social and scientific consciousness' (1961: 379) (see also Chapter 1).

It was perhaps Gandhi alone, a giant even among great men and women, who could contain in his oceanic soul many cultural streams without feeling uprooted, torn apart, or burdened. He too, it may be recalled, combined a denunciation of the 'satanic' British rule and of the evil embodied in Western industrial civilization with an admiration for the moral precepts of Jesus (most notably the Sermon on the Mount) and an approbation of the teachings of modern Western savants such as Emerson, Ruskin, Thoreau and Tolstoy. Similarly, he was deeply concerned with reforming Hindu society—his life-long crusade against untouchability being the best-known example—without abandoning his allegiance to it. In a famous and oft-quoted statement he said that he wanted to keep all the doors and windows open, to let the winds blow in from all directions, while remaining firmly seated in his own house.

While one may not easily associate ambivalence with Gandhi's personality, it is undeniable that he too was in search of a new, forward-looking synthesis, but this was qualitatively different from the liberal nationalist and Hindu reformist exercises. The point that I am trying to make here is that by the twentieth century, westernization had indeed become an integral part of India's historical consciousness, and its political implications had acquired increasing importance since Roy's time. Not to speak of Nehru, even Gandhi's response to the West carried a political load far heavier than what Roy experienced.

The ambivalence and uncertainty of the middle classes in their pursuit of westernization is, of course, nothing peculiar to India, and is general in the non-Western countries. The most confident of modernizers have been afflicted by it, often resulting in the kind of dullness of thought and paralysis of action for which they have been reviled, and not by Third World 'radicals' (such as Frantz Fanon) alone. But it is also instructive to recall that the middle classes have 'success stories' to their credit in some places and at certain times, the most notable in our own times being that of the Japanese.

A comparison of Indian and Japanese responses to westernization would be very instructive because, as is well known, Japan is the only non-Western country which has not only successfully westernized (or modernized) itself but, in fact, turned the tables on the West. Today, Western intellectuals and managers (if this combination of human types appears strange, one has only to be reminded that the role of managers in modern society is in no way less important than that of intellectuals) are writing about what their countries could now learn from Japan, which has been simply judged as 'number one' by the Harvard Japanologist, Ezra Vogel (1979). As another Western scholar puts it, at the beginning of the era of westernization in the late nineteenth century, the slogan was 'Japanese spirit and Western techniques' *(Wakon Yosai)*, but now 'it would make as much sense for Europeans to turn it around and talk of 'Japanese techniques and Western spirit' *(Wasai Yokon)*' (Wilkinson 1982: 170).

By successfully pursuing the goals of Western science and technology, and at the same time claiming to remain Japanese in its social organization and aesthetic and moral sensibilities, Japan has delivered a deadly blow to the arrogant smugness of the tradition-versus-modernity view of the contemporary world in a much more convincing manner than India would be judged to have done. It is of some interest to recall here that one of the first scholars to point this out was the American sociologist Joseph Gusfield (1967). But then, as long ago as 1938, the Japanese intellectual Nyozekan Hasegawa had observed that, not only did the traditional and the modern go hand in hand in Japan, but also that 'in an extremely modern period, something extraordinarily traditional always begins to revive' (1982: 59). This is a judgement which is endorsed by many Japanese intellectuals today.

The whole issue of demonstrating that traditional cultures are not incapable of westernization *(seiyoka)* or modernization *(kindaika)*, which seemed so essential for the self-confidence of the non-Western nations soon after their independence, is today seen as dangerously misleading, for it imposes upon all cultures of the world a single paradigm of modernization (see Madan 1983b). These reservations notwithstanding, or perhaps because of them, a comparison between the responses of India and Japan to westernization seems very worthwhile. More specifically, have the Japanese too suffered from uncertainties as to how to respond to Western culture as the Indians have?

Westernization: Japanese Pragmatism and Indian Acquiescence

Japan's contacts with the West began in the sixteenth century just as they did in India, and as in the Indian case it was the missionaries and the merchants who sought her shores. St Francis Xavier, one of the original members of the Society of Jesus, visited Japan in 1549, just as he came to India, and for the same purpose—to reclaim for Christ Asian heathen peoples—and he rests in peace in Goa. In Japan Christianity was eventually proscribed by Tokugawa Ieyasu in 1614. The Shogunate also shut out all foreigners from the country in 1639, except some Chinese and Dutch merchant traders who were confined to the small island of Dejima at Nagasaki. What is more, no Japanese were allowed to travel abroad. This policy of *sakoku* (no income, no out-go) lasted until modern times. But neither could the Shogun's edict wholly exterminate the Christians, nor could Western influence be kept out completely; thus Western knowledge and techniques in the fields of astronomy and medicine did seep into Japan. This contrasts with the continuously ramifying influence of Western culture during the same period in India.

By the early nineteenth century a consciousness of domestic weakness and foreign threat (*gaikan*) developed in Japan and the same was confirmed by the unequal treaties which the Western powers imposed upon her beginning with the Treaty dictated by Commodore Perry of the US Navy in 1854. The sense of being imposed upon generated a most urgent need to learn about the Western powers and find out the sources of their strength. In a very characteristically pragmatic move the Japanese government established in 1856 an Institute of Barbarian Letters, giving expression both to their contempt and hatred for the Westerners (who were actually called the southern barbarians, *nanbanjin*) and to their determination to learn *even from barbarians* in order to fight them back.

What strikes me as remarkable is the rapidity of the response and not merely its narrowness. As a contemporary Indian historian puts it, 'The Indian mind . . . does not respond to new ideas and events promptly, for as a result of centuries of civilized history, we have acquired a highly discerning mind which refuses to be overwhelmed or hustled by any new idea or any new evidence' (Mookerjee 1967: 1). I quote Mookerjee not because I find his argument wholly convincing, but because it exemplifies a smugness of attitude and a sloth of mind—a Brahmanical superiority—which contrasts sharply with the Japanese alacrity to change.

We are perhaps doing here no more than recalling a distinction made by Hajime Nakamura between the 'passive' or 'contemplative attitude' of the Indian people which, he thought, makes them adaptive, forbearing and averse to activism (1960: 58), and the 'fluid way of thinking' of the Japanese which produces 'an emphasis upon activism' and 'this-worldliness' (ibid.: 414, 540 *et passim*). Regrettably, I do not have the space to examine this contrast in detail here. Suffice it to say, these broad characterizations of national dispositions do seem to contain a kernel of truth.

After the Meiji Restoration in 1868 the rigid dualism of *Wakon Yosai* (Japanese spirit, Western techniques) was abandoned in favour of the state policy of 'Reverence the Emperor, open the country' (*sonnu kaikoku*). The earlier policy of 'reverence the Emperor, expel the barbarian' (*sonnu joi*) had, in fact, been abandoned even before the Restoration when the country's weakness apropos of western military powers had become apparent in the 1850s. For the next two to three decades the attitude of Japanese leadership to the West remained clear and coherent: it was considered the source of all the self-improvement of which she was in need and also capable. Without westernization national survival was considered highly problematic: the unequal treaties had to be repealed or re-negotiated, and to achieve this end one had to be as powerful and efficient as the Westerners themselves. In these circumstances, as Jansen rightly puts it, 'Westernization was a device as well as a policy': 'Whether as sincere admiration or crafty tactic, the Meiji policies of Westernization clearly reflected the overwhelming importance of the West in the latter half of the nineteenth century' (1965: 69–70).

One of the intellectual leaders of the policy of out-and-out westernization was Yukichi Fukuzawa (1835–1901). In some ways he was like Rammohan Roy, in others totally unlike him. He read extensively about the West, and went to Europe and America on historic diplomatic missions the purpose of which was to find out what Japan could obtain or copy from there. His short book, *Conditions in the West* (*Seiyo jijo*, 1886) became modern Japan's first best-seller, 25,000 copies being sold in the first year. While his enthusiasm for the West was as great as Roy's, his approach was basically different, reflecting Japanese pragmatism in contrast to the Indian's preoccupation with fundamentals. This comes out dramatically in their attitudes to Christianity. Roy's reverence for the moral content of Christianity has been mentioned earlier. Fukuzawa was hardly concerned with the moral impact of the teachings of Jesus; he was rather interested in the practical politico-economic advantages that could be derived from Christianity. Hence he advised: 'We do not propose that a majority of our people should become Christians, a small proportion would be enough. All that is necessary is to accept the name of a Christian country' (quoted in Sansom 1950: 457–8).

Some others went to further extremes. It has been recorded that Arinori Mori (1847–89), who was mainly responsible for the reformulation of the post-Meiji educational system, had 'privately' reached the conclusion that, if Japan was to have a strong, effective, modern style educational establishment, the Japanese language would have to be replaced by German or English. This set off quite a lively debate (see Miller 1982: 108). (It may be added here *en passant* that a similar plea for the abandonment of the Japanese language was made by some intellectuals at the end of the Second World War.) These pleas about changes of religion and language reflected pragmatism, but for the Japanese it was soul-stirring pragmatism, for they are a people highly sensitive to situational pressures and, therefore, their responses to them are context-specific. In another book, *An Outline of a Theory of Civilization* (1875), Fukuzawa observed: 'Foreign countries are not only novel and exotic for us Japanese, everything we see and hear about these cultures is strange and mysterious . . . a blazing brand has been thrust into ice-cold water. Not only are ripples and swells ruffling the surface of man's minds, but a massive upheaval is being stirred up at the depths of their souls' (quoted in Wilkinson 1982: 116).

The Japanese might have had their souls stirred, the Indians perhaps simply lost theirs. All the textbooks record that the Battle of Plassey in the plains of Bengal in 1757 laid the foundations of the British *imperium* in India. It is also taught that better guns, better goods, and better government enabled the British to capture India militarily and economically. And yet we might suggest that for India the battle had already been lost, say in 1606, when a Jesuit missionary, Roberto de Nobili, walked the streets of the ancient Hindu city of Madurai, dressed as a Brahman—holy thread and all—possessing knowledge of Hindu scriptures, but converting people (mostly those of the higher castes) to Christianity. He and his successors never made many converts; Christianity had, in fact, arrived in India, if we go by well-established tradition, with the apostle Thomas at the very beginning of the Christian era. What the new missionaries represented was the cultural invasion of Asia by the West. It is in this sense that the Indians may be said to have lost their souls before they lost their territories or markets. Ultimately all the processes were unified. Colonized lands are always populated by colonized minds.

India modernized under the aegis of Western colonialism; it was a matter of imperial and not national policy to westernize the country. In other words, the compulsion to modernize was external, but of a significantly different kind than that experienced by Japan. The British did in India whatever they did to serve, first and foremost, their own domestic and international interests and only then, if at all, the interests of their Indian 'subjects', who were never given the status of the 'citizens' of the empire. In acting thus, Karl Marx pointed out, they were 'actuated by the vilest interests' and, in addition, were 'stupid' in the 'manner of enforcing them'. And yet, Marx believed that, acting as the unconscious hand of destiny, England would fulfil 'a double mission in India': 'the annihilation of old Asiatic society, and the laying of the material foundations of Western Society' (1959: 31). The industries and railways, in the transformative power of which Marx placed much faith, arrived in India (just about the same time that the Meiji era of westernization began in Japan), but the hardware, the nuts and the bolts, came from Britain, contributing more to the prosperity of the latter than of the former. While in Japan westernization brought prosperity in its wake, in India pauperization was the outcome. Neither the economy nor the administrative apparatus could be national in character as in Japan. Though men like Roy and Ranade (and many others) appreciated the establishment of *pax Britannica* in the country, and applauded the West for the values of human dignity and liberty, they were painfully aware that these came nowhere near to being realized in the life of the people of India under British rule.

It was, however, the educational system that the British introduced in India—to produce loyal and reasonably efficient servants of the Raj—which inflicted the worst cultural wounds on Indians. Before this educational system came to hideous fruition, highly gifted and self-educated Indians, such as Rammohan Roy, gave expression to the immense scope for the widening of cultural perspectives. His search for synthesis and rationalism began with his encounter with the Muslim world and the Arabic and Persian languages, before he knew much about Christianity and the classical and modern European languages.

But soon after, under the impact of missionary and government educational institutions, the search for synthesis degenerated into schizophrenia. The split in the consciousness of the affected educated elite damaged the authenticity of their creative response to Western culture and stilled their spontaneity. It is amazing but startlingly true that there has been no one on the national scene in India after Roy who has mastered as many non-Indian languages as he did.

A passive acquiescence in negative Western evaluations became the hallmark of the attitude of the Indian middle classes towards their own culture. Alternatively, they sought refuge in glorified memories of the past, citing for these too the authority of Western scholarship. Thomas Babington Macaulay's disparagement of Sanskrit literature almost inevitably led to Max Müller's panegyrics about it being imprinted, as it were, on the minds of Indian intellectuals. In the process the sense of responsibility to the past, the present, and the future was seriously damaged, if not lost. The situation changed only with the emergence of the national movement, which too was a brainchild of the middle classes, towards the end of the nineteenth century.

Japanese Cultural Rootedness and the Evaluation of Western Culture

By contrast, what strikes me as an outstanding characteristic of the Japanese mode of westernization (*seiyoka*) is the self-consciousness and confidence that marked the choices that were made. No Western power conquered Japan, which was what happened in India. The West was, as it were, dragged (or invited) into Japan. As stated above, the choices that Japan's new leaders made regarding what to borrow and what to emulate pointed to practical rather than philosophical concerns. The model for the new post-Meiji Restoration constitution was Prussian, for the legal code French, for the educational system American and German, for the navy British, and so on. This eclecticism is striking both in terms of its scope and deliberateness. One has only to recall the visits to Europe, England and the USA undertaken by government officials and intellectuals—particularly the historic visit of the top leadership group in 1872. Nothing of a comparable nature happened in India. Our contacts were exclusively with the British and mostly on the individual plane. In fact, there was something tragically appropriate about Rammohan Roy's end-of-the-life visit to Britain, and his death there rather than at home in Bengal.

The Japanese made evaluations—judgements about superiority and inferiority—and expressed fears about being overwhelmed, but there was no sense of defeat as in India. Although both the Japanese and the Indians had known foreigners before their encounter with the West—the Indians for as long as two millennia—the Japanese had also evolved a pragmatic culture of adaption and of dealing with strangers (*tanin*). This they did either by relating to them in emotionally positive terms to the point of being dependent on them (*amae*), or by totally excluding them from their own consciousness (see Doi 1977).

The Japanese had already evolved a cultural homogeneity by the eighth century when their encounter with the mainland giant, China, occurred. It was then that they formulated the doctrine of *Wakon Kansai*, that is Japanese spirit and Chinese knowledge. Confucianism, Buddhism, Taoism, tea, architecture, character writing, literature, drama, and much more, all came from the mainland. But this process of massive borrowing has always been accompanied by the insistence that foreign ideas, knowledge and techniques must be imbued with a characteristically Japanese spirit, best summed up in the ideal of 'harmony' (*wa*), which obviously is a subtler concept than 'synthesis'. Synthesis, it will be agreed, involves the reconciling of opposites dialectically, and is a strenuous process. In contrast, harmony typifies the containment of conflict through consensus. It is also very noteworthy that the educated classes never took to the learning of English or other European languages, thus shutting out European categories of thought *as originally expressed*, and continuing to live in the thought and value worlds of the Japanese tongue. This is a defence mechanism which the Japanese use even today. Not that they have closed their minds: the works of all major European thinkers are available in translation. (A bibliography of Japanese studies on Nietzsche is 300 pages long.) Self-confidence may be shaken temporarily but the Japanese spirit always triumphs again—or so it is claimed.

Erwin Baelz (a German doctor who worked in the Tokyo Medical School and was one of the first Europeans to give detailed impressions of Japan in its early years of modernization) wrote in 1876 (the ninth year of the Meiji era) that cultured Japanese were ashamed of their past. He recorded being told: 'We have no history; our history begins today' (quoted in Ishida 1977: 121). What is important, it would seem, is that this was a Japanese judgement about Japan and, therefore, not quite comparable to, say, Karl Marx's 1853 magisterial pronouncement that 'Indian society has no history at all, at least no known history' (1959: 30). What Indians thought about their own history has already been mentioned above (p. 228) in Ranade's words, which suggest that a break with the past is neither possible nor desirable.

Nor did the Japanese break with their past. The very enthusiasm of the early years of the Meiji era provoked misgivings about the impact of the West. Thus a project was inaugurated in 1870, just two years after the Restoration, for the compilation of national history—a fine example of the reassertion of the Japanese spirit. Westernization was indeed seen by its critics as destructive of an entire way of life, a whole national heritage and national learning (*kokugaku*). Becoming gradually stronger, and using the Emperor as a major symbol of tradition, the reaction against westernization became quite prominent towards the closing years of the century. Japan's victory over China in 1895 further strengthened the reaffirmation of tradition and weakened the obsession with the West.

The idiom of the critical Japanese response to westernization was, however, primarily aesthetic and moral, rather than religious and political as in India. A Japanese Vivekananda would not have made historical sense if he had lived. And a movement for national liberation, too, did not have to be launched: the Meiji Restoration had fulfilled that purpose. As for the artistic and literary expressions of the critical attitude towards Western culture, let me recall here the minor English classic, *The Book of Tea* (1906) by the aesthetician Kakuzo Okakura (1862–1913).

Much concerned about the lack of appreciation in the West of the traditional Asian cultures and their superiority to anything modern in the realm of art, Okakura bemoaned that 'Indian spirituality has been derided as ignorance, Chinese sobriety as stupidity, Japanese patriotism as the result of fatalism' (1964: 3). He came to India in 1902 to meet Rabindranath Tagore (1861–1941) in an obvious effort to consolidate an Asian response to the West. His essay on tea was a poignant critique of modernization through an exposition of the history and art of the tea ceremony (or 'Teaism' as he called it) as an expression of the Japanese tradition, which he held out to the West as something to admire.

Okakura's emphasis was on the positive ideal of aesthetic tranquillity, a quality of the Eastern traditions which the West found deplorable. One may here recall all the rigmarole about Eastern mysticism and quietism, about other-worldliness and lack of achievement. Okakura wrote: 'In religion the Future is behind us. In art the Present is the Eternal' (ibid.: 61). It will be noted that nothing is said about modernization except the fundamental criticism of it so subtly concealed in the observation about the eternal values of art, which (to borrow E. H. Gombrich's phrase) are ideals and not idols.

I would like to mention another classic, Inazo Nitobe's *Bushido, the Soul of Japan*, published in 1905. This work eulogized the samurai ethic and way of life and has continued to sell hundreds of thousands of copies since it first came out. (The copy of the book I personally possess is from the seventy-ninth edition of 1979, and thirteen editions had been published in the previous ten years). What is noteworthy here is the Japanese fascination for, if not attachment to, a medieval value system which is somehow considered by many to express the quintessence of the Japanese world-view. This could hardly be mere nostalgia or romanticism or escapism: it must give expression to something deep and vital that has always animated the Japanese soul, sometimes more intensely and at other times less, and remains largely unaffected by modernization. The historian Aida Yuji has written somewhere—not wistfully but confidently and joy-ously—of the ever-strengthening regression of the present-day Japanese into 'Japaneseness'. His views are echoed by many others.

Let me not, however, oversimplify the situation, for it is the complexity and the ambivalence of attitudes which is a principal concern of this essay. I will, therefore, go back to *Hagakure*, the teachings of the samurai-turned-priest Jocho Yamamoto (1659–1719), which became available to the reading public only after the Meiji Restoration, when its ethic of loyalty was linked to the nation and the nation's prime symbol, the Emperor. *Hagakure* was, however, also criticized under the impact of westernization as supportive of feudalistic ideals and insular attitudes. During the 1930s, the book became very popular again, and was hailed as an expression of 'the unique spirit of Japaneseness' (*yamato-damashii*). *Hagakure*'s central teaching, namely 'I found that the way of samurai is death', made it a national best-seller during the Second World War.

But in post-war Japan it was generally condemned as a jingoistic and pernicious tract, though it never lost its admirers, the most notable among them being, of course, the famous novelist Yukio Mishima, who lived by the letter and the spirit of *Hagakure* to the point of committing *hara-kiri* (or *seppuku* as it is also called). He published an adaptation and interpretation of *Hagakure*, saying that in the 'pitch darkness' in which he believed post-war Japan had become submerged under American occupation and fallen a prey to Western culture, '*Hagakure* radiates its true light' (see Sparling 1978: 5). It is very significant that Mishima confessed his quest for a book in his youth which would not only support his 'loneliness' but, additionally, 'must be a book banned by contemporary society' (ibid.: 6). Does not 'contemporary' here mean 'modern'?

I have written about *Hagakure* at some length to highlight the swings of the pendulum of opinion—between *sakoku* (closure) and *kaikoku* (openness)—that have characterized the response of Japanese intellectuals and opinion-leaders to westernization. Even today there are differences of opinion some of which I was privileged to hear at the centennial symposium of the Kokugakuin University in Tokyo in January 1983. While some of the senior scholars were frankly worried about their Japanese identity (*Nihonjin-ron*), and advocated its preservation through national learning, there were others who made light of the issue, saying that westernization had been made a bogey and that whatever was new in the Japanese way of life—whether values, attitudes, or gadgets—which had not displaced something that existed earlier, could only be called modern and international, not Western. Science and technology had outgrown their historical origins and belonged to everybody, as did the values and attitudes that were a necessary accompaniment of science and technology. In this sense Japan's prolonged search for models had finally come to an end. The impatience of youth was succinctly expressed by a young faculty member of the Kokugukuin University itself who exclaimed: 'I was born after the war. Please do not deify tradition. To me modernization is an unmitigated blessing, not an invader of tradition. It is a beautiful thing!'

It has been pointed out that the early 1970s witnessed a definite search for Japaneseness in the context of the country's splendid recovery from the economic and psychological ravages of the War. The Jews became a new comparison group for the Japanese and, at the same time, the polls also showed a reaffirmation of traditional Japanese values such as filial piety (*oyakoko*) and gratitude (*ongaeshi*). By the close of the decade radical changes of attitudes were, however, again visible. While becoming rich remained as important a guiding principle of life in 1978 as it had been in 1931, 'suiting one's taste' and 'living cheerfully' gained very considerably in importance over the same period, and 'serving society' dropped equally considerably. In conformity with these trends, the feelings of reverence towards the Emperor, which had earlier been an absolute value and the supreme test of patriotism, suffered a decline. These data have led the distinguished Japanese sociologist, Tadashi Fukutake to conclude: 'it is safe to say, at any rate, that contemporary Japanese in general live for their family and their work and are not concerned about outside society' (1982: 148).

Recalling the crucial primacy of the group (ranging from the family to the state) *vis-à-vis* the individual, which has so long been considered the basis of Japanese society, and the importance of which was reaffirmed as recently as 1967 in Chie Nakane's celebrated work on personal relations in a vertical society (see Nakane 1970), the changes Fukutake reports must be judged quite revolutionary in nature. Is Japaneseness, then, being absorbed into a universal modern culture? Perhaps: Shuichi Kato, the historian of ideas, puts it thus: 'once a universal concept is created, no matter who is responsible, it belongs to everybody. We have already accepted that idea where science is concerned, and almost certainly, in the years ahead, we shall come to accept it in contemporary art as well' (1981: 208). Perhaps not: if one reads Aida Yuji rather than Shuichi Kato. The issue of Japanese responses to westernization is not a settled one, but there are new winds blowing.

The Japanese are inevitably opening themselves to foreign influences in areas of life that had earlier remained quite protected. Having established themselves as one of the three top industrial nations of the world (if not yet quite number one as in Ezra Vogel's phrase), they are legitimately seeking a new place of honour and influence in the political capitals of the world and not in its market places alone. The techniques and products of Japanese industry are known, admired and bought all over the world, and these now include military technology, with the USA as a buyer from 1983 onwards! The Japanese themselves are, however, still relatively less known than their goods and skills. The situation has changed dramatically though since 1974 when the Japanese government removed whatever restrictions on travel abroad had still remained in force. Japanese business–promoters and tourists are now visible all over the world all the time.

Equally important is what is happening in scholarly circles. The Japanese also are seeking closer ties with scholars elsewhere and, as a means to this, they are learning foreign languages on an unprecedented scale. The Tokyo University of Foreign Studies is a unique institution in this respect and one of their overseas research projects in the recent past has been located in Tamil Nadu in collaboration with Madras University, and a number of publications in English have become available already. I was told in 1979 by a bright young Japanese economist, specializing on Pakistan, that he deeply regretted that a major and rather technical work on agriculture in India by a distinguished Tokyo University professor had been published in Japanese and not in English. This most certainly represents a new attitude to international communication in the field of scholarship. And it raises a question. Will this decision and drive to have an impact abroad, to communicate better, to cultivate international dialogues, to learn English and other foreign languages weaken Japaneseness? Is there a cultural identity crisis after all in the making for the Japanese?

Or is another scenario in preparation? Writing in the famous national daily newspaper *Asahi Shimbun*, a commentator, Toshio Aoki, pointed out in 1982 that Japanese was increasingly being spoken in the foreign offices and the shopping centres of the Western world. He cautioned that when a 'local' language becomes an international medium, the risk of 'big-power mentality' taking shape is also present. 'Language is where big power hegemony begins', said Mr Aoki (quoted in *Development Forum*, UNU, 10,7,1982, p. 9). His fears may not be far-fetched. Takao Suzuki, the well-known expert on Nihongo (the Japanese language), said in 1978, in the course of a well-attended lecture in Tokyo on the teaching of Nihongo to foreigners, that a religion must be made of Nihongo, that this new religion must be spread throughout the world. He added, obviously carried away by his own rhetoric: 'It is in truth a misfortune for any member of the human race to go to the grave ignorant of the Japanese language' (quoted in Miller 1982: 255). Yet, and paradoxically, Japanese language specialists, including Suzuki himself, have long asserted, and continue to do so, that to learn Japanese you must think like the Japanese, and this is impossible (see ibid.: 279). Hence the interesting and subtle distinction between Nihongo, the language of Japan which the non-Japanese also may learn, and Kokugo, the national language which only the Japanese can master. Their language thus becomes for the Japanese the impregnable armour against cultural invasion from abroad.

Let a cultural anthropologist have the last word here on this very important issue of inter-cultural communication which provides the setting for the westernization of Japan (or India for that matter) as much as for the teaching of Japanese to foreigners. Writes Eiichiro Ishida: 'Perhaps it is difficult for the Japanese to attain a complete understanding of European civilization. At the same time, we may say that for a European to achieve a real and complete understanding of Japanese culture is also difficult. However . . . I think we should study each other's civilizations . . .' (1977: 138–9). As a student of anthropology I agree that the understanding of any culture is to be obtained only through the mutual interpretation of cultures, rather than in the stigmatizing terms of a one-way flow of cultural streams from their Western centres to the world-wide peripheries, such as the process of westernization would convey, or a Eurocentric concept such as Orientalism (see Said 1979) would signify.

This is imperative for whether it is Japan or India, or any other country, a merger of cultures is a reality in today's world. The question we have to answer is 'what are to be the nature and terms of this merger?' Judging by the Japanese example, I would say there is no single answer: there are many roads to modernity, and many definitions of it: nothing is inevitable. As for Western culture itself, it perhaps imposes dualistic modes of thought of a particular kind on other cultures, producing schismatic responses to westernization. In turn, the West too has been bewildered by India and Japan. These aspects of the two encounters are, however, beyond the scope of this limited essay.

Indian Options

Turning back to India, we know that the problem of the merger of cultures and, therefore, of cultural identity has been with us for millennia, but it acquired a new form and content following the encounter with the West. Inevitably 'cultural synthesis' is a key concept in Indian historiography, but it has often only served as a mask for the ambiguity and uncertainty about which I wrote at the beginning of this chapter.

So much has been written, for instance, about the Hindu-Muslim cultural synthesis—not by politicians alone but also by scholars—and yet it has not been the kind of *coincidentia oppositorum* which a genuine dialectic is expected to produce. Referring to the period with which this essay is concerned, we find that the most notable leader of Indian Muslims, who wanted to lead his co-religionists towards westernization, was Syed Ahmed Khan (1817–98). Like Rammohan Roy, he was a rationalist and had great expectations of education that institutions modelled on Cambridge and Oxford could provide to Indian Muslims.

Accordingly he founded a number of schools and finally in 1878 the Muhammadan Anglo-Oriental College at Aligarh. It was proposed to construct a curriculum of which the European sciences would be as essential a core element as Oriental literature. Khan publicly denounced the Islamic sciences as worthless. He was also, to begin with, a confirmed believer in the culturally composite character of north India, the religious divide notwithstanding, and in the common political aspirations of the Indian nation. He earned the wrath of the Muslim orthodoxy for such views. Gradually, Khan changed his views on most of these matters as his contacts with the British government became thicker (See Lelyveld 1978).

This is a long and complex story and the only reason why I mention it here at all is to suggest that, even in a large and culturally diverse country such as India, the new middle class intellectuals did share many basic attitudes towards westernization, including ambivalence, despite regional and religious differences, which it is instructive to compare with the attitudes of the Japanese leaders in the post–Meiji years of the last century.

In all these attempts the dominant concern was to westernize without somehow losing cultural roots completely. Those who would like to reassure us, write of India's historic capacity for absorption and 'encapsulation'; those who take a less sanguine view of the process of synthesis, particularly in recent times, such as V. S. Naipaul, the West Indian writer of Indian origin, simply speak of 'mimicry'. I would like to suggest that ambiguity is inescapable whenever an encounter of cultures takes place. The point rather is, what do we make of it? It is in this context of cultural ambiguity that the liberal nationalist, the Hindu or Muslim reformist, and the Gandhian responses may each be judged to have failed so far to constitute an adequate response to the march of westernization in India.

A persual of available literature reveals three main viewpoints regarding such a response in India. Limitations of space allow only the briefest mention of these.

First, there are those numerous optimists who beckon us all to come out of our caves and cells of primordial loyalties, and participate in a modern, international, civic culture based on 'reason'. They hold that science and technology, and the institutions, values, and attitudes of mind associated with them, will redeem the world. They take the Japanese miracle as proof of the triumph of technology, and consider the persistence of Japanese institutions and values a kind of social 'myth'.

Second, there are those who would like to be called hard-headed

realists and who hold that, good or bad, there is no escape from westernization, and that it is no more than sophistry to press too far the
distinction between westernization and modernization. For them
modernity is good, though perhaps not an unlimited good. I believe
they too would not all take seriously the mystique of Japaneseness
and largely discount a thesis like that of Michio Morishima (1982)
that traditional ethical attitudes, religious values, and institutions
(such as the bureaucracy) have played a crucial role in making Japan
what it is today. There is, therefore, little for Indians to learn from
Japan, for Japan itself has learnt its most crucial lessons from the
West. Morishima also says that it is a 'mistake' to consider Japan as a
model for other countries which lack its cultural ethos (ibid.: 201).

Third and last is the small minority with whose views I have much
sympathy, which does not subscribe to the view that all the paths of
development must lead to the same kind of culture and society, or
that Western society or, for that matter, westernized Japanese society,
provides the rest of the world its best or only paradigm of development. These are the people who would point out that at the core of
the notion of westernization lie the notions of cultural hegemony and
politico-economic power and, therefore, of the so-called 'burden' of
modernizing the world. They maintain that the very 'success' of
Japan highlights the fact that the time for an incisive critique of westernization and modernization is already with us and brooks no
further delay. Time is one of mankind's very scarce resources today.
In this connection, it is noteworthy that a Japanese historian, Minoru
Kasai, has recently pointed out that Gandhi is as relevant to Japan in
her present predicament (he believes that one exists), as he has been
and continues to be to India in her's. In fact, Kasai (1980) emphasizes
the universal import of Gandhi's vision.

One would have liked to elaborate here the idea that the West itself
has of course been changing over the last two hundred years, and that
extremely perceptive and radical critiques of industrial society and
modernization have been advanced by Western intellectuals themselves. Also, there is the important fact that the perceptions of the
'West' among nineteenth century Indian and Japanese intellectuals
were not exactly the same. Limitations of space unfortunately preclude these discussions. From the point of view of the present essay,
however, what is most noteworthy is that, though India was colonized
and Japan was not (at least not formally), for the middle class leadership
of both countries, westernization largely fashioned tastes, formed

mental attitudes, formulated notions of well-being, and defined the skills for achieving the same.

It would thus seem that while the successors to the liberal nationalists, representing the first two viewpoints just mentioned, have reached a dead end rather than their goal, the Hindu reformists have been inexorably overtaken by the flow of events. Together they are the orphans of nationalism. As for the seekers of alternatives, they have really yet to cut their intellectual teeth. Maybe Gandhi has to be retrieved from the scrap–heap and reinterpreted, but this is no easy task.

Concluding Remarks

The doubts, questionings and misgivings that I have tried to outline in this essay reflect at least one of the moods of the 1980s, just as M. N. Srinivas's essays on westernization gave expression to the hopes for the future of three decades ago. His analysis and views still retain their relevance and importance, and ought to be discussed in the light of the experience that we have gained since he wrote them. It is a tribute to his intellectual leadership that his work should still serve as a point of departure for discussion of the problems we face today. The point to ponder is that the experienced reality is far more complex than the extant discourse on westernization perhaps lets us recognize.

REFERENCES

Abu Shahab-ud-Din
1971   Communal Harmony in East Bengal. Mimeo.

1972   Bangladesh and the US Government Policy in Asia. Speech
               delivered at Lincolnland Junior College in Springfield,
               Illinois, 6 January. Mimeo.
Ahmad, Aziz
1964   *Studies in Islamic Culture in the Indian Environment*. Oxford:
               Clarendon Press.

1967   *Islamic Modernism in India and Pakistan, 1857–1940*. London:
               Oxford University Press.
Ahmad, Imtiaz
1965   Social Stratification among Muslims. *The Economic Weekly*
               10: 1093–6.

———
1966   The Ashraf-Ajlaf Dichotomy in Muslim Social Structure in
               India. *The Indian Economic and Social History Review* 3: 268–78.

1972   For a Sociology of India. *Contributions to Indian Sociology*
               (N. S.) 6: 172–8.
Ahmad, Saghir
1970   Social Stratification in a Punjabi Village. *Contributions to
               Indian Sociology* (N. S.) 4: 105–25.
Ahmed, Akbar S
1976   *Millennium and Charisma among Pathans*. London: Routledge
               and Kegan Paul.
Ahmed, Raffiuddin, ed.
1991   *Religion, Nationalism and Politics in Bangladesh*. New Delhi:
               South Asian Publishers.
Alatas, S. H.
1972   The Captive Mind in Developing Studies. *International
               Social Science Journal* 24: 9–25.
Alland Jr., Alexander
1972   *The Human Imperative*. New York: Columbia University
               Press.

Anantha Murty, U.R.
1976   *Samskara, A Rite for a Dead Man.* Trans., A. K. Ramanujan.
               Delhi: Oxford University Press.
Ansari, Ghaus
1960   *Muslim Caste in Uttar Pradesh.* Lucknow: The Ethnographic
               and Folk Culture Society.
Asad, Talal
1973   Introduction. *In* Talal Asad, ed., *Anthropology and the Colonial
               Encounter.* London: Ithaca Press.
Ashraf, K. M.
1959   *Life and Condition of People of Hindustan.* Delhi: Jiwan
               Prakashan.
Ayoob, M. and K. Subrahmanyam
1972   *The Liberation War.* New Delhi: S. Chand and Co.
Bailey, F. G.
1957   *Caste and the Economic Frontier.* Manchester: Manchester
               University Press.

1959   For a Sociology of India? *Contributions to Indian Sociology*
               3: 88–101.

1963   Closed Social Stratification in India. *European Journal of
               Sociology* 4: 107–24.
Baldus, H.
1946   Curt Nimuendaju, 1883–1945. *American Anthropologist*
               48: 238–43.
Bamzai, P. N. K.
1962   *A History of Kashmir.* Delhi: Metropolitan Books.
Bandyopadhyay, Suraj
1977   Caste 'Lost' and Caste 'Regained'. *In* M. N. Srinivas *et al.*,
               eds., *Dimensions of Social Change in India.* Bombay: Allied
               Publishers.
Banton, M.
1964   Anthropological Perspectives in Sociology. *British Journal of
               Sociology* 15: 95–112.
Barnes, J. A.
1967   Genealogies. *In* A. L. Epstein, ed., *The Craft of Social
               Anthropology.* London: Tavistock Publications.
Barnett, Steve, Lina Früzzetti and Ákos Östör
1976   Hierarchy Purified: Notes on Dumont and his Critics. *The
               Journal of Asian Studies* 35, 4: 627–46.

Barth, Fredrik
1960   The System of Social Stratification in Swat, North Pakistan. *In* E. R. Leach, ed., *Aspects of Caste in South India, Ceylon and North-West Pakistan.* Cambridge: Cambridge University Press.

1966   Preface. *In* Richard N. Pehrson, *The Social Organization of the Marri Baluch.* Chicago: Aldine Publishing House.

1970   Introduction. *In* Fredrik Barth, ed., *Ethnic Groups and Boundaries.* London: Allen and Unwin.

Barwick, Diane, Jeremy Beckett and Marie Reay, eds.
1985   *Metaphors of Interpretation. Essays in Honour of W. E. H. Stanner.* Canberra: Australian National University.

Bell, Daniel
1974   *The Coming of Post-Industrial Society.* New Delhi: Arnold Heinemann.

Benedict, Burton
1966   Review of *Family and Kinship* by T. N. Madan (1965). *Man* (N. S.) 1: 584–5.

Berreman, Gerald D.
1960   Caste in India and the United States. *American Journal of Sociology* 66, 2: 120–7.

1962   *Behind Many Masks.* Ithaca, New York: Cornell University Press.

1979   *Caste and Other Inequities.* Meerut: Folklore Institute.

1981   *The Politics of Truth.* New Delhi: South Asian Publishers.

Béteille, André
1991   *Society and Politics in India.* London: The Athlone Press.

Bettelheim, Charles
1968   *India Independent: A History of the Social and Economic Development of India Since 1947.* London: Macgibbon and Kee.

Bharati, Agehananda
1970   The Hindu Renaissance and its Apologetic Patterns. *The Journal of Asian Studies* 29: 267–87.

Bhattacharjee, P. N.
1966   Distribution of the Blood Groups... and the Secretor Factor among the Muslims and the Pandits of Kashmir. *Z. Morph Anthrop* 58, 1: 86–94.

250   *Pathways*

Boas, Franz
1928   *Anthropology and Modern Life*. New York: Norton.
Boel, J.
1968   Review of *Homo hierarchicus: essai sur le système de castes* by
              L. Dumont (1966). *Sociological Bulletin* 17, 1: 103–18.
Boon, James A.
1982   *Other Tribes, Other Scribes*. Cambridge: Cambridge
              University Press.
Bose, Arun
1989   *India's Social Crisis: An Essay on Capitalism, Socialism,
              Individualism and Indian Civilization*. Delhi: Oxford
              University Press.
Bose, N. K.
1971   Review of *Homo Hierarchicus* by L. Dumont (1970). *Man in
              India* 51, 4: 405–10.
Bose, Sarat Chandra
1968   *I Warned my Countrymen*. Calcutta: Netaji Research Bureau.
Brass, Paul
1970   Muslim Separatism in United Provinces. *Economic and
              Political Weekly* 5, 3–5: 167–86.
Broomfield, J. H.
1968   *Elite Conflict in a Plural Society: Twentieth Century Bengal*.
              Berkeley and Los Angeles: University of California Press.
Bühler, G.
1886   *The Laws of Manu*. London: Oxford University Press.
Burridge, Kenelm
1973   *Encountering Aborigines*. New York: Pergamon.
Casagrande, J. B., ed.
1960   *In the Company of Man*. New York: Harper and Row.
Chambers's Twentieth Century Dictionary.
1959   London: W & R Chambers.
Charbonier, G., ed.
1969   *Conversations with Claude Lévi-Strauss*. London: Jonathan Cape.
Chaudhuri, Nirad C.
1951   *The Autobiography of an Unknown Indian*. New York:
              Macmillan.
Clifford, James
1986a   Introduction: Partial Truths. *In* James Clifford and George
              E. Marcus, eds., *Writing Culture: The Poetics and Politics of
              Ethnography*. Berkeley: University of California Press.

1986b   *The Predicament of Culture*. Cambridge, Mass: Harvard
              University Press.

Collingwood, R. G.
1970   *An Autobiography*. London: Oxford University Press.
Confucius
1989   *The Analects of Confucius*. Trans. and annotator, Arthur
               Waley. New York: Vintage Books.
Coomaraswamy, Ananda K.
[1915] 1948   What has India Contributed to Human Welfare? *In* A. K.
               Coomaraswamy, *The Dance of Shiva*. Bombay: Asia Pub-
               lishing House.
Crane, Robert I. ed.
1956   *Area Handbook on Jammu and Kashmir State*. Chicago:
               Chicago University Press for Human Relations Area Files
               Inc. Mimeo.
Das Gupta, Jyotrindra
1970   *Language Conflict and National Development: Group Politics
               and National Language Policy in India*. Bombay: Oxford
               University Press.
Dasgupta, R. K.
1971   *Revolt in East Bengal*. Calcutta: n. p.
Das, Veena
1977   *Structure and Cognition: Aspects of Hindu Caste and Ritual*.
               New Delhi: Oxford University Press.
Desai, A. R.
1948   *The Social Background of Indian Nationalism*. Bombay: Popular.
Dirks, Nicholas
1987   *The Hollow Crown: Ethnohistory of an Indian Kingdom*.
               Cambridge: Cambridge University Press.

1989   The Original Caste: Power, History and Hierarchy in South
               Asia. *Contributions to Indian Sociology* (N. S.) 23, 1: 59–77.
Doi, Takeo
1977   *The Anatomy of Dependence*. Trans., John Bester. Tokyo:
               Kodansha International.
Dube, S. C.
1977   Social and Cultural Factors in Development. *In* UNESCO
               and UN Asian Development Institute, *Asian Rethinking on
               Development*. New Delhi: Abhinav.
Dubois, Abbe J. A.
1959   *Hindu Manners, Customs and Ceremonies*. Third edition.
               Oxford: Clarendon Press.
Dumont, Louis
1957a   For a Sociology of India. *Contributions to Indian Sociology*
               I: 7–22. See Dumont and Pocock 1957.

Dumont, Louis

1957b   *Hierarchy and Marriage Alliance in South Indian Kinship.* London: Royal Anthropological Institute. Occasional Paper no. 12.

1957c   *Une sous-caste de l'Inde du sud. Organisation sociale et religion des Pramalai Kallar.* Paris: Mouton.

1960   Renunciation in Indian Religions. *Contributions to Indian Sociology* 4: 33–62.

1961   Caste, Racism and Stratification. *Contributions to Indian Sociology* 5: 20–43.

1964a   *La civilisation Indienne et nous: esquisse de sociologie comparée.* Paris: A Colin.

1964b   Nationalism and Communalism. *Contributions to Indian Sociology* 7: 30–70.

1966a   A Fundamental Problem in the Sociology of Caste. *Contributions to Indian Sociology* 9: 17–32.

1966b   *Homo hierarchicus: Essai sur le système des castes.* Paris: Gallimard.

1966c   Marriage in India: The Present State of the Question. *Contributions to Indian Sociology* 9: 90–114.

1967a   Caste: A Phenomenon of Social Structure or an Aspect of Indian Culture. *In* A. V. S. de Rueck and J. Knight, eds., *Ciba Foundation Symposium on Caste and Race: Comparative Approaches.* London: J & A Churchill.

1967b   The Individual as an Impediment to Sociological Comparison and Indian History. *In* B. Singh and V. B. Singh, eds., *Social and Economic Change: Essays in Honour of Professor D. P. Mukerji.* Bombay: Allied.

1970a   *Homo Hierarchicus: The Caste System and its Implications.* London: Weidenfeld and Nicolson.

1970b   *Religion, Politics and History in India.* Paris: Mouton.

1971   On Putative Hierarchy and Some Allergies to it. *Contributions to Indian Sociology* (N. S.) 5: 58–78.

Dumont, Louis

1977a   *From Mandeville to Marx: The Genesis and Triumph of Economic Ideology.* Chicago: The University of Chicago Press.

1977b   *Homo aequalis, I, genèse et épanouissement de l'idéologie économique.* Paris: Gallimard.

1979   The Anthropological Community and Ideology. *Social Science Information* 18: 785–817.

1980   *Homo Hierarchicus: The Caste System and its Implications.* Complete revised English edition. Chicago: The University of Chicago Press. Published in India by the Oxford University Press in 1988.

1986a   *A South Indian Subcaste: Social Organization and Religion of the Pramalai Kallar.* Delhi: Oxford University Press.

1986b   *Essays on Individualism: Modern Ideology in Anthroplogical Perspective.* Chicago: The University of Chicago Press.

1987   On Individualism and Equality. *Current Anthropology* 28, 5: 669–72.

Dumont, Louis and David, F. Pocock

1957   For a Sociology of India. *Contributions to Indian Sociology* 1: 7–22. See Dumont 1957a.

1959   Pure and Impure. *Contributions to Indian Sociology* 3: 9–39.

1960   For a Sociology of India: A Rejoinder to Dr. Bailey. *Contributions to Indian Sociology* 4: 82–9.

Durkheim, Emile

1953   Individual and Collective Representations. *In* Emile Durkheim, *Sociology and Philosophy.* Trans., D. F. Pocock. London: Cohen and West.

[1912] 1964a   *The Elementary Forms of the Religious Life.* London: Allen and Unwin.

[1938] 1964b   *The Rules of Sociological Method.* Glencoe, Illinois: The Free Press.

Eglar, Zekiye

1960   *A Punjabi Village in Pakistan.* New York: Columbia University Press.

Eliot, T. S.
1971a   East Coker. *In* T. S. Eliot, *The Complete Poems and Plays,*
               1909–50. New York: Harcourt, Brace and World, Inc.

1971b   The Waste Land. *In* T. S. Eliot, *The Complete Poems and Plays,*
               1909–50. New York: Harcourt, Brace and World, Inc.

Elwin, Verrier
1943   *The Aboriginals.* Bombay: Oxford University Press.

1964   *The Tribal World of Verrier Elwin.* Bombay: Oxford University
               Press.

Epstein, A. L., ed.
1967   *The Craft of Social Anthropology.* London: Tavistock
               Publications.

Evans-Pritchard, E. E.
1951a   *Kinship and Marriage among the Nuer.* Oxford: Clarendon Press.

1951b   *Social Anthropology.* London: Cohen and West.

1956   *Nuer Religion.* Oxford: Clarendon Press.

Fabian, Johannes
1983   *Time and the Other: How Anthropology Makes its Object.* New
               York: Columbia University Press.

Fauq, M. M.
n. d.   *Tarikh-i-Aquam-i-Kashmir* (in Urdu). 3 Vols. Lahore: Zafar
               Brothers.

Fei Hsiao-Tung
1939   *Peasant Life in China.* London: Kegan Paul, Trench and
               Trubner.

Firth, Raymond
1965   Foreward. *In* E. R. Leach, Political Systems of Highland
               Burma. Boston: Beacon Press.

Fortes, Meyer
1949   *The Web of Kinship among the Tallensi.* London: Oxford
               University Press.

Franda, Marcus F.
1971   *Radical Politics in West Bengal.* Cambridge: MIT Press.

1982   *Bangladesh, the First Decade.* New Delhi: South Asian Publishers.
Freeman, J. D.
1970   *Report on the Iban.* London: The Athlone Press.

1983   *Margaret Mead and Samoa: The Making and Unmaking of an*
               Anthropological Myth. Cambridge, Mass: Harvard University
               Press.

Freilich, M. ed.
1970   *Marginal Natives: Anthropologists at Work.* New York:
                Harper and Row.
Fukutake, Tadashi
1982   *The Japanese Social Structure: Its Evolution in the Modern Century.*
                Trans., R. P. Dore. Tokyo: University of Tokyo Press.
Furnivall, J. S.
1945   Some Problems in Tropical Economy. *In* Rita Hinden, ed.,
                Fabian Colonial Essays. London: Allen and Unwin.

1948   *Colonial Policy and Practice.* Cambridge: Cambridge University
                Press.
Gait, E. A.
1911   Caste. *In* J. Hastings and J.A. Selbie, eds., *Encyclopaedia of
                Religion and Ethics.* Edinburgh: T. & T. Clark.
Gandhi, M. K.
[1909] 1939   *Hindu Swaraj or Indian Home Rule.* Ahmedabad: Navjeevan.
Ganguli, B. N.
1975   *Concept of Equality: The Nineteenth Century Indian Debate.*
                Simla: Indian Institute of Advanced Study.
Gascoigne, Bamber
1971   *The Great Moghuls.* New York: Harper and Row.
Geertz, Clifford
1963   The Integrative Revolution, Primordial Sentiments and
                Civil Politics in the New States. *In* Clifford Geertz, ed., *Old
                Societies and New States.* Glencoe: Free Press.
Gellner, E. A.
1963   Concepts and Society. *Proceedings of the 5th World Congress of
                Sociology.* Washington, D. C.
Ghurye, G. S.
1932   *Caste and Race in India.* London: Routledge and Kegan Paul.

1943   *The Aborigines—so-called—and their Future.* Poona: Gokhale
                Institute of Economics and Politics.

1969   *Caste and Race in India.* Fifth edition. Bombay: Popular.
Gibran, Kahlil
1962   *Spiritual Sayings of Kahlil Gibran.* New York: Citadel Press.
Goethe, Johann Wolfgang
1959   *Faust* Part I. Trans., Philip Wayne. Harmondsworth:
                Penguin Books.
Gough, Kathleen
1973   Harijans in Thanjavur. *In* Kathleen Gough and Hari P.
                Sharma, eds., *Imperialism and Revolution in South Asia.* New
                York: Monthly Review Press.

Gould, H. A.
1962   Review of *Caste Ranking and Community Structure in Five Regions of India and Pakistan* by McKim Marriott (1960). *The Eastern Anthropologist* 15: 73–103.

1963   The Adaptive Functions of Caste in Contemporary Indian Society. *Asian Survey* 3, 9: 427–38.

1969   Toward a Jati Model for Indian Politics. *Economic and Political Weekly* 4, 5: 291–7.

Guha, Ramachandra
1989   *The Unquiet Woods: Ecological Change and Peasant Resistance in the Himalayas*. Delhi: Oxford University Press.

Gupta, K. P.
1977   Personal Communication.

Gusfield, Joseph R.
1967   Tradition and Modernity: Misplaced Polarities in the Study of Social Change. *American Journal of Sociology* 72, 4: 351–62.

Hanson, Allan
1989   The Making of the Maori: Culture Invention and its Logic. *American Anthropologist* 91, 4: 890–902.

Harrison, Selig
1960   *India: The Most Dangerous Decades*. Bombay: Oxford University Press.

Hasegawa, Nyozekan
1982   *The Japenese Character: A Cultural Profile*. Trans., John Bester. Tokyo: Kodansha International.

Heesterman, J. C.
1985   *The Inner Conflict of Tradition: Essays in Indian Ritual, Kingship and Society*. Chicago: University of Chicago Press.

Hegel, G. W. F.
1948   *The Philosophy of History*. New York: Dover.

Herskovits, M. J.
1948   *Man and His Works*. New York: Alfred Knopf.

Hughes, T. P.
1935   *A Dictionary of Islam*. London: Allen & Co.

Hunter, W. W.
1885   *The Imperial Gazetteer of India*, Vol. II. London: Oxford University Press.

Hutton, J. H.
1951   *Caste in India*. Bombay: Oxford University Press.

Hymes, Dell
1974   The Use of Anthropology: Critical, Political, Personal. *In* Dell Hymes, ed., *Reinventing Anthropology*. New York: Vintage Books.

Inden, Ronald B.
1976   *Marriage and Rank in Bengali Culture*. New Delhi: Vikas.

1986   Orientalist Constructions of India. *Modern Asian Studies* 20,
               3: 401–46.
Inden, Ronald B. and R. W. Nicholas.
1977   *Kinship in Bengali Culture*. Chicago: The University of
               Chicago Press.
India, Government of
1933   *Census of India, 1931, Jammu and Kashmir*, 24, 2. Jammu: The
               Ranbir Government Press.

1943   *Census of India, 1941, Jammu and Kashmir State*, 22, 3. Village
               Tables and Housing Statistics. Jammu: The Ranbir Govern-
               ment Press.

1966   *Census of India, 1961, Jammu and Kashmir, District Census
               Handbook, I, Anantnag District* by M. H. Kamili. Srinagar:
               Vishinath Printing Press.

1972a   *Census of India, 1971, Series I, Paper I, India, Final Population*.
               Faridabad: Government of India Press.

1972b   *Census of India, 1971, Series I, Paper II, India, Religion*.
               Faridabad: Government of India Press.
Ishida, Eiichiro
[1974] 1977   *Japanese Culture: A Study of Origins and Characteristics*. Trans.,
               Teruko Kachi. Tokyo: University of Tokyo Press.
Jansen, Marius B.
1965   Changing Japanese Attitudes to Modernization. *In* M. B.
               Jansen, ed., *Changing Japanese Attitudes to Modernization*.
               Princeton, N. J.: Princeton University Press.
Jarvie, I. C.
1964   *Revolution in Anthropology*. London: Routledge and Kegan Paul.
Kachru, Braj B.
1969   *A Reference Grammar of Kashmiri*. Urbana: Department of
               Linguistics, University of Illinois. Mimeo.
Kak, R. C.
1936   *Ancient Monuments of Kashmir*. London: Royal Asiatic Soceity.
Karve, Irawati
1953   *Kinship Organization in India*. Poona: Deccan College.

1961   *Hindu Society—An Interpretation*. Poona: Deccan College.

1974   *Yuganta: The End of an Epoch*. Poona: Sangam.

Kasai, Minoru
1980   *Gandhi and the Contemporary World*. Poona: Centre for
               Communication Studies.

Kato, Shuichi
[1971] 1981   *Form, Style, Tradition: Reflections on Japanese Art and Society*.
               Trans., John Bester. Tokyo: Kodansha International.

Kenyatta, J.
1938   *Facing Mount Kenya: The Tribal Life of the Gikuyu*. London:
               Secker and Warburg.

Ketkar, S. V.
1909   *The History of Caste in India*, Vol. I. Ithaca, New York:
               Taylor and Carpenter.

Khan, Abdul Majeed
1960   Research about Muslim Aristocracy in East Pakistan. *In*
               Pierre Bessaignet, ed., *Social Research in East Pakistan*. Dacca:
               Asiatic Society of Pakistan.

Khan, Mohammad Ayub
1967   *Friends not Masters: A Political Biography*. London: Oxford
               University Press.

Khare, R. S.
1976   *The Hindu Hearth and Home*. New Delhi: Vikas.

Kilam, Jia Lal
1955   *A History of Kashmiri Pandits*. Srinagar: G. M. College.

Kluckhohn, Clyde
1950   *Mirror for Man: The Relation of Anthropology to Modern Life*.
               London: George Harrap.

Kolff, Dirk H. A.
1990   *Naukar, Rajput and Sepoy: The Ethnohistory of the Military
               Labour Market in Hindustan, 1450–1850*. Cambridge:
               Cambridge University Press.

Kothari, Rajni
1970   *Politics in India*. New Delhi: Orient Longmans.

Koul, Anand
1924   *The Kashmiri Pandit*. Calcutta: Thacker, Spink & Co.

Kripalani, Krishna
1961   *Rabindranath Tagore: A Biography*. London. Oxford
               University Press.

Kroeber, Alfred Louis
1944   *Configurations of Culture Growth*. Berkeley: University of
               California Press.

Lambert, Richard D.
1959   Factors in Bengali Regionalism in Pakistan. *Far Eastern
               Survey* 28, 4: 49–58.

Lawrence, Walter
1909   *Imperial Gazatteer of India: Jammu and Kashmir*. Calcutta:
               Superintendent Government Printing.

[1895] 1967   *The Valley of Kashmir*. Srinagar: Kesar Publishers.
Leach, E. R.
1961   *Pul Eliya: A Village in Ceylon*. Cambridge: Cambridge
               University Press.

1973   Ourselves and the Others. *The Times Literacy Supplement*
               (London). 6th July, 3722: 770–4.
Lelyveld, David
1978   *Aligarh's First Generation: Muslim Solidarity in British India*.
               Princeton, N. J.: Princeton University Press.
Lévi-Strauss, Claude
1962   *Totemism*. London: Merlin Press.

1963a   The Concept of Archaism in Anthropology. *In* Claude Lévi
               Strauss, *Structural Anthropology*, Vol. I. New York: Basic
               Books INC.

1963b   *Tristes Tropiques*. New York: Atheneum.

1966a   Anthropology: Its Achievements and Future. *Current
               Anthropology* 7, 2: 124–7.

1966b   *The Savage Mind*. London: Weidenfeld and Nicolson.

1967   *The Scope of Anthropology*. London: Jonathan Cape.

1977   The Scope of Anthropology. In Claude Lévi- Strauss,
               Structural Anthropology, Vol. II. London: Allen Lane.
Levy, Reuben
1962   *The Social Structure of Islam*. Cambridge: Cambridge
               University Press.
Lewis, Oscar
1951   *Tepoztlan: Life in a Mexican Village*. Urbana: University of
               Illinois Press.
Linton, Ralph
1955   *The Tree of Culture*. New York: Alfred Knopf.
Lowie, Robert H.
1949   *Primitive Society*. London: Routledge and Kegan Paul.
Macdonell, A. A.
1924   *A Practical Sanskrit Dictionary*. London: Oxford University Press.

Madan, T. N.

1953   Kinship Terms Used by the Pandits of Kashmir. *The Eastern Anthropologist* 7, 1: 37–46.

1961a   Dhirendra Nath Majumdar 1903–60. *American Anthropologist* 63, 2: 369–74.

1961b   Herath: A Religious Ritual and its Secular Aspect. *In* L. P. Vidyarthi, ed., *Aspects of Religion in Indian Society*. Meerut: Kedar Nath.

1961c   Majumdar's Contribution to Anthropology in Uttar Pradesh: A Note. *Research Bulletin of the Faculty of Arts*, University of Lucknow 1: 3–10.

1962a   Is the Brahmanic Gotra a Grouping of Kin? *Southwestern Journal of Anthropology* 18: 59–77.

1962b   The Joint Family: A Terminological Clarification. *International Journal of Comparative Sociology* 3, 1: 7–16.

1963   A Further Note on Pandit Kinship Terminology. *In* L. K. Balaratnam, ed., *Anthropology on the March*. Madras: Social Science Association.

1965   *Family and Kinship: A Study of the Pandits of Rural Kashmir.* Bombay: Asia Publishing House.

1966a   Dhirendra Nath Majumdar. *In: Biographical Memoirs of the Fellows of the National Institute of Sciences of India.* New Delhi: National Institute of Sciences.

1966b   For a Sociology of India. *Contributions to Indian Sociology 9: 9–16.*

1966c   *Politico-economic Change and Organizational Adjustment in a Kashmiri Village. Journal of Karnatak University: Social Sciences* 2: 20–34.

1967   For a Sociology of India: Some Clarifications. *Contributions to Indian Sociology* (N. S.) 1: 90–2.

1968a   D. N. Majumdar. *In* D. Sills, ed., *International Encyclopaedia of the Social Sciences* Vo,. 9: 540–1. New York: Macmillan Free Press.

Madan, T. N.

1968b   Pakistan: The People: Races, Languages, Religions, Cultures.
           Encyclopaedia Britannica Vol. 22: 82–3. Chicago: Encyclopaedia
           Britannica, Inc.

1969   Urgent Research in Social Anthropology in Kashmir. *In*
           B. L. Abbi and S. Saberwal, eds., *Urgent Research in Social
           Anthropology*. Simla: Indian Institute of Advanced Study.

1972a   Religious Ideology in a Plural Society: The Muslims and
           Hindus of Kashmir. *Contributions to Indian Sociology* (N. S.)
           6: 106–41.

1972b   Review of *Society in India* by D. G. Mandelbaum (1970).
           American Journal of Sociology 78, 3: 754–7.

1974   The Dialectic of Ethnic and National Boundaries in the
           Evolution of Bangladesh. *In* S. Navlakha, ed., *Studies in
           Asian Social Development*. New Delhi: Vikas.

1975a   On Living Intimately with Strangers. *In* André Béteille and
           T. N. Madan, eds., *Encounter and Experience: Personal Accounts
           of Fieldwork*. New Delhi: Vikas, Honolulu: University of
           Hawai Press.

1975b   The Gift of Food. *In* B. N. Nair, ed., *Culture and Society,
           Festschrift to Dr. A. Aiyappan*. New Delhi: Thomson Press.

1976   The Hindu Woman at Home. *In* B. R. Nanda, ed., *Indian
           Women: From Purdah to Modernity*. New Delhi: Vikas.

1977a   Inter-regional Cooperation in the Social Sciences: Final Report
           of the Meeting. *In: Interregional Cooperation in the Social Sciences*.
           Paris: UNESCO.

1977b   The Dialectic of Tradtion and Modernity in the Sociology of
           D. P. Mukerji. *Sociological Bulletin* 26, 2: 155–76. Re-
           produced with some changes in *Social Science Information*
           17, 6 (1978): 777–800.

1979   Linguistic Diversity and National Unity: Dimensions of a
           Debate. *In* C. H. Hanumantha Rao and P. C. Joshi, eds.,
           Reflections on Economic Development and Social Change. Delhi:
           Allied Publishers.

Madan, T. N.
1982a   The Ideology of the Householder among the Kashmiri
               Pandits. *In* T. N. Madan, ed. *Way of Life*.

Madan, T. N., ed.
1982b   *Way of Life: King, Householder, Renouncer*. New Delhi:
               Vikas. Second edition, 1988, Delhi: Motilal Banarsidass.

1982c   Anthropology as the Mutual Interpretation of Cultures: Indian
               Perspectives. *In* Hussein Fahim, ed., *Indigenous Anthropology
               in Non-Western Countries*. Durham, N. C.: Carolina Academic
               Press.

1983a   Cultural Identity and Modernization in Asian Countries. *In*:
               Cultural Identity and Modernization in Asian Countries. Tokyo:
               Institute for Japanese Culture and Classics, Kokugakuin
               University.

1983b   *Culture and Development*. New Delhi: Oxford University
               Press.

1984   Coping with Ethnic Diversity: A South Asian Perspective.
               In David Maybury-Lewis, ed., *The Prospects for Plural Societies*.
               Washington D. C.: The American Ethnological Society.

1987   *Non Renunciation: Themes and Interpretation of Hindu Culture*.
               Delhi: Oxford University Press.

1989   *Family and Kinship: A Study of the Pandits of Rural Kashmir*.
               Second enlarged edition. Delhi: Oxford University Press.

1991   Auspiciousness and Purity: Some Reconsiderations. *Contri-
               butions to Indian Sociology* (N. S.) 25,2: 287–94.
Madan, T. N. *et. al.*
1971   Review Symposium on *Homo Hierarchicus* by Louis Dumont
               (1970). *Contributions to Indian Sociology* (N. S.) 5: 1–81.

Maine, Henry Summer
1917   *Ancient Law*. London: J. M. Dent and Sons.
Majumdar, D. N.
1923a   Customs and Taboos Observed by an East Bengal Woman
               from Pregnancy to Childbirth. *Man in India* 3: 232–42.

1923b   Notes on Kali-nauch in the District of Dacca. *Man in India*
               3: 202–16.

Majumdar, D. N.

1923c   The Customs of Burnning Human Effigies. *Man in India*
             3: 97–103.

1936   The Decline of the Primitive Tribes of India. *The Journal of
             U. P. Historical Society* (April).

1937   *A Tribe in Transition: A Study in Cultural Pattern.* Calcutta:
             Longmans, Green & Co.

1939   *Tribal Cultures and Acculturation.* Calcutta: Indian Science
             Congress Association.

1944   *The Fortunes of Primitive Tribes.* Lucknow: Universal
             Publishers Ltd.

1947   *The Matrix of Indian Culture.* Lucknow: Universal Publishers Ltd.

1950   *The Affairs of a Tribe: A Study in Tribal Dynamics.* Lucknow:
             Universal Publishers Ltd.

1951   Tribal Rehabilitation in India. *International Social Science
             Bulletin* 3, 4: 802–12.

1955   Introduction. *In* D. N. Majumdar, ed., *Rural Profiles.*
             Lucknow: Ethnographic and Folk Culture Society.

1956–7   What the Sociologists can do . . . *The Eastern Anthropologist*
             10, 2: 130–43.

1957   *Unemployment among the University Educated: A Pilot Enquiry
             in India* (Co-author: S. K. Anand). Cambridge, Mass: Mas-
             sachusetts Institute of Technology.

1958   *Caste and Communication in an Indian Village.* Bombay: Asia
             Publishing House.

1960   *Social Contours of an Industrial City* (Co-authors: N. S. Reddy
             and S. Bahadur). Bombay: Asia Publishing House.

1962   *Himalayan Polyandry.* Bombay: Asia Publishing House.
Malik, Hafeez, ed.
1971   *Iqbal: Poet-Philosopher of Pakistan.* New York: Columbia
             University Press.

Malinowski, Bronislaw
1922   *Argonauts of the Western Pacific.* London: Routledge and
               Kegan Paul.

1938   Foreword. *In* J. Kenyatta, *Facing Mount Kenya: The Tribal
               Life of the Gikuyu.* London: Secker and Warburg.

1939   Foreword. *In* Fei Hsiao-Tung, *Peasant Life in China.*
               London: Kegan Paul, Trench and Trubner.

1944   *A Scientific Theory of Culture and Other Essays.* Chapel Hill:
               The University of North Carolina Press.

1945   *The Dynamics of Culture Change.* New Haven: Yale
               University Press.

1947   *Freedom and Civilization.* London: Allen and Unwin.

1967   *A Diary in the Strict Sense of the Term.* London: Routledge
               and Kegan Paul, New York: Harcourt, Brace and World. Inc.
Mandelbaum, D. G.
1970   *Society in India,* 2 vols. Berkeley: University of California Press.
Maniruzzaman, Talukder
1983   Bangladesh Politics: Secular and Islamic Trends. *In* Raffiuddin
               Ahmed, ed., *Islam in Bangladesh: Society, Culture and Politics.*
               Dhaka: Bangladesh Itihas Samiti.
Mankekar, D. R.
1971   *Pak Colonialism in East Bengal.* Bombay: Somaiya Publication.
Marcus, George and Michael Fischer
1986   *Anthropology as Cultural Critique.* Chicago: The University
               of Chicago Press.
Marglin, Frédérique A.
1977   Purity, Power and Pollution: Aspects of Caste System Recon-
               sidered. *Contributions to Indian Sociology* (N. S.) 11, 1: 245–70.
Marriott, McKim
1955   Little Communities in an Indigenous Civilization. *In* McKim
               Marriott, ed., *Village India.* Chicago: The University of
               Chicago Press.

1959   Interactional and Attributional Theories of Caste Ranking.
               Man in India 39, 2: 92–107.

1968   Caste Ranking and Food Transactions. *In* Milton Singer and
               Bernard Cohn, eds., *Structure and Change in Indian Society.*
               Chicago: Aldine.

Marriott, McKim
1969   Review of *Homo hierarchicus: essai sur le système de castes* by
               L. Dumont (1966). *American Anthropologist* 71: 1166–75.

1976a   Hindu Transactions: Diversity without Dualism. *In* Bruce
               Kapferer, ed., *Transaction and Meaning: Directions in the Anthro-
               pology of Exchange and Symbolic Behaviour*. Philadelphia:
               Institute for the Study of Human Issues.

1976b   Interpreting Indian Society: A Monistic Alternative to
               Dumont's Dualism. *The Journal of Asian Studies* 36, 1: 189–95.

1985   Anthropology in South Asian 3-D. Lecture delivered at the
               University of Chicago. April 15. Audio tape.

1989   Constructing an Indian Ethnosociology. *Contributions to
               Indian Sociology* (N. S.) 23, 1: 1–40.
Marriott, McKim, ed.
1990   *India Through Hindu Categories*. New Delhi: Sage.

1991   On Constructing an Indian Ethosociology. *Contributions to
               Indian Sociology* (N. S.) 25, 2: 295–308.
Marriott, McKim and Ronald B. Inden
1974   Caste Systems. *Encyclopaedia Britannica* 3: 982–91.
Marx, Karl
1853a   The British Rule in India. *In* Karl Marx and Friedrich
               Engels, 1959.

1853b   The Future Results of the British Rule in India. *In* Marx and
               Engels, 1959.
Marx, Karl and Friedrich Engels
1959   *The First Indian War of Independence 1857–59*. Moscow:
               Progress Publishers.
Mayer, A. C.
1960   *Caste and Kinship in Central India*. London: Routledge and
               Kegan Paul.
Mayer, Albert, *et al.*
1958   *Pilot Project, India: The Story of Rural Development at Etawah,
               Uttar Pradesh*. Berkeley: University of California Press.
McLane, John R.
1966   The Decision to Partition Bengal in 1905. *Indian Social and
               Economic History Review* 2, 3: 221–37.
Mencher, Joan P.
1974   The Caste System Upside Down or the Not-so-mysterious
               East. *Current Anthropology* 15, 4: 469–93.

Mencher, Joan P.
1975   Viewing Hierarchy from the Bottom-up. *In* André Béteille and T. N. Madan, eds., *Encounter and Experience: Personal Accounts of Fieldwork*. New Delhi: Vikas, Honolulu: University of Hawai Press.

Merleau-Ponty, Maurice
1964   *Signs*. Trans., R. C. McCleary. Evanston, New York: Northwestern University Press.

Michener, James A.
1972   A Lament for Pakistan. *New York Times Magazine* 9 Jan. 43.

Miller, Roy Andrew
1982   *Japan's Modern Myth: The Language and Beyond*. New York and Tokyo: Weatherhill.

Mines, Mattison
1992   Individuality and Achievement in South Indian Social History. *Modern Asian Studies* 26, 1: 129–56.

Mookerjee, Girija K.
1967   *The Indian Image of Nineteenth Century Europe*. Bombay: Asia Publishing House.

Morishima, Michio
1982   *Why Has Japan Succeeded?* Cambridge: Cambridge University Press.

Mudimbe, V. Y.
1988   *The Invention of Africa: Gnosis, Philosophy and the Order of Knowledge*. Bloomington: Indiana University Press.

Mukerjee, Radhakamal
1916   *The Foundations of Indian Economics*. Bombay: Longmans Green & Co.

1925   *Borderlands of Economics*. London: Allen and Unwin.

1946   *Planning for the Countryside*. Bombay: Hind Kitabs.
1951   *The Indian Scheme of Life*. Bombay: Hind Kitabs.

Mukerji, D. P.
1924   *Personality and the Social Sciences*. Calcutta: The Book Company.

1932   *Basic Concepts in Sociology*. London: Kegan Paul.

1945   *On Indian History: A Study in Method*. Bombay: Hind Kitabs.

1946   *Views and Counterviews*. Lucknow: Universal.

1948   *Modern Indian Culture*. Bombay: Hind Kitabs.

Mukerji, D. P.
1952   Sociology in Independent India. *Sociological Bulletin* 1, 1: 13–27.

1955   Social Research. *In* K. M. Kapadia, ed., *Professor Ghurye Felicitation Volume*. Bombay: Popular Prakashan.

1958   *Diversities*. New Delhi: People's Publishing House.

1959   Lament for Economics. *Economic Weekly* 11, 46: 1541–2.

1972   *Tagore, A Study*. Calcutta: Manisha.
Mukherjee, Ramkrishna.
1957   *The Dynamics of Rural Society*. Berlin: Akademic–Verlag.

1958a   *The Rise and Fall of East India Company: A Sociological Appraisal*. Berlin: Veb Deutscher Verlag.

1958b   *Six Villages of Bengal*. Calcutta: Asiatic Society of Bengal.

1965   Role of Tradition in Social Change. *In* Ramkrishna Mukherjee, *The Sociologist and Social Change in India Today*. New Delhi: Prentice Hall.

1972   Nation Building and State Formation in Bangladesh. *In* S. P. Varma and I. Narain, eds., *Pakistan: Political System in Crisis*. Jaipur: South Asia Studies Centre.

1976   The Value-base of Social Anthropology: The Context of India in Particular. *Current Anthropology* 17, 1: 71–95.

1977   Trends in Indian Sociology. *Current Sociology* 25, 3: 1–193.

1979   For a Sociology of India: Trends in Indian Sociology. *Contributions to Indian Sociology* (N. S.) 13, 2: 319–32.
Murdock, G. P. *et al.*
1950   *Outline of Cultural Materials*. New Haven: Human Relations Area Files Inc.
Myrdal Gunnar
1968   *Asian Drama, An Inquiry into the Poverty of Nations*. 3 vols. New York: Pantheon.
Nadel, S. F.
1951   *The Foundations of Social Anthropology*. London: Cohen and West.

Nadel, S. F.
1954   *Nupe Religion*. Glencoe, Ill.: The Free Press.
Nakamura, Hajime
1960   *The Ways of Thinking of Eastern Peoples*. Tokyo: Japanese
                National Commission for UNESCO.
Nakane, Chie
1970   *Japanese Society*. Berkeley: University of California Press.
Nandy, Ashis
1983   *The Intimate Enemy: Loss and Recovery of Self Under Colonialism*.
                Delhi: Oxford University Press.
Nehru, Jawaharlal
[1936] 1941   *Toward Freedom: An Autobiography*. New York: Doubleday.

[1956] 1961   *The Discovery of India*. Bombay: Asia Publishing House.
Nitobe, Inazo
1979   *Bushido: The Soul of Japan*. Tokyo: Charles E. Tuttle Company.
Oakeshott, Michael
1962   *Rationalism in Politics and Other Essays*. London: Methuen.
O'Flaherty, Wendy
1984   *Dreams, Illusions and Other Realities*. Chicago: University of
                Chicago Press.
Okakura, Kakuzo
1964   *The Book of Tea*. New York: Dover Publications.
Owen, John E.
1968   Social Structure in Pakistan. *Middle East Forum Quarterly* 44, 3.
Pandit, R. S.
1968   *Kalhana's Rajatarangini: The Saga of the Kings of Kashmir*.
                New Delhi: Sahitya Academy.
Parry, J. P.
1991   *Caste and Kinship in Kangra*. Delhi: Vikas Publishing House.
Paul, B. D.
1953   Interview Techniques and Field Relationships. *In* A. L.
                Kroeber, ed., *Anthropology Today*. Chicago: Chicago
                University Press.
Pehrson, R. C.
1957   *The Bilateral Network of Social Relations in Konkama Lapp
                District*. Bloomington: Indiana University Publications.
                Slavic and East European Series, Vol. 5.
Peirano, Marizo G. S.
1991   For a Sociology of India: Some Comments from Brazil.
                Contributions to Indian Sociology (N. S.) 25, 2: 321–8.
Pike, K.
1954   *Language in Relation to a Unified Theory of the Structure of Human
                Behaviour*. Glendale: Summer Institute of Linguistics.

Pocock, D. F.
1973   The Idea of a Personal Anthropology. Paper presented to the
                Decennial Conference of the Association of Social Anthro-
                pology, Oxford, July 4–11.
Popper, Karl R.
1963   *Conjectures and Refutations*. London: Routledge and Kegan Paul.
Prabhu, P. N.
1954   *Hindu Social Organisation*. New Revised Edition of *Hindu
                Social Institutions* (1940). Bombay: Popular Prakashan.
Qureshi, Ishtiaq Husain
1957   *The Pakistani Way of Life*. London: Heinemann.

1962   *The Muslim Community of Indo-Pakistan Subcontinent* (610–1947),
                'S. Gravenhage: Mouton.
R. A. I. (Royal Anthropological Institute of Great Britain and Ireland).
1951   *Notes and Queries on Anthropology*. Sixth edition. London:
                Routledge and Kegan Paul.
Radhakrishnan, S.
1927   *The Hindu View of Life*. London: Allen and Unwin.

1953   *The Principal Upaniṣads*. London: Allen and Unwin.
Rahim, Muhammad Abdul
1963   *Social and Cultural History of Bengal*. Vol. I, 1201–1576.
                Karachi: Pakistan Publishing House.
Raja Rao
1938   *Kanthapura*. London: George Allen and Unwin.
Ramanujan, A. K.
1986   On the Death of Poem. *In* A. K. Ramanujan, *Second Sight*.
                Delhi: Oxford University Press.
Raonaq Jahan
1980   *Bangladesh Politics: Problems and Issues*. Dhaka: Dhaka
                University Press.
Rashiduzzaman, M.
1967   *Pakistan: A Study of Government and Politics*. Dacca: Ideal Library.
Raychaudhuri, Tapan
1988   *Europe Reconsidered: Perceptions of the West in Nineteenth
                Century Bengal*. Delhi: Oxford University Press.
Raychaudhuri, T. C.
1961   The Pandit and Mohammedan of Kashmir: An Anthropo-
                metric Study. *The Eastern Anthropologist* 14, 1: 84–93.
Redfield, Robert
1930   *Tepoztlan: A Mexican Village*. Chicago: University of
                Chicago Press.

Redfield, Robert
1955.   *The Little Community*. Chicago: University of Chicago Press.

1956   *Peasant Society and Culture*. Chicago: University of Chicago
                     Press.
Rivers, W. H. R.
1900   A Genealogical Method of Collecting Social and Vital
                     Statistics. *Journal of the Royal Anthropological Institute* 30: 74–82.

1910   The Genealogical Method of Anthropological Enquiry. *Socio-
                     logical Review* 3: 1–12. Reprinted in W. H. R. Rivers, *Kinship
                     and Social Organization*. London: The Athlone Press, 1968.

1924   *Social Organisation*. New York: Knopf.
Roosevelt, Eleanor
1953   *India and the Awakening East*. New York: Harper and Brothers.
Roy, Jayanta Kumar
1968   *Democracy and Nationalism on Trial: A Study of East Pakistan*.
                     Simla: Indian Institute of Advanced Study.
Rudolph, Lloyd I. and Susanne H. Rudolph
1967   *The Modernity of Tradition: Political Development in India*.
                     Chicago: University of Chicago Press.
Rushdie, Salman
1988   *The Satanic Verses*. New York: Viking.
Saberwal, Satish
1980   For Renewal. *Seminar* 254: 12–18.
Said Edward W.
[1978] 1979   *Orientalism*. New York: Vintage.
Sansom, G. B.
1950   *The Western World and Japan*. New York: Alfred Knopf.
Santayana, George
1922   *Soliloquies in England and Later Soliloquies*. New York: Scribner's.
Saran, A. K.
1959   India. *In* Joseph S. Roucek, ed., *Contemporary Sociology*.
                     London: Peter Owen Limited.

1962a.   D. P. Mukerji, An Obituary. *The Eastern Anthropologist* 15,
                     2: 167–9.

1962b   Review of *Contributions to Indian Sociology*, No. IV. *The
                     Eastern Anthropologist* 15, 1: 53–68.

1965   The Faith of a Modern Intellectual. *In* T. K. N. Unnithan *et
                     al.*, eds., *Towards a Sociology of Culture in India*. New Delhi:
                     Prentice–Hall.

Schneider, D. M.
1974   Notes Toward a Theory of Culture. *In* K. Basso and H.
               Selby, eds., *Meaning in Anthropology*. Albuquerque: University
               of New Mexico Press.

Seal, Anil
1971   *The Emergence of Indian Nationalism*. Cambridge: Cambridge
               University Press.

Semenov, Yu I.
1980   The Theory of Socioeconomic Formation and World History.
               In E. Gellner, ed., *Soviet and Western Anthropology*. New
               York: Columbia University Press.

Sengupta, Arjun
1971   Regional Disparity and Economic Development in Pakistan.
               Economic and Political Weekly 6, 46: 2315–22.

Shah, A. M.
1973   *The Household Dimension of the Family in India*. New Delhi:
               Orient Longman.

Shahab-ud-Din
1971 and 1972 See Abu Shahab-ud-Din.

Shils, Edward
1961   *The Intellectual Between Tradition and Modernity: The Indian
               Situation. Comparative Studies in Society and History*. Sup-
               plement 1. The Hague: Mouton.

1975a   *Centre and Periphery: Essays in Macro-Sociology*. Chicago:
               University of Chicago Press.

1975b   Tradition. *In* Edward Shils, *Centre and Periphery: Essays in
               Macro-Sociology*. Chicago: University of Chicago Press.

Sidhanta, N. K.
1929   *The Heroic Age of India: A Comparative Study*. London: Kegan
               Paul, Trench, Trubner & Co.

Simmons, D. R.
1976   *The Great New Zealand Myth: A Study of the Discovery and
               Original Tradition of the Maori*. Wellington: Reed.

Singer, Milton
1972   *When a Great Tradition Modernizes*. New York: Praeger.

1984   *Man's Glassy Essence*. Bloomington: University of Indiana
               Press.

Singh, Yogendra
1973   *Modernization of Indian Tradition*. New Delhi: Thomson.

1986   *Indian Sociology*. New Delhi: Vistar Publications.

Smith, M. G.
1971   Some Developments in the Analytical Framework of Pluralism. *In* Leo Kuper and M. G. Smith, eds., *Pluralism in Africa*. Berkeley: University of California Press.

Smith, W. Cantwell
1962   The Ulema in Indian Politics. *In* C. H. Philips, ed., *Politics and Society in India*. New York: Praeger.

Smith, W. Robertson
1903   *Kinship and Marriage in Early Arabia*. London: A & C Black.

Sparling, Kathryn, trans.
1978   *Yukio Mishima on Hagakure: The Samurai Ethic and Modern Japan*. Tokyo: Charles E. Tuttle Company.

Spear, Percival
1967   The Position of the Muslims, Before and After Partition. *In* Philip Mason, ed., *India and Ceylon: Unity and Diversity*. London: Oxford University Press.

Srinivas, M. N.
1942a   *Marriage and Family in Mysore*. Bombay: New Book Company.

1942b   The Family versus the State. *Aryan Path* 13: 68–70.

1951   The Social Structure of a Mysore Village. *The Economic Weekly* Oct. 30: 1051–6.

1952a   A Joint Family Dispute in a Mysore Village. *The Journal of the M. S. University of Baroda* 1, 1: 7–31.

1952b   *Religion and Society among the Coorgs of South India*. Oxford: Clarendon Press.

1955   The Social System of a Mysore Village. *In* McKim Marriott, ed., *Village India*. Chicago: University of Chicago Press.

1956a   A Note on Sanskritization and Westernization. *The Far Eastern Quarterly* 15, 4: 481–96. Reprinted in Srinivas, 1962b.

1956b   Indian Marriages. *Transport* (Bombay), Special Issue.

1956c   Sanskritization and Westernization. *In* L. K. Bala Ratnam and A. Aiyappan, eds., *Society in India*. Madras: Social Sciences Association.

1957   Caste in Modern India. *The Journal of Asian Studies* 16, 4: 529–48. Reprinted in Srinivas 1962b.

Srinivas, M. N.
1958   Hinduism. *Encyclopaedia Britannica* 11: 574–7. Reprinted in
            Srinivas 1962b.

1959   The Dominant Caste in Rampura. *American Anthropologist*
            61, 1: 1–16.

1962a   A Note on Sanskritization and Westernization. *In* M. N.
            Srinivas, *Caste in Modern India and Other Essays*. Bombay:
            Asia Publishing House.

1962b   *Caste in Modern India and Other Essays*. Bombay: Asia
            Publishing House. Fourth Impression, 1977.

1966   *Social Change in Modern India*. Berkeley: University of
            California Press, New Delhi and Bombay: Allied.

1967   Cohesive Role of Sanskritization. *In* Philip Mason, ed.,
            Unity and Diversity: India and Ceylon. London: Oxford
            University Press.

1973   Itineraries of an Indian Social Anthropologist. *International
            Social Science Journal* 25, 1–2: 129–48.

1974   Why I am a Hindu. *The Illustrated Weekly of India* (Bombay),
            November 17.

1976   *The Remembered Village*. New Delhi: Oxford University Press.

1977   The Changing Position of Indian Women. T. H. Huxley
            Lecture (1976). *Man* (N. S.) 12, 2: 221–38.

1978   *The Remembered Village*: Reply to Criticism. *Contributions to
            Indian Sociology* (N. S.) 12, 1: 127–52.

1984a   Some Reflections on the Nature of Caste Hierarchy. *Contributions to Indian Sociology* (N. S.) 18, 2: 151–67.

1984b   *Some Reflections on Dowry*. J. P. Naik Memorial Lecture
            (1983). Delhi: Oxford University Press.

1986   On Living in a Revolution. *In* J. R. Roach ed., *India 2000:
            The Next Fifteen Years*. Maryland: Riverdale.

Srinivas, M. N.
1987   *The Dominant Caste and Other Essays*. Delhi: Oxford
                University Press.

1988   The Image Maker. *The Illustrated Weekly of India*, April 17.

1989   *The Cohesive Role of Sanskritization and Other Essays*. Delhi:
                Oxford University Press.

1992   *On Living in a Revolution and Other Essays*. Delhi: Oxford
                University Press.
Srinivas, M. N. and A. M. Shah
1968   Hinduism. *The International Encyclopaedia of Social Sciences*
                6: 358–66.
Srinivas, M. N. and M. N. Panini
1973   The Development of Sociology and Social Anthropology in
                India. *Sociological Bulletin* 22, 2: 179–215.
Srinivas, M. N., S. Seshiah and V. S. Parthasarthy, eds.
1977   *Dimensions of Social Change in India*. Bombay: Allied Publishers.
Srinivas, M. N., Y. B. Damle, S. Shahani and André Béteille
1959   Caste: A Trend Report and Bibliography. *Current Sociology* 8, 3.
Staley, Eugene.
1954   *The Future of Underdeveloped Countries*. New York: Harper.
Stanner, W. E. H.
1957   Personal Communication (Comments on a Field Work Report).
Steingass, F., compiler.
1957   *Persian–English Dictionary*. London: Routledge and Kegan Paul.
Stryk, Lucien and Takashi Ikemoto, eds. and trans.
1981   *The Penguin Book of Zen Poetry*. Harmondsworth: Penguin
                Books.
Tapper, R.
1985   Review of *Religion and Politics in Muslim Society* by Akbar S.
                Ahmed. (1983). Cambridge University Press, 1983. *Man*
                (N. S.) 20, 3: 562–63.
Tara Chand
1936   *Influence of Islam on Indian Culture*. Allahabad: Kitabmahal.
Thoothi, N. A.
1935   *The Vaishnavas of Gujarat*. Calcutta: Longmans, Green &
                Co. Ltd.
Toynbee, Arnold J.
1956   *East to West*. London: Oxford University Press.
Trautman, Thomas R.
1981   *Dravidian Kinship*. Cambridge: Cambridge University
                Press.

Tyler, Stephen A.
1973   *India: An Anthropological Perspective.* Pacific Palisades. Cal.:
               Goodyear.
Tylor, Edward B.
1871   *Primitive Culture*, 2 vols. London: John Murray.
Uberoi, J. P. S.
1968   Science and Swaraj. *Contributions to Indian Sociology* (N. S.)
               2: 119–23.

1974   New Outline of Structural Sociology, 1945–1970. *Contri-
               butions to Indian Sociology* (N. S.) 8: 135–52.
Vatuk, Sylvia
1972   *Kinship and Urbanization.* Berkeley: California University Press.
Vogel, Ezra F.
1979   *Japan as Number One: Lessons for America.* Cambridge, Mass:
               Harvard University Press.
Wasti, Syed Razi
1964   *Lord Minto and the Indian National Movement: 1905–10.*
               Oxford: Clarendon Press.
Weber, Max.
1930   *The Protestant Ethic and the Spirit of Capitalism.* London: Allen
               and Unwin.

1948   Politics as Vocation. *In* H. Gerth and C. W. Mills, eds.,
               From Max Weber: Essays in Sociology. London: Routledge
               and Kegan Paul.

1958   *Religion of India.* Trans., H. H. Gerth and D. Martindale.
               Glencoe, Ill.: The Free Press.
Whitman, Walt
1980   'A Passage to India'. *In* Walt Whitman, *Leaves of Grass.* Intro-
               duction by Gay Wilson Allen. New York: New American
               Library.
Whyte, W. F.
1953   *Street Corner Society.* Chicago: University of Chicago Press.
Wilkinson, Endymion.
1982   *Misunderstanding: Europe Versus Japan.* Revised Edition.
               Tokyo: Chukoron–Sha.
Wiser, William H.
1936   *Hindu Jajmani System.* Lucknow: Lucknow Publishing House.
Wiser, William H. and Charlotte Wiser
1963   *Behind Mud Walls*, 1920–60. Berkeley: University of California
               Press.

Xian Zhen
1981   Strategy for Economic Development. *Beijing Review* 32,
            August 10.

Yalman, Nur
1969   De Tocqueville in India: An Essay on the Caste System.
            Review Article on *Homo hierarchicus: essai sur le système des
            castes* (1966). *Man* (N. S.) 4, 1: 123–31.

INDEX

Abdali, Ahmad Shah, 206
Abu Shahab-ud-Din, 217
Acculturation, 28, 29, 35
Afghania (North West Frontier), 208, 210n
Afghanistan, 201, 206
Africa, 117, 130n, 139, 145, 153, 156, 157
Agnates, 122, 124
Ahmad, Aziz, 198, 203, 206, 208, 210n, 215n
Ahmad, Imtiaz, 78, 179n, 200n
Ahmad, Saghir, 200
Ahmed, Akbar S., 160
Ahmed, Raffiuddin, 225
Akbar, 181
Alatas, S. H., 138
Aligarh, 242
Alland Jr., Alexander, 222n
All-India Muslim League, 208–11
America, 232
    Latin, 139
    North, 141
Amherst, Lord, 228
Anantha Murty, U. R., 50
Anantnag, 168, 169, 172, 175, 183, 185, 195, 195n
Ancestor(s), 87, 122, 124
Ansari, Ghaus, 200
Anthropology, 4, 24–6, 29, 49, 52, 53, 58, 125–8, 145, 146, 242
    a dialogic, 160
    American cultural, 105
    and sociology at Lucknow University, 30–3
    as critical self awareness, 145–66
    as discourse of power, 165
    as ethnography, 139
    as fieldwork-based discipline, 90, 113, 116–30
    as heightened self awareness, 135–9
    as a shock-absorber, 113
    as study of one's own culture, 156–66
    as study of other cultures, 147–56
    as the mutual interpretation of cultures, 131–46
    classical, 135
    colonial, 145
    cultural, 24, 86
    development of research in, 111, 113
    emergence of, 139
    images of India in American, 85–108
    indigenous, 131, 145
    in India, 139–44, 149
    physical, 24
    pure, 149
    social, 48
    teaching of, 4
    truth of, 160
Aoki, Toshio, 241
Arab(s), 149, 170, 179n 203, 217
Aristotle, 70n
artha, 64, 70, 79–80
Arthaśāstra, 76
Asad, Talal, 138
Ascetic, 97, 172n
Asceticism, 89
Ashoka, 180
Ashraf, K. M., 179n
Asia, 130n, 139, 145, 156, 217, 226–45
    South, 90, 100, 115, 138, 170n, 198, 201, 202, 212n, 222
    South-East, 117, 222

278 Pathways

āśrama (stages of life), 74, 77, 79, 81
Assam, 210n
Auspiciousness, 80, 161
Australian National University,
  53, 115, 117, 158, 172n
Ayoob, M., 215n

Baelz, Erwin, 236
Bailey, F. G. 54, 55n, 68, 69, 77, 78,
  100, 112
Bakarwal (goat herds), The , 170, 175,
  186, 195, 196
Baldus, H., 126
Baluchistan, 208, 210n
Bamzai, P. N. K., 172, 174, 196
Bandyopadhyay, Suraj, 42
Bangladesh, 25, 168, 181n, 202, 215,
  215n, 216, 216n, 217, 219, 221–5
  birth of, 202, 203, 205, 218
Banton, M., 134
Baramulla, 168
Barnes, J. A., 121n, 123n
Barnett, Steve, 105
Barth, Fredrik, 48, 160, 172n 198, 219,
  219n, 220
Barwick, Diane, 151
Battle of Plassey, The, 233
Baviskar, B. S., 226n
Beals, Alan, 46, 49
Belief(s), 8, 24, 25, 29, 30, 38, 45, 47,
  114–7, 127, 133, 134, 145, 148, 177n,
  193
  religious, 25, 142, 179, 227
Bell, Daniel, 151
Benedict, Ruth, 53, 72, 113
Bengal, 24, 25, 73, 162, 181n, 204–10,
  210n, 213, 213n, 216–18, 227, 233, 235
  East, 204
  Muslims of, 206, 211–13, 217, 218,
  221
  violence in, 210
Berreman, Gerald D., 66, 66n, 68,
  95–7, 102, 104, 104n, 105, 127
Béteille, André, 47n, 104n, 111n
Bettelheim, Charles, 71n
Bhadrolok (gentry), 208, 209n
Bhagavadgītā, 69n
Bharati, Agehananda, 22

Bhatta, The, 169, 170, 183
Bhattacharjee, P. N., 170
Biardeau, Madeleine, 78n, 79
Bihar, 26, 113
Birth, 123–5, 156, 158, 171, 174, 176,
  177, 179, 179n, 183, 195, 223
  lowly (mleccha), 186, 191, 192
Boas, Franz, 113, 135
Boel, J., 65n
Bombay University, 4, 38, 39, 140
Boon, James A., 103
Bose, Arun, 84
Bose, N. K., 83, 83n
Bose, Sarat Chandra, 213n
Bouglé, C., 59
Brahman(s), 44, 48, 130n, 169, 178–82,
  181n, 183n, 184–6, 189–92, 196, 199,
  233
  community, 50
  Kashmiri, 169
  life of, 80
  of rural Kashmir, 52
  relationship with kṣatra, 68
  Saraswat, 179
  sect, 171
  Sena, 204
  status of, 77
Brahmanism, 88
Brass, Paul, 207
Britain, 25, 127n, 140, 141, 234, 235
British anthropologists, 85, 100
British Christian Missionaries, 139
Broomfield, J. H., 208, 209, 209n
Buchanan, Francis, 24
Buddhism, 11, 12, 88, 180, 181n, 236
  negativism of, 89
  social and political order of, 204
Buher (Bohra), The, 183
Bühler, G., 74
Bukharin, 10
Bureaucracy, 213
Burridge, Kenelm, 150, 156, 157

Calcutta, 4, 207, 213, 217n
Calcutta University, 4, 24, 25, 140
California University, 43, 226
Cambridge, 26, 104n, 140, 157, 208, 242
Cambridge University, 26

Canberra, 53, 115, 117
Casagrande, J. B., 120, 153
Castaneda, Carlos, 153
Caste(s), 13, 26, 28, 34, 38, 41–7, 51,
  52, 58, 59, 63, 76–9, 91, 92, 95, 100,
  101, 112, 114, 136, 140, 142, 160–2,
  168, 171n, 174n, 179, 189, 198–201
  analogues, 189
  assembly, 63
  differentiation, 35
  dominant, 41, 42, 63
  endogamous, 60, 169, 182, 183
  exterior, 28
  gradition, 60n
  hierarchy, 96
  higher/upper, 46, 142, 161, 204, 233
  ideology of, 62, 95, 136
  in India and the US, 96
  jurisdiction, 63
  leaders, 38
  low, 40, 95, 180, 204
  mobility, 43
  Muslim, 200
  nature of, 58–71
  non-antagonistic, 95
  organization, 68
  preoccupation with, 71–3
  relationship, 89
  restrictions, 181n
  status, 48, 172n
  substitutes, 189, 199
  system, 40, 43, 83n, 89, 91, 94–6,
    136, 142, 162, 163, 179, 189, 199
  theory of, 63, 64
  trading, 183
  twice-born, 40
  untouchable, 94
  Vaishya, 179
Chamba Valley, 183n
Charakasamhita, 104n
Chatterjee, Bankim Chandra, 18n
Chattopadhyay, K. P., 140
Chaudhuri, Nirad C., 208n, 216n
Chicago, 83, 99n, 105
China, 32n, 89, 156, 236, 237
Christ, 231
Christian(s), 211n, 233
Christianity, 43, 149, 231, 233–5

Civilization(s), 8, 37, 64, 68, 131,
  135, 242
  European, 135, 241
  great, 88
  history of, 142
  Indian, 16, 76, 91, 92, 98, 142
  industrial, 9
  Western, 149–51, 229
Class(es),
  antagonistic, 95
  Bengali Muslim middle, 209n
  conciousness, 13
  conflict, 13, 31, 95
  hierarchy of, 45
  Hindu middle, 209n
  Indian middle, 10–12, 227–31, 235
Clifford, James, 104, 147, 160
Collingwood, R. G., 10n
Colonialism, 131, 147, 148, 152, 156
  academic, 138
  British, 90
  Western, 234
Communalism, 76, 84, 221
Community Development
  Programme, 29, 34, 86
Comte, Auguste, 148
Conflict, 18, 20, 26, 42, 81, 123, 125,
  205, 221, 236
  among kinsfolk, 129
  class, 13, 31, 95, 205
Confucianism, 236
Confucius, 1
Coomaraswamy, Ananda K., 104n,
  131, 139
Coorg(s), The, 38–42
Cosmos, 81
Crane, Robert I., 168n
Cutural difference, 101, 103, 149, 164,
  165, 203, 204, 216, 218, 220
Cultural invasion, 27, 234, 241
Cultural pluralism, 13, 90, 198, 202,
  202n, 212, 212n, 220
Cultural relativism, 96, 103, 125, 150,
  151, 155, 164
Cultural synthesis, 6, 9–11, 14, 16,
  18–20, 23, 24, 29, 71, 98, 104n, 134,
  168, 199, 205, 213n, 236, 242
  desire for, 228, 229

Cultural synthesis, (continued)
    Hindu-Muslim, 168, 198, 242
    process of, 13, 20, 242
    search for, 234, 235
    validity of, 9
Culture(s), 13, 17, 19, 27, 30, 42, 46,
    86, 92, 93, 102, 103
    adjustment, 28
    base of a, 26
    change, 25, 29, 33
    contact, 25, 26
    crises, 29
    development of, 24–36
    diversity in, 152
    dominant, 27
    exclusion of, 134
    gradition of, 27
    homogeneity, 211, 236
    human, 87, 94, 113
    Indian, 3, 10, 11, 16, 28, 87, 154
    Islamic, 208
    levels of, 35
    modern Indian, 11–14
    mutual interpretation of, 131–5,
        146, 159
    natural category, 107
    non-Western, 131, 132
    Occidental, 87
    primitive, 26
    progress, 27
    scientific theory of, 132
    stagnant, 87–90
    static, 89
    study of, 113
    theories of, 25
    the study of other, 147–56
    traditional, 10, 36, 227
    trait, 25, 168
    tribal, 28, 156
    Western, 35, 93, 149, 150, 154, 156
Cushing, Frank, 126, 153
Custom(s), 8, 25, 27, 38, 41, 46, 74,
    95, 102, 139, 201, 204
    diversity of, 76
    marriage, 38
    of tribes and castes, 24
    traditional, 175

Dacca, 208, 217
Dacca University, 212, 216n
dakshinā, 121
Das Gupta, Jyotirindra, 213n, 221n
Dasgupta, R. K., 210n, 213n
Das, Veena, 66n, 67, 78n, 80, 143
Death, 123, 124, 177, 181, 201
    ceremonies, 38
Decolonialization, 138
Delhi, New Delhi, 57, 58, 83n, 210,
    215n, 222n
Delhi University, 83n
Democracy, 34, 92, 222, 224
Democratization, 92
de Nobili, Roberto, 233
Desai, A. R., 72
De-sanskritization, 41
Devadasis, 161
dharma, 64, 70, 80, 81, 192
    varnāśrama, 74, 75
Dharmashāstra, 124
d'Humiers, M. Gilles, 83n
Dilthey, W., 16
Dirks, Nicholas, 162
Division of labour, 37, 60
    principal of, 31⁻
    sexual, 44
    traditional, 60, 63 (*see also* Jajmani
        system)
Doi, Takeo, 236
Dualism, 60, 232
Duality, 54, 56, 77n, 128, 134, 199
Dube, S. C., 36
Dubois, Abbe, The, 74
Dumont, Louis, v, 16, 39, 52–84, 98,
    100, 103, 107, 112, 123n, 126–8,
    134–7, 142, 143, 155, 156, 158, 159,
    161, 162, 164, 184n, 191, 194, 198,
    198n, 199, 200, 207n
Durkheim, Emile, 53, 62n, 67, 77,
    100, 132
Dutta, Michael Madhusudan, 18n

East India Company, The, 73, 206
Egalitarianism, 59, 62
Eglar, Zekiye, 171n
Eliot, T.S., 7n, 18n, 109, 202

Elwin, Verrier, 27, 229
Emerson, Ralph Waldo, 86, 229
Engels, Friedrich, 18n
England, 14, 15, 18n, 58, 86, 111, 140,
  142, 234, 235
Epstein, A. L., 112
Epstein, Scarlett, 46, 49
Equality, 7, 59, 68, 95, 101
Equalitarianism, 227
Ershad, H. M., 224
Europe, 127n, 135, 139, 140, 150,
  232, 235
Evans-Pritchard, E. E., 39, 47, 53,
  126, 132

Fabian, Johannes, 102, 150
Family, The, 38, 46, 52, 72, 81, 91,
  118, 119, 120, 122n, 161, 162, 170,
  171, 176, 177, 188, 194, 195, 195n,
  223, 240
  Brahman, 181
  change in the structure of joint, 89
  extended/joint, 38, 115, 162
  Hindu, 81, 183n, 216
  name, 170, 171, 183n
  natal, 182
  nuclear, 162
  organization, 72
  origin of, among the Pandits, 120
  priest, 184
Fanon, Frantz, 229
Fauq, M. M., 183n
Fei Hsiao-Tung, 156
Firth, Raymond, 154
Fischer, Michael, 154
Fortes, Meyer, 53
Foucault, Michel, 147, 165
Franda, Marcus F., 213, 215n, 223, 224
Frazer, James, 51, 135
Freeman, J. D. (Derek), 116, 117,
  154, 158
Freilich, M., 112
French holism, 100
Fukutake, Tadashi, 240
Fukuzawa, Yukichi, 232, 233
Fumon, 226
Functionalism, 26, 39, 40, 72, 127,
  142, 221

Fundamentalism, 166
Fürer-Haimendorf, C. von, 66, 66n, 157
Furnivall, J. S., 218, 218n

Gadamer, Hans-Georg, 159
Gait, E. A., 170n
Galey, Jean-Claude, 58, 76, 78n, 82
Gandhi, M. K., 20, 32, 165, 229,
  244, 245
Gandhi, Ramchandra, 78n
Ganguli, B. N., 228
Gascoigne, Bamber, 171n
Geddes, Patrick, 140
Geertz, Clifford, 50, 51, 162, 221
Gellner, E. A., 125
Ghazni, Mahmud, 203
Ghurye, G. S., 23, 27, 38–40, 55, 72,
  72n, 101, 140, 141, 158
Gibran, Kahlil, 111
Giddings, Franklin, 13, 23
Goa, 231
Goethe, Johann Wolfgang, 135, 147
Gombrich, E. H., 238
Gor (Brahman priests), The, 182–4,
  189, 190, 191
Gorakhpur, 52
gotra, 123, 124, 177, 182
Gough, Kathleen, 95
Gould, H. A., 92, 171n
Guha, Ramachandra, 96
Gujar (cowherds), The, 170, 175, 186,
  195, 196
Gujarat, 75
Gupta, K. P., 8n, 20, 49
Gusfield, Joseph R., 230

Hanson, Allan, 160
Harijan, 45
Harrison, Selig, 221, 221n
Hasegawa, Nyozekan, 230
Heesterman, J. C., 66n, 67, 68, 78,
  81, 82
Hegel, G. W. F., 7, 14n, 70n, 88n
Hegelian ideology, 29
Heller, Clemens, 83n
Heritage, 17, 35, 168, 182
Herodotus, 148
Herskovits, M. J., 150

Hierarchization, 56
Hierarchy, 52, 60, 62–6, 62n, 68, 69,
    79, 94, 112, 136, 189, 191
    Indian, 155
    low caste, 96
    notion of, 55
    of values, 8
    revolving, 79
Himalayas, The, 168
Hindu(s), The, 9, 11, 12, 14, 18n, 26,
    40, 41, 57, 59, 64, 69, 69n, 74, 78, 81,
    85–8, 92–4, 99, 100, 102, 105, 107,
    108, 114, 121, 149, 157, 161, 162,
    167, 169, 170n, 171, 172, 178,
    179–81, 181n, 192, 194, 196, 198,
    198n, 200n, 201, 204–7, 207n, 209n,
    210, 211n, 213n, 214, 215n, 216, 217,
    223, 224, 229
    behaviour, 107
    belief, 179
    Bengali, 208n
    caste system, 179, 189
    city, 233
    cognitive categories, 99, 102, 164
    concept of strands (*guṇa*), 107
    cosmology, 94, 107
    culture, 97, 105
    domination, 209
    ethic of ritual purity, 198
    high/upper caste, 95, 204
    leap year, 181n
    low caste, 205
    lunar calendar, 189
    medicine, 107
    moral philosphy, 107
    Muslim contact with, 207n
    Muslim rule, 213
    of Kashmir, 179–85, 192–8
    pilgrims, 121
    reformists, 243, 245
    renaissance, 22
    rule, 209n
    scriptures, 233
    social life, 77
    social order, 39
    social organization, 75
    society, 12, 37, 62, 66, 67, 74, 76,
        85, 97, 98, 100, 141, 143, 158, 161

socio-cultural identity of, in rural
    Kashmir, 167–201
    strands (*guṇa*), 107
    symbolism, 209n
    tradition, 20n, 70
    ways of life, 79, 207
Hinduism, 40, 41, 44, 45, 58, 74, 93,
    142, 180, 198n, 205, 227
Hinduization, 157
Hindustan, 14
Hos, The, 26, 29
Householder(s), 80–2
Hughes, T. P., 169, 177n, 180, 193n
Humanitarianism, 227
Hume, David, 48
Hunter, W. W., 204, 205
Huq, A. K. Fazlul, 209, 213
Husserl, Edmund, 18n, 19n
Hutton, J. H. 174n, 182n, 183, 200
Hyderabad (Pakistan), 208n
Hymes, Dell, 144
Hypergamy, 63

Iban, The, 116, 117
Identity, 218, 219
    Bangladeshi, 222, 224
    cultural, in rural Kashmir, 167–201,
        203, 212, 217, 241, 242
    ethnic, 212, 215, 217, 218
    Islamic, 224, 225
    Japanese (*Nihonjin-ron*), 239
Ieyasu, Tokugawa, 231
Impurity, 59, 60, 62, 63, 66, 186,
    193, 194
Inauspiciousness, 80, 187
Inden, Ronald, 78n, 80, 92, 143,
    162, 171n
India, 6, 9, 11, 13, 14n, 16, 20, 22, 26,
    31, 35, 38, 40, 48, 49, 112, 126, 131,
    138, 143, 151, 157, 158, 160, 163,
    164, 168, 169, 173n, 183, 185n, 197,
    198n, 208, 210, 216, 219, 221, 222n,
    225, 234–7, 242
    ancient 58, 140
    another, 96–100
    anthropology of/in, 37, 139, 141,
        143, 144
    as a Hindu country, 223

India (continued)
  British rule in, 12, 14, 162, 206,
    226–31, 233
  caste in modern, 43
  caste in rural, 51
  civilization of, 142
  communal divisions in, 11
  cultural specificity of, 4n, 149
  decline of primitive tribes in, 26
  eternal, 90–4
  future of, 16
  images of, in American
    anthropology, 85–108
  independent, 12, 30
  Islamization of, 204
  Muslims in, 203, 209–11, 217n
  medieval, 149, 207
  modern, 58, 207, 228
  modern education in, 157, 234
  North, 121, 121n, 123n, 161, 207
  opportunity for field work in, 44
  partition of, 12, 16, 209
  past of, 15
  progressive groups of, 32
  social reality of, 17, 42
  sociology of/in, 3, 43, 52–84, 142,
    155, 164
  tribes of, 29
  traditions of, 14
  westernization of, 227
Individualism, 59, 62, 76, 79, 84, 98,
  136, 155, 156, 160
  values of, 162
Indology, 54, 58, 59, 79, 100, 140, 142
Indonesia, 219
Industrialization, 43, 71n, 91, 92, 151
Inequlaity, 59, 62
Iqbal, Muhammad, 208, 215, 215n
Ishida, Eiichiro, 236, 241
Islam vi, 11, 12, 177–9; 181, 181n, 195,
  196, 198n, 203, 205, 208, 216n, 222–5
  advent of, 203–6
  arrival of, in India, 180
  conversions to, vi, 177, 198n,
    204, 205
  return to, 205
Islamism, 215
Islamization, 41, 180, 204
Isogamy, 63

Jain, Ravindra, 49, 87
Jajmani system, 63, 199
Jammu, 168
Japan, 72, 89, 230–9, 241, 242, 244
Jarvie, I. C., 125
jāti, 62, 75, 77, 171, 171n (see also caste)
Jaunsar Bawar, 34, 35
Jesus, 228, 229, 231, 233
Jews, The, 239
Jinnah. M. A., 212, 215

Kachru, Braj B., 170, 191
Kak, R. C., 180n, 181
Kalhana, 179, 179n, 180, 182
kāma, 80
Kanpur, 35
Kanthapura, 50
Kantowsky, Detlef, 66n, 68, 70
Karkun, 182–4, 190
karma, 10n, 74, 160, 161, 178
Karnataka, 38, 44–6, 50, 51
Karnatak University, 54
Karve, Irawati, 53, 72, 72n, 75, 117
Kasai, Minoru, 244
Kashmir, v, vi, 52, 114, 115, 120, 121,
  129, 168, 168n, 169, 172n, 174, 183,
  204, 208
  rural, vi, 115, 118n, 167–210
Kashmiri Pandit(s), The, 72, 115, 117,
  118, 122, 123, 127, 128, 130, 130n,
  170, 172, 174, 177n, 178, 184, 185,
  185n, 190, 195, 196, 200, 200n
  conversion to Islam, of 177
  cultural identity of, 192, 201
  culture, 120, 125, 129
  family names of, 183n
  gotra among, 182, 182n
  kinship system of, 114, 116, 119, 124
  relationship with Muslims, of,
    118n, 186, 189, 191, 192, 197, 199
  occupations of, 186
  of Utrassu Umanagri, 185–8
  patrons/customers of Muslims, as,
    188, 199
  religious ceremonies of, 193
  society, 118, 121
  zat among, 183
Kato, Shuichi, 240
Kenya, 156

Kenyatta, Jomo, 156
Ketkar, S. V. 60n
Khalida, Begum, 224
Khan, Abdul Majeed,. 205, 217
Khan, Ali Akbar, 88
Khan, Mohammad Ayub, 214
Khan, Syed Ahmed, 242, 243
Khare, R. S., 66n, 67, 68, 161
Kilam, Jia Lal, 182
Kingship, 58, 76, 80
Kinsfolk, 111, 118–25
Kinship, 38, 52, 53, 58, 72, 72n, 76–80,
    83n, 117, 123n, 124, 125, 142, 153
    Hindu, 117
    study of, 114, 116
    system, 53, 115, 116, 116n, 118,
        123n, 124
    terminology, 38, 86, 114
    ties, 125, 175
kokugaku (national learning), 237, 239
Kokugakuin University, 239
Kolff, Dirk, H. A., 161
Koran, The, 176, 177n, 178, 179n,
    193, 193n
Kothari, Rajni, 71n, 222n
Koul, Anand, 182
Kripalani, Krishna, 216n
Krishna, 98
Kroeber, Alfred Louis, 87–90, 88n,
    102, 104n, 113
Kshatriya, 179, 180

Lahore, 209
Lambert, Richard D., 209n, 217n
Land reforms, 51
Lawrence, Walter, 168n, 170n, 173n,
    174, 182, 183, 195n, 196n, 200
Leach, Edmund, 50, 66, 66n, 67, 115,
    116, 116n, 130n
Lelyveld, David, 248
Lenin, V. I., 10
Lévi-Strauss, Claude, 53, 75, 103, 104,
    128, 131, 133, 136, 139, 145, 148–52,
    159, 199
Levy, Reuben, 179n, 195
Lewis, Oscar, 112
Lineage, 80, 91
Linton, Ralph, 87–90, 102

London, 54, 160
Lowie, Robert, 157
Lucknow, 4, 24n, 34, 53, 114, 115
Lucknow University, 3, 4, 24, 26, 30,
    52, 113, 117, 141, 157, 161
Lyall, J. C., 204
Lynch, Owen, 47

Macaulay, Thomas Babington, 157, 235
Madan, T. N., 24n, 44, 52, 54–7, 72,
    73, 76, 78, 78n, 80, 82, 111n, 117,
    212n, 123, 127, 137–9, 162, 168n,
    169, 172, 177n, 182n, 185, 185n, 188,
    193, 193n, 197, 200n, 210n, 222,
    226n, 230
Madras, 93
Madras University, 241
Madurai, 233
Mahābhārata, 72n, 79
Maharashtra, 228
Main, Henry Summer, 65
Majumdar, D. N., 4, 24–30, 33–6, 52,
    72, 112–15, 141, 157, 161
Malabar, 203
Malamoud, Charles, 78n, 79, 80
Malaysia, 219
Malik, Hafeez, 215n
Malinowski, Bronislaw, 25, 26, 39, 53,
    113, 116, 128, 130n, 132, 135, 141,
    154, 156
Mandelbaum, D. G., 37, 67, 73, 90–3,
    102, 104, 104n, 105
Maniruzzaman, Talukder, 223
Mankekar, D. R., 210n, 213, 215n, 216n
Manu, 60n, 100
Manusmrti, The, 74, 104n
Marcus, George, 154
Marglin, Frederique A., 78n, 80, 161
Marriage, 35, 38, 46, 52, 53, 58, 63, 76,
    77, 79, 83n, 99, 123, 124, 153, 175,
    176, 178, 187, 193
Marriott, Mckim, 56, 62, 63, 73, 86,
    93, 97–100, 99n, 103–8, 143, 164, 171n
Marxism, 4n, 16, 18n, 20, 20n, 23, 32n,
    72, 143n
Marx, Karl, 7, 14, 14n, 15, 18n, 43, 65,
    90, 100, 151, 234, 236
Mauss, Marcel, 50, 100, 158

māyā, 91
Mayer, A. C., 48, 50, 55n, 62, 78n, 80,
    86, 123n
McLane, John R., 208
Mead, Margaret, 135, 154
Mecca, 177
Mencher, Joan P., 94, 104n
Merleau-Ponty, Maurice, 18n, 167
Mexico, 92, 112, 142
Michener, James A., 215n
Miller, Roy Andrew, 233, 241
Mines, Mattison, 84
Mishima, Yukio, 238, 239
Mobility, 12, 43, 65, 91, 175, 194, 226
Modernism, 100
Modernity, 3–23, 86, 102, 230, 242, 244
Modernization, 5, 8, 16–22, 35, 36n,
    70, 71n, 89, 91, 101, 143, 152, 165,
    166, 227, 230, 236–9, 244
    concept of, 5, 8n
    costs of, 8
    forces of, 91
    nature of, 7, 20
    of India, 15
    paradigms of, 227
    path of genuine, 5, 13
    process of, 36, 227
    quest for, 5
mokṣa, 80
Mongol(s), The, 149, 203
Mookerjee, Girija K., 231
Moore, G. E., 6
Morgan, Lewis Henry, 86, 87, 103
Mori, Arinori, 233
Morishima, Michio, 244
Mudimbe, V. Y., 153
Müller, Max, 140, 235
Mughal(s), The, 170, 173n, 195, 195n,
    196, 214
    empire, 206
Muhammad, The Prophet, 176, 177,
    179n, 195
Mukerjee, Radhakamal, 4, 30, 33, 36,
    75, 141
Mukerji, D. P., 3–23, 30, 30–3, 31n,
    36, 113, 115n, 141, 161
Mukherjee, Ramkrishna, 23, 73, 143n,
    144, 205, 209n, 212, 214n

Mukhopadhyay, Bhudev, 163
Murdock, G. P., 112
Musalman, The, 169, 170n, 195n, (*see
    also* Muslim)
Muslim(s), The, 12, 14, 45, 87, 118,
    118n, 149, 167, 169, 170, 172–81n,
    185–201, 235, 242, 243
    Bengali, 202–25
    distribution of, in India, 204
    dynamism, 89
    Hindu contacts with, 207n
    Indian, 206–8, 211, 215, 215n, 242
    of rural Kashmir, 167–201
    kings, 70, 180, 204
    leaders, 207
    orthodox, 243
    political authority of, 206
    reformist, 243
    separatism among, 205
    ways of life, 207
    zamindars, 173, 191, 193
Myrdal, Gunnar, 21
Mysore, 44, 50

Nadel, S. F., 39, 114, 115, 115n, 157
Nagasaki, 231
Naipaul, V. S., 243
Najibu-l-Daulah, 206
Nakamura, Hajime, 232
Nakane, Chie, 46, 72, 136, 240
Nandy, Ashish, 160, 163
Nangar (non-agricultural artisan
    group in rural Kashmir), 172, 174–6
Narayan, R. K., 50
Nationalism, 76, 79, 84, 94, 245
Nation-building, 42, 202
Nehru, Jawaharlal, 228
New Ghinea, 153
New Zealand, 160
Nicholas, Ralph, 78n, 80, 143
Nilgiri Hills, The, 90

Oakeshott, Michael, 18, 18n
O'Flaherty, Wendy, 98
Ogden, C. K., 72n
Okakura, Kakuzo, 237
Orientalism, 105
Orissa, 161

Oudh, 30, 207
Owen, John, 216n
Oxford, 40, 44, 242
Oxford University, 39, 40

Pakistan, 168, 201, 206, 208n, 214n,
     216n, 217, 218, 219, 224, 241
   break-up of, 13
   creation of, 207, 210n, 217n
   cultural pluralism in, 212
   demand for, 203, 210
   East, 211, 211n, 214, 215n
   languages of, 213
   name of, 208
   population/people of, 211, 214
   Punjab in, 171n
   West, 211, 212, 214, 215, 217n
pañcamahāyajña, 74
panda, 121–3, 121n
Pandit, R. S., 174, 179n
Panini, M. N., 4n
Parochialization, 93
Parry, J. P., 78n, 80
Patrilineal ideology, 121, 123
Paul, B. D., 126
Pedigree(s), 121, 121n, 123,
     123n, 124
Pehrson, R. C., 48, 126
Peirano, Marizo G. S., 55n
Personality, The concept of, 4–9
Pike, K., 132
Pilgrim(s), 121–3
Pilgrimage, 177
Plato, 70, 70n, 148
Pocock, D. F., 39, 47, 53, 54, 55n,
     69, 76, 77, 78n, 82, 126, 127, 137
Politicization, 71, 91, 92
Pollution, 39, 124, 182n, 185
   notion of, 194
   period of, 123, 187
   purity and, 45, 60n, 62
   ritual, 193
   sources of, 191
Popper, Karl R., 3, 18n, 134
Positivism, 134
Power, 42, 62–4, 63n, 67–9, 77, 78, 95,
     97, 100, 138, 148, 164, 165, 174n,
     224, 234

   balance of, 202
   distinction between status and, 100
   distribution of, 60, 138
   female, 80
   imperial, 206
   Muslim, 206
   political, 95, 162, 218, 225
   royal, 80, 161
   Western, 231, 234, 235
Prabhu, P. N., 75
Priest(s), 62, 80, 184
Progress, 7–9, 24, 33
Punjab, 171n, 182n, 183n, 208, 210n
Purity, 39, 80, 100, 161, 205 and
   pollution, 45, 60n, 62
   Islamic, 206, (*see also* Pollution)
Puruṣārtha, 57, 74, 75, 77–9, 81, 107

Qureshi, I. H., 203, 206, 210n, 224

Radcliffe-Brown, A. R., 39, 44, 47,
     53, 141
Radhakrishnan, S., 74
Radin, Paul, 154
Raghavan, V., 104n
Raghu, 80
Rahim, Muhammad Abdul, 205
Rahman, Sheikh Mujibur, 210n, 215,
     222–5
Raja Rao, 50
Rajput(s), 123n, 173n, 195n
Ramanujam, A. K., 85
Rampura, 38, 41, 43, 45–8, 50
Ranade, M. G., 228, 234, 237
Ranchi, 114
Raonaq Jahan, 223
Rashiduzzaman, M., 213
Ravi Shankar, 88
Raychaudhuri, Tapan, 163
Raychaudhuri, T. C., 170
Red Indians, 87
Redfield, Robert, 92, 93, 112, 142
Reflexivity, 57
Religion(s), 13, 25, 41, 45, 60, 63, 64,
     117, 142, 163, 178, 192, 199, 222, 237
   absence of, 223
   and society, 46
   appeal of, 219

Religion(s) (continued)
  as an integrative force, 211
  as cultural difference, 150
  authority of, 177n
  bond of, 203
  books on, 38, 39
  casteless, 181n
  change of, 233
  difference of, 216, 243
  discussion of, 49
  domain of, 30
  followers of, 181
  new, 241
  of Bangladesh, 224, 225
  popular, 217
  primitive, 153
  salience of, 219
  state and, 42
  study of, 114
Renunciation, 54, 64, 76, 77, 79–81,
  86, 160, 161
Risely, H. H., 62
Rite(s), 27, 38, 187–9
Ritual(s), 38, 39, 115–17, 119, 123,
  127, 133, 140, 181n, 184, 200
  conduct of, 129, 163
  functionaries, 121
  impurity, 191
  liturgies, 189, 199
  marriage, 187
  pollution, 138, 161, 182, 193
  purity, 188, 196, 198
  ranking of caste, 68
  status, 42, 197
  temple, 161
Rivers, W. H. R., 25, 117n, 121, 140
Roosevelt, Eleanor, 86
Roy, Jayanta Kumar, 213
Roy, Rammohan, 17, 227–9, 232, 234,
  235, 242
Roy, S. C., 25
Rudolph, Lloyd. I., 71n, 92
Rudolph, Susanne, H., 71n, 92
Rural development, 151
Rushdie, Salman, 164
Ruskin, John, 229

Saberwal, Satish, 82n

Sacrifice, 39, 74, 82
Sagan, Carl, 153
Said, Edward W., 242
Samoa, 135
Saṁsāra, 99
Sanskritization, 40–3, 142, 226, 211n
Saran, A. K., 5, 6, 20, 21, 31n, 54, 55n,
  77, 78
Schneider, D. M., 18n, 78
Schweitzer, Albert, 100
Seal, Anil, 204, 205, 207
Secularism, 51, 215, 219, 222–4
Secularization, 43, 91
Selwyn, Tom, 78n
Semenov, Yu I., 51
Sengupta, Arjun, 211
Shah, A. M., 38, 41
Shah, K. J., 78n, 79
Shils, Edward, 18n, 138, 152, 162
Shiva, 188
shrāddha, 121
Shudra, 179
Sidhanta, N. K., 72n
Sikandar, 180, 181
Sikh(s), The, 169, 206
Simmons, D. R., 160
Siṅ, 39
Sind, 203, 2065, 208, 210n
Singer, Milton, 21, 66n, 68, 70, 71, 86,
  92–4, 102, 104n, 105, 142
Singh, Yogendra, 14, 21, 73n
Sita, 80
Smith, M. G., 212n
Smith, S. Percy, 160
Smith, W. Cantwell, 206
Smith, W. Robertson, 116
Social forces, 20, 32, 37
Socialism, 151
Social Organization, 25, 34, 39, 40, 60,
  75, 86, 92, 94, 95, 101, 168, 179, 181,
  200, 201, 204, 212n, 213, 228
Social reality, 6, 50, 60, 61, 63, 77, 80,
  93, 143
  dimensions of, 132
  native models of, 200
  of India, 17, 73, 94
Society, 8, 10, 17, 25, 45–8, 112
  American, 135

Society (continued)
    capitalist, 15
    technology-oriented, 21
    Western, 15
Sociology, 3, 6, 6n, 11, 15, 21, 22, 33,
    55, 57, 58, 113, 141
    anthropology and, at Lucknow
        University, 30–3
    African, 42
    French, 59
    of India, 40, 44; 69, 70–7, 80, 82,
        142, 155, 164, 226
Sparling, K., 239
Spear, P., 181n, 203
Sri Lanka, 116n
Srinagar, 114, 117, 119, 168, 169,
    183–5, 183n, 184n, 189n, 193n, 195n
Srinivas, M. N., 4n, 37–51, 55, 73, 83,
    90, 92, 104n, 128, 136, 137, 141, 142,
    158, 159, 161, 222n, 226, 227, 245
Staley, Eugene, 86
Stanner, W. E. H., 116, 151, 167
Status, 67, 68, 80, 100, 104, 105
    development of ascribed, 89
    distinction between power and, 100
    of Brahmans, 77
    of women, 163
    social, 40, 162, 171n
Steingass, F., 171
St Francis Xavier, 231
Stratification, 58, 95
Structuralism, 59, 134, 212, 212n
Subrahmanyam, K., 215n
Suhrawardy, H. S., 209, 213n
Suzuki, Takao, 241
Swami Vivekananda, 149

Taboos, 3, 25
Tagore, Rabindranath, 17, 18n, 216, 237
Tambiah, S. J., 78n, 79, 81
Tamilnadu, 76, 240
Taoism, 236
Tapper, R., 160
Tara Chand, 203
Tarascon, a French folk festival, 75
Tax, Sol, 44, 46, 55
Thapar, Romila, 78n, 81
Thoothi, N. A., 74, 75

Thoreau, Henry David, 86, 229
Thucydides, 148
Tokyo, 236, 239–41
Tolstoy, L., 229
Toynbee, Arnold, 86
Tradition(s) 4, 8, 32, 36n, 41, 71, 72,
    82, 102, 121, 127n, 130n, 152, 161,
    162, 165, 174, 175, 216n, 230, 234, 239
    ancient, 50
    Asian, 37n
    cultural, 101, 155, 163
    empiricist, 73, 79
    ethnographic, 24
    French sociological, 59, 70n
    great, 92, 93, 142
    Hindu, 7, 10, 162
    Indian, 84
    intellectual, 143n
    Japanese, 237
    literary, 158
    little, 92, 142
    Maori, 160
    oral, 98, 158
    pre-British, 14
    taboos of a, 3
    Vedic, 81
    village, 189
    Western sociological, 99
Trautman, Thomas R., 87
Tribe(s), 27, 28, 35, 100, 132, 139, 140,
    161, 174n
    decline of, 26
    in transition, 26
    of India, 29, 141
    problems of, 115
    rehabilation of, 113
    works of the colonial period on, 38
Trotsky, L., 10
Truth(s), 6n, 20, 146, 150, 163, 241
    affirmed by anthropology, 148, 160
    distinction between essential and
        general, 127
Turkistan, 180
Turk(s), The, 149, 203
Tyler, Stephen A., 96, 97
Tylor, E. B., 25, 103, 104n

Uberoi, J. P. S. (Jit, Jit Singh), 66n, 67, 138

Unemployment, 34
United Kingdom, The, 202n
United States (U. S. A.), The, 58, 96, 111, 127, 202n, 235, 240
Universalization, 93
Upanishad(s), The, 9, 12
Urbanization, 65, 91, 92
Uttar Pradesh, 34, 63, 113, 171n, 200n
Utrassu-Umanagri (village in Kashmir), 117, 118, 120, 121, 172, 173, 173n, 175, 177, 183, 185–91, 185n, 193, 194n, 195, 197, 198, 200n, 201

Vaishya, 179
Value(s), 11, 18, 19, 27, 45, 57, 59–61, 67, 73, 76, 77, 101, 128, 130, 134, 144, 161, 186, 188, 198n, 199, 203, 207n, 227, 236, 240, 243
  creation of new, 81
  cultural, 142, 152, 154
  inversion of, 136
  Islamic, 16, 192
  fundamental, 9
  hierarchy of, 8, 42
  kinship, 115
  moral, 118
  of egalitarianism, 62, 95
  of human dignity and liberty, 234
  of individualism, 62, 162
  pattern of, 31
  primacy of, 32
  problem of balancing of, 8
  religious, 16, 63, 162, 184, 244
  Sanskritic, 40
  sociology of, 66
  study of, 116, 117
  system of, 29, 61, 94, 127, 238
  traditional, 17, 18, 20
  traditional Japanese, 239
  Western liberal, 43
Varna, 62, 74, 75, 77
Varnāśrama-dharma, 74, 75
Vatuk, Sylvia, 121n

Vedānta, 20, 23
Vogel, Ezra F., 230, 240
Vyasa, 100

Wa (principle of harmony in Japanese culture), 236
Wakon Kansai (Japanese spirit and Chinese knowledge), 236
Wakon Yosai (Japanese spirit and Western techniques), 230, 232
Wasai Yokon (Japanese technique and Western spirit), 230
Wasti, Syed Razi, 208
Weber, Max, 41, 57, 100, 165, 166
West Bengal, 213, 217n
Westernization, 15, 43, 65, 152, 157, 226–45
  Japanese mode of (*seiyoko*), 235
  process of, 41, 227, 242
  under the Meiji era, 234
Whitman, Walt, 85, 86
Whyte, W. F., 126
Wilkinson, E. 230, 233
Winkle, Rip van, 86
Wiser, C., 90n
Wiser, W. H., 90n
Wissler, Clarke, 25

Xian Zhen, 32n

Yajamān, 182n, 183
Yamamoto, Jocho, 238
Yamato-damashii (the unique spirit of Japaneseness), 238
Yuji, Aida, 238, 240

Zamindar(s) (agriculturists), 172, 175
  Muslim, 173, 191, 193
Zamindar(s), (Muslim servant class), 186, 187
zāt, 171, 171n, 175–7, 183, 195, 196, 199
Zia-ur-Rahman, 223, 224